READING PHILO

READING PHILO

A Handbook to Philo of Alexandria

Edited by

Torrey Seland

WILLIAM B. EERDMANS PUBLISHING COMPANY

GRAND RAPIDS, MICHIGAN / CAMBRIDGE, U.K.

Published 2014 by
Wm. B. Eerdmans Publishing Co.
2140 Oak Industrial Drive N.E., Grand Rapids, Michigan 49505 /
P.O. Box 163, Cambridge CB3 9PU U.K.
www.eerdmans.com

Printed in the United States of America

20 19 18 17 16 15 14   7 6 5 4 3 2 1

Library of Congress Cataloging-in-Publication Data

Reading Philo: a handbook to Philo of Alexandria / edited by Torrey Seland.
    pages   cm
    Includes bibliographical references and index.
    ISBN 978-0-8028-7069-8 (pbk.: alk. paper)
    1. Philo, of Alexandria.   I. Seland, Torrey, editor.

    B689.Z7R43   2014
    181'.06 — dc23

                                        2014031213

The author has received substantial support for his writing of chapters 3 and 7
by a grant from *Det faglitterære fond, Norway*

Contents

Contributors

PER JARLE BEKKEN is associate professor at the University of Nordland, Bodø, Norway. http://www.uin.no/omuin/ansattoversikt/Pages/VisAnsatt. aspx?EmpID=1376&Guid=b03016f2-e081-410a-9782-0ffcaea648f4&Lang= NO

ELLEN BIRNBAUM is an independent scholar living in Cambridge, Massachusetts, U.S.A.

PEDER BORGEN is professor emeritus at the University of Trondheim, Norway (now Norwegian University of Science and Technology). http://no.wikipedia.org/wiki/Peder_Borgen

ERKKI KOSKENNIEMI is an independent scholar and adjunct professor of biblical studies at Åbo Akademy University, Finland. http://www.koskenniemi .fi

ADELE REINHARTZ is professor, Department of Classics and Religious Studies at the University of Ottawa, Canada. http://www.cla-srs.uottawa.ca/eng/faculty/reinhartz.html

DAVID T. RUNIA is master of Queen's College and professorial fellow in the School of Historical and Philosophical Studies at the University of Melbourne, Australia. http://divinity.yale.edu/core/philo-alexandria-runia

KARL-GUSTAV SANDELIN is professor emeritus of New Testament exegesis, Åbo Akademy University, Finland. http://eurojewishstudies.org/scholar_shortdisplay.php?idscholar=926

TORREY SELAND is professor emeritus, School of Mission and Theology, Stavanger, Norway. http://www.torreys.org/cv

GREGORY E. STERLING is Reverend Henry L. Slack Dean of Yale Divinity School and Lillian Claus Professor of New Testament, Yale Divinity School, Yale University, New Haven, Connecticut, U.S.A. http://divinity.yale.edu/sterling

Preface

This project had its beginning in a Scandinavian project of a somewhat larger scale, initiated by the Finnish scholar Professor Karl-Gustav Sandelin. When that project turned out not to be realizable, I — after some time — asked Professor Sandelin if I could take over his idea in a somewhat modified form, and if he would be willing to contribute. Happily, he immediately responded positively to both requests. I am very grateful for that graciousness and for his valuable contribution to this volume.

I then approached my two Norwegian friends and Philo scholars alike, Associate Professor Dr. Per Jarle Bekken and Prof. Emeritus, Dr.Theol., and Ph.D. Peder J. Borgen, if they would join me in the project of writing *A Handbook to Philo.* As they both agreed, the main outline and a suggestion of coauthors was worked out over a fine dinner in an Indian restaurant in Oslo. I am very grateful for their interest, encouragement, and help in this project, especially in its early stages.

At first we talked about making this a Scandinavian project, but it soon turned out that this idea was too ambitious and hardly realizable. There are not that many Philo scholars in the Scandinavian or Nordic countries, and some of those that might have contributed were not able to do so. Hence we looked to some of our other friends and Philo scholars in the wider scholarly world, made up a list, contacted them, and asked for their possible contributions. The result, I believe, has been a group of very representative and distinguished Philo scholars who each approach him from their special angle of interest and expertise. The ensuing book, I hope, will prove itself to be relevant and interesting for all those wanting to approach the works of Philo, whether they want to study him as a Diaspora Jew, an Alexandrian theologian, philosopher, or politician, or as a person who has had an immense influence on early Christian theology. While the primary group of readers may be beginning M.A. and Ph.D. students, I am convinced that others will also find here something of interest when it comes to reading Philo.

TORREY SELAND
Stavanger, Norway
March 3, 2014

Acknowledgments

First of all, I am immensely grateful to all my coauthors in this project. When asked, they all responded positively to my request for a contribution. That made my work as an editor so much easier.

Two of the chapters in this volume have been published earlier in identical or somewhat altered form; the others are completely new and written for this volume. I am grateful to Adele Reinhartz, who willingly accepted my request to use her piece "Philo's *Exposition of the Law* and Social History: Methodological Considerations," originally printed in *Society of Biblical Literature 1993 Seminar Papers,* ed. Eugene H. Lovering Jr. (Atlanta: Scholars, 1993) 6-21, and to Wm. B. Eerdmans Publishing Co. for allowing their author Peder Borgen to reuse his work "Philo of Alexandria as Exegete," here in a slightly modified form (originally published in *A History of Biblical Interpretation.* Vol 1: *The Ancient Period,* ed. Alan J. Hauser and Duane F. Watson [Grand Rapids: Eerdmans, 2003] 114-43).

Then I myself was greatly helped in getting time to write my contributions by a two-month scholarship in 2011 from *Det faglitterære fond, Norway,* a support for which I am most grateful.

Finally, it was a great inspiration to present the project to Eerdmans, represented by their senior editor Allen Myers. Eerdmans at once agreed to take upon themselves the burden of publishing this book. They have seen the manuscript pass through the various stages of production with an eagle's eyes, and I am very grateful for their encouraging support.

Abbreviations

GENERAL

AB	Anchor Bible
ABD	*Anchor Bible Dictionary,* ed. David Noel Freedman. 6 vols. New York: Doubleday, 1992.
AGJU	Arbeiten zur Geschichte des antiken Judentums und des Urchristentums
AJP	*American Journal of Philology*
ALGHJ	Arbeiten zur Literatur und Geschichte des hellenistischen Judentums
AnBib	Analecta biblica
ANRW	*Aufstieg und Niedergang der Römischen Welt: Geschichte und Kultur Roms Im Spiegel der Neueren Forschung,* ed. Hildegard Temporini and Wolfgang Haase. Berlin: de Gruyter, 1972–.
ANTC	Abingdon New Testament Commentaries
ASP	American Studies in Papyrology
BA	*Biblical Archaeologist*
BAR	*Biblical Archaeology Review*
BASP	Bulletin of the American Society of Papyrologists
BBR	*Bulletin for Biblical Research*
BEATAJ	Beiträge zur Erforschung des Alten Testaments und des antiken Judentum
BETL	Bibliotheca ephemeridum theologicarum lovanensium
BJS	Brown Judaic Studies

BRS	Biblical Resources Series
BWANT	Beiträge zur Wissenschaft vom Alten und Neuen Testament
BZ	*Biblische Zeitschrift*
BZNW	Beihefte zur Zeitschrift für die neutestamentliche Wissenschaft
CBQMS	Catholic Biblical Quarterly Monograph Series
CP	*Classical Philology*
CPJ	*Corpus papyrorum Judaicarum*, ed. Victor A. Tcherikover, Alexander Fuks, and Menahem Stern. 3 vols. Cambridge, MA: Harvard University Press, 1957-64.
CQ	*Classical Quarterly*
CRINT	Compendia rerum iudaicarum ad Novum Testamentum
DMOA	Documenta et monumenta Orientis antiqui
DNP	*Der Neue Pauly: Enzyklopädie der Antike,* ed. Hubert Cancik und Helmuth Schneider. Stuttgart: Metzler, 1996–.
EBib	*Etudes bibliques*
EPRO	Etudes préliminaires aux religions orientales dans l'empire romain
HDR	Harvard Dissertations in Religion
Hen	*Henoch*
HNT	Handbuch zum Neuen Testament
HSS	Harvard Semitic Series
HTR	*Harvard Theological Review*
HUCA	*Hebrew Union College Annual*
JAAR	*Journal of the American Academy of Religion*
JBL	*Journal of Biblical Literature*
JEA	*Journal of Egyptian Archaeology*
JECS	*Journal of Early Christian Studies*
JQR	*Jewish Quarterly Review*
JRS	*Journal of Roman Studies*
JSJ	*Journal for the Study of Judaism*
JSJSup	Supplements to Journal for the Study of Judaism
JSNT	*Journal for the Study of the New Testament*
JSOTSup	Journal for the Study of the Old Testament Supplement Series
JSP	*Journal for the Study of the Pseudepigrapha*
JTS	*Journal of Theological Studies*
LCL	Loeb Classical Library
LNTS	Library of New Testament Studies
LSTS	Library of Second Temple Studies
MDAI	*Mitteilungen des Deutschen archäologischen Instituts*

MGWJ	Monatschrift für Geschichte und Wissenschaft des Judentums
Mus	*Muséon*
NedTT	*Nederlands theologisch tijdschrift*
NovT	*Novum Testamentum*
NovTSup	Supplements to Novum Testamentum
NTS	*New Testament Studies*
PACS	Philo of Alexandria Commentary Series
PCW	Leopold Cohn, Paul Wendland, Siegfried Reiter, and Hans Leisegang, eds. *Philonis Alexandrini opera quae supersunt.* 7 vols. Berlin: Reimer, 1896-1930; repr., Berlin: de Gruyter, 1962-63.
PG	Patrologia graeca, ed. J.-P. Migne. 162 vols. Paris: Lutetiae, 1857-86.
PL	Patrologia latina, ed. J.-P. Migne. 217 vols. Paris, 1844-64.
PRSt	*Perspectives in Religious Studies*
PW	*Paulys real-encyclopädie der classischen Altertumswissenschaft,* ed. August Friedrich von Pauly. New ed. Georg Wissowa. Stuttgart: Metzler, 1894–
RAC	*Reallexikon für Antike und Christentum,* ed. Theodor Klauser et al. Stuttgart: Hiersemann, 1950–.
REG	*Revue des études grecques*
REJ	*Revue des études juives*
RGG⁴	*Religion in Geschichte und Gegenwart,* ed. Hans Dieter Betz. 4th ed. 9 vols. Tübingen: Mohr, 1998-2007.
SBLDS	Society of Biblical Literature Dissertation Series
SBLPS	Society of Biblical Literature Pseudepigrapha Series
SBLTT	Society of Biblical Literature Texts and Translations
SC	Sources chrétiennes. Paris: Cerf, 1943–.
SEG	Supplementum epigraphicum graecum
SHR	Studies in the History of Religions (supplement to *Numen*)
SIG	*Sylloge inscriptionum graecarum,* ed. Wilhelm Dittenberger. 4 vols. 3rd ed. Leipzig: Hirzel, 1915-24.
SJ	Studia judaica
SJLA	Studies in Judaism in Late Antiquity
SNTSMS	Society for New Testament Studies Monograph Series
SPhAn	*Studia Philonica Annual*
SPhilo	*Studia Philonica*
SPhilMon	Studia Philonica Monograph
SR	*Studies in Religion*

ST	*Studia theologica*
STAC	Studien und Texte zu Antike und Christentum
STDJ	Studies on the Texts of the Desert of Judah
Str-B	Hermann L. Strack and Paul Billerbeck, *Kommentar zum Neuen Testament aus Talmud und Midrasch*. 6 vols. Munich: Beck, 1922-61.
SUNT	Studien zur Umwelt des Neuen Testaments
SVTP	Studia in Veteris Testamenti pseudepigraphica
ThH	Théologie historique
TSAJ	Texte und Studien zum antiken Judentum
TTKi	*Tidsskrift for Teologi og Kirke*
TUGAL	Texte und Untersuchungen zur Geschichte der altchristlichen Literatur
VC	*Vigiliae christianae*
VCSup	Supplements to Vigiliae christianae
VTSup	Supplements to Vetus Testamentum
WBC	Word Biblical Commentary
WUNT	Wissenschaftliche Untersuchungen zum Neuen Testament
ZNW	*Zeitschrift für die neutestamentliche Wissenschaft*

PHILO

Abr.	*De Abrahamo/On the Life of Abraham*
Aet.	*De aeternitate mundi/On the Eternity of the World*
Agr.	*De agricultura/On Agriculture*
Anim.	*De animalibus/Whether Animals Have Reason*
Cher.	*De cherubim/On the Cheribim*
Conf.	*De confusione linguarum/On the Confusion of Tongues*
Congr.	*De congressu eruditionis gratia/On the Preliminary Studies*
Contempl.	*De vita contemplativa/On the Contemplative Life*
Decal.	*De decalogo/On the Decalogue*
Deo	*De Deo/On God*
Det.	*Quod deterius potiori insidari soleat/That the Worse Attacks the Better*
Deus	*Quod Deus sit immutabilis/That God Is Unchangeable*
Ebr.	*De ebrietate/On Drunkenness*
Flacc.	*In Flaccum/Against Flaccus*
Fug.	*De fuga et inventione/On Flight and Finding*

Gig.	*De gigantibus*/On Giants
Her.	*Quis rerum divinarum heres sit*/Who Is the Heir?
Hypoth.	*Hypothetica*
Ios.	*De Iosepho*/On the Life of Joseph
Leg.	*Legum allegoriae*/Allegorical Interpretation
Legat.	*Legatio ad Gaium*/On the Embassy to Gaius
Migr.	*De migratione Abrahami*/On the Migration of Abraham
Mos.	*De vita Mosis*/On the Life of Moses
Mut.	*De mutatione nominum*/On the Change of Names
Opif.	*De opificio mundi*/On the Creation of the World
Plant.	*De plantatione*/On Planting
Post.	*De posteritate Caini*/On the Posterity of Cain
Praem.	*De praemiis et poenis*/On Rewards and Punishments
Prob.	*Quod omnis probus liber sit*/That Every Good Person Is Free
Prov.	*De providentia*/On Providence
QE	*Quaestiones et solutiones in Exodum*/Questions and Answers on Exodus
QG	*Quaestiones et solutiones in Genesin*/Questions and Answers on Genesis
Sacr.	*De sacrificiis Abelis et Caini*/On the Sacrifices of Cain and Abel
Sobr.	*De sobrietate*/On Sobriety
Somn.	*De somniis*/On Dreams
Spec.	*De specialibus legibus*/On the Special Laws
Virt.	*De virtutibus*/On the Virtues

Introduction and Motivation

Philo of Alexandria: An Introduction

Torrey Seland

Who was Philo of Alexandria? Why is it important to study him? And how are we to study him? These are some of the questions that this *Handbook to Philo* will address. Whether you are an M.A. or Ph.D. student, a student of the New Testament or Judaism in general, or just happened to pick up this book, we do hope that a reading of the chapters contained here will prove both interesting and rewarding for your studies.

There are, admittedly, several other introductions to Philo available on the market.[1] The present one is meant to be a very practical resource for reading and understanding this important Hellenistic Jewish philosopher. This book is not meant, however, to be read in isolation from, or in preference for, reading the works of Philo himself. Nothing can substitute a reading of his works directly, whether in a good translation or, preferably, in Greek or with access to the Greek text. One of the chapters in this collection is especially designed as a practical help in how to read Philo's works — focusing on what text editions, translations, and other auxiliary tools are available and particularly useful in trying to understand Philo's works and significance.[2]

This handbook is designed as a firsthand introduction to the works and significance of Philo of Alexandria, written by experienced and well-known Philo experts. The intended readership is M.A. and Ph.D. students who are just embarking on a study of Philo. Here is a presentation and discussion of

---

1. See Seland, "Why Study Philo? How?" below.
2. See Seland, "Why Study Philo? How?" below.

aspects and issues considered especially relevant for a reader who wants to learn more about Philo as a Jewish philosopher, scholar, writer, or politician. Hence whether your intention is to gain knowledge of New Testament background, or become better acquainted with how a Jewish theologian and philosopher in Alexandria might present himself and his ideas, or just study Philo as an example of a first-century C.E. Jew living and working in the Diaspora, your knowledge will be considerably enhanced. Perhaps, however, you have other interests, or your purpose may be somewhat vague as you open this book. It is hoped that you will find something here to digest and enjoy. Perhaps your interest will even be piqued to pursue the authors' suggestions for further research.

Philo of Alexandria is a fascinating person, but at the same time also somewhat of an enigma, even to scholars who have long tried to understand him, his works, and his position in the social world of Alexandria at the beginning of our era. In this brief introduction we shall first deal with biographical aspects often considered relevant for understanding Philo and then provide an overview of the various contributions that follow and their role in assessing the importance and value of Philo for students of antiquity.

Some Biographical Issues

Philo of Alexandria, Philo Alexandrinus, or Philo Judaeus, as he is most commonly called, is known primarily through his legacy of books, written in Greek, that are still available to us. But he is also mentioned in several other sources, including Josephus — the first-century C.E. Jewish historian — and several of the church fathers. From what is available about him from these sources, we are able to gather that he wrote somewhat more than seventy treatises, of which about fifty are still extant in whole or in part. This tremendous production is in itself enough to make one curious about his biography, thoughts, work, and influence.

With regard to Philo's life, we encounter a number of problems, represented in no small number by the many "unknowns" or "uncertainties." Yet compared with what we know about other individuals from approximately the same period, our knowledge is nevertheless fairly good. While the dates of his birth and death, for instance, cannot be given with exactitude, they can be plausibly determined. Most probably his lifetime spanned the period between 20-15 B.C.E. to 45-50 C.E., although we have no solid indicators to be more exact. Such is the case with many other persons from antiquity. What we do know indicates that he is to be considered a contemporary of both Jesus of Nazareth and the apostle Paul. There is little reason, however, to presume that they knew each other or that there was any mutual knowledge of the writings now being associated with Paul or Philo. Paul does not mention Philo, nor does any serious scholar today suggest that Philo mentions the Christians in any of his writings.[3]

Philo belonged to a rich and influential family in Alexandria.[4] His brother Alexander Lysimachus was "alabarch," perhaps an office concerned with administration of the paying of taxes and customs.[5] That his family was rich is strongly indicated by Josephus, who says that Alexander "surpassed all his fellow citizens both in ancestry and in wealth" (*Ant.* 20.100). Philo thus undoubtedly belonged to the elite segment of the Jewish Alexandrian community.[6] Josephus also tells us that Alexander once lent a large amount of money to Agrippa, one of the kings-to-be in the Land of Israel, or more accurately, to Agrippa's wife Cypros, because he did not trust Agrippa (*Ant.* 18.159). Alexander also disclosed his wealth and demonstrated his reverence for the temple of Jerusalem by clothing nine of its ten gates with gold and silver (*J. W.* 5.205). Alexander's position in the Alexandria of his day was also witnessed in his close relationship to the later emperor Claudius and his mother Antonia. Gaius Calicula (emperor 37-41 C.E.), however, had Alexander thrown in jail, but Claudius released him when he became emperor in 41 C.E. (*Ant.* 19.276).

One of Alexander's sons, Marcus Julius Alexander, was married to Berenice, the daughter of Agrippa (*Ant.* 19.277). Another son is mentioned more often in our sources, namely, Tiberius Julius Alexander.[7] According to Jose-

3. That was not always so. Cf. F. H. Colson in *Philo IX* (LCL; London: Heinemann and Cambridge, MA: Harvard University Press, 1941) 106-8; and David T. Runia, *Philo in Early Christian Literature* (CRINT 3/3; Assen: Van Gorcum; Minneapolis: Fortress, 1993).

4. For a recent discussion of Philo's family, see Daniel R. Schwartz, "Philo, His Family, and His Times," in *The Cambridge Companion to Philo,* ed. Adam Kamesar (Cambridge: Cambridge University Press, 2009) 9-31.

5. Cf. the comments in Josephus, *Ant.* 18.159 (LCL).

6. See also my summary in Torrey Seland, *Establishment Violence in Philo and Luke: A Study of Non-conformity to the Torah and Jewish Vigilante Reactions* (Biblical Interpretation 15; Leiden: Brill, 1995) 82-93; and now also Peder Borgen, *Philo of Alexandria: An Exegete for His Time* (NovTSup 86; Leiden: Brill, 1997) 14-26.

7. On Tiberius, see Robert Ernest Bennett, "The Prefects of Roman Egypt 30 B.C.-69 A.D." (Ph.D diss., Yale University, 1971) 134-47; E. G. Turner, "Tiberius Iulius Alexander," *JRS* 44 (1954) 54-64; and now esp. Katherine G. Evans, "Alexander the Alabarch: Roman and Jew," in *Society*

phus, Tiberius did not persevere in the traditions of his fathers (*Ant.* 20.100; τοῖς γὰρ πατρίοις οὐκ ἐνέμεινεν οὗτος ἔθεσιν) — that is, he probably left Judaism[8] — and he had a great career in the service of the Romans. In ca. 46-48 C.E. he was procurator of Judea (*Ant.* 20.100; *J. W.* 2.220), and in ca. 66-70 he was prefect of Egypt (cf. *J. W.* 2.309.492-98). Tiberius also participated actively in the campaigns against Jerusalem in 66-70 C.E. (*J. W.* 5.45-46; 6.237).

Philo must have had — at least for some time — close contact with his nephew Tiberius. It is almost generally accepted among scholars that Tiberius figures directly or indirectly as a debater with his uncle in two of Philo's writings. In *De providentia* they discuss whether the world is governed by the providence of God, an issue Tiberius doubts. In *De animalibus*[9] the topic of discussion is whether animals have reason. Philo here discusses a work possibly written by Tiberius Alexander. These insights into Philo's family indicate that it must have been both rich and influential, and that at least one of Philo's close relatives was an apostate.[10]

Scholars often try to study Philo's attitudes to Greco-Roman culture by investigating his views of the encyclical education, the *enkyklios paideia*.[11] It seems to be Philo's view that these institutions represent an issue of "adiaphora": they are in and by themselves neither only good nor only bad (cf.

---

of Biblical Literature 1995 Seminar Papers, ed. Eugene H. Lovering Jr. (Atlanta: Scholars, 1995) 576-94.

8. For a discussion of Tiberius's apostasy, see Joseph Mélèze Modrzejewski, *The Jews of Egypt: From Rameses II to Emperor Hadrian,* trans. Robert Cornman (Edinburgh: T. & T. Clark, 1995) 185-90; and Gottfried Schimanowski, *Juden und Nichtjuden in Alexandrien: Koexistenz und Konflikte bis zum Pogrom unter Trajan (117 n. Chr.)* (Münsteraner Judaistische Studien 18; Berlin: LIT, 2006) 135-39.

9. Cf. Abraham Terian, "A Critical Introduction to Philo's Dialogues," in *ANRW* 2.21.1 (1984) 272-94.

10. Against this background of the wealth of his family it is somewhat strange to read Philo's negative comments about wealth and prosperity. He even refers to "us poor people" (*Spec.* 2.20). These sayings are probably not to be taken as expressions of personal poverty but are related to the traditions he addresses in various contexts. See David L. Mealand, "Philo of Alexandria's Attitude to Riches," *ZNW* 69 (1978) 258-64; "The Paradox of Philo's Views on Wealth," *JSNT* 24 (1985) 111-15; F. Gerald Downing, "Philo on Wealth and the Rights of the Poor," *JSNT* 24 (1985) 116-18.

11. Alan Mendelson, *Secular Education in Philo of Alexandria* (Monographs of the Hebrew Union College 7; Cincinnati: Hebrew Union College Press, 1982); Aryeh Kasher, "The Jewish Attitude to the Alexandrian Gymnasium in the First Century A.D.," *American Journal of Ancient History* 1 (1976) 148-61; *The Jews in Hellenistic and Roman Egypt: The Struggle for Equal Rights* (TSAJ 7; Tübingen: Mohr Siebeck, 1985).

Congr. 35; *Fug.* 212-13). According to Philo, they are in fact only preliminary to the study of the real and genuine philosophy represented by the law, i.e., by Judaism.

Several references in his works can be taken as indicating that Philo himself had undergone the encyclical education (*Congr.* 74-76). It is not quite clear, however, in what setting he received this education. Harry Austryn Wolfson[12] believed that the Jews had such educational institutions of their own, but surmised that Philo's sayings may not be related to actual education. Aryeh Kasher[13] argues that the Jews had no desire to receive the Greco-Roman education of the encyclia, since that in fact represented apostasy. The dissension in recent research on this question stems from the fact that the education of the encyclia was necessary to obtain the rights of citizenship, and it is not quite clear whether the Jews enjoyed these rights at the time of Philo. Presupposing that such education, however, was accessible to some Jews, at least to the rich and elite members of Jewish families, and due to the fairly good knowledge of these institutions evidenced in the writings of Philo, it is commonly held among scholars today that he received his education in a Greco-Roman cultural setting, most probably in a Greek gymnasion.[14]

Hence it comes as no surprise that Philo's writings demonstrate that he had a fairly good knowledge of Greco-Roman culture, and not least of the various philosophers and their ideas. Influence from the works of Plato, Pythagoreanism, and Stoicism is especially prominent in Philo.[15]

Considering his education, one might also ask what Philo's profession was. What prompted him to write his many books? Was he a teacher, and if so, who were his students? Such questions are among those most discussed in Philonic research. Philo himself nowhere directly indicates his profession, and references that might be used for constructing a professional image of Philo are very few and ambiguous indeed.

In *Ant.* 18.259, Josephus comments on the Alexandrian delegation that was sent to Rome to intercede for the Jews with Emperor Gaius Caligula in 38 C.E. Josephus here presents Philo as "a man held in the highest honor, brother of Alexander the alabarch, and no novice in philosophy." It is also

---

12. Harry Austryn Wolfson, *Philo: Foundations of Religious Philosophy in Judaism, Christianity, and Islam* (Cambridge, MA: Harvard University Press, 1948) 1:79ff.

13. Kasher, "The Jews in Hellenistic and Roman Egypt."

14. Cf., e.g., Schwartz, "Philo, His Family, and His Times," 18.

15. Quotations and allusions to various philosophers are numerous. Wolfson (*Philo*, 1:93) lists twenty-three philosophers whom he finds cited in the works of Philo.

obvious from Philo's own writings that he held official positions in the city, and the story of the delegation to Rome is told in his *Legatio ad Gaium*. It is, however, not obvious what kind of office he did hold, and for how long. Erwin R. Goodenough[16] emphasizes that "his duties were of a judicial character," but admits that "this cannot be demonstrated." An autobiographical section in *Spec.* 3.1-5 has been interpreted as indicating that first, and for a rather long period, Philo was primarily concerned with his philosophy and his writing. He later was drawn reluctantly into the political life of the Jewish community in Alexandria. This is a possible interpretation, but it is very difficult to say anything more explicit about when it became necessary for Philo to indulge in the political affairs of his city (contra Goodenough). The reference in *Spec.* 3.1-5 may primarily indicate Philo's frustration over political responsibilities overcoming his activity as a philosopher, in which he had much more delight (cf. also *Spec.* 2.44).[17]

Those who focus on Philo's literary activities have suggested that he must have had a thorough education, and some suggest that he might also have been a teacher himself. Gregory E. Sterling has set forth a fascinating hypothesis about Philo's scholarly activities: "I suggest that Philo had a private school in his home or personally owned structure for advanced students which were similar to schools of higher education run by individuals throughout the Greco-Roman world."[18] Evidence for this is, certainly, circumstantial, as Sterling himself admits. Sterling nevertheless offers several arguments in support of this view. First, he points to the plausibility that Philo worked within an exegetical tradition, as his references to other exegetes, whether literalists or allegorists, seem to indicate.[19] Second, Philo probably employed some types of sources (cf. *Mos.* 1.4); third, he was probably aware of other extant Diaspora-Jewish works (Aristobulus; Pseudo-Aristeas; Ezekiel the Tragedian), hence he was working within a tradition that also continued after him. Sterling also points to other indicators in Philo's own texts, including his descriptions of the Therapeutae. The very nature of several of his works, e.g., his two books on *Questions and Answers* and his several commentaries, point to Philo's involvement in educational

16. Erwin R. Goodenough, "Philo and Public Life," *JEA* 12 (1926) 77-79.

17. For more discussion on Philo's possible political activities, see the chapter below by Seland, "Philo as a Citizen: Homo politicus."

18. Gregory E. Sterling, "The School of Sacred Laws: The Social Setting of Philo's Treatises," *VC* 53 (1999) 150.

19. Cf. David M. Hay, "Philo's References to Other Allegorists," *SPhilo* 6 (1979-80) 41-75; Montgomery J. Shroyer, "Alexandrian Jewish Literalists," *JBL* 55 (1936) 261-84.

activities.[20] Hence it is possible that he functioned as a teacher, working in a setting comparable to those known of others approximately contemporary. Such a context would represent an appropriate setting for many of his works.[21]

What This Book Is About

The first five chapters in this handbook deal with Philo of Alexandria in context (pp. 19-154). First, the Finnish scholar Karl-Gustav Sandelin focuses on Philo as a Jew (pp. 19-46). However one might describe Philo, there is no doubt that he was a Jew, both by ethnicity and by conviction. Just what constituted the nature of Philo's Jewishness has been discussed, but there is no doubt that he was very much committed to the Jewish people and its traditions.[22] Sandelin addresses some of the standard views of Philo's Jewishness, but he himself favors Philo as a representative of the Jewish wisdom tradition.[23] Here he attempts to illuminate Philo as a Jew from three perspectives: (1) What should be said in general terms of Philo as a Jew; i.e., how is Philo a Jew like any other Jews of his time? Here Sandelin presents and briefly discusses issues including Philo's view of God; the Bible and the law; and such aspects of Jewish practice as Sabbath observance, dietary laws, sexuality and marriage, and temple service. (2) What is it in Philo's Judaism that makes it distinctive? Sandelin here points in particular to the realms of Wisdom and the Word and the place of humans within these two realms. He then discusses Philo's views on the ideal Jew. (3) Judaism in Philo's time was not a monolithic phenomenon, and several Jewish groups existed. Does Philo adhere to the views and practices of any of these? Philo mentions in particular the Essenes and the Therapeutae. What does he say about them? Philo does not mention

20. Sterling, "'The School of Sacred Laws,'" 154-60.

21. For related issues, see below the chapters by Sandelin ("Philo as a Jew"), Koskenniemi ("Philo and Classical Education"), and Sterling ("'The Jewish Philosophy': Reading Moses via Hellenistic Philosophy according to Philo").

22. Cf. here Samuel Sandmel, himself a Jew, who considers Philo as fully immersed in Hellenistic culture and Greek philosophy yet nevertheless staunchly Jewish; *Philo's Place in Judaism: A Study of Conceptions of Abraham in Jewish Literature* (augmented ed.; New York: Ktav, 1971), xxiv.

23. See further Karl-Gustav Sandelin, *Wisdom as Nourisher: A Study of an Old Testament Theme, Its Development Within Early Judaism, and Its Impact on Early Christianity* (Acta Academiae Aboensis ser A: Humaniora 64/3; Åbo: Åbo Akademi, 1986); *Sophia och hennes värld: Exegetiska uppsatser från fyra årtionden* (Studier i exegetik och judaistik utgivna av Teologiska fakulteten vid Åbo Akademi 6; Åbo: Åbo Akademi, 2008).

the Pharisees or the Sadducees, but Sandelin briefly discusses Philo's views in relation to what we know about these two Palestinian groups. According to Sandelin, if we look for texts that represent views similar to Philo's, the book of Wisdom comes close, as does *Fourth Maccabees* (see, e.g., *4 Macc* 1:13-30; 5:34). Hence, Philo is not an isolated Jewish thinker in antiquity. Furthermore, he is not a Pharisee, still less a Sadducee. He sympathizes with the Essenes and admires the Therapeutae, although he is not a member of either. Yet as a theologian he does not stand isolated from other Jews.

The next chapter, by the editor of this volume, Torrey Seland, represents an investigation of the political aspects of Philo's public life, that is, an attempt at describing Philo as a citizen, as a *Homo politicus* (pp. 47-74). The main part of the essay is devoted to Philo's descriptions of Roman rule and his own activities as a politically active citizen. After some introductory comments on Philo's social location and his background as coming from a family of politicians, the chapter is divided into three main sections: recent studies on Philo and his politics; issues of political theory in Philo; and Philo as a practical politician. The first section discusses the contributions of Sterling Tracy, Erwin R. Goodenough, Samuel Sandmel, and Ray Barraclough. In the next section, Seland presents Philo's views on the role of Israel in the world, of himself as a cosmopolite, and the Torah as the Law of Nature. He then addresses Philo's much-discussed views on Joseph as a politician. In the final section, Seland deals with the picture of Philo as a practical politician as drawn from his writings. Here the interpretation of *Spec.* 3.1-6 is crucial, as are Philo's descriptions of, and his attitude to and possible role in, the conflicts in Alexandria in 38-41 C.E. Finally, Seland points out some major problems in interpreting Philo's narratives as well as other problems and prospects in understanding him as a politician.

Whatever one might think about Philo as a politician, one thing is certain, that Philo was an interpreter of the Jewish Scriptures. The Norwegian doyen of Philo studies, Peder Borgen, addresses this topic in his chapter "Philo — An Interpreter of the Laws of Moses" (pp. 75-101).[24] Among Philo's

---

24. Borgen has written extensively on this topic. A student of Philo familiarizing herself with these issues should be acquainted with these works: Peder Borgen, *Bread from Heaven: An Exegetical Study of the Concept of Manna in the Gospel of John and the Writings of Philo* (NovTSup 10; Leiden: Brill, 1981); *Philo of Alexandria, An Exegete for His Time*. See also Borgen's collection, *Philo, John, and Paul: New Perspectives on Judaism and Early Christianity* (BJS 131; Atlanta: Scholars, 1987). The present chapter is a revised version of "Philo of Alexandria as Exegete," in *A History of Biblical Interpretation*. Vol 1: *The Ancient Period*, ed. Alan J. Hauser and Duane F. Watson (Grand Rapids: Eerdmans, 2003) 114-43.

writings, the expository works are of central interest for understanding him as an exegete. In these writings, Philo demonstrates his primary role as an interpreter of the Pentateuch (his works provide only a few references to nonpentateuchal books). Borgen first discusses Philo's expository treatises, which fall into two main categories: those rewriting the Pentateuch and his exegetical commentaries, comprising the *Allegorical Commentary* on Genesis and the *Questions and Answers* on Genesis and Exodus. He briefly presents the most important of Philo's hermeneutical presuppositions under three headings: God's laws proclaimed to the Greek-speaking world; the Mosaic law and the cosmic law; and the deeper meanings. He then looks at several aspects of Philo's exegesis. Here he finds that "Philo moves from one level of meaning to another by proceeding from macrocosm to microcosm, from individuals to the virtues and vices they embody, from specific command-ments to their ethical meanings, and by anthropomorphic statements and etymologies. Angels are seen as means of communication between the levels" (pp. 81-82). Borgen notes Philo's use of several exegetical approaches and forms: question and answer, direct exegesis, contrast, paraphrastic rewriting, rewriting of the Bible, and commentary. Finally, Borgen discusses the historical writings *Against Flaccus* and *On the Embassy to Gaius* as a report on a struggle for the interpretation and application of the laws of Moses in the context of the Jewish community and its status in Alexandria as well as in Palestine. The chapter ends with a brief overview on the use of Philo's works by the church fathers.

The matter of Philo's education has been much discussed, with views ranging from Philo as a most conservative Jew to a Jew very much accultur-ated to Greco-Roman society and its educational ideals. The Finnish scholar Erkki Koskenniemi concentrates on these issues in his chapter "Philo and Classical Education" (pp. 102-28).[25] His study presents what we generally know of Greek education and explores the options Jews had — and were willing to employ in Greek Alexandria. Koskenniemi investigates what Philo himself says on the topic, details how Philo uses or mentions Greek philos-ophers and poets, and estimates how well he was versed in secular literature. While exploring Philo's secular training, the chapter also contributes to our knowledge of Greek education in general.

25. Relevant studies include Erkki Koskenniemi, "Moses — A Well-Educated Man: A Look at the Educational Idea in Early Judaism," *JSP* 17 (2008) 281-96; "Philo and Classical Drama," in *Ancient Israel, Judaism, and Christianity in Contemporary Perspective: Essays in Memory of Karl-Johan Illman,* ed. Jacob Neusner et al. (Lanham: University Press of America, 2006) 137-51.

The chapter opens with an informative review of what we know and what we do not know about classical education as represented by the Greek gymnasion. Koskenniemi's main thesis here is that the educational systems were not identical in every place and every time, and in particular that we are not able to define a fixed curriculum, or even claim that everyone studied the same matters, ἐγκύκλιος παιδεία having all too often been considered an early and clearly defined set of studies. The gymnasion was a very important institution in the Greek world, but it was certainly not consistent throughout. The duration of the training varied greatly, and apparently so did the number of non-Greeks attending the gymnasion.

The scattered evidence does not allow an accurate presentation of the education and educational institutions in Greek Egypt in general, and in Alexandria in particular. As for Philo and his education, Koskenniemi contends that, for the sake of accuracy, Philo does not speak specifically of the gymnasion and the training given there, but of gymnasial training, which leaves open the place and the institution. In explaining the commandments to his Jewish audience, Philo assumes that parents had provided this kind of education for their children. It would be simplest to say that Philo refers only to the gymnasion. But if only a small part of the Jewish population was admitted to that institution, Koskenniemi asks whether those Jews were the only ones who received that kind of education.

The last section of his study is devoted to Philo's knowledge of the Greek philosophers and poets (pp. 121-27), and Koskenniemi sees here evidence that Philo was among those who had enjoyed access to the Greek gymnasion, an access that was not only endangered, but also probably denied to Jews at the end of his life (cf. the letter of Claudius to the Alexandrians). The chapter thus demonstrates that there is much we do not know about Philo and the social conditions of the Jews in Alexandria. Perhaps this study will whet the appetite of some readers to seek more knowledge.

Gregory E. Sterling, in his chapter "'The Jewish Philosophy': Reading Moses via Hellenistic Philosophy according to Philo" (pp. 129-54), follows up on the last section of Koskenniemi's essay and deals explicitly with the question of Philo's relations to philosophy. After reflecting on how other authors regard Philo as a philosopher, Sterling addresses the issue of philosophy in the works of Philo. He argues that it is impossible to read Philo without some understanding of his relationship to Hellenistic philosophical traditions. Acknowledging the insights of Philo's Alexandrian predecessors (Aristobulus, Pseudo-Aristeas, the allegorists), Sterling demonstrates that Philo stood within a line of philosophically oriented interpreters, thus working within a tradition; he had both predecessors and contemporary figures who were deeply indepted to philosophy. Philo himself, however, should be considered as an eclectic thinker; he drew upon what he considered to be the best from several traditions and incorporated that into his thought. Hence he was deeply influenced by Platonism, Stoicism, Aristotle, the Peripatetics, Neopythagoreans, and other influential philosophers. However, as an expositor of the Jewish Scriptures Philo was primarily an exegete and not a philosopher. Commenting on Moses' Pentateuch was the focus of his life. Yet he was reading the texts philosophically by means of allegory, as is especially evident in his great allegorical commentaries. Sterling thinks that Philo taught in a kind of school and that he believed "that Hellenistic philosophy — at least the traditions he accepted — and the Jewish faith came together at the most important juncture: the understanding of the divine" (pp. 153-54).

Why, then, should a person study Philo? And how should one go about it? With an emphasis on the second question, the five chapters in the second main part of this handbook all deal with various aspects of why and how to study Philo.

The first of these, by Torrey Seland, is meant to be a very practical introduction in how to proceed when embarking on a study of Philo of Alexandria. Accordingly, it deals not only with where to begin among Philo's many writings, but also with available text editions, translations, indexes, and lexica, as well as how to read Philo on the computer, whether using programs containing his texts or by means of various searching resources. The chapter also lists and comments on bibliographies, reviews, and other handbooks as well as commentaries and introductions. Hence the beginning M.A. or Ph.D. student might find here some very practical help not usually available elsewhere.

Philo's works are often scrutinized in searches for philosophical and/or theological topics, whether as part of background studies for New Testament studies, for example, or as part of Philo's own thought world. The works of Philo also represent a significant resource for understanding social issues and the social history of the Jewish life in the Diaspora. Adele Reinhartz's chapter, "Philo's *Exposition of the Law* and Social History: Methodological Considerations" (pp. 180-99), remains a valuable resource dealing precisely with such matters.[26] It represents an initial attempt to address whether it may

---

26. First publishd in *Society of Biblical Literature 1993 Seminar Papers,* ed. Eugene H. Lovering Jr. (Atlanta: Scholars, 1993) 6-21; cf. http://www.torreys.org/philo-art/reinhartz.pdf.

be possible to draw social-historical data from Philo's exegetical discussions in the *Exposition*.[27]

In her study, Reinhartz carefully lays out the problems and prospects of using both Philo's renderings of the Jewish Torah as well as his interpretations of the same. In employing his works, one should pay careful attention to the relationship between biblical legislation and Philo's exegesis; his preferences and concerns may be based on the realities of Jewish family life in Alexandria. Especially interesting are the passages in which Philo extends the scope of biblical law to cover areas not mentioned in the biblical texts. Furthermore, Reinhartz suggests, one should also pay attention to Philo's "tone, length, and content of a particular comment." In addition, Philo's "throwaway" comments and references to contemporary issues and events may also provide hints concerning social structures and norms. However, whatever use one might want to make of Philo, the findings must also be investigated while drawing on other sources and data; in this way they may be corroborated or corrected. Thus, looking for source material for understanding and describing the social Jewish world of the Diaspora, Philo's works should not be studied in isolation, but may nevertheless yield important insights.

The next three contributions to this handbook deal not so much with methodology proper (the how question), as with what fields, areas, and subjects of study might receive helpful insights from a reading of Philo (the why question). The three areas represented are Judaism, the New Testament, and the early church fathers.

Jewish scholar Ellen Birnbaum provides a very informative chapter, "Philo's Relevance for the Study of Jews and Judaism in Antiquity" (pp. 220-225), representing a fresh consideration of how Philo should be viewed as important for the study of Judaism.

Philo's works provide abundant information regarding his contemporaries. One should keep in mind that, as a representative of the elite segments in Alexandria, Philo was not typical of most Jews there. Nevertheless, as Birnbaum argues, his volumes shed light on both the commonality and the diversity among these and other Jews. She therefore offers comprehensive insights into seven areas in which Philo's works contribute to our under-

---

27. As such it was a preliminary study for her investigations into Jewish family life in the Diaspora. Cf. Adele Reinhartz, "Parents and Children: A Philonic Perspective," in *The Jewish Family in Antiquity*, ed. Shaye D. Cohen (BJS 298; Atlanta: Scholars, 1993) 61-88; "Philo on Infanticide," *SPhAn* 4 (1992) 42-58.

standing: Jewish practices; beliefs and ideas; community institutions; the Bible and exegesis; Jews and Jewish identity; Jews' attitudes towards non-Jews and their culture; and historical events pertaining to the Jews. Birnbaum's review of the relevant issues also draws attention to several aspects that are in need of further studies.

The Norwegian scholar Per Jarle Bekken[28] addresses Philo's relevance for the study of the New Testament (pp. 226-67). While some might think it would be most pertinent to proceed from book to book in the New Testament, looking for similarities and parallels in Philo's works,[29] Bekken has chosen a thematic approach. He surveys a vast range of representative topics and texts which might show how a study of Philo is relevant for a New Testament student. The main sections of this chapter are Scripture and exegesis; beliefs, motifs, and metaphors; Jews' relation to non-Jews and pagan society; inner-Jewish conflicts and punishments; and historical information. The information gathered here witnesses to the wide variety of topics that have been dealt with in New Testament studies utilizing insights from Philo. Bekken's presentation is a valuable introduction to the usefulness of knowing Philo when studying the New Testament.

It was not the Jews, however, who preserved Philo's works for future generations. Rather, he was so embraced by Christians in the immediately following centuries that he actually fell out of favor in the struggling Jewish communities. Although particulars regarding the early preservation of his works remain hidden in obscurity, the church fathers provide ample evidence of how they employed his works and of their value for the emergent Christian communities, theologians, and theologies.[30] Hence it is only pertinent that this handbook includes a chapter on Philo and the patristic traditions.

28. Bekken, a former student of Peder Borgen, wrote his dissertation on Paul and Philo (1998) and is now working particularly on Philo and John. His dissertation has been published as *The Word Is Near You: A Study of Deuteronomy 30:12-14 in Paul's Letter to the Romans in a Jewish Context* (BZNW 144; Berlin: de Gruyter, 2007). See also Bekken, "Abraham og Ånden: Paulus' anvendelse av Genesis 15:6 i Galaterbrevet 3:6 belyst ut fra jødisk materiale," *TTKi* 71 (2000) 265-76; "Misjon og eskatologi: Noen observasjoner til Paulus' misjonsteologi på bakgrunn av eskatologiske forventninger i tidlig jødedom," *Norsk Tidsskrift for Misjon* 54 (2000) 85-104; "The Controversy on Self-Testimony According to John 5:31-40; 8:12-20 and Philo, Legum Allegoriae III.205-208," in *Identity Formation in the New Testament,* ed. Bengt Holmberg and Mikael Winninge (WUNT 227; Tübingen: Mohr Siebeck, 2008) 19-42.

29. The most recent review using this book by book procedure is Folker Siegert, "Philo and the New Testament," in Kamesar, *The Cambridge Companion to Philo,* 175-209.

30. An instructive review is to be found in Runia, *Philo in Early Christian Literature.*

Rather than a survey of the range of use and importance of Philo's works for the church fathers,[31] the final chapter of this handbook constitutes a list compiled by David T. Runia that aims to include every explicit reference to Philo in Christian sources up to 1000 C.E. This list will be of great value, for instance, for those who want to investigate how and/or to what extent a particular Christian author uses Philo's works.[32] Where possible, texts are cited for modern critical editions (full details can be found in the peerless volumes of the *Clavis patrum graecorum* and *Clavis patrum latinarum*), and brief summaries of the contents are provided. Preceding the list is a brief look at how Philo's writings survived and his influence on early Christian thought.

It is the hope of the editor and his coauthors that this handbook to Philo may prove itself valuable for those coming to the works of Philo in order to pursue studies of the man and his world, of Philo in his own context and of his influence even after he had laid down his pen. If none of Philo's works had survived his own times, we would indeed be much poorer not only in understanding antiquity, but also in understanding much that remains with us in the form of Scriptures, traditions, and values.[33] *Tolle lege.*

---

31. A brief introduction to such issues can be found in David T. Runia, "Philo and the Early Christian Fathers," in Kamesar, *The Cambridge Companion to Philo,* 210-30.

32. The list is based on two previous publications of Runia: *Philo in Early Christian Literature,* 348-56; "References to Philo from Josephus until 1000 AD," *SPhAn* 6 (1994) 111-21.

33. Cf., e.g., Abraham Terian, "Had the Works of Philo Been Newly Discovered," *BA* 57 (1994) 86-97; Gregory E. Sterling, "'Philo Has Not Been Used Half Enough': The Significance of Philo of Alexandria for the Study of the New Testament," *PRSt* 30 (2003) 251-69.

PHILO OF ALEXANDRIA IN CONTEXT

Philo as a Jew

Karl-Gustav Sandelin

Introduction

The thought and praxis of Philo of Alexandria is a synthesis of biblical, early Jewish, and non-Jewish traditions in the Hellenistic and Roman world. To separate these threads in Philo's writings from one another is a difficult matter. Philo is a Jew whose theological reflections are embedded in Greek, Hellenistic, and Roman patterns of thought.[1] The following short statement by Roberto Radice gives, I think, an apt characterization: "Philo believed only in those principles which are true according to both Moses and Plato."[2] Starting from these premises, the task to present Philo as a Jew must from the very beginning lead to a somewhat one-sided picture of him. It is notwithstanding an important task. There is no doubt that Philo considers himself a Jew who is committed to the Jewish nation and its traditions. Samuel Sandmel, who strongly emphasizes the Hellenistic element in Philo, nevertheless is able to state that Philo was a "staunch Jew."[3] But in present-

---

1. See, e.g., Earle Hilgert, "Philo Judaeus et Alexandrinus: The State of the Problem," in *The School of Moses: Studies in Philo and Hellenistic Religion in Memory of Horst R. Moehring,* ed. John Peter Kenney (BJS 304; SPhilo Monograph 1; Atlanta: Scholars, 1995) 1-15. Cf. Maren Ruth Niehoff, "Jewish Identity and Jewish Mothers: Who Was a Jew according to Philo?" *SPhAn* 11 (1999) 31-54, esp. 32-34.

2. Roberto Radice, "Observations on the Theory of the Ideas as the Thoughts of God in Philo of Alexandria," *SPhAn* 3 (1991) 126-34, esp. 129.

3. Samuel Sandmel, *Philo's Place in Judaism: A Study of Conceptions of Abraham in Jewish Literature* (augmented ed.; New York: Ktav, 1971), xxiv.

ing Philo's Jewish ideas, one cannot avoid taking into account his indebtedness to modes of thought prevalent in the non-Jewish contemporary culture.

Recent studies pose different answers regarding the extent to which Philo the Jew is a hellenized Jew. Erwin Ramsdell Goodenough maintained that Philo was representive of a kind of Jewish mystery religion.[4] Notwithstanding important observations pointing in such a direction, Goodenough's view has not gained very broad support.[5] On the other hand, an effort such as that by Harry Austryn Wolfson to make Philo a figure with very close ties to Palestinian and later rabbinic Judaism has been severely criticized.[6] But Wolfson is also very well aware that Philo was indebted to Greek philosophy even though he criticized the philosophers.[7]

Philo's position in relation to the Judaism of Palestine and to Greek philosophy remains an important issue. A dependence on Greek philosophy is strongly stressed today by scholars like David Runia.[8] On the other hand, the question of Philo's relationship with Palestinian Jews was addressed in the late 1970s by Richard D. Hecht, who referred appreciatively to the scholarship of Samuel Belkin, who already before Wolfson had attempted to show that Philo was dependent on contemporary Palestinian oral law.[9] More recently, with a distinction between Pharisaism and rabbinic literature drawn more energetically than previously,[10] Philo's relationship to the Pharisees

4. Erwin Ramsdell Goodenough, *Jewish Symbols in the Greco-Roman Period* (New York: Pantheon, 1957-68) 6:122-25, 173, 187, 191ff., 198-217.

5. See Karl-Gustav Sandelin, *Wisdom as Nourisher: A Study of an Old Testament Theme, Its Development Within Early Judaism, and Its Impact on Early Christianity* (Acta Academiae Aboensis ser A: Humaniora 64/3; Åbo: Åbo Akademi, 1986) 135-40; for critics of Goodenough, see p. 135 n. 183; for a defense of certain aspects of Goodenough's theory, see pp. 137-40.

6. Harry Austryn Wolfson, *Philo: Foundations of Religious Philosophy in Judaism, Christianity, and Islam* (Cambridge, MA: Harvard University Press, 1948) 2:90-93, 95-96. See Hilgert ("Philo Judaeus, et Alexandrinus," 11), who refers to the articles by Yehoshua Amir.

7. Wolfson, *Philo*, 93-95, 101.

8. David T. Runia, *Philo of Alexandria and the Timaeus of Plato* (Philosophia antiqua 44; Leiden: Brill, 1986) 434-36; *On the Creation of the Cosmos according to Moses: Introduction, Translation and Commentary* (PACS 1; Leiden: Brill, 2001) 32-36.

9. Samuel Belkin, *Philo and the Oral Law* (HSS 11; Cambridge, MA: Harvard University Press, 1940) 219-70, esp. 256. Belkin (p. 27) characterizes Philo as "a *Pharisaic Halakist*, that is, one who applied the principles of the oral law in interpreting the Bible." For an evaluation of Belkin's contributions see Richard D. Hecht, "Preliminary Issues in the Analysis of Philo's *De Specialibus Legibus*," *SPhilo* 5 (1978) 1-55, esp. 2, 42-43.

10. See, e.g., Jacob Neusner, *Method and Meaning in Ancient Judaism* (ser. 1; BJS 10; Missoula: Scholars, 1979) 59-75. Cf. Cristina Termini, "Philo's Thought within the Context of

does not seem to have been in focus.[11] The question of whether there is any link between Philo and the Dead Sea Scrolls, however, has been addressed in standard volumes such as the revised edition of Schürer's large work, *The History of the Jewish People in the Age of Jesus Christ*, as well as in articles published for instance in the *Studia Philonica Annual*.[12] An aspect of Philo hitherto not often observed has been recently articulated by Maren R. Niehoff, who emphasizes the Roman element in Philo's thought and life.[13]

As for my own research into Philo, I started to study him in order to find an alternative to the hypothesis that those were Gnostics who according to Paul said "there is no resurrection from the dead" (1 Cor 15:12).[14] I made some observations concerning the exegesis of Gen 2:7 in Paul (1 Cor 15:45), Gnostic texts, and Philo and tried to show that Paul lay closer to Philo than to the Gnostics.[15] In the course of my work I became aware of the research that had been done by Burton Lee Mack, who saw Philo as a representative of Jewish wisdom tradition.[16] This gave me the direction also for my future

Middle Judaism," in *The Cambridge Companion to Philo*, ed. Adam Kamesar (Cambridge: Cambridge University Press, 2009) 95-123, esp. 114.

11. Benny Lévy, *Le logos et la lettre: Philon d'Alexandrie en regard des pharisiens* (Lagrasse: Verdier, 1988), has not been available to me. See an abstract by Roberto Radice in *SPhAn* 3 (1991) 361. I have found some references to the question of Philo's relation to Pharisaism in Lutz Doering, *Schabbat: Sabbathalacha und -praxis im antiken Judentum und Urchristentum* (TSAJ 78; Tübingen: Mohr Siebeck, 1999) 359, 385; see also "Namen und Sachregister: Pharisäer," p. 675. For Philo and rabbinic literature, see Peder Borgen, "Philo of Alexandria: A Critical and Synthetical Survey of Research since World War II," in *ANRW* 2.21.1 (1984) 98-154, esp. 124-26. On the question of Philo's relationship to rabbinic and earlier Palestinian halakah, see the discussion by David Winston, "Philo and Rabbinic Literature," in Kamesar, *The Cambridge Companion to Philo*, 231-53, esp. 248-51.

12. Emil Schürer, *The History of the Jewish People in the Age of Jesus Christ (175 B.C.–A.D. 135)*, rev. and ed. Geza Vermes and Fergus Millar (3 vols.; Edinburgh: T. & T. Clark, 1973-87) 2:555-97. Joan E. Taylor, "Philo of Alexandria on the Essenes: A Case Study on the Use of Classical Sources in Discussions of the Qumran-Essene Hypothesis," *SPhAn* 19 (2007) 2-4, with bibliography. See also four articles introduced by John J. Collins in the same volume (pp. 81-142) by Florentino García Martínez, Hindy Najman, Katell Berthelot, and Loren T. Stuckenbruck.

13. Maren Ruth Niehoff, *Philo on Jewish Identity and Culture* (TSAJ 86; Tübingen: Mohr Siebeck, 2001).

14. Karl-Gustav Sandelin, *Die Auseinandersetzung mit der Weisheit in 1. Korinther 15* (Meddelanden från Stiftelsens för Åbo Akademi forskningsinstitut 12; Åbo: Åbo Akademi, 1976) 5-8.

15. Sandelin, *Die Auseinandersetzung mit der Weisheit*, 24-47.

16. Burton L. Mack, *Logos und Sophia: Untersuchungen zur Weisheitstheologie im hellenistischen Judentum* (SUNT 10; Göttingen: Vandenhoeck & Ruprecht, 1973) 108-95.

research. When as a lecturer at the Åbo Akademi University I prepared lectures on the *Didache,* I had the feeling that I was acquainted with the vocabulary used in the eucharistic prayers in that text. This resulted in the volume *Wisdom as Nourisher,* which includes a substantial chapter on Philo.[17] Inspired by Professor Peder Borgen, I then became engaged with the question of how Jews in antiquity were occasionally attracted to non-Jewish religion. A result was the article "The Danger of Idolatry According to Philo of Alexandria."[18]

In the present chapter I shall try to illuminate Philo as a Jew from three sides: (1) What should be said in general terms of Philo as a Jew; i.e., how is Philo a Jew like any other Jew in his time? The premise here is naturally that we are able to say something general about Judaism in antiquity. The Jews in Philo's time read the Scriptures both in public and in private. They practiced circumcision. They observed the Sabbath and celebrated other feasts. They followed specific regulations concerning food and sexual behavior. Does Philo join other Jews in such matters? (2) What is it in Philo's Judaism that gives it a profile of its own? To answer such a question is, of course, dependent on how one looks at Philo from the perspective of a particular student of philonic texts. Does Philo look at the world like a prophet or a transmitter of heavenly revelations? Or is he more of a lawyer and halakist? Or is his intention the attainment of mystical insights about God and humankind? The risk of locking Philo into categories like these is obvious. The perspective may be very subjective and is, of course, highly dependent on the erudition of the student who makes the characterization. Being well aware of the exigency here, I myself, as already noted, see Philo as a representative of Jewish wisdom tradition. From the very beginning this tradition had ties to non-Israelite streams of thought, and this is certainly the case also in Philo's time. (3) Judaism in Philo's time is not a monolithic phenomenon. Several Jewish groupings existed. From the Holy Land, the Pharisees, the Sadducees, and the Essenes are well known. Philo himself also refers to a group that he calls Therapeutae. Does Philo in any respect adhere to the

---

17. Sandelin, *Wisdom as Nourisher,* 82-150.

18. *Temenos* 27 (1991) 109-50. See also "Jews and Alien Religious Practices during the Hellenistic Age," in *Ancient Israel, Judaism, and Christianity in Contemporary Perspective: Essays in Memory of Karl-Johan Illman,* ed. Jacob Neusner et al. (Lanham: University Press of America, 2006) 365-92; "Philo and Paul on Alien Religion: A Comparison," in *Lux Humana, Lux Aeterna: Essays on Biblical and Related Themes in Honour of Lars Aejmelaeus,* ed. Antti Mustakallio et al. (Helsinki: Finnish Exegetical Society; Göttingen: Vandenhoeck & Ruprecht, 2005) 211-46.

views and practices of these groups? Such questions will be briefly discussed at the end of this essay.

Philo's Judaism in General Terms

God

Philo believes in God who is for him the Creator of All (*Ebr.* 42; *Fug.* 12; *Somn.* 1:76). Philo is also of the opinion that it is possible for a human being to arrive at a knowledge of the existence of God by rational observation of the world (*Fug.* 12; *Opif.* 8-9; *Leg.* 3.97).[19] To apprehend the real substance (οὐσία) of the Ruler of the universe is, however, beyond the mental capacities of humankind (*Spec.* 1.32-44; cf. *Praem.* 39-40).[20]

According to Philo, the created world has not existed from eternity and will not exist for ever (*Opif.* 7, 171). In maintaining this, Philo takes a stand against the thought of Greek philosophers.[21]

Philo defends Jewish monotheism against polytheism and pantheism.[22] If the divine beings were many, this would cause a chaotic situation, mob rule (ὀχλοκρατία) in heaven (*Opif.* 171) and atheism (ἀθεότης) and strife among human beings (*Ebr.* 110; *Conf.* 42). If, on the other hand, God and the universe would be identical, an idea that Philo often labels as the "Chaldean creed," creation instead of the Creator would be the object of religious devotion (*Migr.* 184; *Her.* 97; *Congr.* 49; *Virt.* 212-13).[23] Actually, Philo thinks that polytheists also deify and worship created objects (*Ebr.* 110).[24] Thus both pantheism and polytheism for Philo are two sides of the same coin. Philo

19. For a discussion of the passages referred to from Philo, see Wolfson, *Philo,* 2:74-78.

20. Wolfson, *Philo,* 2:73; Runia, *Philo of Alexandria and the Timaeus of Plato,* 436; Gregory E. Sterling, "'The Queen of the Virtues': Piety in Philo of Alexandria," *SPhAn* 18 (2006) 103-23, esp. 115.

21. Wolfson, *Philo,* 2:74, maintains that Philo has Aristotle in mind in *Opif.* 7. Possibly the Stoics are his target, however. See Runia, *On the Creation of the Cosmos,* 121-23.

22. For this theme, see Sandelin, "The Danger of Idolatry."

23. Sandelin, "The Danger of Idolatry," 113-14. Scholars often see an attack on Stoicism in Philo's denouncement of the Chaldeans. See, e.g., Wolfson, *Philo,* 2:78; Alan Mendelson, *Secular Education in Philo of Alexandria* (Monographs of the Hebrew Union College 7; Cincinatti: Hebrew Union College Press, 1982) 24. This understanding may be too narrow. See, e.g., Sandmel, *Philo's Place in Judaism,* 158 n. 261; Sandelin, "The Danger of Idolatry," 132-33; Runia, *On the Creation of the Cosmos,* 112, 207-9.

24. Cf. Sandelin, "The Danger of Idolatry," 140.

vehemently attacks the worship of images of the pagan gods (*Post.* 165; *Mos.* 2.205; *Decal.* 72-74). But in doing so and in spite of his great indebtedness to Plato, Philo does not, like the former, make any distinction between the images of the gods and the divinities they represent.[25] Here Philo stands in continuity with biblical tradition (e.g., Isa 44:9-20).

The God of "Abraham, Isaac, and Jacob" (*Mos.* 1.76) is also the God of the people of Israel which stems from Abraham (*Her.* 277-79) and is called by Philo the race "beloved of God" (*Migr.* 113-14). The people was saved from slavery in Egypt by God, who appointed Moses their leader (*Mos.* 1.71-73, 148-49) and who in different ways supported the people (ἔθνος) during their wandering in the desert toward the land of Canaan (*Mos.* 1.163-66, 173-75, 197-203). At Mount Sinai God the Lawgiver (νομοθέτης), through Moses, gave the law to Israel (*Mut.* 125-26; *Spec.* 3.125).

Philo does not in any substantial way address the history of Israel after the wandering in the desert. Biblical figures from Joshua onward are only sporadically mentioned (e.g., *Cher.* 49; *Deo* 5-15; *Conf.* 149; *Migr.* 196). Babylonia is not described as the land of the Jewish exile, but belongs instead to the region where Abraham was brought up (e.g., *Abr.* 188), even though Philo is also aware of the Jewish population there in his own time (*Legat.* 282). Nor does Philo refer to Cyrus, the liberator of the exiled Jews. Nevertheless, when referring to a very critical contemporary moment in Jewish history Philo expresses his confidence in God's providence. As a leading member of a Jewish Alexandrian embassy to Emperor Caligula, Philo, having been informed about the emperor's plans to erect a statue of himself in the Jerusalem temple, admonishes his listeners and readers to let their souls "retain indestructible the hope in God our Savior (σωτήρ) who has often saved the nation (ἔθνος) when in helpless straits" (*Legat.* 196).[26] Those of Israel who adhere to the law and repent of their sins God will bring to a blissful end (*Praem.* 79-97, 164-68).[27] Philo may even have a messianic figure in mind when, referring to God's aid to the holy, he speaks of a warrior and cites the words "a man shall come forth," found in Num 24:7 LXX (*Praem.* 95).[28]

---

25. Karl-Gustav Sandelin, "Philo's Ambivalence towards Statues," in *In the Spirit of Faith: Studies in Philo and Early Christianity in Honor of David Hay,* ed. David T. Runia and Gregory E. Sterling (SPhAn 18; BJS 332 [2001]) 122-38, esp. 133-34.

26. Cf. Peder Borgen, "Application of and Commitment to the Laws of Moses: Observations on Philo's Treatise *On the Embassy to Gaius,*" in Runia and Sterling, *In the Spirit of Faith,* esp. 97.

27. Wolfson, *Philo,* 2:408-13, Schürer, *The History of the Jewish People,* 2:507-9.

28. Wolfson, *Philo,* 2:414. For a discussion on the topic see Peder Borgen, " 'There Shall

The Bible and the Law

Philo's thought is biblically orientated, or in the words of Peder Borgen, "Philo is primarily an exegete."[29] The majority of scriptural references in his writings are from the Septuagint version of the five books of Moses.[30]

Much of Philo's literary production consists of commentaries on the five books of Moses. He also wrote a number of treatises commenting on the biblical books, using either historical or allegorical methods. Following Borgen, we may divide the writings of Philo into three categories:[31] (A) The Pentateuch in rewritten form: books including *On the Life of Moses; On the Creation of the World; On the Life of Abraham;* and *On the Decalogue.* (B) Exegetical commentaries: treatises such as *Questions and Answers on Genesis and Exodus; Allegorical Interpretation* 1-3; *On the Sacrifices of Abel and Cain; On Planting;* and *On the Migration of Abraham.* (C) Pentateuchal principles applied to contemporary issues and events: tracts such as *On the Contemplative Life* and *On the Embassy to Gaius,* both of which contain references

---

Come Forth a Man': Reflections on Messianic Ideas in Philo," in *The Messiah: Developments in Earliest Judaism and Christianity,* ed. James H. Charlesworth et al. (First Princeton Symposium on Judaism and Christian Origins; Minneapolis: Fortress, 1992) 341-61, esp. 349, 352-53, 357-58; Burton L. Mack, "Wisdom and Apocalyptic in Philo," in *Heirs of the Septuagint: Philo, Hellenistic Judaism and Early Christianity. Festschrift for Earle Hilgert,* ed. David T. Runia, David M. Hay, and David Winston (SPhAn 3; BJS 230; Atlanta: Scholars, 1991) 21-39, esp. 22, 31-39; Thomas H. Tobin, "Philo and the Sibyl: Interpreting Philo's Eschatology," *SPhAn* 9 (1997) 84-103, esp. 94-103; Lester L. Grabbe, "Eschatology in Philo and Josephus," in *Judaism in Late Antiquity,* pt. 4: *Death, Life-after-Death, Resurrection and the World-to-Come in the Judaisms of Antiquity,* ed. Alan J. Avery-Peck and Jacob Neusner (HO 1: Der Nahe und Mittlere Osten 49; Leiden: Brill, 2000) 163-85, esp. 170-171. For apocalyptic traditions of a different kind, see Loren T. Stuckenbruck, "To What Extent Did Philo's Treatment of Enoch and the Giants Presuppose a Knowledge of the Enochic and Other Sources Preserved in the Dead Sea Scrolls," *SPhAn* 19 (2007) 131-42.

29. Peder Borgen, "Philo of Alexandria," in *The Literature of the Jewish People in the Period of the Second Temple and the Talmud,* vol. 2: *Jewish Writings of the Second Temple Period: Apocrypha, Pseudepigrapha, Qumran Sectarian Writings, Philo, Josephus,* ed. Michael E. Stone (CRINT 2/2; Assen: Van Gorcum; Philadelphia: Fortress, 1984) 233-82, esp. 259.

30. See the Scripture Index compiled by J. W. Earp in Vol. 10 of *Philo,* ed. F. H. Colson and G. H. Whitaker (LCL 275; London: Heinemann; Cambridge, MA: Harvard University Press, 1934) 189-264.

31. I will here follow Borgen's treatment in *Philo, John, and Paul: New Perspectives on Judaism and Early Christianity* (BJS 131; Atlanta: Scholars, 1987) 17-59. Cf. Borgen, "Philo of Alexandria," in Stone, *Jewish Writings of the Second Temple Period,* 233-52.

to the Pentateuch.[32] The Pentateuch as a whole served as Philo's "conceptual unit" and his "point of reference."[33]

Philo does, however, also refer to other books in the Jewish Bible, the Tanak. One finds references to the Prophets, the Psalms, and Wisdom books.[34] In *Contempl.* 25 he hints at a threefold division of the Scriptures. One might therefore maintain that the works of Philo bear witness to the notion of the Jewish canon as established already in the first century C.E.[35]

According to Philo, the content of the Pentateuch does of course have its origin in divine revelation. However, he distinguishes between different kinds of laws. The Ten Commandments are directly given by God, whereas the "special laws" are given through the mouth of Moses the Lawgiver (νομοθέτης). Philo sees the Ten Commandments as main headings (κεφάλαια) under which the specific rulings (τὰ ἐν μέρει διατάγματα) are ordered (*Decal.* 17-20, 168; *Spec.* 1.1; 4.132).[36] The reason that God restricts himself to the Ten Commandments, which do not contain penalties, is his goodness. To lay down penalties and punish sins is left for subsequent lawgivers and subordinate powers (*Decal.* 175-79). Philo is not, however, entirely consistent concerning this view. In *Mos.* 2.192-245 he presents four cases where God delivered ordinances directly as answers to questions posed to him by Moses, who was hesitant in making the right decisions (esp. 201-2, 217-18, 228ff., 237-38). In subsequent paragraphs of the same tractate, Philo provides four examples in which the prophet Moses made pronouncements under divine inspiration (κατ᾽ ἐνθουσιασμὸν τοῦ προφήτου; *Mos.* 2.246-87).

---

32. For *Legat.*, see Borgen, "Application of and Commitment to the Laws of Moses," 88-97; for *Contempl.*, see Sandelin, *Wisdom as Nourisher,* 146.

33. So Naomi G. Cohen, *Philo's Scriptures: Citations from the Prophets and Writings: Evidence for a Haftarah Cycle in Second Temple Judaism* (JSJSup 123; Leiden: Brill, 2007) 52.

34. For a detailed treatment, see Cohen, *Philo's Scriptures,* 61-173.

35. Thus Wolfson, *Philo,* 1:117; Roger T. Beckwith, *The Old Testament Canon of the New Testament Church and Its Background in Early Judaism* (London: SPCK, 1985; Grand Rapids: Eerdmans, 1986) 117. The commoon view that Philo's "canon" was only the Pentateuch is articulated by Folker Siegert, "Die Inspiration der Heiligen Schriften: Ein philonisches Votum zu 2Tim 3,16," in *Philo und das Neue Testament. Wechselseitige Wahrnehmungen. I. Internationales Symposium zum Corpus Judaeo-Hellenisticum 1.-4. Mai 2003, Eisenach/Jena,* ed. Roland Deines und Karl-Wilhelm Niebuhr (WUNT 172; Tübingen: Mohr Siebeck, 2004) 205-22, esp. 206-7. As for the Psalms, Cohen (*Philo's Scriptures,* 155) notes that they "apparently had a special degree of holiness" for Philo.

36. According to Cristina Termini, this is an original contribution by Philo and reflects a notion prevalent in the Roman Empire; "Taxonomy of Biblical Laws and φιλοτεχνία in Philo of Alexandria: A Comparison with Josephus and Cicero," *SPhAn* 16 (2004) 1-29, esp. 28-29.

In functioning as interpreter of the Ten Commandments by issuing the special laws, Moses is filled by the divine spirit (ἔνθεος πνεῦμα; *Decal.* 175).[37] Philo also sees Moses as the author of "the five books in which the Holy Laws are written" (*Abr.* 1-2; cf. *Aet.* 19; *Opif.* 1; *Det.* 135-39; *Migr.* 14; cf. *Mos.* 2.188).

In discussing the reasons for circumcision, Philo contends that the interpretation of the laws has been continued after Moses by those who have "made deep research into the writings of Moses." He himself is prepared to offer additional reasons for this ritual. In the context he even speaks of the lawgivers in the plural (*Spec.* 1.8-9).[38]

Although such notions might have predisposed Philo toward moderate flexibility concerning what the Scriptures say, in reality he had a very rigid understanding of the text wherein he found the various aspects of the law codified, i.e., the Septuagint version of the Pentateuch. In his account of the translation of the Hebrew (Chaldean) text of the Law into Greek, Philo differs in particular from Pseudo-Aristeas. Whereas the latter has the seventy-two translators compare and correct their translations, Philo says that they produced their texts without consulting one another, and because they became, "as it were, possessed (ἐνθουσιῶντες)," arrived at identical translations "as though dictated to each by an invisible prompter" (*Mos.* 2.37).[39]

The Jewish Way of Life

In *Migr.* 89-93 Philo takes a stand against those who stress the symbolic meaning of the laws but neglect their literal sense.[40] Philo does not deny that the precepts contain doctrinal and symbolic teachings. But laws concerning the Sabbath, annual feasts, circumcision, and the sanctity of the temple should be observed in correspondence with the letter of the laws.

Philo does not compromise regarding the precepts which he sees as

37. For a discussion of Moses and the Scriptures as "inspired," see Siegert, "Die Inspiration der Heiligen Schriften," 213-18; Jens Herzer, "'Von Gottes Geist durchweht': Die Inspiration der Schrift nach 2Tim 3,16 u. bei Philo von Alexandrien," in Deines and Niebuhr, *Philo und das Neue Testament,* 223-40, esp. 229-33.

38. This passage is seen as an example of "unwritten laws" in Philo by Wolfson, *Philo,* 1:188-95, esp. 193. For interaction with Wolfson, see Sandmel, *Philo's Place in Judaism,* 17-19.

39. Cf. Siegert, "Die Inspiration der Heiligen Schriften," 210-13.

40. For the relationship between *Migr.* 89-93 and the treatise as a whole, see David M. Hay, "Putting Extremism in Context: The Case of Philo, *De Migratione* 89-93," *SPhAn* 9 (1997) 126-42, esp. 135-40.

given by God. Without question, he stands in common with the large majority of Jews in antiquity. Although it is difficult to present hard evidence, the fact that Julius Caesar and Augustus granted the Jews important religious privileges probably enabled them to feel confident in practicing their religious life.[41] Indeed, documentation of apostasy from Judaism is fairly limited.[42] Further indication of widespread devotion to the law is found in an extant portion of Philo's treatise *Hypothetica,* which records combinations or "clusters" of laws that also appear in the writings of Josephus and Pseudo-Phokylides.[43] Philo's attachment to the law can be seen in his views on a number of central issues: circumcision, Sabbath observance, dietary laws, and sexuality and marriage.

Circumcision

In *Migr.* 89-92, Philo refers to those Jews who do not believe that physical circumcision is required. According to this position, circumcision should be understood allegorically and spiritually. Philo accepts such an understanding, but still insists that circumcision of the flesh is necessary for all Jews.[44] Even proselytes are bound by this rule. According to Philo, one does not become a Jew through circumcision (*QE* 2.2), but a person who has converted to Judaism is obliged to be circumcised in obedience to God's ordinance.[45]

Normally circumcision should be performed on the eighth day after the birth of a boy (Gen 17:12; *QG* 3.49). Although Philo in *QG* 3.45-52 answers several questions posed by the text of Gen 17:10-14, he does not discuss such halakic questions as, for instance, by whom circumcision should be exe-

41. See Schürer, *The History of the Jewish People,* 2:270-76; 3:121: ". . . a lasting and substantial alteration of the existing situation did not occur until the later imperial period" (3:121).

42. See Sandelin, "Jews and Alien Religious Practices."

43. Gregory E. Sterling, "The Place of Philo of Alexandria in the Study of Christian Origins," in Deines and Niebuhr, *Philo und das Neue Testament,* 21-52, esp. 36-38 and n. 95 with bibliog.

44. Cf. John M. G. Barclay, "Paul and Philo on Circumcision: Romans 2.25-9 in Social and Cultural Context," *NTS* 44 (1998) 536-56, esp. 541-43. Barclay says that Philo "is deeply concerned about a 'pure' allegorical programme, which omits, or seriously downgrades, the literal practice" (p. 540). Cf. Hay, "Putting Extremism in Context," 128-29.

45. Thus Borgen, *Philo, John, and Paul,* 67. At this point Ellen Birnbaum is more cautious; *The Place of Judaism in Philo's Thought: Israel, Jews, and Proselytes* (BJS 290; SPhilo Monographs 2; Atlanta: Scholars, 1996) 200.

cuted, what instruments should be used, or if it ought to be performed even on a Sabbath.[46]

Sabbath Observance

According to Philo, an Israelite is bound to keep the Sabbath command-ment.[47] This is one of the issues where he differs from those who would follow the Sabbath commandment only symbolically without actually prac-ticing it literally (*Migr.* 89-91). Although Philo accepts a symbolic interpre-tation of the meaning of the Sabbath, he nevertheless without hesitation accepts and explicates the account in Num 15:32-36 in which a man who collected wood on a Sabbath was sentenced to death by stoning (*Spec.* 2.250-51). This is one of the cases where Moses turned to God for advice concerning how the execution ought to be performed (*Mos.* 2.209-20). The breaking of the Sabbath is seen as a capital crime in Exod 31:14 and 35:2, which Philo probably sees underlying Moses' statement that the action of the offender in Num 15:32 "deserved death" (*Mos.* 2.217). Lutz Doering sees this, however, as a "theoretical ideal" in Philo, one which probably never was put into practice.[48]

Philo mentions a number of activities forbidden on the Sabbath. He contends that the one who broke the law by collecting wood (Num 15:32) also acted against the rule not to light a fire on the Sabbath (Exod 35:3). In place of the LXX use of the word ξύλα, Philo says that the man went out to gather "firewood" (φρυγανισμός; *Mos.* 2.213). The offender thus committed a double crime (*Mos.* 2.220).

In *Migr.* 91, in addition to carrying loads and lighting fires, Philo men-tions tilling the ground, bringing a charge in court, sitting in judgment, asking return of property, and recovering loans as nonpermissible activities on the Sabbath. According to *Mos.* 2.211, on that day one should abstain from "work, and profit-making crafts and professions, and business pursued for gaining a livelihood." Even employing slaves or beasts of burden or herds, or cutting shoots or breaches or leaves, or plucking fruit is forbidden because

46. Cf. Richard D. Hecht, "The Exegetical Contexts of Philo's Interpretation of Circum-cision," in *Nourished With Peace: Studies in Hellenistic Judaism in Memory of Samuel Sandmel*, ed. Frederick E. Greenspahn, Earle Hilgert, and Burton L. Mack (Homage Series 9; Chico: Scholars, 1984), 43-79, 63-64.

47. On this theme, see above all Herold Weiss, "Philo on the Sabbath," *SPhAn* 3 (1991) 83-105; Doering, *Schabbat*, 315-86.

48. Doering, *Schabbat*, 360-66, esp. 365.

the Sabbath extends even to these, so that they might live, as it were, in freedom on that day (*Mos.* 2.21-22; cf. *Spec.* 2.66-67).[49]

Although Philo criticizes those who spend their time in "burst of laughter or sports or shows of mimes," he nevertheless believes that those who keep the Sabbath should hold "high festival (πανηγυρίζειν) through hours of cheerful gaiety." This consists of the pursuit of "true philosophy" (*Mos.* 2.211-12). Thus the Sabbath is not a day of idleness, but should be filled with another kind of activity than on the other six days of the week, i.e., of study. During the time in the wilderness it was customary on every day, says Philo, but preeminently on the seventh day, to pursue "the study of wisdom with the ruler (i.e., Moses), expounding and instructing the people in what they should say and do, while they received edification and betterment in moral principles and conduct" (*Mos.* 2.215).

As for his own day, Philo says somewhat exaggeratedly that "each seventh day there stand wide open in every city thousands of schools (διδασκαλεῖα)" where instruction on the four cardinal virtues is given to attentive listeners. The intention of the teachers is to promote a better life. Two principles exist above all, "one of duty to God as shown by piety and holiness, one of duty to men as shown by humanity and justice" (*Spec.* 2.62-63; cf. *Mos.* 2.216). A final important aspect of Sabbath observance according to Philo is his recommendation that individuals examine themselves "with the laws as their fellow-examiners" whether "any offense against purity had been committed in the preceding days." They should account for their words and deeds in order to "correct what had been neglected and to take precaution against repetition of any sin" (*Decal.* 98).

Dietary Laws

In the last part of his treatise *On the Special Laws,* Philo discusses the dietary laws in a section under the general commandment "Thou shalt not covet" from Exodus 20 (*Spec.* 4.78, 100-125). He offers arguments in support of the dietary laws given especially in the books of Leviticus and Deuteronomy.[50] There exist unclean and clean animals among beasts, fish, and fowl. To eat meat from swine is prohibited because of its fatness and deliciousness (100-101). Also forbidden are "wild beasts that feed on human flesh," partly be-

---

49. Philo gives arguments regarding some of the Sabbath rules, but not for all. See Doering, *Schabbat,* 330, 333, 338, 344, 347.

50. Alan Mendelson, *Philo's Jewish Identity* (BJS 161; Atlanta: Scholars, 1988) 68-69.

cause these also provide a tasty meal and partly because of the risk that retaliation against a foe could be implied (103-4). Ten varieties of grass-eating animals that have parted hooves and chew the cud are clean, whereas those which lack one or both of these characteristics are unclean (104-9). Among Philo's reasons: chewing the cud symbolizes a pupil who carefully digests his teacher's instructions; the parted hooves show the importance of making distinctions between good and bad concepts (106-8). On the other hand, a horse is unclean because the unparted hoof shows that no distinction is made between good and bad (109). In a similar way, Philo discusses animals living in the water (110-12), reptiles, and other creeping things (113-14). An exception is the grasshopper, which has legs above its feet and is able to resist the weight of its body and leap from the ground. In the same way, there are human beings who are able to resist the weight that "would pull them down" and, after having been instructed, can leap heavenward (114).

Following his discussion of clean and unclean creatures flying in the air (117-18), Philo treats the prohibitions against eating flesh from animals that have been torn by wild beasts or which have died a natural death (119-22). Regarding the former, Philo comments that a human being should not "be table mate with savage brutes." On the latter, Philo presents sanitary arguments. Finally (122-24), he discusses questions concerning strangled animals and consumption of blood and of fat (cf. Lev 3:17). Blood is the essence (οὐσία) of the soul and "should be allowed to run freely away." Philo here distinguishes between the soul which "we and the irrational animals possess in common" and the rational soul, whose essence is the divine spirit breathed by God into the face of humankind when the latter was created.[51]

Sexuality and Marriage

"No Jewish writer ever protested so much against sexual irregularities as Philo." The statement belongs to Samuel Belkin, who, in his study on Philo and the oral law among other halakic rules, investigated Philo's principles concerning marriage and sexual morality.[52]

First of all, Philo states that because of the fact that we have been "endowed with generative organs" with a view to "the persistence of the race," we should strive for such unions only "which are the lawful means of prop-

---

51. For different conceptions of the "soul" in man according to Philo, see, e.g., Sandelin, *Die Auseinandersetzung mit der Weisheit,* 26-44.

52. Belkin, *Philo and the Oral Law,* 219-70, esp. 256.

agating the human race" (*Det.* 102). We do not know anything about Philo's wife or children,[53] but we may safely conjecture that he was married.

Regarding specific issues within marital law, Philo adheres to the rules concerning prohibited degrees of marriage given in Lev 18:6-18 (*Spec.* 3.12-28). In *Spec.* 3.29, Philo also discusses the prohibition in Deut 7:3-4 against marrying women among the Canaanites and other peoples, understanding this to mean marriage alliances with members of all foreign nations. He sees a danger therein that the generation succeeding such a marriage may easily "unlearn the honor due to the one God." He designates children from such unions as "base-born" (*Virt.* 224), by which he indicates that they are illegitimate.[54] Alan Mendelson notes, however, that Philo, when referring to the non-Israelite women Hagar, Bilhah, Zilpah, and Zipporah, "either minimizes the foreign element in the marriage or ennobles the pagan partner." Mendelson continues: "Philo's laxness on the subject may be a sign that such unions were not unknown and that the better part of wisdom was to hope for the conversion of the non-Jewish partner."[55]

As would be expected, Philo very severely denounces adultery, i.e., committing a sexual act with someone other than the legal husband or wife (*Spec.* 3.11, 52,). Philo does not hesitate in pronouncing the penalty for such an offense as death (*Spec.* 3.11, 58; cf. Lev 20:10; Deut 22:22). Whether it was possible to effect such a punishment in his day and setting is another question.[56] According to Philo, the marital union begins with betrothal. The law concerning adultery therefore is to be applied also to the betrothed because they constitute a married couple (*Spec.* 3.72-74). This stance was apparently not shared by all of Philo's Jewish contemporaries in Alexandria or elsewhere.[57]

Philo also has very hard words concerning prostitution. A whore is "a pest, a scourge, a plague-spot to the public." She ought to be stoned to death (*Spec.* 3.51). But in contrast, Philo also reckons with the possibility that a harlot may repent, "discard her trade," and assume a "decent and chaste demeanor." To marry such a woman is lawful, although not for a priest (*Spec.* 1.102).[58]

---

53. Daniel R. Schwartz, "Philo, His Family, and His Times," in Kamesar, *The Cambridge Companion to Philo,* 9-31, esp. 11.

54. Belkin, *Philo and the Oral Law,* 232-35.

55. Mendelson, *Philo's Jewish Identity,* 73-74.

56. Cf. the discussion by Katell Berthelot concerning capital punishment in the case of apostasy; "Zeal for God and Divine Law in Philo and the Dead Sea Scrolls," *SPhAn* 19 (2007) 113-29, esp. 124-29.

57. See Belkin, *Philo and the Oral Law,* 241-49.

58. Cf. Belkin, *Philo and the Oral Law,* 257.

Philo provides a very idealized picture of Jewish sexual behavior when he writes: "Before the lawful union we know no mating with other women, but come as virgin men (ἀγνοί) to virgin maidens" (*Ios.* 43). In *Spec.* 3.79-83 he has a long explanation of the law in Deut 22:13-21 dealing with the problem of prenuptial unchastity. He does not, however, discuss the penalty for a girl if she has lived with another man before betrothal. Belkin concludes that there is no reason to think that "Philo demanded the death penalty for the girl betrothed as a virgin but later found not to be."[59]

Several other aspects of Philo's perspective on the Jewish way of life can be noted briefly, e.g., his descriptions of the temple service and his comments on the great festivals, especially the Day of Atonement and the Passover (*Spec.* 2.140-222). For Philo the temple service is of high importance (*Spec.* 1.67-75).[60] He is quite explicit in his comments about the high priest.[61] But at Passover the distinction between priests and the rest of the people is suspended, because on this occasion "the whole nation perform the sacred rites" and are raised to "the dignity of priesthood." The Passover for Philo is a "reminder and thank-offering" for the great migration from Egypt, but also a remainder of the thank-offering itself performed after the flight (*Spec.* 2.145-46; cf. *Mos.* 2.224; *QE* 1.10). Mendelson notes that sacrifices by individuals are not prescribed in Deuteronomy 16 or related biblical passages. This independence of priests then "points in the direction of a measure of religious autonomy on the part of Alexandrian Jewry."[62] Accordingly, Mendelson finds that Philo's approach to the Passover and to ordinary sacrifice is "characterized by a flexible and liberal spirit."[63] However, neither quality is evident in his treatment of the Day of Atonement,[64] which has "paramount

---

59. Belkin, *Philo and the Oral Law,* 266.

60. Cf. Wolfson, *Philo,* 2:241-42, 247.

61. See Wolfson, *Philo,* 2:337-45.

62. Mendelson, *Philo's Jewish Identity,* 64.

63. Mendelson (*Philo's Jewish Identity,* 64) does not, however, find any "evidence to suggest that paschal sacrifices were made in Alexandria or that Philo would have sanctioned them." The opposite position is taken by Nils Martola, "Eating the Passover Lamb in House-Temples in Alexandria: Some Notes on Passover in Philo," in *Jewish Studies in a New Europe: Proceedings of the Fifth Congress of Jewish Studies in Copenhagen 1994 under the Auspices of the European Association for Jewish Studies,* ed. Ulf Haxen, Hanne Trautner-Kromann, and Karen Lisa Goldschmidt-Salamon (Copenhagen: Reitzel, 1998) 521-31; Nicholas de Lange, "The Celebration of the Passover in Graeco-Roman Alexandria," in *Manières de penser dans l'Antiquité méditerranéenne et orientale: Mélanges offerts à Francis Schmidt par ses élèves, ses collègues et ses amis,* ed. Christophe Batsch and Mǎdǎlina Vârtejanu-Joubert (JSJSup 134; Leiden: Brill, 2009) 157-166, 165.

64. Mendelson, *Philo's Jewish Identity,* 66.

importance" for him as "the greatest of feasts" (*Spec.* 2.194). Mendelson continues: "The Day of Atonement was to have a central place in the lives of Alexandrian Jews, for Philo says that the fast was 'carefully observed not only by the zealous for piety and holiness but also by those who never act religiously in the rest of their life (Spec. 1.186)." [65]

Profile of Philo as a Jew: Student and Teacher of Wisdom

Wisdom and the Word

In Philo's thinking, there are two important powers mediating between God and humankind: Wisdom (σοφία) and the Word (λόγος). They seem to be understood in personal terms. Both powers are also seen as images of God (*Leg.* 1.43; *Her.* 230-31) and are described as radiant "light" (*Migr.* 40; *Somn.* 1.75). Philo is here clearly dependent on a tradition manifested in the Bible and in early Judaism (e.g., Proverbs 8–9; Wisdom 6–10; 18:15; Sirach 24). To delineate the relationships between God, the Word, and Wisdom is not easy in Philo because he is not quite consistent in these matters.[66] Even if he positions the Word as a "second God" (*QG* 2.62; cf. *Leg.* 2.86), this certainly does not mean that he would categorize himself among those who adhere to polytheism.[67]

Several biblical concepts and persons serve for Philo as metaphors for both Wisdom and the Word. Among those which symbolize Wisdom are the "land" promised to Abraham (*Her.* 96-102), the "rock" in the desert (*Leg.* 2.84-86; cf. Deut 8:15), "Sarah," the "wife" of Abraham (*Cher.* 9-10) and "mother" of Isaac (Leg. 2.82; cf. *Cher.* 7-9), and the "river" of Euphrates (*Her.* 315-16; cf. Gen 15:18). Philo also sees the Word as symbolized, like Wisdom, by a "river" (*Somn.* 2.246-47; cf. Ps 46:4) and probably by the "cloud" in the desert (*Her.* 203-4; cf. *Wisd* 10:17-18).[68]

Mack has demonstrated how Philo conceives of the universe as consisting of two stories, the one being the intelligible (κόσμος νοητός) and the other the visible world (κόσμος αἰσθητός; *Opif.* 16). The higher realm is that of Wisdom and the lower forms the dominion of the Logos or Word.[69] But

---

65. Mendelson, *Philo's Jewish Identity,* 67.

66. Cf. Sandelin, *Wisdom as Nourisher,* p. 101.

67. I am somewhat critical of the position taken by Niehoff, *Philo on Identity and Culture,* 77-78. Cf. Sandelin, "The Danger of Idolatry," 111, 113, 119-20.

68. Sandelin, *Wisdom as Nourisher,* 106-7.

69. Mack, *Logos und Sophia,* 112-14.

the realms are not quite separate. Philo also defines Wisdom as "the land of the Word" (*Migr.* 28). With more or less mythological language, Philo is able to describe the relationship between God, Wisdom, and the Word in terms of family, God being the father, Wisdom representing the mother, and the Word being their son (*Fug.* 108-9).[70] Philo presents this understanding through an allegorical interpretation of the words regarding the high priest in Num 35:25, a figure that Philo sees as the Word (cf. *Somn.* 1.215).[71]

The Realm of Wisdom

According to Philo, the land God gave Abraham to inherit (Gen 15:7) is Wisdom. It cannot be perceived by the senses, but "is apprehended by a wholly pure and clear mind" (*Her.* 96-98). Philo also identifies Wisdom with the desert tabernacle (Exod 33:7) in which "the wise man tabernacles and dwells." But, he says, it is established "outside the body" (*Leg.* 3.46). Actually, God has constructed the earthly tabernacle as an image of heavenly Wisdom identical with divine Virtue (*Her.* 112). In a couple of instances, Philo conceived Wisdom as occupying a place in heaven. Thus the wise man's soul has heaven as his fatherland, and he sees the house of Wisdom as his own (*Agr.* 65). The good man, i.e., the wise man, has "Wisdom for both city (πόλις) and dwelling" (*Leg.* 3.3). Philo regards the patriarch Isaac as the wise man who dwells in the land of Wisdom. He is "self-taught and self-instructed" (αὐτομαθὴς καὶ αὐτοδίδακτος), which in reality means that he is instructed from heaven, i.e., by Wisdom (*Migr.* 27-29; *Fug.* 166-67; cf. *Prob.*13).[72]

The abode of Wisdom is described in *Fug.* 50 as a "calm and fair haven." The context consists of an allegorical interpretation of Isaac's admonition to his son Jacob to take a wife from the "house of Bethuel" (Gen 28:2). According to Philo, the name Bethuel means "the daughter of God" and therefore signifies Wisdom. That Bethuel is the father of Rebecca indicates that Wisdom in her relationship to human beings is masculine. But in her relationship to God, she is feminine because she comes after him, occupying the second place (*Fug.* 51). Nevertheless, Philo is able also to categorize Wisdom as feminine in her relationship to the Word and to creation. She is the mother of the

---

70. Cf. Mack, *Logos und Sophia*, 144-46.

71. For Philo's understanding of the Logos as the Son of God, see Florentino García Martínez, "Divine Sonship at Qumran and in Philo," *SPhAn* 19 (2007) 85-99, esp. 97-99.

72. Sandelin, *Wisdom as Nourisher*, 89-90.

Word, but also in a sense of the world (κόσμος) because she brought to completion what God, the father of the world, had engendered (*Fug.* 108-9).[73]

The Realm of the Word

In some accounts, Philo understands the Logos or Word in somewhat Stoic fashion as the structural principle of the world. The Logos is "the bond (δεσμός) of all existence" which "fills up all things with its being" (*Fug.* 112; *Her.* 188).[74]

But Philo's writings also feature other ways of speaking about the Word in its relationship to the world. In commenting upon the creation, Philo cites Gen 1:3 in discussing the notion that God is "light," an idea he finds in Ps 26:1 (LXX). God is not only light, but also the archetype of every other light, prior to and high above every archetype, in essence, the model of the model (παράδειγμα).[75] The model or pattern was the Word (λόγος), which contained all of God's fullness — light; for, as the lawgiver tells us, "God said, 'let light come into being,'" whereas he himself resembles none of the things which have come into being (*Somn.* 1.75). Philo understands the biblical text to convey the idea of the creation of the Logos as a pattern. God spoke, and the Logos came into being.[76] According to Philo, the entire world is a copy (μίμημα) of the archetypal seal (ἀρχέτυπος σφραγίς), which in turn is an image (εἰκών) of God (*Opif.* 25). In other of Philo's works, the Logos is not only the pattern and archetype of the created beings, but also an instrument (ὄργανον) used by God in creating the visible world (*Leg.* 3.96). In Philo the notion of the Logos as an instrument is combined with the Platonic concept of the sphere of ideas. In God's mind, i.e., in his Logos, God draws a design of the world. This design is called the κόσμος νοητός, the intelligible world, which is a world of ideas (*Opif.* 16-17).[77] Thus in Philo's view the Logos has

73. Cf. Mack, *Logos und Sophia*, 145.

74. Cf. Mack, *Logos und Sophia*, 148-50.

75. Colson emends here because he finds it necessary to postulate that Philo has used the word "model" twice. God is the model of the Word, which in turn also serves as a model (*Philo,* 5:337).

76. Concerning the relationship between the phrase "God said" in Genesis and the Logos, see Gregory E. Sterling, "'Day One': Platonizing Exegetical Traditions of Genesis 1:1-5 in John and Jewish Authors," *SPhAn* 17 (2005) 118-40, esp. 133-34.

77. For Philo's indebtedness to *Timaeus* of Plato and the Platonic tradition here see Runia, *Philo of Alexandria and the Timaeus of Plato*, 159-65. Cf. Sterling, "'Day One,'" 131.

two aspects, an instrumental and a noetic one.[78] In Platonic terms, the Logos is a combination of the sphere of ideas and the demiurge.[79]

The concept of the Logos as an instrument probably emanates from biblical and Jewish notions concerning the wisdom of God (Ps 104:24; Prov 3:19; 8:22-31; Wis 7:22; 9:9).[80] The concept that the Word is a power which structures the world seems to have roots in the same tradition. In discussing the figure of Wisdom, Gerhard von Rad made an important and perhaps controversial observation that we do not have here a quality of God that has been made an object or a hypostasis, but an aspect of the world in which humankind lives, a power which approaches humankind and creates order in his life.[81]

The Place of Humans within the Two Realms

As a part of creation the first human being was formed as an image of a paradigm.[82] So Philo contends in his tractate *On the Creation of the World*. According to Gen 1:26-27, humankind was created in — or after — the image of God (κατ' εἰκόνα θεοῦ). Philo is not consistent in interpreting these verses.[83] On the one hand, he understands them as a description of the creation of the first human being (*Opif.* 25, 69-88). Actually, the "image of God" only concerns the "mind (νοῦς), the sovereign element of the soul (ψυχή)" (*Opif.* 69). Less noble parts were created by powers subordinate to God, a notion Philo derives from the words "let *us* make man" (*Opif.* 72-75). On the other hand, according to Philo, Gen 1:27 describes a man that was a "kind of idea"

78. Cf. Runia, *Philo of Alexandria and the Timaeus of Plato*, 447.

79. Runia (*Philo of Alexandria and the Timaeus of Plato*, 439) states: "The demiurge is up-graded by as much as the ideas are down-graded."

80. Cf. Mack, *Logos und Sophia*, 69, 144.

81. Gerhard von Rad, *Weisheit in Israel* (Neukirchen-Vluyn: Neukirchener Verlag, 1970) 204. Wolfson sees Philo's different descriptions of the Word (the mind of God, the sum of ideas, the immanent Word, the Word as an instrument) as different stages in the existence of the Logos; *Philo*, 2:518, index.

82. Runia, *On the Creation*, 333, notes that Philo himself does not use the name Adam in *Opif.* nor elsewhere in his entire exposition of the Law: "For Philo the first man is more a type than a historical personage" (p. 351).

83. Thomas H. Tobin explains some of the inconsistencies as a result of differences in interpretations that Philo inherited from earlier tradition; *The Creation of Man: Philo and the History of Interpretation* (CBQMS 14; Washington: Catholic Biblical Association of America, 1983) 25-35, 125-30.

(ἰδέα τις) or "type (γένος) or seal (σφραγίς), intelligible (νοητός), incorporeal, neither male nor female (!), by nature incorruptible" (*Opif.* 134). Philo does not discuss here whether the ideal man is a seal with which the earthly, sense-perceptible man also described in this passage has been stamped. But this interpretation does occur in *QG* 1.4, a passage explaining Gen 2:7. According to Philo, the man "formed" here is "the perceptible man and a likeness of the intelligible type." In addition, the intelligible man is a likeness and a copy of the original seal which is the Logos, the "archetypal idea." In *Opif.* 25; *Leg.* 3.95-96; and *Her.* 230-31 we find similar interpretations of Gen 1:27, but here Philo does not mention the image which lies between the Logos and man. God is the archetype of the Logos, which in turn is the image (εἰκών) of God and an archetype of man, or more precisely of his mind. Man is not a direct image of God, but created "after the image" (κατ᾽ εἰκόνα θεοῦ).[84]

The first human being was created in a composite nature consisting of body and soul (ἐκ σώματος καὶ ψυχῆς συνεστώς; *Opif.* 134). He was created mortal, i.e., mortal in respect of the body, but immortal with respect to the mind (νοῦς), because God breathed the soul (ψυχή) into him, in reality a divine breath (πνεῦμα θεῖον; *Opif.* 135). Philo describes the first human being using the classical Greek expression καλὸς καὶ ἀγαθός, lit., "beautiful and good" (*Opif.* 136). His body was composed of the best material of the earth and was most proportionate (*Opif.* 137-38).[85] His soul was also most excellent because the Logos was the pattern after which it was made (*Opif.* 139).

The first human was also wise. In *Opif.* 148, Philo describes his wisdom in terms similar to those he uses for the wise in heaven, the realm of Wisdom. He says that the first human being was "self-taught and self-instructed" (cf. above under "The Realm of Wisdom").[86] Although initially he was alone in the world, he nevertheless communicated with beings belonging to a

---

84. Cf. Tobin, *The Creation of Man*, 25-26, 58-65; Sandelin, *Die Auseinandersetzung mit der Weisheit*, 26-28. The texts are not exactly easy to interpret in every detail. See therefore the discussion by Runia, *On the Creation*, 321-25.

85. Runia (*On the Creation*, p. 333) notes that Philo's assessment of the body is very positive in *Opif.* 136-47, in contradistinction to many other passages in his writings. He has an "inclination to a platonizing devaluation of the corporeal." But not even Plato was "always negative about the body."

86. Colson and Whitaker (*Philo*, 1:117), translate part of *Opif.* 148 rather freely, but in my opinion to the point: "the first man was wise with a wisdom taught by Wisdom's own lips." Cf. Runia (*On the Creation*, 350), who with reference to *Opif.* 149 maintains that the first human being obtained his wisdom "directly from God."

larger realm. In that "Great City" there existed creatures that were spiritual and divine, some without bodies and some carrying bodies "such as are the stars" (*Opif.* 142-44). Even if Philo does not call that reality the realm of Wisdom, this idea still comes very close. The structure of the two-story universe can easily be detected in these passages.

The first human was also characterized by his highly ethical way of life. He "endeavored in all his words and actions to please the Father and the King" and followed God "step by step in the highways (ὁδοὶ λεωφόροι) cut out by virtues (ἀρεταί)" (*Opif.* 144).

In Paradise the first human being had access to the tree of life, meaning "reverence towards God" (θεοσέβεια), "by means of which the soul attains immortality" (*Opif.* 154). But the man's life in paradise took a tragic turn following creation of the woman (*Opif.* 151). Through her, pleasure (ἡδονή; *Opif.* 152), also symbolized by the serpent (*Opif.* 158), took hold of him. The coveting for pleasure resulted in passion (πάθος; *Opif.* 166-67). Together with his wife the first human approached the tree of life, and they were punished with a hard life instead of having gathered an existence "long and happy" (*Opif.* 156, 167-68).

The descendants of the first human being had the same composite constitution as he. They consisted of body and soul (*Opif.* 146). But in comparison with their first forefather, they were of a much inferior character in every respect (*Opif.* 141-42). They were prone to be attacked by pleasure, which drove them to passions of a most different kind (*Opif.* 161-63).

Notwithstanding the weakness of the bodily and spiritual gifts of human beings, their goal ought to be to reach the higher realm where the soul has its real home, the sphere of Wisdom and the wise heavenly beings (*Cher.* 114-15; *Gig.* 61; *Agr.* 65; *Migr.* 27-30).[87] They should therefore free themselves from their inclination to pleasure and their passions, which tie them to the world of the body, often symbolized by Egypt (*Det.* 4, 9; *Conf.* 88-97).[88] Pleasure should be constrained by self-restraint (ἐγκράτεια; *Opif.* 164; *Spec.* 2.195).[89] The way to do this is to lead a virtuous life (*Det.* 95; *Migr.* 18, 148-51; *Virt.* 181-82).[90] This is the area in which Philo demonstrates his Jewishness.

---

87. Cf. Walther Völker, *Fortschritt und Vollendung bei Philo von Alexandrien* (TUGAL ser. 4, vol. 49/1; Leipzig: Hinrich, 1938) 181; Wolfson, *Philo,* 1:401-4; Mack, *Logos und Sophia,* 118-22, for detailed expositions.

88. For details, see Völker, *Fortschritt der Vollendung,* 126-54, esp. 138.

89. Cf. Niehoff, *Philo on Jewish Identity and Culture,* 94-95.

90. Concerning passions and the "healing" of them, see also Carlos Lévy, "Philo's Ethics," in Kamesar, *The Cambridge Companion to Philo,* 146-71, esp. 154-64.

The Ideal Jew

If the goal for a human being, according to Philo, is heaven or the realm of Wisdom, his view of the perfect human being is the wise man residing in that realm. In particular, the patriarch Isaac serves here as a model (*Migr.* 28-30). Isaac also serves as exemplification of a wise man on earth (*Conf.* 81; *Mut.* 256), as does Adam before his fall (*Opif.* 148) and Moses (*Leg.* 2.87; *Mos.* 2.67, 204). All three are described as perfect, excellent (*Somn.* 1.162; *Opif.* 135-45; *Leg.* 2.91), and virtuous (*Sobr.* 8; *Opif.* 144; *Mos.* 1.48). Philo often refers to the four so-called cardinal virtues (e.g., *Spec.* 2.62). But for him, it is the Mosaic law which provides the basic ethical guidelines which he considers universal and in harmony with the laws of nature (*Mos.* 1.48; 2.48). Philo's description of the Jewish way of life has been discussed above. We have observed how he deals with the precepts of Moses by presenting arguments in their favor. One such argument briefly touched upon is the function of the laws to lead the Jew to avoid pleasure and the passions and instead to lead a virtuous life (cf. *Sacr.* 20, 27-33; *Gig.* 40-44).

As noted, Philo considers circumcision to be necessary for a Jew. But he also accepts an allegorical or spiritual understanding, according to which circumcision means "excision of pleasures and all passions (ἡδονῆς καὶ πάντων παθῶν ἐκτομή)" (*Migr.* 92).[91]

According to Philo, Moses also gave the dietary laws in order to restrict pleasures and curb passion (*Spec.* 4.95-101). Philo regards gluttony as an evil "very dangerous both to soul and body" (*Spec.* 4.100). The lawgiver bridled food and drink with ordinances which would lead to self-restraint (ἐγκράτεια), humaneness, and piety (*Spec.* 4.97, 101).[92] Therefore he forbade the "members of the sacred Commonwealth" to eat animals whose "flesh is the finest and fattest," the pig's being the most delicious. Such food only excites pleasure (ἡδονή; *Spec.* 4. 100-101; cf. 122).

Philo opens his exposition of the sixth commandment by indicating that he thinks it appears first in the second tablet because "pleasure (ἡδονή) is a mighty force felt throughout the whole inhabited world" (*Spec.* 3.8). Animals and humans alike are cast under its domination. Thus it can lead to unchastity even within a marriage (*Spec.* 3.9). In line with this, Philo contends that the "offspring of the Hebrews" do not become man and wife in order to achieve pleasure, but with the end of begetting "lawful children"

---

91. Cf. Barclay, "Paul and Philo on Circumcision," 539.
92. Niehoff, *Philo on Identity and Culture*, 105-7.

(*Ios.* 42-43).[93] Self-restraint is important also in efforts to regulate sexuality (*Spec.* 3.22). Nevertheless, Philo is not extremely rigid in sexual matters. "Natural pleasure," he says, "is to blame only when the craving for it becomes "immoderate and insatiable" (*Spec.* 3.9). Philo does give some value to sexual pleasure, which has a positive effect because it leads to creation of life (*Opif.* 161).[94]

The Jew who strives for ethical perfection is not left alone in his endeavors. He receives instruction from both Wisdom and the Word, by which he is strengthened in his efforts. In *Opif.* 157-58; *Post.* 120-22, Philo contrasts an exaggerated consumption of earthly food with the reception of heavenly nourishment, which he understands as instruction. The voluptuous lover of pleasure is dragged downward like the serpent in paradise, the symbol of pleasure. He does not feed on "heavenly nourishment, which Wisdom by means of discourses and doctrines proffers to lovers of contemplation" (*Opif.* 158). By contrast, "among those for whom the soul's life is an object of honor," Philo declares, "the Divine Word dwells and walks." He continues that "those who are fattened by Wisdom, which nourishes virtue-loving souls, acquire a firm and settled vigor" (*Post.* 122). In *Leg.* 3.161-77, Philo also treats earthly and heavenly nourishment as opposites. The latter, meaning the word of God, is symbolized by the manna in the desert and has the peculiar effect of bringing about "congealment in all that part of us that is earthly, bodily and sense-bound" (*Leg.* 3.172). This perhaps somewhat strained interpretation of Exod 16:14 shows that Philo understands the word of God as having an ethical effect.

An important role in the process of instruction is played by the Sabbath gatherings. For Philo, the manna which symbolizes wisdom from above, i.e., teaching, is actually shed from heaven on the Sabbath (*Mut.* 259).[95] In the Sabbath meetings in the διδασκαλεῖα, people sit orderly and listen attentively to one of the more experienced men who sets forth what "will make the whole of life grow into something better" (*Spec.* 2.62).

The festivals of Passover and the Day of Atonement also serve a similar end, according to Philo.[96] "Passover," he says, "is the passage from the life of

93. Cf. Belkin, *Philo and the Oral Law,* 220.

94. Cf. the nuanced discussion by Niehoff, *Philo on Identity and Culture,* 95-101.

95. Peder Borgen, *Bread from Heaven: An Exegetical Study of the Concept of Manna in the Gospel of John and the Writings of Philo* (NovTSup 10; Leiden: Brill, 1965) 112-13; Sandelin, *Wisdom as Nourisher,* 129. Critical toward this interpretation is Weiss, "Philo on the Sabbath," 102 n. 55.

96. Cf. Mendelson, *Philo's Jewish Identity,* 66-67, cf. Niehoff, *Philo on Identity and Culture,* 108-10.

passions to the practice of virtue" (*Sacr.* 63; cf. *Spec.* 2.147). For the Day of Atonement Philo uses the term "Fast" (*Spec.* 1.186; cf. Num 29:7). In *Spec.* 2.193-96, he has an anonymous inquirer ask what kind of feast this is that completely lacks food, drink, and entertainment. The wise Moses saw the ignorance in such an attitude and gave the feast the name "Sabbath of Sabbaths" (cf. Lev 16:31 LXX). The Greek equivalent, "seven of sevens," would mean "holier than the holy." Philo supplies a number of reasons for this. First, the fast entails self-restraint (ἐγκράτεια), control of the "tongue, the belly, and the organs below the belly." There are certain things that should be despised which promote pleasure (ἡδονή) "with all its powers of mischief." Second, this day is devoted to "prayers and supplications." The participants seek "earnestly to propitiate God and ask for remission of their sins (παραίτησιν ἁμαρημάτων)." Thereby they do not look "to their own merits but to the gracious nature of him who sets pardon before chastisement."[97]

Philo and Other Jewish Groups

Philo mentions two varieties of Jewish groups: the Essenes, in *That God Is Unchangeable* and in the *Hypothetica;* and the Therapeutae, in *On the Contemplative Life.*[98]

Philo's description of the Essenes is more than just a report. It is a presentation with apologetic overtones, probably intended for non-Jewish readers, and therefore presents the Essenes in philosophical, notably Stoic, categories.[99] Through analysis of Philo's account, one may derive certain characteristics such as are mentioned by Joan E. Taylor: "Philo's Essenes are numerous, autonomous, old, male, celibate representatives of the goodness and truth of the fundamental principles of Jewish law and philosophy."[100]

97. Cf. Völker, *Fortschritt der Vollendung,* 115-22, 200-207.

98. One could perhaps mention a third: interpreters of the Bible who would understand different commands in the Scriptures in an allegorical sense only (*Migr.* 89-92). But here we probably are dealing with, as David M. Hay says, a "class of individuals who are inclined to disregard the literal for the sake of concentrating on the allegorical," rather than a well-defined religious group. See Hay, "Putting Extremism in Context," 141. For different types of allegorists and literalists in Alexandria, see Hay, "Philo's References to Other Allegorists," *SPhilo* 6 (1979-80) 41-75, esp. 44-46, 49.

99. See Taylor, "Philo of Alexandria on the Essenes," 7-8; Borgen, *Philo, John, and Paul,* 46.

100. Taylor, "Philo on the Essenes," 26-27.

Many traits in the attitudes and practices of the Essenes as depicted by Philo have their counterparts in those of his own. Thus he describes the Essenes as law-abiding Jews who gather together on the Sabbath in their synagogues. There they listen to readings from books, their instruction being conducted by means of symbols (*Prob.* 80-82). It is of course difficult to determine what in Philo's account is authentically Essene and what are his own projections. But because many such features are also described as Essene by Josephus, one may find reason to claim historicity at many points.[101] According to Philo, the Essenes lived in villages in "Palestinian Syria," sharing housing, property, clothes, and meals (*Prob.* 75-76, 84-86). In this regard, and particularly because of their celibate lifestyle, Philo could not have been an Essene of the type he describes. Nevertheless, he treats them with great sympathy, pointing to their virtuous and frugal way of life (*Prob.* 84).

Concerning the Essenes, we are faced with a significant problem: how do Philo's and Josephus's descriptions of the Essenes relate to the Jewish group which produced the Dead Sea Scrolls?[102] No doubt the religious developments reflected in the Dead Sea Scrolls differ in many respects from what we find in Philo. Still, there exist similarities at several points. Note the observations by John J. Collins on Philo and the Scrolls: "They have a common basis in the Torah and its interpretation. They may have some common exegetical traditions, although much remains to be explored in this regard. They have a surprising affinity in the high value placed on zeal for the law. They both testify to the pursuit of spiritual perfection, even if they understand it in somewhat different ways."[103]

Philo mentions neither the Pharisees nor the Sadducees. The accounts

101. See Taylor, "Philo on the Essenes," p. 9. For possible sources used by both Philo and Josephus, see Per Bilde, "The Essenes in Philo and Josephus," in *Qumran between the Old and New Testaments*, ed. Frederick H. Cryer and Thomas L. Thompson (JSOTSup 290; Sheffield: Sheffield, 1998) 32-68; Randal A. Argall, "A Hellenistic-Jewish Source on the Essenes in Philo, *Every Good Man is Free* 75-91 and Josephus, *Antiquities* 18.18-22," in *For a Later Generation: The Transformation of Tradition in Israel, Early Judaism, and Early Christianity*, ed. Randal A. Argall, Beverly A. Bow, and Rodney A. Werline (Harrisburg: Trinity Press International, 2000) 13-24.

102. See, e.g., Curtis Hutt, "Qumran and the Ancient Sources," in *The Provo International Conference on the Dead See Scrolls — Technological Innovations, New Texts, and Reformulated Issues*, ed. Donald W. Parry and Eugene Ulrich (STDJ 30; Leiden: Brill, 1999) 274-93.

103. Collins provides a summary of recent essays on Philo and the Dead Sea Scrolls in *The Studia Philonica Annual* in "Special Section: Philo and the Dead Sea Scrolls," *SPhAn* 19 (2007) 81-142, esp. 83.

concerning the Pharisees in the writings of Josephus, the New Testament, and in Jewish tradition from the Mishnah onward differ very much in content and emphasis. Precise determination of the views and practices of the "historical Pharisees" is therefore difficult.[104]

Philo believes in eternal life for the soul. In this he differs from the Sadducees but is in accordance with the teachings of the Pharisees, if we follow Josephus (*J. W.* 2.162-64). In contradistinction to the Sadducees, however, the Pharisees according to the New Testament seem to have believed in some kind of bodily resurrection (Acts 17:31-33), as supported in Josephus's account (*J. W.* 2.163). This distances them from Philo.[105] According to both Josephus and the New Testament, the Pharisees further referred to a "tradition of the fathers" or the "elders" separate from Scripture (*Ant.* 13.297-98; Mark 7:3; cf. Gal 1:14). Philo does refer to earlier interpretations of Moses by those who have "made deep research into the writings of Moses" (*Spec.* 1.8). However, this does not make Philo pharisaic, because other religious groups, e.g., the Essenes or the early Christians, also had tradition on which to build, either written on unwritten.[106]

As we have seen, Philo understands every male Jew to be a priest when the Passover is celebrated. He also refers to Exod 19:6, implying the priesthood of the Israelites (*Sobr.* 66; *Abr.* 56). Here we find a resemblance to the pharisaic view that a Jew is a priest in his own house, where the purity laws of the cult in the temple, e.g., the cleansing of pots or washing of hands, should be observed (cf. Mark 7:1-4).[107] But Philo does not seem to generalize his understanding of the Passover and apply it to everyday meals. Neither is cleansing of pots a concern for him. Indeed, he omits verse 28, which deals with such cleansing when he discusses the rules for the priests in Lev 6:24-30 (LXX 6:17-23; *Spec.* 1.239-46). Philo does refer to the washing of hands re-

---

104. See Jacob Neusner and Bruce D. Chilton, eds., *In Quest of the Historical Pharisees* (Waco: Baylor University Press, 2007), esp. the concluding essay by William Scott Green, "What Do We Really Know about the Pharisees, and How Do We Know It?" 409-23, esp. 410. Cf. in the same volume Jacob Neusner, "Rabbinic Traditions about the Pharisees before 70 CE: An Overview," 297-31, esp. 310-11.

105. Cf. Steve Mason, "Josephus's Pharisees: The Philosophy," in Neusner and Chilton, *In Quest of the Historical Pharisees*, 41-66.

106. Cf. Neusner, *Method and Meaning in Ancient Judaism*, 67-70; Doering, *Schabbat*, 385.

107. Jacob Neusner, *Major Trends in Formative Judaism*, vol. 3: *The Three Stages in the Formation of Judaism* (BJS 99; Chico: Scholars, 1985) 17; *Judaic Law from Jesus to the Mishnah: A Systematic Reply to Professor E. P. Sanders* (South Florida Studies in the History of Judaism 84; Atlanta: Scholars, 1993) 259; *The Rabbinic Traditions about the Pharisees before 70*, vol. 3: *Conclusions* (South Florida Studies in the History of Judaism 204; Atlanta: Scholars, 1999) 244-46.

quired of the sacrificing priest (Exod 30:20-21), but he does not extend this to practice at meals outside the temple (*Mos.* 2.138; cf. *Spec.* 1.198).

Philo's description of the Therapeutae living in the vicinity of Alexandria has many similarities with that of the Essenes. Like the Essenes, they gather for meetings on the Sabbath and listen to a sermon (*Cont.* 30-31). This practice is also found as a part of the annual symposium or vigil described in detail in *Cont.* 64-90. On this occasion they carefully listen to explications of the Scriptures, which they understand allegorically (*Cont.* 75-78). The Therapeutae also conducted a celibate life, but in contradistinction to the Essenes the group comprised both men and women (*Cont.* 32, 68). Unlike the Essenes, they did not meet for common meals daily, but their annual vigil did include a communal meal (*Cont.* 81-82). Unlike the Essenes, the Therapeutae did not live in common residences but in separate dwellings (*Cont.* 24-25).[108]

Philo was not a member of the community of the Therapeutae.[109] But some features in Philo's description do show that they represent for him a kind of religious ideal.[110] They are law-abiding Jews who serve God (*Cont.* 2, 25). Instructed by personified Wisdom (*Cont.* 35), they practice self-restraint (*Cont.* 34) and spurn bodily pleasure (*Cont.* 68).[111]

As for texts which represent views similar to Philo's, the book of Wisdom comes close, as does the Fourth Book of Maccabees (e.g., *4 Macc* 1:13-30; 5:34). Moreover, Philo is not an isolated Jewish thinker in antiquity.[112] As an allegorist he has colleagues and predecessors such as Aristobulus.[113]

108. For similarities between Philo's description of the Therapeutae and the Qumran community, see Hindy Najman, "Philosophical Contemplation and Revelatory Inspiration in Ancient Judean Traditions," *SPhAn* 19 (2007) 101-11, esp. 106-11. For a comprehensive study on the Therapeutae, see Joan E. Taylor, *Jewish Women Philosophers of First-Century Alexandria: Philo's "Therapeutae" Reconsidered* (Oxford: Oxford University Press, 2003) reviewed by David M. Hay in *SPhAn* 16 (2004) 290-94.

109. Does Philo describe a community that actually existed? See the response of Mary Ann Beavis, "Philo's Therapeutai: Philosopher's Dream or Utopian Construction?" *JSJ* 14 (2004) 30-42, to Troels Engberg-Pedersen, "Philo's *De vita Contemplativa* as a Philosopher's Dream," *JSJ* 30 (1999) 40-64.

110. Cf. David Runia, "The Theme of Flight and Exile in the Allegorical Thought-World of Philo of Alexandria," *SPhAn* 221 (2009) 1-24, esp. 22.

111. On Wisdom as an instructor, see Sandelin, *Wisdom as Nourisher*, 88, 142, 146.

112. Discussing in detail the relationship between the book of Wisdom and Philo, David Winston suggests that the Wisdom of Solomon may even be dependent on Philo rather than vice versa. See his commentary, *The Wisdom of Solomon* (AB 43; Garden City: Doubleday, 1979) 59-63.

113. See, e.g., Karl-Gustav Sandelin, "Zwei kurze Studien zum Alexandrinischen Judentum," *ST* 31 (1977) 147-52, esp. 147-49.

To conclude: Philo is not a Pharisee, still less a Sadducee. He sympathizes with the Essenes and admires the Therapeutae, although he is not a member of these groups. But as a theologian, he does not stand isolated from other Jews.

In terms of opportunities for future studies on Philo as a Jew, one should take into account that in recent decades much work has been done on various forms of Judaism. It is now fairly obvious that Pharisaism had its own profile which differed from later rabbinic Judaism. How does Philo relate to "historical Pharisaism," and to what extent does rabbinic Judaism preserve postbiblical traditions already evident in Philo? Apparently, some concepts in Philo have their counterparts in the Dead Sea Scrolls, which therefore deserve closer examination. Philo was not an apocalypticist. Still, he had ideas concerning the future of Israel and other themes which create points of contact to apocalyptic literature, calling for deeper investigation. The first Christian generation was largely Jewish, and Philo's works were transmitted by Christians, whereas in antiquity the Jews themselves had forgotten him. The lines between early as well as patristic Christianity and Hellenistic Judaism, of which Philo was one of its most important representatives, are also open for scholarly endeavors.

Summary

Philo is a practicing, law-abiding Jew. He is firmly Bible-oriented, taking the Septuagint, especially the five books of Moses, as his chief authority. Philo is of the opinion that the laws given through Moses must be observed literally. As a theologian, he builds very much upon Jewish wisdom tradition, which he further develops, organizing the universe into two realms, that of Wisdom and that of the Word. The goal for the human soul is the heavenly realm of Wisdom. To a large extent, Philo interprets the Scriptures allegorically. Interpreting the precepts of the law, he argues for a life characterized by self-restraint and the renunciation of pleasure. Although Philo's manner of articulating his religion differs from other important trajectories of Judaism in his day, he does not stand isolated from other Jews, either in his thinking or in his way of life.

Philo as a Citizen: *Homo politicus*

Torrey Seland

The present chapter will focus on Philo as a citizen in the Greco-Roman Alexandria of his time, emphasizing his life as a politically active person, a *homo politicus*. The main part of the essay will be devoted to his descriptions of Roman rule and his own activities as a politically active citizen. Philo's more theoretical expositions of what might be called his political theory will have to reside more in the background of our discussion. It is, however, not possible to overlook them completely, as theory and praxis are often interrelated. Perhaps the great twentieth-century Philo scholar Erwin R. Goodenough will seem to some to have too great a role in what follows, but one would be unable to discuss Philo and politics without to some extent dealing with Goodenough's views. His stance is indeed strong and clearly set forth, although some may find it insufficient. While the topic at hand touches upon many aspects and issues related to our understanding of Philo and his life and thought, an overview of Philo and politics may also reveal the many uncertainties with which we must cope. Nevertheless, as in all areas of research, that should not be considered an obstacle, but a challenge.

Political Aspects of Philo's Social World

We cannot provide a comprehensive picture of the social world of Philo and his place within it, but may focus on some issues we consider especially important in trying to understand him as a politician.

47

The Jews in Alexandria and Their Political Institutions

Jews had a long history as inhabitants of Egypt and also of Alexandria. Whether one traces back to the sixth-century B.C.E. influx of Jewish refugees or the conquest of Alexander the Great in the fourth century, by the time of Philo there had been Jews in Egypt for centuries.[1] When Alexander established Alexandria, the city's prospects also attracted Jews, and it soon had a great Jewish community. Over time there were several reasons for these Jewish immigrants coming to Egypt: political (whether as exiles or as refugees); commercial (business); or social (e.g., adventure, reuniting families).

Apparently from the second century B.C.E., a special quarter was granted to the Jews in Alexandria, the Delta section.[2] Philo says that at his time most of the Jews lived in two areas of the city (*Flacc.* 55), but also that there were synagogues in other sections (*Legat.* 132); hence the Jews were not confined to only one or two parts of the city.

Jews in the Diaspora, at least in Alexandria, had two important institutions of pivotal cultural value: they had their synagogues, and in Philo's time they were probably organized as a *politeuma* (πολίτευμα), an ethnic political entity ruled in Alexandria by a *gerousia* (γερουσία), or council of elders.

The most important institution for the Jews in Alexandria was the synagogue. According to both Philo and some rabbinic traditions, there was a great and well-known synagogue in the city;[3] and according to Philo, there were several other synagogues in the city (*Legat.* 132). These institutions served several social functions: they were the centers for communal prayer and worship, they served as town halls and courts, and they were also socializing institutions in the form of schools, transmitting knowledge and insight in the Torah. Wealthy and influential persons could serve as patrons

---

1. For a fuller description of the history of the Jews in Egypt, see Victor Tcherikover, *Hellenistic Civilization and the Jews*, trans. S. Applebaum (New York: Atheneum, 1985); E. Mary Smallwood, *The Jews under Roman Rule: From Pompey to Diocletian* (2nd ed.; SJLA 20; Leiden: Brill, 1981); Joseph Mélèze Modrzejewski, *The Jews of Egypt: From Rameses II to Emperor Hadrian*, trans. Robert Cornman (Edinburgh: T. & T. Clark, 1995); John M. G. Barclay, *Jews in the Mediterranean Diaspora: From Alexander to Trajan (323 BCE–117 CE)* (Edinburgh: T. & T. Clark, 1996); Gottfried Schimanowski, *Juden und Nichtjuden in Alexandrien: Koexistenz und Konflikte bis zum Pogrom unter Trajan (117 n. Chr.)* (Münsteraner judaistische Studien 18; Berlin: LIT, 2006). The introduction in vol. 1 of *CPJ* is also indispensable.

2. Smallwood, *The Jews under Roman Rule*, 225.

3. *Legat.* 132-4; *t.Sukkah* 4, 6; *b.Sukkah* 51b; *y.Sukkah* 51, 55a.

for the synagogues, and various other functions or offices are amply attested in a number of inscriptions.[4]

The cities of the Diaspora seem to have been made up of several *politeumata*.[5] Jewish *politeumata* are attested for a number of these cities, and their structures are relatively well known.[6] The Jewish *politeuma* in Alexandria had its own record office,[7] and the *gerousia* was probably composed of seventy-one members. At its head stood an ethnarch (ἐθνάρχης). According to Philo (*Flacc.* 74), however, Augustus replaced the "genarch" (γενάρχης) with a senate *(gerousia)* after the genarch died. As to the different terms ethnarch and genarch used by Josephus and Philo, the prevailing view in most recent research is that they denote the same function. The existence of this institution was important, as the Greeks were not allowed to have their own court, or *boule* (βουλή), during this period.[8] While some scholars now deny the existence of a *politeuma*,[9] the institution still has strong support.[10] Here might be opportunity for further research.

Thus the Jews had a sociopolitical organization of some sort, whether it was a *politeuma* or not, that was acknowledged by the authorities, an insti-

---

4. See Jean Baptiste Frey, *CPJ*, vol. 1.

5. "Such a corporation was a quasi-autonomous civic unit with administrative and judicial powers over its own members, distinct from and independent of the Greek citizen body and its local government"; Smallwood, *The Jews under Roman Rule*, 139.

6. See Sterling Tracy, *Philo Judaeus and the Roman Principate* (Williamsport: Bayard, 1933) 7-11; Smallwood, *The Jews under Roman Rule*, 225-26.

7. E. Mary Smallwood, *Philonis Alexandrini Legatio ad Gaium* (2nd ed.; Leiden: Brill, 1970) 6. This is possibly the setting for the registration mentioned in *Spec.* 1.63, which refers to those who are "registered in the commonwealth of the laws."

8. See Naphtali Lewis, *Life in Egypt Under Roman Rule* (Oxford: Clarendon, 1983) 27-30.

9. Cf. Joseph Mélèze-Modrzejewski, "How To Be a Greek and Yet a Jew in Hellenistic Alexandria?" in *Diasporas in Antiquity*, ed. Shaye J. D. Cohen and Ernest S. Frerichs (BJS 288; Atlanta: Scholars, 1993) 77-78; Sarah Pearce, "Jerusalem as 'Mother-City' in the Writings of Philo of Alexandria," in *Negotiating Diaspora: Jewish Strategies in the Roman Empire*, ed. John M. G. Barclay (LSTS 45; London: T. & T. Clark, 2004) 19-36; Barclay, *Jews in the Mediterranean Diaspora*, 43 n. 73, 64-65; and esp. Gert Lüderitz, "What Is the Politeuma?" in *Studies in Early Jewish Epigraphy*, ed. Jan Willem Van Henten and Pieter Willem van der Horst (AGJU 21; Leiden: Brill, 1994) 183-225.

10. Peder Borgen, "Judaism: Judaism in Egypt," in *ABD* 3:1061-72; Daniel R. Schwartz, "Philo, His Family and His Times," in *The Cambridge Companion to Philo*, ed. Adam Kamesar (Cambridge: Cambridge University Press, 2009), 16-17; Andrew Harker, *Loyalty and Dissidence in Roman Egypt: The Case of the* Acta Alexandrinorum (Cambridge: Cambridge University Press, 2008) 212-20; Sandra Gambetti, *The Alexandrian Riots of 38 c.e. and the Persecution of the Jews: A Historical Reconstruction* (JSJSup 135; Leiden: Brill, 2009) 57-59.

tution with its own constitution and administration which could perform certain internal functions and also had some judicial character. These rights were limited, however, as the Jews lacked the right to impose capital punishment, even though in several cases the Torah prescribed such measures.

The existence of such an institution is important for understanding the riots in Alexandria, the delegations that were sent to the emperor in Rome, and the important issues of citizenship at stake for the Alexandrian Jews.

Philo's Family: A Family of Politicians?

Philo belonged to a rich and influential family in Alexandria. His brother Alexander Lysimachus was "alabarch," probably an office concerned with administration for the paying of taxes and customs.[11] Josephus says that Alexander "surpassed all his fellow citizens both in ancestry and in wealth" (*Ant.* 20.100). Josephus also reports that Alexander once lent a large amount of money to Agrippa, or more correctly, to Agrippa's wife Cypros because he did not trust Agrippa (*Ant.* 18.159). Alexander disclosed his wealth and demonstrated his reverence for the temple of Jerusalem by clothing nine of its ten ports with gold and silver (*J. W.* 5.205). Alexander's position of honor in Alexandria was also evident in his close relationship to Claudius and his mother Antonia. Gaius Galicula, however, had Alexander thrown into jail, but Claudius released him upon becoming emperor (*Ant.* 19.276). One of Alexander's sons, Marcus Julius Alexander, was married to Berenice, the daughter of Agrippa (*Ant.* 19.277). But it is another son who is mentioned more often in our sources, Tiberius Julius Alexander.[12] According to Josephus, Tiberius left Judaism (*Ant.* 20.200)[13] and had a great career in the service of the Romans. In ca. 46-48 C.E. he was procurator of Judea (*Ant.*

---

11. Cf. the comments on Josephus *Ant.* 18.159 by Louis H. Feldman, trans., *Josephus,* vol. 90: *Books XVIII-XIX* (LCL 433; London: Heinemann; Cambridge, MA: Harvard University Press, 1965). See further Katherine G. Evans, "Alexander the Alabarch: Roman and Jew," in *Society of Biblical Literature 1995 Seminar Papers,* ed. Eugene H. Lovering Jr. (Atlanta: Scholars, 1995) 576-94.

12. On Philo's family, see Schwartz, "Philo, His Family and His Times"; Robert Ernest Bennett, "The Prefects of Roman Egypt 30 B.C.–69 A.D." (Ph.D diss., Yale University, 1971) 134-47; E. G. Turner, "Tiberius Iulius Alexander," *JRS* 44 (1954)54-64; and now esp. Evans, "Alexander the Alabarch."

13. For a critical assessment of this, however, see Stéphane Etienne, "Réflexion sur l'Apostasie de Tibérius Julius Alexander," *SPhAn* 12 (2000) 122-42; Schimanowski, *Juden und Nichtjuden in Alexandrien,* 135-39.

20.100; *J. W.* 2.220), and ca. 66-70 C.E. he was prefect of Egypt (cf. *J. W.* 2:309, 492-98). He also participated actively in the campaigns against Jerusalem in 66-70 C.E. (*J. W.* 5.45-46; 6.237).

Philo thus undoubtedly belonged to the elite segment of the Jewish Alexandrian community. To be rich at this time and in this world also implied power, and power meant influence. While we do not know exactly how and where Philo is to be fitted into these family structures — he might have been a solitary scholar caring little for the turmoil of both social and political life — we might surely conclude that he would have lived close to influential people in the city.

Philo as a Politician

In the following we shall first briefly review representative analyses of Philo's politics and political views and various aspects considered important toward understanding him as a politician: his statements in *Spec.* 3.1-6; Philo's views on Joseph as a politician; his report on the delegation to Emperor Gaius Caligula in 38-40 C.E. Finally, we will consider further possibilities for interpretating Philo as a political writer.

Sterling Tracy's 1933 study[14] concerns Philo's attitudes to the Roman principate and thus focuses primarily on *In Flaccum* and *Legatio ad Gaium*. Considering Philo's personal political status, Tracy claims it is important to distinguish Philo as a member and leader of the Jewish *politeuma* in Alexandria, as a member of the larger Jewish Diaspora community, as a resident of Alexandria, and as a subject of the Roman emperor (pp. 9-21). Tracy does not question the existence of such Jewish *politeumata* in Alexandria, and argues that the executive powers within the community lie with a special *gerousia* (pp. 9-10): "Certainly it was all-powerful in the time of Philo" (p. 13), and Tracy considers Philo to have been a member and leader of this Jewish *politeuma* (p. 14). Concerning Philo's place as a Jew in Alexandria, Tracy does not consider him a Greek or Roman citizen, but interprets the statements in Philo's work on citizenship (e.g., *Flacc.* 53.172) to be concerned with membership in the Jewish *politeuma* (pp. 16-19). With regard to *In Flaccum* and *De Legatione,* Tracy argues that the general political aim of Philo in these works is clear: "Both are undisguised attacks on Roman policy. Both advance the idea that a peculiar sanctity hedges

14. Tracy, *Philo Judaeus and the Roman Principate.*

about the Jewish people, that no Roman emperor can harm them with impunity" (p. 23).

In the last chapter of his relatively brief study, Tracy sharpens the negative profile of Philo concerning the Roman imperial system: "Political allusions in his philosophical works antedating the *In Flaccum* and *Ad Gaium* indicate that he had long recognized the fundamental incompatibility of the Roman imperial system and the polity of the Jewish people" (p. 48). He points to an understanding of Philo's writing that a few years later would be further developed by Goodenough, namely that Philo's works include both direct statements concerning the Roman administration and indirect criticisms of Roman practices and institutions.[15] Tracy further notes that Philo nowhere outside *Ad Gaium* and *In Flaccum* has any words of praise for the emperor or Roman rule as such, and he finds that several aspects of Philo's descriptions of Moses' leadership are presented in terms that indicate its superiority to the Roman rule. Furthermore, in describing and dissecting the practical politician in *De Iosepho,* Philo had in mind the current prefect of Egypt (p. 53). Hence, when Philo does praise Roman rule or rulers, it is primarily for apologetic purposes (p. 51).

Goodenough's book *The Politics of Philo Judaeus,* published in 1938,[16] remains today probably the most comprehensive study of these aspects in Philo's works. A central thesis in Goodenough's work is that Philo is to be read as an opponent of the Romans, and one writing against the Romans both openly and in coded form. He argues that Philo was at the same time both a privileged citizen and an alien in Alexandria. He belonged to the elite segments of the Jewish communities in the city, but at the same time he was an outsider, not having access to the same privileges as the Roman citizens. And Philo was not an admirer of the Roman authorities: "he loved the Romans no more than the skipper of a tiny boat loves the hurricane."[17] In such circumstances, Goodenough argues, any opponent of the Romans had to be careful in what he said about the Roman authorities; if he was to mention them at all, he might preferably have to do it cryptically or rhetorically (cf. *Somn.* 2.82-91).[18] Hence Goodenough suggests that Philo deals with politics in three ways: directly, primarily in his *In Flaccum* and *De Legatio;* in code, as in *De Somniis* (especially *Somn.* 1.219-25; 2.61-64.78-91;

---

15. See, e.g., *Spec.* 2.90-95; 3.157-68 concerning Roman tax collections.

16. E. R. Goodenough, *The Politics of Philo Judaeus: Practice and Theory* (New Haven: Yale University Press, 1938); cf. "Philo and Public Life," *JEA* 12 (1926) 77-79.

17. Goodenough, *The Politics of Philo Judaeus,* 7.

18. Goodenough, *The Politics of Philo Judaeus,* 4-6.

2.116-33); and by innuendo, that is, by negative, indirect allusion. This latter method is to be found in *De Iosepho,* a treatise written primarily for Gentiles[19] and in which Joseph is read in light of the Roman prefect in Egypt at Philo's time.[20]

Concerning the addressees of *In Flaccum,* Goodenough argues that it was written for a Gentile audience after the death of Gaius, and possibly for the new prefect in Alexandria.[21] *De Legatione,* on the other hand, he surmises was written after the accession of Claudius, and as a presentation to just that emperor.[22] Be that as it may, it seems obvious to most readers that these important political works of Philo are written for both Jews and Gentiles, possibly even including the Roman authorities. Goodenough also finds some messianism in the works of Philo, but it is described in such a veiled way that "what he does say shows that there was much more thought of it than he dares to write."[23] Many scholars are of the opinion that Goodenough overstates his case,[24] but the issue of hidden agendas in Philo's style of writing has also gained some support. David M. Hay discusses Philo's politics and exegesis in the treatise *De Somniis* and finds that Philo here offers both overt political criticism (*Somn.* 1.219-25; 2.78-91; 2.115-33) and allegory as within the allegorical treatises (*Somn.* 2.42-64; 2.283-99). Hence he concludes that "part of Philo's purpose in writing *De Somniis* was to present answers to some of the political problems which he and his fellow Jews were facing."[25] Furthermore, the Danish scholar Per Bilde, in investigating *In Flaccum* and *Legatio,* finds a "threatening tone" in these works, and that Goodenough is right in interpreting them as hidden warnings to the Roman elite: If the traditional positive politics of the Romans were changed into a negative one,

---

19. See esp. Erwin R. Goodenough, *An Introduction to Philo Judaeus* (2nd ed.; Oxford: Blackwell, 1962; repr. Brown Classics in Judaica; Lanham: University Press of America, 1986) 61-62.

20. Cf. Goodenough, *The Politics of Philo Judaeus,* 21-41; *An Introduction to Philo Judaeus,* 61.

21. Goodenough, *The Politics of Philo Judaeus,* 10-11; *An Introduction to Philo Judaeus,* 59; Pieter Willem van der Horst, *Philo's Flaccus: The First Pogrom: Introduction, Translation, and Commentary* (PACS 2; Leiden: Brill, 2003) 15-16.

22. Goodenough, *The Politics of Philo Judaeus,* 19.

23. Goodenough, *The Politics of Philo Judaeus,* 115.

24. See, e.g., Ray Barraclough, "Philo's Politics: Roman Rule and Hellenistic Judaism," in *ANRW* 2.21.1 (1984) 448-49.

25. David M. Hay, "Politics and Exegesis in Philo's Treatise on Dreams," in *Society of Biblical Literature 1987 Seminar Papers,* ed. Kent Harold Richards (Atlanta: Scholars, 1987), 438.

such a change would call forth an armed Jewish resistance that would represent severe difficulties for Rome.[26]

Samuel Sandmel, Goodenough's former student, has a brief chapter on Philo's political theory in his introductory book to Philo.[27] Considering Philo as a citizen and practical politician, he agrees to a large extent with Goodenough. Sandmel notices the somewhat surprising silence in Philo's works about the state of affairs in Judea, and also the almost complete absence of any allusion to David as a king or to his dynasty. This indicates to Sandmel that "Philo is concerned more with the situation of the Jewish community in Alexandria as part of a unique politeuma than with the Judean situation and experience."[28] He also to a large degree supports Goodenough's view that Philo was criticizing the Roman Empire in a veiled way, in describing the ideal constitution by drawing on the Scriptures. Hence, for instance, Philo's description of Joseph in the *Allegorical Commentary* is a veiled description of a wicked Roman official. Thus by allegory and by describing the constitution of the Jews as ideal, Philo can indicate the Roman shortcomings.

The study by Ray Barraclough is probably the best and most comprehensive in dealing with various sides of Philo's politics, on both the theoretical and practical level.[29] Here Barraclough focuses both on Philo and the Roman world and on Philo's theory of rule. He is critical of several of Goodenough's views concerning the addressees of Philo's political writings and on the Roman rule. He considers *De Legatione* to have been written for a wider Gentile audience, perhaps even for some with considerable political power, but also for those among the Jews who were "wavering in their faith that their God was still sovereign over the affairs of mankind."[30] *In Flaccum*, moreover, was probably written for the new prefect as well as for Claudius himself. Barraclough does not agree with Goodenough, however, that Philo

---

26. Per Bilde, "Filon som polemiker og politisk apologet: En undersøgelse af de to historiske skrifter Mod Flaccus (In Flaccum) og Om delegationen til Gaius (De legatione ad Gaium)," in *Perspektiver på jødisk apologetik,* ed. Anders Klostergaard Petersen and Kåre Sigvald Fuglseth (Antikken Og Kristendommen 4; Copenhagen: ANIS, 2007) 178. Cf. also Ellen Birnbaum on *In Flaccum:* "Philo . . . may also wish to sound a warning to Gentiles to stop their maltreatment of his people"; *The Place of Judaism in Philo's Thought: Israel, Jews, and Proselytes* (BJS 290; SPhilo Monographs 2; Atlanta: Scholars, 1996) 21.

27. Samuel Sandmel, *Philo of Alexandria: An Introduction* (New York: Oxford University Press, 1979).

28. Sandmel, *Philo of Alexandria,* 103.

29. Barraclough, "Philo's Politics."

30. Barraclough, "Philo's Politics," 450-51.

failed to appreciate the benefits of Roman rule. The Roman order was much more in accord with the conditions he considered most desirable in a state than Goodenough's interpretations allow.[31]

Issues of Political Theory in Philo

Describing Philo as a *homo politicus* must necessarily also include considerations of his political theory. This is, however, such a wide topic that we will have to restrict ourselves to just a few aspects.[32]

Philo as a Jew and Cosmopolites and the Torah as the Law of Nature

Philo had a very high view of Israel and its role in the world. The special situation of the Jews is depicted in terms of honor, with emphatic attention to their distinctiveness as a people in comparison with other peoples. According to Philo, the Jewish nation is "a nation dearest of all to God" (*Abr.* 98). They are "the best of races" (*Congr.* 51) and are "preferred and chosen" by God (*Conf.* 56; *Migr.* 60). In this last passage Philo cites Deut 7:7, where God's election is grounded in his love alone. In *Spec.* 4.181, however, it is grounded in the "precious signs of righteousness and virtue shown by the founders of the race."[33] The Jews, further, are "God's portion" (*Spec.* 4.159, 179-80; *Legat.* 3; *Post.* 89, 93; cf. Deut 32:7-9). They stand in a special relation to God, and this distinctiveness is related to their law: "they are living under exceptional laws" (cf. *Spec.* 4.179; *Ios.* 42; *Conf.* 141). The law is here described as both marking them out in relation to the other nations and constituting their special relation to God. The law is the special prerogative of Israel, as Israel is the special portion of God, set apart for him alone.[34] The Jews thus constitute a singularity in the world.

Philo's conception of the people of Israel is thus firmly grounded in their God-given law: it is observance of the law that constitutes them as the people of God and thereby functions as the element qualifying who is to be regarded as kinsfolk (συγγενεῖς), e.g., *Spec.* 3.155 (cf. also 4.159 and 1.317):

31. Barraclough, "Philo's Politics," 452, 472.

32. For other issues, see Barraclough, "Philo's Politics," 506-51.

33. Cf. *Praem.* 166, where the patriarchs are said to be supplicants for the Jews.

34. Cf. Philo's use of Exod 19:5 in addressing the prophetic and priestly aspects of the people; see esp. *Abr.* 56, 98; *Mos.* 1.149; *Sobr.* 66. On the prophetic aspect, see *Abr.* 98.

Those whom we call our kinsfolk (συγγενεῖς) or within the circle of kins-men our friends are turned into aliens by their misconduct when they go astray: for agreement to practice justice and every virtue makes a closer kinship (συγγένεια) than that of blood, and he who abandons this enters his name in the list not only of strangers and foreigners but of mortal enemies.

Accordingly, although kinship by blood is important, there is a kind of kinship ranked above that of blood: the one based on observance of the law and thus on the honoring of God, "which is the indissoluble bond of all the affection which makes us one" (*Spec.* 1.52; cf. 1.317).[35] Thus proselytes also belong to this συγγένεια, as they are "incomers" who have come to "the clear vision of truth and the worship of the one and truly existing God" (*Virt.* 102; cf. 179). In somewhat exaggerated fashion, Philo can say that "Moses himself was the best of all lawgivers in all countries, better in fact than any that have ever arisen among either the Greeks or the barbarians" (*Mos.* 2.12). A few sections later he says that "not only Jews but almost every other people, particularly those which take more account of virtue, have so far grown in holiness as to value and honor our laws" (*Mos.* 2.17). At the same time, how-ever, he cherishes the eschatological hope that when Israel prospers, "each nation would abandon its peculiar ways, and, throwing overboard their an-cestral customs, turn to honoring our laws alone" (*Mos.* 2.44).[36]

Philo is also describing himself as a cosmopolites and the law of Israel as the natural law of the world. To Philo, the Torah is not only the particular law of the Jews; it is also in accord with the natural law of the world. Here the Jewish particularism seems to be rising to a higher level of a particular kind of universalism.

The patriarchs can be described as living laws (*Abr.* 5.276); even before

35. For a brief overview of the meaning of *nomos* in Philo, see Adele Reinhartz, "The Meaning of Nomos in Philo's Exposition of the Law," *SR* 15 (1986) 337-45.

36. For a review of the possible extent of eschatology in Philo's works, see the various views of Ulrich Fischer, *Eschatologie und Jenseitserwartung im hellenistischen Diasporajuden-tum* (BZNW 44; Berlin: de Gruyter, 1978) 184-213; J. De Savignac, "Le Messianisme de Philon d'Alexandrie," *NovT* 4 (1960) 319-24; Richard D. Hecht, "Philo and Messiah," in *Judaisms and Their Messiahs at the Turn of the Christian Era*, ed. Jacob Neusner, William Scott Green, and Ernest Frerichs (Cambridge: Cambridge University Press, 1987) 139-68; Peder Borgen, "'There Shall Come Forth a Man': Reflections on Messianic Ideas in Philo," in *The Messiah: Develop-ments in Earliest Judaism and Christianity*, ed. James H. Charlesworth et al. (First Princeton Symposium on Judaism and Christian Origins; Minneapolis: Fortress, 1992) 341-61.

the Torah had been given, the patriarchs were living in accordance to the law because they were living according to nature, the original and living laws. And the Torah as containing written and particular laws constituted copies of the unwritten laws (*Abr.* 5):

> for in these men we have laws endowed with life and reason, and Moses extolled them for two reasons. First he wished to shew that the enacted ordinances are not inconsistent with nature; and secondly that those who wish to live in accordance with the laws as they stand have no difficult task, seeing that the first generations before any of the particular statutes were set in writing followed the unwritten law with perfect ease, so that one might properly say that the enacted laws are nothing else than memorials of the life of ancients, preserving to a later generation their actual words and deeds.

According to Sidney Sowers,[37] by stating that the patriarchs bore in their souls the law on which the Torah is based, Philo was seeking to provide support and legitimation for the Torah within the context of contemporary Hellenism. The Torah is thus not only the particular law of the Jews, but it is in harmony with the law of nature (*Mos.* 2.48). While there has been debate concerning whether Philo was the first to frame in Greek the concept of natural law, it appears now probable that he was drawing on Stoic ideas.[38] But in his sphere of thought, this realization gave the law of the Jews, the Torah, its universal importance. Hence, when tempted by Potiphar's wife, Joseph says that "We children of the Hebrews follow laws and customs which are especially our own" (*Ios.* 42), there is no contradiction, for these laws were to be considered identical to the laws of nature. Philo could hardly have given a stronger expression of the importance of the Jewish people and their Torah.

37. Sidney G. Sowers, *The Hermeneutics of Philo and Hebrews: A Comparison of the Interpretation of the Old Testament in Philo Judaeus and the Epistle to the Hebrews* (Basel Studies of Theology 1; Richmond: John Knox, 1965) 45.

38. Cf. Helmut Koester, "ΝΟΜΟΣ ΦΥΣΕΩΣ: The Concept of Natural Law in Greek Thought," in *Religions in Antiquity: Essays in Memory of Erwin Ramsdell Goodenough*, ed. Jacob Neusner (SHR 14; Leiden: Brill, 1968) 521-41, and contra Koester: Richard A. Horsley, "The Law of Nature in Philo and Cicero," *HTR* 71 (1978) 35-59. See also David Winston, "Philo's Ethical Theory," in *ANRW* 2.21.1 (1984) 372-416, esp. 381-86; Hindy Najman, "The Law of Nature and the Authority of the Mosaic Law," *SPhilo* 11 (1999) 55-73; and the articles in David T. Runia, Gregory E. Sterling, and Hindy Najman, eds., *Laws Stamped with the Seals of Nature: Law and Nature in Hellenistic Philosophy and Philo of Alexandria* (SPhAn 15; BJS 337; Providence: Brown University Press, 2003).

Philo on Joseph as a Politician

For those acquainted with the career of Joseph in Egypt as it is recorded in Genesis, it comes as no surprise that when Philo begins his treatise on Joseph, he introduces him as a statesman, ὁ πολιτικός (*Ios.* 1). Further consequences of this view are spelled out in his treatises *De Somniis* and *De Iosepho*. However, scholars are somewhat confused over the tensions between Philo's descriptions and evaluations of Joseph in *De Iosepho* and in the allegorical commentaries (especially *Somn.* 2). This problem has been approached in several ways.[39] Goodenough sees these works as focused on two different audiences, Gentiles and Jews, respectively. Hence, in the allegorical commentaries Goodenough reads Philo as writing in code; in *De Iosepho,* by innuendo, by negative and indirect statements.

In *De Somniis,* Goodenough views the descriptions of Joseph as a "clever piece of double entendre, a fierce denunciation of the Roman character and oppression, done in a way, and in a document, which would give it fairly wide currency among Jews, but would seem quite innocuous if, as was unlikely, it fell into Roman hands."[40] What Goodenough presents here is, in fact, an allegorical reading of these volumes. Joseph becomes a type of the governor or prefect of Egypt (*Somn.* 2.43), and the negative characterizations of this type are for Goodenough a way for Philo to "vent his secret hate of not just the politician, but specifically of that Roman ruler who was immediately over Philo and his own circle." He attaches significance to three terms or characterizations of Joseph: κενὴ δόξα, empty opinion; τῦφος, mist or confusion; and arrogance. Joseph, and thus the Roman politicians, are "additions" to true society.[41] These characterizations function for Goodenough as code references that need decoding to be understood (in *Somn.* 2, especially 2.42-43, 61-64, 78-81, 91-92, 115-33, as well as 1.219-22). The picture

---

39. On Joseph in Philo's work, see esp. Goodenough, *An Introduction to Philo Judaeus,* 52-74; *The Politics of Philo Judaeus,* 21-63; Earle Hilgert, "A Survey of Previous Scholarship on Philo's *De Josepho,*" in *Society of Biblical Literature 1986 Seminar Papers,* ed. Kent Harold Richards (Atlanta: Scholars, 1986) 262-70; Thomas H. Tobin, "Tradition and Interpretation in Philo's Portrait of the Patriarch Joseph," in Richards, *Society of Biblical Literature 1986 Seminar Papers,* 271-77; Maren Niehoff, *The Figure of Joseph in Post-Biblical Jewish Literature* (AGJU 16; Leiden: Brill, 1992) 54-83; Sarah J. K. Pearce, *The Land of the Body: Studies in Philo's Representation of Egypt* (WUNT 208; Tübingen: Mohr Siebeck, 2007) 112-19. The two last works do not have much to say about Joseph as a politician.

40. Goodenough, *The Politics of Philo Judaeus,* 21.

41. Goodenough, *The Politics of Philo Judaeus,* 23, 33.

emerging from Goodenough's reading is not that of a fanatic apocalyptic, at least not in the usual sense. Philo knew how to hold his tongue, avoiding apocalyptic imagery, yet saying enough to reveal to his Jewish readers where he stood: he "knew that as long as the Messiah had not yet come, one must get on with the Romans in the most conciliating spirit possible. So Philo kept his Messianism to himself. But one could secretly think, hope and hate. And Philo seems to me to be assuring his Jewish friends that he was passionately doing all three."[42]

Philo's allegories thus also become, in Goodenough's reading, a call "for Jews, to remain Jews, to conciliate Romans when necessary" and rest assured that "the God of justice would some day overturn these Roman upstarts and give to Jews their proper place at the head of the world."[43]

The other treatise, *De Iosepho,* is intended more for Gentiles, perhaps those seriously interested in Judaism, and Joseph is described in a much more favorable light. He is still a type of the Roman prefect, but now more an ideal person. Joseph was trained for this role in several ways: first by means of the lore of the shepherd's craft, then through household management, and with emphasis on continence of self-control. All in all, Philo seems to have an ambiguous attitude to the role of the politician. Thomas H. Tobin[44] has pointed out inconsistencies in the text of *De Iosepho.* In general it is formed as an encomium on Joseph. But in three more allegorical expositions (*Ios.* 28-36; 54-79; 125-56), Philo focuses more on the role of the statesman, and the picture becomes darker, and even ambiguous: at best the politician is an interpreter of dreams; at his worst he is a slave of the populace.

Goodenough argues that Philo draws much of his emphases and imagery from the Hellenistic ideals of kingship, and by describing Joseph in this way he is also describing the Roman prefect: "It is difficult to see how Philo could have made it more clear that in Joseph he saw the type of the Roman prefect."[45] In taking this approach, and by the descriptions he confers on Joseph, Philo is exaggerating and flattering the Romans. He did not like the type of Joseph, but it could be useful in presenting him to the Romans, as to guide them into patronage of the Jews. It might also have been useful to remind the Romans that Egypt had at least once been ideally governed — by a Jew.

---

42. Goodenough, *The Politics of Philo Judaeus,* 25.
43. Goodenough, *The Politics of Philo Judaeus,* 32.
44. Tobin, "Tradition and Interpretation."
45. Goodenough, *The Politics of Philo Judaeus,* 55.

Goodenough's allegorical readings have not found universal approval,[46] several scholars finding them too subtle to be obvious to the first readers.[47] Also debatable is whether Philo, coming from a family so close to the Romans, could have cherished such negative attitudes toward the Romans. Others argue that the differences between these treatises are not that great, and not at all irreconcilable.

Philo as a Practical Politician

From his works *In Flaccum* and *De Legatione,* we can observe Philo as a practicing politician. We can also find several politically flavored statements in his other works, for his politics is rooted in his wider ideology.[48] However, we do not know for how long Philo was engaged in politics, for it seems obvious from the following passage that he was not always engaged in political endeavors, nor was it his chosen path in life.

Philo on Spec. 3.1-6

There are not many autobiographical remarks in the works of Philo. One of the most extensive concerns his relationship to political life in Alexandria. The passage is not easy to decipher, hence it is worth quoting in extenso:

> There was a time when I had leisure for philosophy and for the contemplation of the universe and its contents, when I made its spirit my own in all its beauty and loveliness and true blessedness, when my constant companions were the divine themes and verities, wherein I rejoiced with a joy that never cloyed or sated. I had no base or abject thoughts nor grovelled in search of reputation or of the wealth or bodily comforts, but seemed always to be borne aloft into the heights with a soul possessed by some God-sent inspiration, a fellow-traveller with the sun and moon and the whole heaven and universe. Ah then I gazed down from the upper air, and straining the

46. As mentioned above, Hay and Bilde have offered support: Hay, "Politics and Exegesis in Philo's Treatise on Dreams"; Bilde, "Filon som polemiker."

47. On Joseph, see Hilgert, "A Survey of Previous Scholarship."

48. See, e.g., the study of Borgen, who has characterized *In Flaccum* and *De Legatione* as works applying the principles of the Torah; *Philo of Alexandria: An Exegete for His Time* (NovTSup 86; Leiden: Brill, 1997), 158-93.

mind's eye beheld, as from some commanding peak, the multitudinous worldwide spectacles of earthly things, and blessed my lot in that I had escaped by main force from the plagues of mortal life. But, as it proved, my steps were dogged by the deadliest of mischiefs, the hater of the good, envy, which suddenly set upon me and ceased not to pull me down with violence till it had plunged me in the ocean of civil cares, in which I am swept away, unable even to raise my head above the water. Yet amid my groans I hold my own, for, planted in my soul from my earliest days I keep the yearning for culture which ever has pity and compassion for me, and lifts me up and relieves my pain. To this I owe it that sometimes I raise my head and with the soul's eyes — dimly indeed because the mist of extraneous affairs has clouded their clear vision — I yet make shift to look around me in my desire to inhale a breath of life pure and unmixed with evil. And if unexpectedly I obtain a spell of fine weather and a calm from civil turmoils, I get me wings and ride the waves and almost tread the lower air, wafted by the breezes of knowledge which often urges me to come to spend my days with her, a truant as it were from merciless masters in the shape not only of men but of affairs, which pour in upon me like a torrent from different sides. Yet it is well for me to give thanks to God even for this, that though submerged I am not sucked down into the depths, but can also open the soul's eyes, which in my despair of comforting hope I thought had now lost their sight, and am irradiated by the light of wisdom, and am not given over to lifelong darkness.

Philo seems to state at least three things in this passage. First, there was a time when he could devote himself fully to his beloved theological and philosophical studies: "There was a time when I had leisure for philosophy and for the contemplation of the universe and its contents" (3.1). This period is described as the golden years of his life, a time when he "rejoiced with a joy that never cloyed or sated." He does not record, alas, at what stage of his life this period is to be located, or how long it lasted. Then second, something happened which is described in terms that are even more difficult to decipher: something happened that "ceased not to pull me down with violence till it had plunged me in the ocean of civil cares, in which I am swept away, unable to raise my head above the water." This is probably his way of stating to the readers, or even reminding them, that he had been a scholar for some time before he had to indulge in political issues and activity. "As it stands, the passage is a cry against his having had to abandon a life of contemplation in order to devote himself to political matters."[49] This represents the actual time of his writing this text and thus his current conditions; he is engaged in some public work. From time to time, however, he is able to find some time away from his official duties and indulge in more philosophical matters: "if unexpectedly I obtain a spell of fine weather and a calm from civil turmoils, I get me wings and ride the waves and almost tread the lower air, wafted by the breezes of knowledge which often urges me to come to spend my days with her, a truant as it were from merciless masters in the shape not only of men but of affairs, which pour in upon me like a torrent from different sides" (3.5). In these periods he is able to do some studying, and even some teaching, to "unfold and reveal what is not known to the multitude" (3.6). The main aspects of Goodenough's explanation of this period might be accepted as probable: "What the passage tells us is that Philo spent a time in his youth as a recluse (probably with the Therapeutae), but felt that his people needed him so much that he returned to them, and thereafter consoled himself during his leisure hours with writing about the mystic message of the Scriptures, while he devoted his main career to public service."[50] But several questions nevertheless remain: For instance, when did it become necessary that Philo leave his life of contemplation, and for what reasons, and what was his new occupation? These are questions to which scholarly research has not yet provided simple and indisputable answers.

An older interpretation of when Philo had to leave his work of contemplation and writing takes *Spec.* 3.1-6 as referring to his having to travel to Rome in 38-39 C.E. as a leader of the delegation to Emperor Gaius Caligula, to negotiate with him concerning the situation of the Jews in Alexandria as a result of the pogrom in 38 C.E.[51] Most scholars now reject this view,[52] the main reason being that if the events of 38 C.E. were the background of *Spec.* 3.1-6, this would necessitate a late dating for works such as *Spec.* 3, *De virtutibus*, and *De praemiis et poenis*.[53]

---

49. Goodenough, *The Politics of Philo Judaeus*, 66.

50. Goodenough, *The Politics of Philo Judaeus*, 68. His reference to Philo staying with the Therapeutae is, however, more dubious.

51. E.g., Isaak Heinemann, *Philons griechische und jüdische Bildung: Kulturvergleichende Untersuchungen zu Philons Darstellung der jüdischen Gesetze* (Breslau: Marcus, 1932; Hildesheim: Olms, 1962).

52. Borgen too considers the possibility and seems to vacillate a bit in *Philo of Alexandria: An Exegete for His Time*, but finally rejects it (pp. 171-75, 181).

53. Some still argue that *Spec.* 3.1-6 is written after the events of 38-40 C.E. See, e.g., Mi-

The third question related to the understanding of *Spec.* 3 is what kind of work Philo might have had on the basis of this text. Goodenough contends that "there can be no doubt that Philo actually spent the major part of his life in some public office."[54] Later in the same article he surmises that "his duties were of a judicial character, in which he had to administer Jewish law in harmony with the Hellenistic law of Alexandria, though this cannot be demonstrated."[55] In *The Jurisprudence of the Jewish Courts in Egypt*, Goodenough suggests that Philo was "a practical political administrator of some kind during much of his life,"[56] but he admits that this is a guess. Most scholars have not followed Goodenough's rather precise definition of Philo's work, but would probably agree that he must have held some degree of public responsibility in order to be elected as a representative of the Jews in Alexandria to the emperor in Rome.

Philo and the Conflicts in Alexandria 38-41 C.E.

Relations between the Jews and the other peoples in Alexandria escalated into a series of severe conflicts in the period of 38-41 C.E. The Jews had by then a history in the city going back centuries,[57] and relations between the Jews, the native Egyptians, and the so-called Greeks, who represented more a political than an ethnic category, had witnessed changing circumstances and various degrees of relationship. We cannot address extensive details of this history here, nor provide more than an outline of the conflicts in this

---

chael F. Mach, "Choices for Changing Frontiers: The Apologetics of Philo of Alexandria," in *Religious Apologetics — Philosophical Argumentation,* ed. Yossef Schwartz and Volkhard Krech (Religion in Philosophy and Theology 10; Tübingen: Mohr Siebeck, 2004) 319-33. See also R. A. Kraft, who argues for a late date for Philo's descriptions of Joseph; "Tiberius Julius Alexander and the Crisis in Alexandria According to Josephus," in *Of Scribes and Scrolls: Studies of the Hebrew Bible, Intertestamental Judaism and Christian Origins Presented to John Strugnell on the Occasion of His Sixtieth Birthday,* ed. Harold W. Attridge, John J. Collins, and Thomas H. Tobin S.J. (Lanham: University Press of America, 1990) 175-84.

54. Goodenough, "Philo and Public Life," 77.

55. Goodenough, "Philo and Public Life," 79.

56. Goodenough, *The Jurisprudence of the Jewish Courts in Egypt: Legal Administration by the Jews under the Early Roman Empire as Described by Philo Judaeus* (1929; repr., Amsterdam: Philo, 1968) 9.

57. See, e.g., Smallwood, *The Jews under Roman Rule,* 220-35; Modrzejewski, *The Jews of Egypt;* Sandra Gambetti, "The Jewish Community of Alexandria: The Origins," *Hen* 29 (2007) 213-39.

period: "The problems are formidable, and the answers inevitably tentative."[58] By addressing the problems with which a historian must cope — relating Philo to the events and seeking to understand his descriptions and personal viewpoints and interpretations — we may demonstrate the intricacies involved in considering Philo as a *homo politicus*. Hence we shall first provide an outline of the major conflictual events of this period; then consider some historical problems inherent in the descriptions of these events; and finally sketch Philo's own theological-political views as crucial for understanding his attitudes and descriptions.

Main Episodes of the Conflict

The Jews, in general, welcomed the Romans when they incorporated Egypt under their rule, and Philo has many positive statements about Augustus Caesar, the first emperor. In his treatise *In Flaccum,* he is also positive in references to the local governor Flaccus, up to a certain point (*Flacc.* 1-5). But Flaccus, who was a friend of Tiberius Caesar and enjoyed his patronage, faced a changed situation when Tiberius died and Gaius Caligula was made emperor. Gaius was not one whom Flaccus could expect would be warmly disposed toward him, hence his procuratorship was in danger. According to Philo (*Flacc.* 16-24), Flaccus was led into a plot against the Jews by three somewhat enigmatic characters named Dionysius, Lampo, and Isidorus. Flaccus, again according to Philo, now became an enemy of the Jews in Alexandria (*Flacc.* 24), discriminating against them, first indirectly and then more openly. Then a visitor arrived in Alexandria, and that greatly exaggerated tensions in the city.

The visit of Agrippa to Alexandria, August 38 (*Flacc.* 25-39, 103). The Jewish Agrippa (10 B.C.E.–44 C.E.), grandson of Herod the Great, had been in Rome for some time. He had received there responsibility for the tetrachy formerly ruled by Philip and had also been given the title of king.[59] According to Philo, Gaius advised Agrippa to return home via Alexandria. When arriving in the city, he did not sail into the harbor in daytime, but waited till night had fallen, so that he might disembark and reach the house of his host

58. Erich S. Gruen, *Diaspora: Jews amidst Greeks and Romans* (Cambridge, MA: Harvard University Press, 2002) 54.

59. Agrippa had a rather tumultuous history. He is mentioned by Josephus (e.g., *Ant.* 18.6), Philo, and the New Testament (Acts 12). For his biography, see David C. Braund, "Agrippa," in *ABD* 1:98-100; Daniel R. Schwartz, *Agrippa I: The Last King of Judaea* (TSAJ 23; Tübingen: Mohr Siebeck, 1990).

without being seen (*Flacc.* 37). Philo supplies no other reasons for his arrival than that he "only wanted to get a short route for his journey home" (*Flacc.* 28). Nevertheless, Philo does report that people of Alexandria observed "his bodyguard of spear men, decked in armor overlaid with gold and silver" (*Flacc.* 30), so Agrippa's presence in the city was not entirely secret. Flaccus's advisors incited his jealousy, complaining that the entire visit was an act of disgrace to the local prefect. Flaccus, however, did not shame Agrippa directly or in public, but permitted what Philo calls "the mob" to slander the king. They jeered Agrippa, parading a lunatic named Carabas dressed as a king, whom they hailed as *marin*, "Lord" (*Flacc.* 36-39). Although Flaccus could have intervened, he did nothing to prevent it, thus in Philo's view demonstrating his acceptance of the plot.

Desecration of the Synagogues (*Flacc.* 41-52; *Legat.* 132-35). Thus incited, the "mob" proceeded to ravage the Jewish synagogues. Some were burned, others desecrated by the installation of images of Gaius (*Flacc.* 41; *Legat.* 134). Still Flaccus did nothing to prevent these acts, leading Philo to conclude that they were carried out, if not on the order of Flaccus, at least with his consent.

Flaccus's edict (*Flacc.* 53-54). Flaccus then proceeded more openly against the Jews, issuing an edict in which, according to Philo, he "denounced us as foreigners and aliens (ξένους καὶ ἐπήλυδας) and gave us no right of pleading our case but condemned us unjudged" (*Flacc.* 54). This represented "the destruction of our citizenship (τὴν τῆς ἡμετέρας πολιτείας ἀναίρεσιν), so that when our ancestral customs and our participation in political rights (μετουσίας πολιτικῶν), the sole mooring on which our life was secured, had been cut away, we might endure the worst misfortunes."

Ghettoization and pogrom (*Flacc.* 55-96; *Legat.* 120-31). The resulting devastation for conditions of the Jews in Alexandria has been labeled a pogrom and the first Jewish ghetto in history. The Jews, who so far had been living in all five sectors of the city, although mostly in two, were now all driven into one sector. Their homes and workshops were damaged and plundered, and many of the Jews were hindered from their regular employment. The ensuing hunger and overcrowding prompted many to attempt to escape, but they were captured and killed, according to Philo, some by burning, some even by crucifixion. The leaders of the Jewish community, thirty-eight of them, were arrested, stripped, and lacerated with "scourges commonly used for the degradation of the vilest malefactors" (*Flacc.* 75; cf. 80). The Jewish homes were searched for weapons, but according to Philo, none were found. Flaccus seems to have played a more active role in these events.

Philo interprets the events politically, especially the scourging, as the gravest dishonoring of the Jews.

The account of these Alexandrian conflicts preserved in Philo's *In Flaccum* ends with the arrest and subsequent deportation and execution of Flaccus, but other sources support and supplement his narrative.

Embassies to Rome (*Legat.* 181-83, 349-72; Josephus *Ant.* 18.257-60). *De Legatione* is Philo's account of the embassies sent to the emperor in Rome representing both sides of the conflict, the Jews and their opponents. When the new governor, C. Virasius Pollio, had taken up his duties, the situation cooled down. The Jews were probably able to return home, resume their work, and reconsecrate their synagogues. Nevertheless, the situation was still tense and unstable, and both sides appointed delegations to go to Rome.

According to Josephus, Philo was the leader of the Jewish embassy of five persons, and the opposing Alexandrian delegation is said to have included Apion, Isidorus, and perhaps Lampo.[60] The chronology of events in Rome is, at best, "uncertain and controversial."[61] Philo reports that they first received a brief hearing by the emperor, who promised to listen to their case more fully later. It was several months, however, before that second hearing took place. In the meantime, Gaius ordered a statue of himself to be set up in the Jerusalem temple, an action Philo details in *Legat.* 184-98, 207-348. When the meeting finally came about, the emperor received them in a garden, talking to them while he inspected the arrangements and a house there. The entire scene demonstrated that Gaius was not much interested in their case at all: "In a sneering, snarling way he said: Are you the god-haters who do not believe me to be a god, a god acknowledged among all the other nations but not to be named by you?" (*Legat.* 353). The opposing delegation seized the opportunity to slander the Jews. The Jews protested, but as they all proceeded through the garden, the emperor continued to inspect a house, asking a few questions, but providing scarce time to listen to their response. He brought the meeting to an end, declaring that "They seem to me to be people unfortunate rather than wicked and to be foolish in refusing to believe that I have the nature of a god" (*Legat.* 366).

The delegation to Rome thus failed completely to achieve positive results. Neither Philo nor Josephus indicate any further decision by the emperor in this matter. And Philo's *De Legatione* ends somewhat abruptly: "So now I have told in a summary way the cause of the enmity which Gaius had

---

60. See Josephus *Ant.* 18.257; Smallwood, *The Jews under Roman Rule,* 242.
61. Smallwood, *The Jews under Roman Rule,* 243.

for the whole nation of the Jews, but now I must also describe the palinode" (373). We have no further knowledge of what the "palinode" contained, if it was ever written.

Edict of Claudius (Josephus *Ant.* 19.280-85). Gaius was murdered shortly thereafter (24 January 41 C.E.), and his uncle Claudius was elected as his successor. The delegations probably remained in Rome, hoping to present their cases before the new emperor. When news of Gaius's death reached Alexandria, there was a new outbreak of violence, this time initiated by the Jews. The prefect quelled the revolt and sent a report to the emperor. Claudius appears to have dealt with the Alexandrian issue, probably hearing both sides, and then issued an edict, recorded by Josephus (*Ant.* 19.280-85). The edict concludes: "I do not wish the Jewish race to lose any of its rights because of Gaius's madness, but I wish their former privileges to be preserved as long as they follow their national customs; and I instruct both sides to take the utmost care to ensure that there are no disturbances after this edict of mine has been published." This edict was to be followed by a letter to the Alexandrians.

Letter of Claudius. Peace was not yet reestablished in Alexandria, despite Claudius's edict. Tensions prevailed, if not even violent conflicts. During spring or summer 41 the Greeks sent a new delegation, comprising twelve men, to congratulate Claudius and offer him honors and to reopen the case against the Jews. According to the ensuing letter by the emperor, it seems that another delegation was also sent from the Jews, so possibly two Jewish delegations presented their case to the emperor. This *Letter to the Alexandrians* (10 November 41 C.E.) is attested neither by Josephus nor by Philo, and was generally unknown to scholars until published by H. Idris Bell in 1924.[62]

In this letter, the legal situation of the Jews in Alexandria was returned to what it had been before the conflicts occurred in 38 C.E. Claudius, in undisguised threats, told the Alexandrians "to stop this destructive and obstinate mutual enmity" and ordered that the customs of the Jews should not be further dishonored; they were allowed to keep their own ways. The Jews, for their part, were told "not to aim at more than they have previously had and not in the future to send two embassies as if they lived in two cities, . . . and not to intrude themselves into the games presided by the gymnasiarchoi and the kosmetai, since they enjoy what is their own, and in a city which is

---

62. H. Idris Bell, *Jews and Christians in Egypt: The Jewish Troubles in Alexandria and the Athanasian Controversy* (London: Oxford University Press, 1924); *CPJ* 2:36-55.

not their own they possess an abundance of all good things. Nor are they to bring in or invite Jews coming from Syria or Egypt."

Hence the issues were probably settled in Alexandria and Egypt for some time. However, new conflicts arose in 66 and especially in 115-17 C.E, with devastating results for the Jewish communities.[63]

Major Problems of Interpretation

This brief sketch of the conflicts involving the Jews in Alexandria raises several matters that are still discussed by scholars. Philo obviously was not a neutral observer, nor an unbiased reporter. Although we must acknowledge the great value of his narratives, several issues nevertheless remain open for further analyses. These are compounded by the fact that there is no consensus in current research for understanding the legal and social conditions of the Jews even before the conflicts broke out. Did they have a *politeuma* of their own?[64] If so, what kind of legal rights did it represent for the Jews? Did the Jews have Alexandrian citizenship in general, or was it a prerogative for only a few, primarily the elites? Was the conflict over Jews claiming Alexandrian citizenship while the Greeks opposed these claims? Or was it rather related to the rights of their *politeuma*?[65] Scholars remain quite divided on these issues.[66]

One might ask further: Why did Agrippa come to Alexandria? Some think it may have been to visit Alexander, the brother of Philo.[67] Others surmise that he actually had duties to carry out there on behalf of the emperor.[68]

---

63. On the latter, see Smallwood, *The Jews under Roman Rule,* 356-427.

64. See notes 9 and 10 above.

65. This is the view most ardently argued by Aryeh Kasher; *The Jews in Hellenistic and Roman Egypt: The Struggle for Equal Rights* (TSAJ 7; Tübingen: Mohr Siebeck, 1985).

66. See Smallwood, *The Jews under Roman Rule,* 224-35; *Philonis Alexandrini Legatio ad Gaium,* 6-12; Shimon Applebaum, "The Legal Status of the Jewish Communities in the Diaspora," in *The Jewish People in the First Century: Historical Geography, Political History, Social, Cultural and Religious Life and Institutions,* ed. Shmuel Safrai and M. Stern (CRINT 1/1; Assen: Van Gorcum; Philadelphia: Fortress, 1974) 1:420-63; Modrzejewski, *The Jews of Egypt,* 161-83; Barclay, *Jews in the Mediterranean Diaspora,* 60-71; Horst, *Philo's Flaccus,* 18-24. For a general discussion of the Jewish rights in the works of Josephus, see Miriam Pucci Ben Zeev, *Jewish Rights in the Roman World: The Greek and Roman Documents Quoted by Josephus Flavius* (TSAJ 74; Tübingen: Mohr Siebeck, 1998).

67. See, e.g., Schwartz, *Agrippa I,* 74-76.

68. Most innovative here is probably Gambetti, who suggests that Agrippa came to Alexandria to deliver imperial mandata to Flaccus; *The Alexandrian Riots of 38 C.E.,* 151-65.

Inconsistencies in Philo's account trigger such questions, but provide little help in answering them. Many, if not most, scholars tend to believe that Philo is underscoring something here regarding Agrippa's visit to Alexandria.

Another issue still debated concerns the identity of the opponents of the Jews. Who were the main persons responsible for the conflicts, and for what reasons?[69] E. Mary Smallwood[70] refers consistently to "the Greeks," but also the "nationalists." Philo himself does not speak of "the Greeks" as opponents, but rather of the "Alexandrians" and "Egyptians," which is much more helpful.[71] John Collins surmises whether there might have been some Graecized Egyptians among them,[72] while Erich Gruen[73] represents a minority position, seeming to argue that the opponents were the Egyptians. Probably some Egyptians were involved, if not the only antagonists.[74] The roles of persons like Isidorus and Lampo are also enigmatic.[75] The identity of the opponents would thus throw light on the central issues in the conflicts. Furthermore, how should one explain that two Jewish embassies presented themselves to Claudius? Several scholars take this as evidence of a split within the Jewish Alexandrian community, surfacing while Philo remained in Rome. According to this view, Philo's

69. Gruen, *Diaspora,* 62, lists eight distinct, but partly intersecting and overlapping views.

70. In her *Philonis Alexandrini Legatio ad Gaium,* 12, she calls them "a party of extreme patriots or nationalists."

71. On Philo and the Greeks, both here and in general, see Ellen Birnbaum, "Philo on the Greeks: A Jewish Perspective on Culture and Society in First-Century Alexandria," in *In the Spirit of Faith: Studies in Philo and Early Christianity in Honor of David Hay,* ed. David T. Runia and Gregory E. Sterling (SPhAn 18; BJS 332 [2001]) 37-58.

72. John J. Collins, "Anti-Semitism in Antiquity? The Case of Alexandria," in *Ancient Judaism in Its Hellenistic Context,* ed. Carol Bakhos (JSJSup 95; Leiden: Brill, 2005) 9-29, esp. 13-14.

73. See Gruen, *Diaspora,* 63-66. For the Egyptians in the symbolic universe of Philo, see Pearce, *The Land of the Body.*

74. Peter Schäfer, *Judeophobia: Attitudes Toward the Jews in the Ancient World* (Cambridge, MA: Harvard University Press, 1997) 136-60, esp. 145: "If we can safely assume that the mob who executed the pogrom consisted mainly of Egyptians, it even seems plausible that the Greek faction deliberately used the Egyptians in order to achieve their goal"; see also 159-60.

75. At first they entice Flaccus against the Jews (*Flacc.* 20); then, when Flaccus is brought as a prisoner to Emperor Gaius, they appear as his accusers (*Flacc.* 125-45), and later as the opponents of Philo in Rome (*Legat.* 155). A great literature developed around the role and fate of these persons, today usually labeled the *Acta Alexandrinorum* or *Acts of Alexandrian Martyrs.* For the texts, see *CPJ* 2:55-60. Smallwood, *The Jews under Roman Rule,* 250-55, discusses them briefly. For the most recent and extensive scholarly monograph on these texts, see Harker, *Loyalty and Dissidence in Roman Egypt.* There is room for another study of the enigmatic figure Isidorus.

delegation represented the moderate and elite Jews who wished to restore the status quo, while the second faction was more radical, possibly even more militant, desiring more privileges than they had before the conflicts began.[76]

Although additional scholarly disagreements regarding this period could be noted, the above may demonstrate the complexity of the research concerning these issues. While this might appear daunting to a M.A. or Ph.D. student trying to navigate the wilderness, it can also present opportunity and a challenge for further research.

Philo as a Politician and Political Writer

In the preceding sections we have used Philo as a major source for the conflicts in Alexandria without focusing on his own particular interpretations of these events. Here we will elaborate on his views as found in *In Flaccum* and *De Legatione*.

Philo nowhere states explicitly why he wrote a treatise such as *In Flaccum*, and that work contains no preface as in the Gospel of Luke (1:1-3) or the beginning of Josephus's *Jewish War* (*J.W.* 1.1). However, in the last section of *In Flaccum* Philo does contain a theological statement that underscores much of his focus and intentions for the book. After Flaccus has been imprisoned, sentenced to exile on the island of Andros, and then finally executed there by the minions of Gaius Caligula, Philo concludes his somewhat detailed exposition of the end of Flaccus with the following: "Such was the fate of Flaccus also, who thereby became an indubitable proof that the help which God can give was not withdrawn from the nation of the Jews" (*Flacc.* 191).

This expression of assurance of the reliability of divine help is further closely associated with the political struggles the Jews had endured under the rule of Flaccus. Toward the end of the treatise, Philo has Flaccus utter this prayer confessing his mistakes concerning the Jews (*Flacc.* 170, 173):

> King of gods and men, so then Thou dost not disregard the nation of the Jews, nor do they misreport Thy Providence, but all who say that they do

76. The rebuke in the *Letter of Claudius* against the Jews for sending two embassies is our primary evidence for the existence of two such delegations, but their positions remain enigmatic. See Barclay, *Jews in the Mediterranean Diaspora*, 56-57. See also *CPJ* 2:50-53. For a brief review of recent scholarship, see Gambetti, *The Alexandrian Riots of 38 c.e.*, 224 n. 38.

not find in Thee a Champion and Defender, go astray from the true creed. I am a clear proof of this, for all the acts which I have madly committed against the Jews I have suffered myself. . . . I cast on them the slur that they were foreigners without civic rights (ὠνείδισά ποτε ἀτιμίαν καὶ ξενιτείαν αὐτοῖς ἐπιτίμοις οὖσι κατοίκοις), though they were inhabitants with full franchise.

This prayer sums up much of what the treatise is about, namely the civic rights of the Jews as understood by Philo, here also theologized as a part of God's providence and care. The statement made here by Flaccus coincides with what Philo describes as the height of the offenses carried out by Flaccus against the Jews in the early stages of the conflicts. In *Flacc.* 53, Philo laments that Flaccus "issued a proclamation in which he denounced us as foreigners and aliens and gave us no right of pleading our case but condemned us unjudged." To Philo that amounts to "the destruction of our citizenship, . . . when our ancestral customs and our participation in political rights, the sole moorings on which our life was secured, had been cut away."

The issues at stake in *In Flaccum* are thus the political rights of the Jews. This is evident throughout the treatise and demonstrates the politician Philo at work. In Alexandria he identifies two kinds of inhabitants, "us and them" (*Flacc.* 43) — "us" being the Jews, "them" being all the others. As for the Jews, Philo says that not only were there a million residing in Alexandria and Egypt, but also they had settled in most countries (*Flacc.* 46; cf. *Legat.* 281):

> For so populous are the Jews that no one country can hold them, and there-fore they settle in very many of the most prosperous countries in Europe and in Asia, both in the islands and on the mainland, and while they hold the Holy City where stands the sacred Temple of the most high God to be their *mother city* (μητρόπολις), yet those which are theirs by inheritance from their fathers, grandfathers, and ancestors even farther back, are in each case accounted by them to be their fatherland (πατρίδας νομίσοντες) in which they were born and reared, while to some of them they have come at the time of their foundation as immigrants (i.e., colonists) (ἤλθον ἀποικίαν στειλάμενοι) to the satisfaction of the founders.

While Philo on the one hand acknowledges Jerusalem to be their mother city, and thus their presence in Egypt to be comparable to the Greek and Roman colonies, Alexandria is nevertheless considered by many to be their fatherland (cf. *Conf.* 78). This is a very strong assertion of allegiance to Alexandria and Egypt, hence Philo can also characterize Alexandria as "our city" (*Flacc.* 123). Philo is fighting for what he characterizes as their citizenship and political rights in that city. The Jews had a senate appointed to take charge of Jewish affairs, an institution established "by our savior and benefactor Augustus" (*Flacc.* 74). This is also the background for Philo's anger in dealing with the punishments inflicted on their leaders, namely the disgracing "scourges commonly used for the degradation of the vilest malefactors" (*Flacc.* 75).

This is what we might surmise through a surface reading of Philo. But when we try to go further in asking the historical questions, we enter a minefield, like looking at a map containing several blank spots. What kind of citizenship did Philo have in mind, and for whom? Citizenship of Alexandria, or the more limited one of their own *politeuma* and its rights? The letter of Claudius to Alexandria in 41 C.E., which Philo does not mention,[77] seems to resolve some of these questions. Here the emperor states that the Jews were living in a city not their own. But at the same time, the Alexandrians are told "to behave gently and kindly towards the Jews who have inhabited the same city for many years, and not to dishonor any of their customs in their worship of their god, but to allow them to keep their own ways, as they did in the time of the god Augustus and as I too, having heard both sides, have confirmed" (lines 83-85). Claudius tried to be fair to both sides, and the letter probably settled the case for some time, but not for very long. After the conflicts in 115-17 C.E. the Jewish communities in Egypt were never again to attain a comparable measure of influence. But by then, Philo had rested in his grave for decades.

Problems and Prospects: An Open Ending

Philo was a citizen of Alexandria, at the time one of the three largest cities in the Roman Empire. He belonged to the elite segments among the Jews, being a member of a very rich and probably also very influential family in the city. He might have been a Roman citizen, and he might have received a thorough Greek education in the gymnasium (*Congr.* 74-76). He felt free to attend such social gatherings as parties and symposia (*Leg.* 3.155-59) and could watch sporting events (*Agr.* 110-21) and frequent theaters (*Ebr.* 177;

77. Perhaps *De Legatione* was written before the letter was written or known in Alexandria.

Prob. 141). He might to some extent be considered an acculturated Jew, but far from being assimilated.[78] In spite of the fact that he was a productive writer, providing us with a voluminous library that still informs, inspires, and challenges scholars, he remains nevertheless somewhat enigmatic, as we see him arguing in behalf of his people's political role in the city and clearly distinguishing between "us and them."

According to Peder Borgen, Philo was a Jew on the brink of being absorbed into the Greco-Roman culture. This was not because Philo compromised his Judaism or merged Hellenism and Judaism, but because of his efforts to conquer the Greco-Roman culture by asserting that all the good to be found therein in fact stemmed from Judaism.[79] Thus Borgen coined the phrase that Philo was "a conqueror, on the verge of being conquered."[80] Others, however, have applied other characterizations. Victor Tcherikover[81] considered Philo as a Jew that struggled for Jewish "emancipation," while a Jewish scholar like Aryeh Kasher has been discerned as making Philo into a very conservative Jew, primarily seeking to secure the rights of their own Jewish *politeuma.*[82] Goodenough tried to convince his readers that Philo was a mystic, while his biographer points out that Goodenough to a large degree considered mysticism to be the essence of religion.[83] What all this amounts to is to remind us that a scholar's social location and his or her hermeneutic might play a considerable interpretative role that should not be overlooked. None of us are socially detached readers or writers.

78. Such descriptions are relevant, but one must be careful about how one defines these terms. As two examples of a somewhat different use, see Barclay, *Jews in the Mediterranean Diaspora,* 82-124, 320-35; and Torrey Seland, "'Conduct yourselves honorably among the Gentiles' (1 Peter 2:12): Assimilation and Acculturation in 1 Peter," in *Strangers in the Light: Philonic Perspectives on Christian Identity in 1 Peter* (Biblical Interpretation 76; Leiden: Brill, 2005) 147-89.

79. Peder Borgen, "Philo of Alexandria: A Critical and Synthetical Survey of Research Since World War II," in *ANRW* 2.21.1 (1984) 154. Cf. "Filo, Diasporajøde Fra Aleksandria," in *Blant skriftlærde og fariseere: Jødedommen i oldtiden,* ed. Hans Kvalbein (Oslo: Verbum, 1984) 154.

80. Cf. Borgen, "Philo of Alexandria: A Critical and Synthetical Survey," 150: This characterization has been adopted by D. T. Runia, "How to Read Philo," in *Exegesis and Philosophy: Studies on Philo of Alexandria* (Collected Studies Series; Aldershot: Variorum, 1990) 185-98, esp. 190; cf. in the same volume "Philo, Alexandrian and Jew," 16: ". . . can hardly be bettered."

81. Tcherikover, *Hellenistic Civilization and the Jews.*

82. Esp. Aryeh Kasher, "The Jewish Attitude to the Alexandrian Gymnasium in the First Century A.D.," *American Journal of Ancient History* 13 (1976) 148-61.

83. See Robert S. Eccles, *Erwin Ramsdell Goodenough: A Personal Pilgrimage* (Chico: Scholars, 1985).

Another challenging problem in reading Philo is how to understand his political terminology. In addition to there probably being a certain fluidity in the use of several of these terms in general, we might also be hampered in our understanding of Philo because of variations in his usage of terms that are not easy to decipher today. Sandra Gambetti's important study[84] is challenging not least for her assessment of some of Philo's terminology, but also for some of her positions regarding the chronology of the events of the late 30s c.e. Another challenge is how to consider the *Acts of the Alexandrian Martyrs*. The recent contributions of both Gambetti and Andrew Harker[85] demonstrate the importance of not overlooking these artifacts.

Recently, the hermeneutic of postcolonialism has come to be applied increasingly in historical studies of antiquity. Some studies have tried to apply this approach to Philo, one for example subscribing to Goodenough's view of Philo's relation to the Romans, another dealing with colonial education and class formation. Time will tell if this avenue is helpful.[86]

Still more problems and prospects could be mentioned, but it is to be hoped that the preceding presentation of some of the relevant aspects and issues concerning Philo as a politician might inspire further research and scholarly discussions.

84. Sandra Gambetti, *The Alexandrian Riots of 38 c.e.*
85. Harker, *Loyalty and Dissidence in Roman Egypt.*
86. See Torrey Seland, " 'Colony' and 'Metropolis' in Philo: Examples of Mimicry and Hybridity in Philo's Writing Back from the Empire?" *Études Platoniciennes 7: Philon d'Alexandrie*, ed. J.-F. Pradeau (Paris: Les Belles Lettres, 2010) 13-36; Royce M. Victor, *Colonial Education and Class Formation in Early Judaism: A Postcolonial Reading* (LSTS 72; London: T. & T. Clark, 2010).

Philo — An Interpreter of the Laws of Moses

Peder Borgen

Philo's Expository Writings

Among Philo's writings, his expository treatises are of main interest for a presentation of him as an exegete.[1] They deal primarily with material from the Pentateuch.[2] In addition to Philo's expository works, references will be made at times to the two historical treatises, *Against Flaccus* and *On the Embassy to Gaius*, since they provide glimpses into problems connected with the interpretation of the laws of Moses in the life of the Alexandrian community.[3] Philo's expository treatises fall into two main groups: those rewriting the Pentateuch and his exegetical commentaries.

---

1. For an analysis of Philo's writings from the perspective of rhetoric, see Manuel Alexandre Jr., *Rhetorical Argumentation in Philo of Alexandria* (BJS 322; SPhilo Monographs 2; Atlanta: Scholars, 1999). For an understanding of Philo's *Exposition of the Laws of Moses* against the background of *Tractatus Coislinianus* (its date is debated), a treatise on literary criticism, and the classification of genres given by Diomedes (second part of the fourth century of the Common Era), see Adam Kamesar, "The Literary Genres of the Pentateuch as Seen from the Greek Perspective: The Testimony of Philo of Alexandria," in *Wisdom and Logos: Studies in Jewish Thought in Honor of David Winston*, ed. David T. Runia and Gregory E. Sterling (SPhAn 9; BJS 312; Atlanta: Scholars, 1997) 143-89.

2. For further reading on Philo, see Peder Borgen, *Philo of Alexandria: An Exegete for His Time* (NovTSup 86; Leiden: Brill, 1997).

3. Cf. Kenneth Schenk, *A Brief Guide to Philo* (Louisville: Westminster John Knox, 2005) 14-22.

Rewriting the Pentateuch

Philo's works that rewrite the Pentateuch are his expositions of the laws of Moses, *On the Life of Moses,* and *Hypothetica.* The extant writings representing the expositions of the laws of Moses are *On the Creation, On Abraham, On Joseph, On the Decalogue, On the Special Laws, On the Virtues,* and *On Rewards and Punishments.* E. R. Goodenough[4] named this collection of treatises *The Exposition of the Laws of Moses. On the Life of Moses* was formerly classed in a group of miscellaneous writings, but Goodenough has shown that these treatises and the *Exposition* were companion works.[5] The preserved fragments of the *Hypothetica (An Apology for the Jews)* deal with events and laws that cover parts of the Pentateuch from Jacob (Genesis 25) to the conquest of Palestine in the books of Joshua and Judges. In this work the emphasis is placed on a characterization of Judaism in Philo's own time, mainly as a response to criticism leveled against the Jews.

Exegetical Commentaries

Philo's exegetical commentaries include the *Allegorical Commentary on Genesis* and the literal and allegorical *Questions and Answers on Genesis and Exodus.* The *Allegorical Commentary on Genesis* consists of the *Allegorical (Interpretation of the) Laws* 1-3, *On the Cherubim, On the Sacrifices of Cain and Abel, That the Worse Attacks the Better, On the Posterity and Exile of Cain, On the Giants, On the Unchangeableness of God, On Husbandry, On Noah's Work as a Planter, On Drunkenness, On Sobriety, On the Confusion of Tongues, On the Migration of Abraham, Who Is the Heir of Divine Things, On Mating with the Preliminary Studies, On Flight and Finding, On the Change of Names, On Dreams* 1-2. This series covers the main parts of Genesis 2–41. In general they have the form of verse-by-verse commentary on the biblical texts.

   Questions and Answers on Genesis and Exodus is a brief commentary in the form of questions and answers on sections of the two first books of the Pentateuch. The extant text of *Questions and Answers on Genesis* begins at

4. E. R. Goodenough, "Philo's Exposition of the Law and His De Vita Mosis," *HTR* 26 (1933) 109-25.

5. Goodenough, "Philo's Exposition of the Law"; Jenny Morris, "The Jewish Philosopher Philo," in Emil Schürer, *The History of the Jewish People in the Age of Jesus Christ (175 B.C.–A.D. 135),* rev. and ed. Geza Vermes and Fergus Millar (3 vols.; Edinburgh: T. & T. Clark, 1973-87) 3/2:854-55.

Gen 2:4 and ends at 28:9 (with lacunae), and *Questions and Answers on Exodus* covers parts of Exod 12:2–28:34 (LXX). All but a small portion of the Greek original has been lost, and for the bulk of the work we must depend on the ancient Armenian version.[6]

In common with the commentaries which have been found among the Dead Sea Scrolls, Philo's *Allegorical Commentary* and *Questions and Answers on Genesis and Exodus* are largely running commentaries that interpret biblical texts mainly in sequence, verse-by-verse. Some of the rabbinic midrashim also consist of running commentaries on the Pentateuch and other parts of the Hebrew Bible.[7]

Hermeneutical Presuppositions

Here we will identify some of the hermeneutical presuppositions that guided Philo in his expository enterprise.

God's Laws Proclaimed to the Greek-speaking World

Some clues to Philo's hermeneutical presuppositions may be found in *Mos.* 2.1-65. Here Philo makes clear that in the Diaspora setting of the Alexandrian Jews the translation of the laws of Moses into Greek was a major revelatory event. The giving of the laws in the Hebrew language at Mount Sinai was for the barbarian half of the human race, while the translation of these laws into Greek on the island of Pharos at Alexandria made them known to the Greek half of the world (*Mos.* 2.26-27). This second event took place under Ptolemy Philadelphus, the third in succession to Alexander, the conqueror of Egypt (*Mos.* 2.25-40).

In *Mos.* 2.25-40 Philo gives a summary of the traditional account of the origin of the Greek translation:[8] according to Philo, the reason for the translation was not lack of knowledge of Hebrew among Alexandrian Jews, but

---

6. Earle Hilgert, "The Quaestiones: Texts and Translations," in *Both Literal and Allegorical: Studies in Philo of Alexandria's Questions and Answers on Genesis and Exodus,* ed. David M. Hay (BJS 232; Atlanta: Scholars, 1991) 1-15.

7. Gary G. Porton, "Midrash." In *ABD* 4:818-22, here 820.

8. Henry Barclay Swete, *An Introduction to Old Testament in Greek* (Cambridge: Cambridge University Press, 1902) 12; cf. Henry G. Meecham, *The Oldest Version of the Bible: "Aristeas" on Its Traditional Origin* (London: Holborn, 1932) 121-24.

the need for the laws of the Jewish nation, which at the same time were the one God's cosmic and universal laws, to be made known to all nations.

In his works, then, Philo continues this *proclamatio Graeca* with the same aim in mind. Philo was involved in cross-cultural communication, and his works reflect this dual context.[9] It should be remembered that Judaism as a whole is — in different degrees and in different ways — to be understood within the sphere of Hellenism.[10]

The glimpse given by Philo of the Septuagint festival on the island of Pharos shows that there was a large number of non-Jews in Alexandria who were sympathizers with Judaism and took part in at least one Jewish festival, and by implication probably in several of the activities in the Jewish community. These sympathizers, together with the Alexandrian Jews, celebrated the Greek translation of the laws of Moses. Thus, there is reason for believing that Philo largely had in mind the kind of people present at these Septuagint festivals when he wrote, and that setting for his writings comprises both the Jewish community and its borderline to the surrounding world, such as non-Jewish sympathizers with Judaism.

The Mosaic Law and the Cosmic Law

According to Philo, Moses receives from within a share of the divine being. On this, Yehoshua Amir stresses the contrast between Philo and the rabbis: "Even the fact that in two passages [Exod 4:16 and 7:11] the Torah conditionally refers to Moses as 'God' — a fact that the rabbis did their best to explain away — is enthusiastically welcomed by Philo."[11] But Amir overlooks the rabbinic midrash *Tanchuma:* "he [God] called Moses 'God,' as it is said, 'See, I have made you a god to Pharaoh' (Exod 7:1)."[12] Even so, Moses is primarily the Lawgiver.

9. Cf. David T. Runia, *Philo of Alexandria and the Timaeus of Plato* (Philosophia antiqua 44; Leiden: Brill, 1986) 32-37.

10. Martin Hengel, *Judaism and Hellenism,* trans. John Bowden (2 vols.; Philadelphia: Fortress, 1974).

11. Yehoshua Amir, "Authority and Interpretation of Scripture in the Writings of Philo," in *Mikra: Text, Translation, Reading and Interpretation of the Hebrew Bible in Ancient Judaism and Early Christianity,* ed. Martin Jan Mulder and Harry Sysling (CRINT 2/1; Assen: Van Gorcum; Philadelphia: Fortress, 1988) 421-54, here 436.

12. *Midrash Tanchuma,* ed. Solomon Buber (Wilna: Romm, 1885) 4:51-52. See Wayne A. Meeks, *The Prophet-King* (NovTSup 14; Leiden: Brill, 1967) 193.

The laws of Moses had authority for Philo because they contain the revelation of God in words, in events in history, and in creation.[13] The relationship between the law and God's creation, cosmos, is a central theme in Philo's works.[14] He deals with this theme most fully in *Mos.* 2.45-52. In *Mos.* 2.47b Philo considers why Moses began his lawbook *(nomothesia)* with history, even back to creation. Part of his answer is:

> in relating the history of early times, and going for its beginning right to the creation of the universe, he [Moses] wished to shew two most essential things: first that the Father and Maker of the cosmos was in the truest sense also Lawgiver, secondly that he who would observe the laws will accept gladly the duty of following nature and live in accordance with the ordering of the universe, so that his deeds are attuned to harmony with his words and his words with his deeds. (*Mos.* 2.48)

This harmony is also dealt with in *Mos.* 2:52: "the particular enactments . . . seek to attain to the harmony of the universe." These particular enactments are the specific laws and regulations in the Mosaic laws. This conclusion is supported by *Abr.* 3, where the patriarchs are understood to be archetypes pointing to particular laws in the treatises *On the Decalogue* and *On the Special Laws*.

From this analysis a hermeneutical key can be formulated:

> The particular ordinances of the Jewish Law coincide with the universal cosmic principles. Thus to Philo universal and general principles do not undercut or cancel the specific ordinances or events of the Mosaic law.[15]

Philo furthermore applies the Stoic idea of the cosmos as a city[16] to the biblical story of the creation: Moses "considered that to begin his writings

---

13. Cf. Amir, "Authority and Interpretation of Scripture"; Folker Siegert, "Early Jewish Interpretation in a Hellenistic Style," in *Hebrew Bible: The History of Its Interpretation*, vol. 1/1: *Antiquity*, ed. Magne Sæbø (Göttingen: Vandenhoeck & Ruprecht, 1996) 130-98, here 171.

14. Harry Austryn Wolfson, *Philo: Foundations of Religious Philosophy in Judaism, Christianity, and Islam* (Cambridge, MA: Harvard University Press, 1948) 2:189-92; Valentin Nikiprowetzky, *Le Commentaire de l'écriture chez Philon d'Alexandria* (ALGHJ 11; Leiden: Brill, 1977) 117-55.

15. Cf. Per Jarle Bekken, *The Word Is Near You: A Study of Deuteronomy 30:12-14 in Paul's Letter to the Romans in a Jewish Context* (BZNW 144; Berlin: de Gruyter, 2007) 127-28, 138-42.

16. Hans Friedrich August von Arnim, *Stoicorum veterum fragmenta* (Leipzig: Teubner, 1903-24) 1:262; Cicero *De natura deorum* 154.

with the foundation of a man-made city was below the dignity of the laws . . . , [and] inserted the story of the genesis of the "Great City," holding that the laws were the most faithful picture of the world-polity" (*Mos.* 2.51; cf. *Spec.* 1.3-14; *QE* 2.1, 4; *Opif.* 142-44).

By calling the laws of Moses the most faithful picture of the cosmic *politeia,* Philo makes an exclusive claim for these laws. They are both the picture of and the revelatory means by which one can perceive the cosmic commonwealth and its law and live accordingly. The laws of Moses are "stamped with the seals of nature itself" (*Mos.* 2.14).[17]

Israel is a chosen people that has a universal role, just as its law is modeled on the cosmic law. This understanding is formulated in *QE* 2.42, where Exod 24:12c ("the law and the commandment which I have written . . .") is interpreted: "rightly does He legislate for this race [the contemplative race, i.e., Israel], also prescribing [its law] as a law for the world, for the chosen race is a likeness of the world, and its Law [is a likeness of the laws] of the world."[18] In this role the people function as the priesthood of all humankind, and their temple and sacrifices have cosmic significance (*Abr.* 56, 98; *Mos.* 1.149; *Spec.* 1.66-67, 76, 82-97; 2.163-67; *Fug.* 108-9; *Her.* 84; *Somn.* 2:188, 231; cf. Josephus *Ant.* 3.179-87).[19]

The presupposition of these ideas is the biblical tradition that the God of Israel is also the Creator and that the books of the Mosaic law begin with the story of creation. There was a broad Jewish tradition built on this biblical idea. In Sirach the concept of Wisdom was thought to pervade the cosmos and to have made her home in Israel, in Jerusalem (Sir 24:3-12). Sirach identified Wisdom with Torah (Sir 24:23).

Also in rabbinic writings creation and the revealed Torah are connected in such a way that the Torah is the cosmic law: heaven and earth cannot exist without Torah (*b. Ned.* 32a), and God consulted the Torah when he created the world (*Gen. Rab.* 1:2). Of special interest is Josephus's statement that everything in the Mosaic law is set forth in keeping with the nature of the universe (*Ant.* 1.24). At the same time it should be remembered that Philo does not draw a distinction between private and public laws or between religious and secular laws: "As the Torah was the revealed will of God, it was the primary source for all Jewish legislation."[20]

---

17. Nikiprowetzky, *Le Commentaire de l'écriture,* 117-55.

18. Nikiprowetzky, *Le Commentaire de l'écriture,* 118.

19. Jean Laporte, *La doctrine eucharistique chez Philon d'Alexandrie* (ThH 16; Paris: Beauchesne, 1972) 75-190.

20. Torrey Seland, *Establishment Violence in Philo and Luke: A Study of Non-conformity to the Torah and Jewish Vigilante Reactions* (Biblical Interpretation 15; Leiden: Brill, 1995) 12.

The Deeper Meanings

The hermeneutical insights drawn from these observations are that Philo can in different ways interpret one and the same biblical text basically on two, sometimes three, levels, for example, on concrete and specific levels, or on the level of the cosmic and general principles and on the level of the divine realm of the beyond.[21]

It should be mentioned that a two-level exegesis is present also in other Jewish writings, for example, in such a way that both levels may be pictured in concrete and specific terms. Thus, in the book of *Jubilees* Noah, Abraham, and others are said to have observed and enjoined the laws on *earth,* but the laws are the ones inscribed on *heavenly* tablets, which were later given to Moses (*Jub* 6:17; 15:1; 16:28, passim; cf. *Abr.* 276).[22]

In general support of the understanding of Philo's two-level exegesis outlined above, one might refer to the hermeneutical function of Philo's ascents according to *Spec.* 3.1-6. Philo states that his soul ascended to the heavenly sphere. This and other ascents enable him to unfold and reveal in the laws of Moses their deeper meaning, which is not known to the multitude (*Spec.* 3:6). This deeper meaning may often be expressed in allegory, but is not limited to it, as is evident from Philo's *Exposition of the Laws of Moses,* of which *On the Special Laws* 3.1-6 is a part. In this comprehensive work of Philo, allegorical interpretations as such are not prominent. The general (ethical) meaning behind the specific commandments and regulations are, however, brought out by Philo.

Aspects of Philo's Exegesis

Philo moves from one level of meaning to another by proceeding from macrocosm to microcosm, from individuals to the virtues and vices they embody, from specific commandments to their ethical meanings, and by an-

---

21. Cf. Irmgard Christiansen, *Die Technik der allegorischen Auslegungswissenschaft bei Philon von Alexandrien* (Beiträge zur Geschichte der biblischen Hermeneutik 7; Tübingen: Mohr, 1969), 134.

22. Wilhelm Bousset, *Die Religion des Judentums im späthellenistischen Zeitalter,* rev. Hugo Gressmann (3rd ed.; HNT 21; Tübingen: Mohr, 1926) 125, n. 3; 126 n. 1; Ephraim E. Urbach, *The Sages: Their Concepts and Beliefs,* trans. Israel Abrahams (Jerusalem: Magnes, Hebrew University, 1975) 1:335.

thropomorphic statements and etymologies. Angels are seen as means of communication between the levels.

From Macrocosm to Microcosm

In many cases Philo builds his exegesis on the correspondence between macrocosm and microcosm. As seen within a macrocosmic context, for Abraham to become a proselyte (*Abr.* 68-84) meant to migrate from the Chaldean search for God within the created order, in astrology, to the recognition that the world is not sovereign but dependent on its Maker. From a microcosmic point of view, Abraham's migration was an ascent via a microcosmic apprehension of a person's invisible mind as the ruler of the senses (Philo connects the name of Haran with the Greek root *charran,* "hole," i.e., sense organ):[23] "It cannot be that while in yourself there is a mind appointed as a ruler which all the community obeys, the cosmos . . . is without a king who holds it together" (*Abr.* 74). Philo's ideas about macrocosm and microcosm should not be seen as alien to rabbinic tradition, since they are also expressed by rabbis.[24]

More associative analogies can also be found. For example, Moses compares passion to a tiger, the animal least capable of being tamed (*Leg.* 1.69). In Pythagorean fashion numbers in the biblical text are often interpreted within a cosmic context as well as in the microcosmic context of humanity. Of special importance is the connection between the number seven and the celebration of the completion of the world, the Sabbath, as outlined in *Opif.* 89-128 and *Leg.* 1.8-12. The properties of the number seven are seen in things incorporeal, in external creation as heavenly bodies (the seven planets), in the stages of humanity's growth, in all visible existence, and in grammar and music, and as given as a commandment in the Decalogue. On a more limited state, Aristobulus developed a similar interpretation already in the second century B.C.E. Clement of Alexandria also has arithmological sections in which the number seven is seen in the cosmic realm, as in the planets, and in anthropology (*Strom.* 6.16.139-45).[25]

---

23. Lester L. Grabbe, *Etymology in Early Jewish Interpretation: The Hebrew Names in Philo* (BJS 115; Atlanta: Scholars, 1988) 218.

24. See Rudolf Meyer, *Hellenistisches in der rabbinischen Anthropologie* (BWANT 74; Stuttgart: Kohlhammer, 1937) 39-40, 43-44, 126-27, 148-49.

25. Annewies van den Hoek, *Clement of Alexandria and His Use of Philo in the Stromateis* (VCSup 3; Leiden: Brill, 1988) 201-5; Paul Heinisch, *Der Einfluss Philos auf die älteste christliche Exegese* (Alttestamentliche Abhandlungen 1/2; Münster: Aschendorff, 1908) 105.

Etymologies

Philo makes extensive use of etymologies of names, using both the Hebrew and Greek languages.[26] For example, on the basis of Hebrew, the term "Israel" is interpreted to mean "the one who sees God," "Abram" as "uplifted father," and "Abraham" as "elect father of sound" (*Abr.* 82). From Greek etymology, the river Pheison is interpreted to mean "sparing" (*Leg.* 1.66). Etymologies were widely used in Christian exegesis as well, as by Clement. Some of Clement's Hebrew etymologies occur in contexts in which he draws on Philo,[27] and Clement uses the same etymological explanations of Abram and Abraham (*Strom.* 5.1.8).[28]

Angelology, Etc.

Philo's references to and interpretations of angels and on personifications of concepts are both complex and extensive. In general, they are either seen as spiritual entities distinct and different from the level of the external world of the senses or they may serve as means for different activities which take place between these two levels. For example, in *Conf.* 146, Logos, the Word, is called the "archangel." In *Fug.* 109, the high priest is not a man, but a divine Logos, his father being God, who is likewise the Father of all, and his mother is Sofia, Wisdom.[29] Logos can be called the Second God (*QG* 2.62).

Philo also lifts a specific person, Moses, up to the divine level. He seems to be seen as an angel ascending and descending on Sinai (*Somn.* 1.141-43 with reference to Exod 20:19). Moreover, Moses "was made god and king (Exod. 7:1 and 4:16) of the whole nation, and entered, it is told (Exod. 20:21) into the darkness where God was, that is into the unseen, invisible, incorporeal and archetypical essence of existing things." Amir[30] maintains that the rabbis did their best to explain away that the Torah refers to Moses as "God." Amir here overlooks the rabbinic midrash *Tanḥuma*: "He [God] called Moses 'God', as it is said, 'See I have made you a god to Pharaoh' (Exod 7:1)."[31] Also in the Dead Sea Scrolls, in the frag-

---

26. Grabbe, *Etymology in Early Jewish Interpretation.*
27. Van den Hoek, *Clement of Alexandria and His Use of Philo,* 222.
28. Heinisch, *Der Einfluss Philos,* 109.
29. Wolfson, *Philo,* 1:259
30. Amir, "Authority and Interpretation of Scripture," 430.
31. *Tanḥ.* 4:51ff. (ed. Buber). See Meeks, *The Prophet-King,* 193.

ments 4Q374 and 4Q377, Moses is given divine and angelic status, accord-ing to C. H. T. Fletcher-Louis.[32]

Individuals as Embodiments of Virtues and Vices

In ways other than by etymologies, specific persons can be seen as embod-iments of general virtues and vices or of other properties. A central plate in Philo's educational philosophy is the view that Abraham, when he failed at first to have a child by Sarah, that is, by wisdom and philosophy, he took the maid Hagar, general education, in her place. Here Philo follows an allegorical interpretation of Homer's Penelope, as is found in Pseudo-Plutarch: those who wear themselves out in general studies and fail to master philosophy are like the suitors who could not win Penelope and contented themselves with her maids.

By applying this tradition to Abraham's relation to Hagar, Philo brings it into a Jewish context. The relationship between Judaism (Abraham) and non-Jewish culture (Hagar and general education) is a central matter:[33] properly used, pagan education may in a positive way prepare for the re-vealed wisdom of the laws of Moses and be a useful help for the Jews.

Specific Commandments and Their Ethical Meaning

In his expositions, Philo fuses together the specific commandments and observances and their ethical and philosophical meanings. Thus his inten-tion is not to instruct his readers in the practical specifics of Jewish life. In his interpretation of the dietary laws, he does not ignore observance, but he also takes them as having deeper ethical meanings. In this he is dependent on exegetical traditions, as can be seen from the agreements with Pseudo-Aristeas. For example, both say that the laws concerning clean animals, those with parted hooves, teach humanity that it must distinguish between virtu-ous and bad ways of life (*Spec.* 4.106-9; Pseudo-Aristeas 150). One clue to

32. Crispin H. T. Fletcher-Louis, *All the Glory of Adam: Liturgical Anthropology in the Dead Sea Scrolls* (STDJ 42; Leiden: Brill, 2002) 236-342.

33. Peder Borgen, "Philo of Alexandria," in *The Literature of the Jewish People in the Period of the Second Temple and the Talmud*, vol. 2: *Jewish Writings of the Second Temple Period: Apocrypha, Pseudepigrapha, Qumran Sectarian Writings, Philo, Josephus*, ed. Michael E. Stone (CRINT 2/2; Assen: Van Gorcum; Philadelphia: Fortress, 1984) 233-82, here 255.

such ethical interpretations was the idea that observance made it possible to live an orderly, harmonious, and healthy life free of gluttony and extravagance. Thus Moses approved neither a life of rigorous austerity, like the Spartan legislator, nor of luxurious living, as taught to the Ionians and Sybarites (*Spec.* 4.100-102).

Anthropomorphic Statements, Etc.

One criterion that may show that the literal understanding is to be discarded and a deeper meaning is meant is formulated by Philo in this way: "to say that God uses hands or feet or any created part at all is not the true account" (*Conf.* 98). Thus Philo is a pointed representative of the broad tendency among Jews, seen also in the Septuagint, Aristobulus, the Targums, and the midrashic commentaries, to remove anthropomorphic statements about God by reading deeper meanings into them.[34]

Details in the text may indicate that a deeper meaning is intended. One such criterion is formulated by Philo in *On Flight and Finding:* Moses "never puts in a superfluous word." Thus since the phrase "let him die the death" (Exod 21:12) refers redundantly to death, it actually refers to two deaths: bad people are spiritually dead already while living (*Fug.* 54-55).

The Deeper and Literal Meanings

Although Philo in exceptional cases discards the literal meaning (e.g., *Det.* 95, 167), his basic principle and attitude are that the deeper meaning does not invalidate the literal meaning. Accordingly, the deeper meanings of the observances enjoined in the laws are not to be understood in such a way as to mean the abrogation of the practice of these laws. "Nay we should look on all these outward observances as resembling the body, and their inner meaning as resembling the soul" (*Migr.* 93).

In the employment of these (and other) methods of exegesis, Philo fol-

---

34. Siegmund Maybaum, *Die Anthropomorphien und Anthropathien bei Onkelos und den spätern Targumim* (Breslau: Schletter, 1870); Jacob Z. Lauterbach, "The Ancient Jewish Allegorists in Talmud and Midrash," *JQR* n.s. 1 (1991) 291-333, 503-31; Charles T. Fritsch, *The Anti-Anthropomorphisms of the Greek Pentateuch* (Princeton: Princeton University Press, 1943); Wolfson, *Philo,* 1:56-60; 2:127-28; Borgen, "Philo of Alexandria," in Stone, *Jewish Writings of the Second Temple Period,* 278.

lows approaches that existed within Jewish expository traditions in general, including rabbinic exegesis, and that shared features with methods of interpretation in the broader Hellenistic context. In comparison with rabbinic expositions (committed to writing from the late second century on), an important difference is that Philo to a larger extent finds in the texts Greek philosophical ideas, mainly of a Platonic and Stoic bent.

Philo as an Exegete in Context

Philo was an exegete among other exegetes, and he refers to many others, though not by name.[35] Here only two examples will be mentioned to indicate different hermeneutical approaches. In *Migr.* 89-93, Philo criticizes some spiritualists who in their interpretation of the Sabbath, feasts, and circumcision were in danger of separating the specific and concrete level from the higher level of general ideas and convictions. Philo keeps both levels together. It is then interesting to note that the specific and concrete levels do not just refer to biblical texts, but to biblical and traditional laws as they were to be practiced in Jewish community life.

Philo also refers to exegetes who do not look for a higher general and cosmic meaning if it is not stated in the text itself. Some examples of this approach are: in Deut 34:4, God humiliates Moses by not permitting him to enter the promised land (*Migr.* 44-45); in Gen 11:7-8, the confusion of tongues refers to the origin of the Greek and barbarian languages (*Conf.* 190); Gen 26:19-32 tells about the actual digging of wells (*Somn.* 1.39); and in Exod 22:26-27, the material return of the garment is meant (*Somn.* 1.92-102).

Moreover, Philo may deal with concrete and specific human experiences and events, at times seen together with biblical examples. Thus in *Praem.* 11-14, the idea of hope is illustrated by examples from various professions, such as the meaning of hope in the life of a tradesman, a ship captain, a politician, an athlete, and others. Then the biblical figure of Enos expresses every person's need for setting hope in God.

Within Philo's two- or three-level hermeneutical perspective there is room for various emphases. Thus the focus may be set on the level of specific

---

35. Montgomery J. Shroyer, "Alexandrian Jewish Literalists," *JBL* 55 (1936) 261-84; David M. Hay, "Philo's References to Other Allegorists," *SPhAn* 6 (1979-80) 41-75; Borgen, "Philo of Alexandria," in Stone, *Jewish Writings of the Second Temple Period,* 126-28; Kåre Sigvald Fuglseth, *Johannine Sectarianism in Perspective* (NovTSup 119; Leiden: Brill, 2005) 93-104.

historical events, interpreted by ideas from the higher level of cosmic principles and divine guidance. The treatises *Against Flaccus* and *On the Embassy to Gaius* belong to this kind of writing. The focus may also primarily be placed on the higher level of general cosmic principles and God's realm above the created world. The *Allegorical Commentary* qualifies for this classification.

Another possibility was to place both the concrete and the deeper levels together in immediate sequence, as especially is the case in several entries in the *Questions and Answers on Genesis and Exodus* and parts of *On Abraham* and *On Joseph.*[36] Various aspects of both levels may be woven together, as is largely the case in Philo's rewriting of the laws of Moses in *On the Life of Moses, On the Decalogue, On the Special Laws, On the Virtues,* and *On Rewards and Punishments.*

Some Exegetical Approaches and Forms

In this section we will discuss the forms of question and answer, direct exegesis, contrast, paraphrastic rewriting, rewriting of the Bible, and commentary.

Question and Answer

The exegetical form of question and answer is central for a formal analysis of the works of Philo, since it occurs in the *Exposition of the laws of Moses, On the Life of Moses,* the *Allegorical Commentary,* and the *Questions and Answers in Genesis and Exodus.*[37] As seen by its title, *Questions and Answers on Genesis and Exodus* is a collection of such questions and answers. Other examples are

---

36. Peder Borgen, *Philo, John, and Paul: New Perspectives on Judaism and Early Christianity* (BJS 131; Atlanta: Scholars, 1987) 22-23, 53-54; Sze-kar Wan, "Philo's *Quaestiones et solutiones in Genesim*: A Synoptic Approach," in *Society of Biblical Literature 1993 Seminar Papers,* ed. Eugene H. Lovering Jr. (Atlanta: Scholars, 1993) 22-53, here 35, 39.

37. Peder Borgen and Roald Skarsten, "Quaestiones et Solutiones: Some Observations on the Forms of Philo's Exegesis," *SPhilo* 4 (1976-77) 1-15; repr. in Borgen, *Paul Preaches Circumcision and Pleases Men* (Relieff 8; Trondheim: Tapir, 1984) 191-201; Nikiprowetzky, *Le Commentaire de l'écriture,* 170-80; "L'exegese de Philon d'Alexandrie dans le *De Gigantibus et le Quod Deus,*" in *Two Treatises of Philo of Alexandria: A Commentary on De Gigantibus and Quod Deus sit immutabilis,* ed. David Winston and John Dillon (BJS 25; Chico: Scholars, 1983) 5-75; Hay, *Both Literal and Allegorical;* Wan, "Philo's *Quaestiones et solutiones in Genesim.*"

seen in *Leg.* 1.33-41, 48-52, 70-71, 85-87, 90, 91-92a; 2.19-21, 42-43, 44-45; 3.18-19, 49ff., 66-68, 77-78; also *Cher.* 21-22, 55ff.; *Sacr.* 128ff.; *Det.* 57ff., 80ff.; *Post.* 33ff., 40ff., 153; *Gig.* 55ff.; *Mut.* 11-12; and *Somn.* 1.5ff.; 12-13.

In the *Exposition of the Laws,* Philo uses the exegetical form of question and answer at many points. One is the account of the creation of humankind (*Opif.* 72-88). Another is in connection with the central event of the giving of the law at Mount Sinai, where it is asked why, when all the many thousands were collected in one spot, God thought it good to proclaim the Ten Commandments to each person, not as to several persons, but with singular "Thou shalt not . . ." (*Decal.* 36-43). Other questions treat the desert as an unusual place for setting up a code of laws (*Decal.* 2-17), the lack of penalties for future transgressors of the ten commandments (*Decal.* 176-78), and Moses' unusual use of a story of the creation of the world to begin his legislation (*Mos.* 2.47ff.).

Broadly speaking, Philo's own context is reflected in some passages. The questions asked in *Mos.* 2.47ff. and *Decal.* 176-78 refer to some special features of the Mosaic law when compared with other laws (the creation as introduction to the laws, the lack of specified penalties with the Ten Commandments).

With regard to why the laws were given in the desert, Philo characterizes cities as places of countless evils, such as vanity, pride, and polytheistic worship. This point had special relevance against the background of life in a large city such as Alexandria.

In both *Opif.* 72ff. and *Conf.* 168ff., it is asked why the creation of humanity is ascribed not to one Creator but to plural creators. *Leg.* 1.101-4 and *QG* 1.15 ask why, when giving the charge to eat of every tree of the garden, God addresses the command to a singular person, but when prohibiting any use of that which causes evil and good, God speaks to plural persons (Gen 2:16-17).[38] But the answers differ in these two passages. Philo (or a synagogal school tradition behind him) could give different answers to the same question and could express them in the same expository structure of question and answer. Moreover, parallel usage can be found, as in *Opif.* 77 and in *QG* 2.43, where the problem of an unexpected order and rank in two sections of the pentateuchal story is addressed.

This question-and-answer form is also seen in rabbinic exegesis, and Philo and the rabbis even sometimes draw on the same traditions. For example, why Adam was created last is asked several times in rabbinic writings

38. Borgen and Skarsten, "Quaestiones et Solutiones," 2-5.

(*Gen. Rab.* 8:1ff.; *Lev. Rab.* 14:1; the *Midrash* on Psalm 139; *Tanḥuma* 132;[39] *t. Sanh.* 8:7; *y. Sanh.* 4:9). Of special interest is the parallel in form and content between Philo, *Opif.* 77 — "One should ask the reason why man comes last in the world's creation, for, as the sacred writings show, he was the last whom the Father and Maker fashioned — and *t. Sanh.* 8:7 and 9: "Man was created last. And why was he created last?"[40]

Furthermore, one answer to this question is shared between the two texts, and it is an answer that goes beyond the text of Genesis:[41]

> Just as givers of a banquet, then, do not send out the summonses to supper till they have put everything in readiness for the feast . . . in the same way the Ruler of all things, like some provider . . . of a banquet, when about to invite man to the enjoyment of a feast . . . made ready beforehand the material . . . in order that on coming into the world man might at once find . . . a banquet . . . full of all things that earth and rivers and sea and air bring forth for use and enjoyment. (*Opif.* 78)

> Another matter: So that he might enter the banquet at once. They have made a parable: To what is the matter comparable? To a king who built a palace and dedicated it and prepared a meal and [only] afterwards invited the guests. And so Scripture says, "The wisest of women has built her a house" (Prov. 9:1). This refers to the King of the kings of kings, blessed be He, who built his world in seven days by wisdom. "She has hewn out her seven pillars" (Prov. 9:1) — these are the seven days of creation. "She has killed her beasts and mixed her wine" (Prov. 9:2) — These are the oceans, rivers, wastes, and all the other things which the world needs. (*t. Sanh.* 8:9)[42]

Moreover, this tradition also occurs elsewhere in the rabbinic writings (*y. Sanh.* 4:9; *b. Sanh.* 38a; *Jalkut, Shemone* 15; cf. *Gen. Rab.* 8:6) and in church

---

39. Ed. Buber.

40. Moses Samuel Zuckermandel, ed., *Tosefta, Mischna und Boraitha in ihrem Verhältnis zueinander, oder pälastinische und babylonische Halacha* (Frankfurt: Band, 1908).

41. Peder Borgen, "Man's Sovereignty over Animals and Nature according to Philo of Alexandria," In *Texts and Contexts,* ed. T. Fornberg and D. Hellholm (Oslo: Scandinavian University Press, 1995) 369-89, here 377-79; David T. Runia, *Philo of Alexandria: On the Creation of the Cosmos according to Moses* (PACS 1; Leiden: Brill, 2001) 250.

42. According to Jacob Neusner, trans., *The Tosefta: Fourth Division: Neziqin* (New York: Ktav, 1981) 224.

writings, such as Gregory of Nyssa *De hominis opificio 2,* and so was widespread and originated at the time of Philo or before.

Scholars have observed that the question-and-answer form is found both in the Jewish Alexandrian writer Demetrius (*On the Kings of Judea,* frag. 2) and in Greek commentaries on Plato's *Theaetetus* (*Anonymous Commentary on Theaetetus* 34.9-14; 34.33-35, 44) and on the writings of Homer (*Scholia Venetus A on Iliad* 1.52, etc.). It was frequently used also in Christian exegesis. Early on, it often reflected controversies between the orthodox and heretic. From the fourth century on, the commentaries treated traditional problems rather than live issues. Thus, the question-and-answer form represented a very broad and varied exegetical tradition in antiquity.[43]

This analysis has demonstrated the central importance that the exegetical use of the form of question and answer has in Philo's expository writings. The locus of this exegetical method and form seems to be activities in learned settings within Judaism as well as in the wider Hellenistic context. In Jewish communities these learned settings may be located in synagogal or similar contexts, as suggested by Philo's report on the expository activity among the Therapeutae: "the President of the company . . . discusses *(zētei)* some questions arising in the Holy Scriptures or solves *(epilyetai)* one that has been propounded by someone else."

Against this background the term *dialegomai,* "hold converse with," "discuss," when used of expository activity, probably refers to the use of the question-and-answer method (*Cont.* 31, 79; *Spec.* 2.62; *Mos.* 2.215). Against the background of such expository activity in community meetings, learned persons would themselves employ the same expository method, partly as a rhetorical and literary device. Thus, instead of discussing the possible dependence of the *Allegorical Commentary* on the *Question and Answer Commentary,* as done by scholars,[44] one should discuss how far Philo is dependent on traditions and on learned (synagogal) school activity in his extensive use of this form of exegesis.[45]

---

43. Christoph Schaublin, *Untersuchungen zu Methode und Herkunft der antiochenischen Exegese* (Theophaneia 23; Cologne: Hanstein, 1974) 74:49-51; Heinrich Dörrie and Hermann Dörries, "Erotapokriseis," in *RAC* 6 (1966) cols. 342-70, here 347-70.

44. See Borgen, *Philo, John, and Paul,* 30; Hay, *Both Literal and Allegorical.*

45. Cf. Gerhard Delling, "Perspektiven der Erforschungen des hellenistischen Judentums," *HUCA* 45 (1974) 133-76, here 41; Nikiprowetzky, *Le Commentaire de l'écriture,* 174-77.

Direct Exegesis

Valentin Nikiprowetzky[46] suggests that the technique of question and answer was behind Philo's expositions in general. This view is too one-sided. There is thus a need for examining other exegetical forms that might be found in Philo's expositions. A large body of such expositions may be classified as direct exegesis, that is, small or large units in which no exegetical question is formulated.

A typical exegetical term used in such direct exegesis is *toutestin,* "this is," "this means," or "that is to say."[47] By means of this phrase a word or a phrase is explained by another word, phrase, or sentence. For example, *Leg.* 1.24: "'And all the grass of the field,' he says, 'before it sprang up' (Gen. 2:5), that is to say, 'before' the particular objects of sense 'sprang up.'" There are many other examples (*Leg.* 1.45, 65; 2.38, 41, 45; 3.11, 16, 20, 28, 46, 52, 95, 142, 143; *Cher.* 17; *Sacr.* 62, 86, 119; *Det.* 10, 59, 119; *Post.* 53, 150, 168, 182; *Gig.* 53, 54; *Plant.* 42, 116; *Ebr.* 40, 53, 70, 95, 125; *Heres* 304; *Congr.* 49; *Fug.* 135, 192, 201; *Somn.* 1.112; 2.76; *Spec.* 1.306).

Other such exegetical terms used by Philo are phrases built on the word *ison,* "equal (to)," as, for example, in *Leg.* 1.36: "'Breathed into' (Gen. 2:7), we note, is equivalent to inspired." There are many other examples (*Leg.* 1.65, 76; 2.16, 21; 3.51, 119, 189, 247, 253; *Cher.* 7.119; *Sacr.* 12.112; *Det.* 38, 70, 96, 169; *Agr.* 166; *Plant.,* 90.114; *Sobr:* 15; *Conf.* 72, 84, 111, 150, 160, 189; *Migr.* 5, 7, 27, 42, 101; *Congr.* 158, 172; *Spec.* 3.133; *Aeter.* 46).

Contrast

Besides question and answer and direct exegesis, many other exegetical terms and methods are used. One meaning may be discarded in contrast to the proper meaning by the contrast "not — but." This is exemplified in *Leg.* 1.1, where Gen 2:1 is cited: "And the heaven and the earth and all their world were completed." Philo's exposition rejects one interpretation over against another: "He [Moses] does not say that either the individual mind or the particular sense perceptions have reached completion, but that the originals have done so."

46. See his *Le Commentaire de l'écriture,* 179-80; and "L'exegese de Philon d'Alexandrie," 55-75
47. Cf. Maximilianus Adler, *Studien zu Philon von Alexandreia* (Breslau: Marcus, 1929) 23.

A contrast may be used to confirm a certain reading of the text against an alternative one.[48] In *Migr.* 1 and 43, the contrast offers a confirmation of the reading of the text of Gen 12:1: "into the land that I will show you": "He says not 'which I am shewing,' but 'which I will shew *(deichō)* thee.'" Such philological confirmation of the reading of a text is used in rabbinic exegesis, as in *Mek. on Exod.* 15:11: "Doing wonders: It is not written here 'Who did *('ś)* wonders,' but 'who does *('śh)* wonders,' that is, in the future." A New Testament example is found in Gal 3:16: "'and to his offspring': It does not say 'and to offsprings,' as referring to many, but, referring to one, 'and to your offspring,' which is Christ."

The contrast may correct a certain reading, as is the case in *Det.* 47-48: "'Cain rose up against Abel his brother and slew him *(auton)*' (Gen. 4:8). . . . It must be read in this way, 'Cain rose up and slew himself *(heauton),*' not someone else." *Mek. On Exod.* 16:15 has a rabbinic parallel: "'Man did eat the bread of strong horses (Ps. 78:25). Do not read 'of strong horses' *('byrym),* but 'of the limbs' *('ybrym),* that is, 'bread' that is absorbed by the 'limbs.'" When the Greek verb is translated back into Hebrew, John 6:31-32 is seen to be a parallel: "'Bread from heaven he gave *(edōken/natan)* them to eat.' . . . Truly, truly I say to you, 'not Moses gave *([d]edōken/nātan) you* the bread from heaven, but my Father gives *(didōsin/nōtēn) you* the true bread from heaven'" (cf. Exod 16:4, 15; Ps 78:24).[49]

In his expositions Philo often moves from one level of meaning to another one. He may do so by using a modified form of contrast to indicate that he accepts both levels of meaning: "not only — but also." For example, *Spec.* 4.149-50: "'Thou shalt not remove thy neighbor's landmarks which thy forerunners have set up.' Now this law, we may consider, applies not merely to allotments and boundaries of land . . . but also to the safeguarding of ancient customs."

Paraphrastic Rewriting

In some forms of exegesis the biblical material has been interpreted by means of rewriting as a paraphrase. One such form draws on the formulation of

48. Peder Borgen, *Bread from Heaven: An Exegetical Study of the Concept of Manna in the Gospel of John and the Writings of Philo* (NovTSup 10; Leiden: Brill, 1965) 62-65.

49. Borgen, *Bread from Heaven,* 40-41; Maarten J. J. Menken, *Old Testament Quotations in the Fourth Gospel: Studies in Textual Form* (Contributions to Biblical Exegesis & Theology 15; Kampen: Kok Pharos, 1996) 47-65.

blessings and curses from the Bible. Philo builds on this form in his rewriting of biblical material in *Praem.* 79-162, drawing mainly on parts of Leviticus 26 and Deuteronomy 28. The future blessings are surveyed in *Praem.* 85-125, and the description of the curses follows in *Praem.* 127-62. Philo ties the two sections together in § 126: "These are the blessings invoked upon good men, men who fulfill the laws by their deeds, which blessings will be accomplished by the gift of the bounteous God, who glorifies and rewards moral excellence because of its likeness to Himself. We must now investigate the curses delivered against the law-breakers and transgressors."

Another form of paraphrase is a list of biblical persons or events. Philo lists a series of biblical persons in *Virt.* 198-210. Here Adam, Noah, Abraham, and Isaac are surveyed and characterized.[50] This series of cases from the laws of Moses serves as an argument against the view that nobility of ancestry as such is a criterion of nobility and for the view that the criterion is rather the virtuous life of the person himself. It is worth noticing that, although Philo here illustrates a general principle, he at the same time keeps the idea of Jewish superiority, since he maintains that non-Jews obtain nobility by following Abraham's example and becoming proselytes.

The theme of predestination is illustrated by a chain of biblical examples in *Leg.* 3.69-106: Noah, Melchizedek, Abraham, Isaac, Jacob and Esau, Manasseh and Ephraim, those who sacrifice the Passover (Num 9:1-8), Bezalel, and Moses. Outside of Philo's works, one might mention as a parallel Paul's discussion of predestination in Romans 9, in which he gives a brief list in verses 7-18: Abraham, Isaac, Jacob and Esau, and Pharaoh.[51] In both *Leg.* 3.88 and Rom 9:10-12, 20-23, the idea illustrated is God's foreknowledge and election of two contrasting persons, Jacob and Esau, even before their birth. Moreover, in both cases God is pictured as a maker of clay pots. These agreements make it probable that Philo and Paul draw here on a common tradition of exposition of Gen 25:23.

Jewish and early Christian literature contain numerous reviews of biblical history varying in content and length, and each adapted to its own context and interpretative function. Lists of biblical persons are found in many places (Sir 44:1–49:16; Wis 10:1-21; 1 Macc 2:49-64; *3 Macc* 2:1-20; 6:1-15; *4 Macc* 16:16-23; 18:11-13; *Apoc. Zeph.* 9:4; *4 Ezra* 7:106-10; Heb 11:1-39; *1 Clem.*

---

50. Armin Schmitt, "Struktur, Herkunft, und Bedeutung der Beispielreihe in Weish 10," *BZ* n.s. 21 (1977) 1-22.

51. James D. G. Dunn, *Romans* (2 vols.; WBC 38a, 38b; Waco: Word, 1988) ad loc.; Joseph A. Fitzmyer, *Romans* (AB 33; New York: Doubleday, 1993) ad loc.

4:7-6.4; 9:2–12:8.[52] In Hebrews 11, Abel, Enoch, Noah, Sarah, Abraham, Isaac and Jacob, Moses, and heroes and events from the time of the judges, the monarchy, and other times are listed to illustrate faith. In *1 Clem.* 4:7–6:4, Christian persons are added to Old Testament figures to illustrate the struggle against envy.

Rewriting of the Bible

Reviews of material from the Old Testament may also have the form of continuous rewriting in chronologically ordered narratives. A body of laws may be included in the historical scheme. An example is *Virt.* 51-174, which deals with the virtue *philanthropia*, "love of people," "philanthropy." Philo exalts Moses' *philanthropia* by recording some events in his life and by presenting a selection from the Mosaic laws. There seems to be a corresponding structure in parts of the preserved fragments of Philo's *Hypothetica*. Fragment 8, 6:1-9 reviews biblical history from Abraham to the exodus and the Hebrews' settlement in Palestine. Then Philo describes the Mosaic constitution and presents the admonitions, prohibitions, and injunctions (frag. 8, 6:10–7:20). Josephus gives a corresponding account of the Jewish laws in *C. Ap.* 2.145-56 (286). His stated purpose is to refute criticism of Judaism from Apollonius Molon, Lysimachus, and others. Like Philo in *Virt.* 51-174 and *Hypothetica* 8, 6:1–7:19, Josephus also begins with a characterization of Moses and events connected with the exodus (*C. Ap.* 2.157-63). Josephus gives a direct polemical response to his critics (*C. Ap.* 2.164-89), and then a selection of the laws follows.[53]

The basic structure of this form is already found in Deuteronomy, which contains a revised repetition of a large part of the history and laws of the first four books of the laws of Moses.[54] This model can also be traced in Josephus, *Ant.* 4.176-331, where Josephus gives a summary of the laws and events from biblical history, drawing largely on Deuteronomy (*Ant.* 4.199-301).

Philo also rewrites biblical events and laws in *On the Decalogue* (cf. *Heres* 167-73) and *Spec.* 1-4. As the title indicates, *On the Decalogue* is a paraphrase of the event at Sinai and a paraphrasing elaboration of the Decalogue,

---

52. See Harold W. Attridge, *The Epistle to the Hebrews* (Hermeneia; Philadelphia: Fortress, 1989) 305-7; Schmitt, "Struktur, Herkunft und Bedeutung."

53. John M. G. Barclay, *Flavius Josephus: Against Apion* (Translation and Commentary 10; Leiden: Brill, 2007) 242-47, esp. 353-61.

54. Moshe Weinfeld, "Deuteronomy, Book of," in *ABD* 2:168-83.

which understands the Ten Commandments to be headings for the grouping of laws. In *Spec.* 1-4, Philo generally begins with an elaboration on a given commandment, similar though fuller than in *On the Decalogue,* and then discusses particular requirements that Philo thinks may be set under the commandment. He seems to develop in a more systematic fashion a notion also found in Palestinian tradition, that the Decalogue contained *in nuce* all the other commandments of the Mosaic laws.[55] In general, Philo follows in these two treatises the biblical chronology.

Philo's entire exposition of the law of Moses, his *Exposition of the Laws of Moses,* is divided into treatises tied together by transitional statements in which he gives his own perspective and understanding.[56] Thus we find in them systematic motifs that demonstrate that Philo is not just an eclectic editor, but is largely an author. The introductory and transitional statements indicate that he has organized and interpreted traditional material with three systematic aspects in view, *Praem.* 1: (1) the creation of the world, (2) history, and (3) legislation. The treatises may then be grouped as follows: (1) Moses describes the creation of cosmos and humans, *On the Creation of the World* (cf. *Praem* 1b). (2) In the historical part, he gives a record of good and bad lives and sentences passed in each generation on both: *On Abraham,* [*On Isaac; On Jacob*]; *On Joseph* (cf. *Praem.* 2a). (3) Having related the lives of the good men, the patriarchs (and their contrasting counterparts), who are portrayed in Scripture as archetypes and founders of "our nation," Philo presents the written laws of Moses. Here there are two subdivisions: (a) the ten headings or summaries, *On the Decalogue,* and then (b) the specific ordinances, *On the Special Laws* 1 to 4.132 (cf. *Praem.* 2b).

Moreover, Philo renders the virtues that Moses assigned to peace and war which are common to all commandments; cf. *On the Special Laws* 4.133-238 and *On the Virtues* (cf. *Praem.* 3a). Finally, Philo proceeds to the rewards and punishments that the good and the bad respectively can expect, *On Rewards and Punishments* (cf. *Praem.* 3b).

This outline shows that Philo followed some overriding concepts when he interpreted various traditional materials in his *Exposition.* Although he is not a systematic philosopher, he has some overarching perspectives when he fuses Jewish and Greek traditions, ideas, and notions together.

---

55. See Peder Borgen, "Philo of Alexandria: A Critical and Synthetical Survey of Research since World War II," in *ANRW* 2.21.1 (1984) 98-154, here 126; "Philo of Alexandria," in Stone, *Jewish Writings of the Second Temple Period,* 239-40, and n. 30; *Philo, John, and Paul,* 26-27.

56. Peder Borgen, "Philo of Alexandria — A Systematic Philosopher or an Eclectic Editor?" *Symbolae Osloenses* 71 (1996) 115-34.

In this *Exposition of the Laws of Moses,* Philo, nevertheless, basically follows the form found in other Jewish books that rewrite (parts of) the Pentateuch. Philo covers the biblical story from creation to Joshua's succession. *Jubilees* narrates the story from creation to the giving of the laws on Mount Sinai. The Qumran *Genesis Apocryphon,* preserved only in parts, covers Genesis from the birth of Noah to Gen 15:4. The *Biblical Antiquities* of Pseudo-Philo contain an abstract of the biblical story from Genesis 5 to the death of Saul. In his *Jewish Antiquities,* Josephus begins with creation and relates the whole span of biblical history and goes beyond even to the beginning of the Jewish War in his own time.[57]

Commentary

In the rewritten Bible, the *Exposition of the Laws of Moses,* Philo ties the different parts together with interpretative transitional statements and outlines the content of larger units of the work in summary statements. There is a kinship between the *Exposition* and the *Allegorical Commentary* in that both have been subject to extensive editorial activity. In both, references and transitions bind various parts together. But the *Allegorical Commentary* and the *Questions and Answers* differ from the *Exposition* in their general structure since they appear in the form of running commentaries on parts of the pentateuchal text and not as rewritten Scripture. In the *Questions and Answers,* transitional statements are used only in a limited degree.

In the *Allegorical Commentary,* Philo has built up the treatises as a running commentary. Their structures and outline vary, however. For example, the complexity of the expositions in the first three treatises, *Leg.* 1-3, increases from the first to the second and from the second to the third. The exposition of seventeen verses (Gen 2:1-17) in the first treatise fills twenty-eight pages in one edition, the exposition of nine verses (2:18–3:1) in the second treatise covers twenty-two pages, and the exposition of eleven verses (3:8b-19) in the third treatise fills fifty-six pages.[58]

---

57. Borgen, "Philo of Alexandria," in Stone, *Jewish Writings of the Second Temple Period,* 233-34; Borgen, *Philo, John, and Paul,* 18, 20; George W. E. Nickelsburg, "The Bible Rewritten and Expanded," in Stone, *Jewish Writings of the Second Temple Period,* 97-110; Philip S. Alexander, "Retelling the Old Testament," in *It Is Written: Scripture Citing Scripture: Essays in Honour of Barnabas Lindars, SSF,* ed. Donald A. Carson and Hugh G. M. Williamson (New York: Cambridge University Press, 1988) 99-121.

58. Adler, *Studien zu Philon von Alexandreia,* 8-24.

In *Leg.* 3, and to a lesser degree also in *Leg.* 1 and 2, Philo has used the running commentary on the verses from Genesis as headings for related expositions on other parts of the Pentateuch. Thus, the commentary on Gen 3:8 in *Leg.* 3.1-48 (Adam hiding himself) leads into a lengthy exposition of other pentateuchal verses dealing with the theme of hiding and flight. Similarly, God's cursing of the serpent, Gen 3:14, is quoted in *Leg.* 3.65 and 107, and this leads into a broad exposition of the contrast between lives of pleasure and of virtue based on a list of examples from various parts of the Pentateuch. Such extensive expositions of interrelated passages are quite common in the other treatises of the *Allegorical Commentary* as well.

Among the specific problems of Philo's own time that he deals with are temptations at banquets (*Leg.* 2.29; 3.155-56, 220-21); temptations of wealth, honors, and offices (2.107); and the temptation to use education only for building one's political career regardless of Jewish values and commitments (3.167).

In *Leg.* 1-3 and *Cher.,* the exegesis deals with the stories of Adam and Eve and paradise. *On the Cherubim* is a commentary on two verses, Gen 3:24 and 4:1. The biblical story of Cain and Abel is dealt with in *On the Sacrifices of Cain and Abel* (on Gen 4:2-4), *The Worse Attacks the Better* (on Gen 4:8-15), and *On the Posterity and Exile of Cain* (on Gen 4:16-22, 25). The story of the appearance of giants on earth, Gen 6:1-4a, 4b-9, 11-12, is interpreted in the twin treatises *On the Giants* and *On the Unchangeableness of God.*

On Husbandry, On Noah's Work as a Planter, and *On Drunkenness* all deal with the same text, Gen 9:21-22, and consist of well-organized sections on themes suggested by words in the text. *On Sobriety* interprets Gen 9:24-27, on Noah's return to sobriety and the curses he then uttered, and follows the structure of a running commentary. Transitional statements tie these treatises together.

The various parts of *On the Confusion of Tongues* are brought together at the beginning by the umbrella quotation of Gen 11:1-9, the story of the tower of Babel. A running commentary follows. The treatise serves as a defense of the laws of Moses against scoffers who state that the laws contain myths, such as the story of the tower of Babel. *On the Migration of Abraham* covers Gen 12:1-4, 6, with a topical and running commentary. The long treatise *Who Is the Heir?* (of Abraham) is a running commentary on Gen 15:2-18.

On Mating, with Preliminary Studies is a running commentary of Gen 16:1-6a, on Abraham's mating with his handmaid Hagar. The text is applied to Philo's contemporary setting, in which the question of Greek general education was an issue. *On Flight and Finding* follows then and interprets Gen 16:6b-9, 11-12. Philo ties the two treatises together with a transitional statement: "Having in the preceding treatise said what was fitting about the courses of Preliminary training and about evil entreatment, we will next proceed to set forth the subject of fugitives" (*Fug.* 2). The text is cited in an umbrella quotation in *Fug.* 1.

On the Change of Names gives a running exposition of Gen 17:1-5, 15-21, on the names of Abram and Sarai and the promise of a son to Abraham and Sarah. Sections 60-129 are a thematic excursus on the change of names. It serves as a defense against scoffers who ridicule the idea that a change of a letter in a name should have any importance. Finally, the fragment of *On God* is extant only in Armenian. It concerns the revelation to Abraham at the oak of Mamre.

In the two treatises *On Dreams,* the form of running commentary serves only as a subordinate element in expositions of dreams in Genesis. The form thus approaches that of *On the Virtues* and *On Rewards and Punishments.* Philo classifies the dreams in three groups: those in which God on his own initiative sends visions to a sleeping person, those in which a person's mind is God-inspired and foretells future events, and those in which the soul, setting itself in motion, foretells the future. This classification seems to follow one such as the one Cicero, *De Divinatione* 1.30.64 ascribes to Poseidonius. The treatise for Philo's first group of dreams is lost. The first extant treatise deals with the two dreams of Jacob, the ladder (Gen 28:10-22) and the flock with varied markings (Gen 31:10-13). The second treatise deals with the dreams of Joseph (Gen 37:8-11), of Pharaoh's baker and butler (Gen 40:9-11, 16-17), and of Pharaoh (Gen 41:17-24). Allusions and references to Philo's own time are sometimes built into the exposition, as for example in *Somn.* 2.123, where he reports on a dream of his own that a governor of Egypt had attempted to interfere with the Jewish observance of the Sabbath and other laws.

The Laws of Moses in the Alexandrian Conflict

The conflict in Alexandria and Jerusalem during the reign of Emperor Gaius Caligula and the governor Flaccus was a struggle about the way in which the laws of Moses should be interpreted and practiced in society as civil rights, as a way of life, and as institutional life centered on the synagogues and the temple. Philo's *Against Flaccus*[59] and *On the Embassy to Gaius*[60] give ample support

---

59. Pieter Willem van der Horst, *Philo's Flaccus: The First Pogrom: Introduction, Translation and Commentary* (PACS 2; Leiden: Brill, 2003) 29-30, 129, 141, 146-47, 159, 202-3, 204.

60. Peder Borgen, "Greek Encyclical Education and the Synagogue: Observations from

for this understanding: the Alexandrian Jews experienced an attack on their laws, synagogues, temple and ancestral customs (see *Flacc.* 41, 47, 50, 53 and *Legat.* 6-7, 115, 117, 152-57, 161, 170, 200, 232, 236, 240, 249, 256). Thus these two treatises should be understood as a report on a struggle for the interpretation and application of the laws of Moses in the context of the Jewish community and its status in Alexandria as well as in Palestine. Thus, to Philo the relationship between the Jewish community and its non-Jewish surroundings was a central factor in his interpretation of the laws of Moses and their role in the life of the Jewish community.

Epilogue: Philo in Early Christian Literature

David T. Runia sums up the main points about Philo's place in early Christian literature and states that it has not been possible to demonstrate beyond doubt that Philo was known to apologists such as Justin, Athenagoras, and Theophilus of Antioch.[61] The teachers of the catechetical school in Alexandria — Pantaenus, especially Clement,[62] and Origen — made use of Philo's writings in making the connection between the biblical sources and philosophical ideas and categories. They also followed Philonic methods of exegesis. A main difference was, of course, that their expositions were written in a setting basically located outside the Jewish community. Moreover, their presupposition was that Christ, not the laws of Moses, was the center of revelation.[63]

Clement's worldview was akin to that of Philo, and he worked similarly with exegesis on two or more levels. For example, that which belonged to the temple signifies cosmic entities (*Strom.* 5.32.2): "Now, connected with

---

Philo of Alexandria's Writings," in *Libens Merito: Festskrift til Stig Strømholm på sjutioårsdagen 16 sept. 2001*, ed. O. Matsson, Aa. Frändberg, M. Hedlund, S. Lunell, and G. Sedin (Uppsala: Kungl. Vetenskapssamhället I Uppsala, 2001) 61-71; Ellen Birnbaum, *The Place of Judaism in Philo's Thought: Israel, Jews, and Proselytes* (BJS 290; SPhilo Monographs 2; Atlanta: Scholars, 1996) 105-7, 189-92; David T. Runia, "Philo of Alexandria, 'Legatio Ad Gaium' 1-7," in *Neotestamentica et Philonica: Studies in Honor of Peder Borgen*, ed. David E. Aune, Torrey Seland, and Jarl Henning Ulrichsen (NovTSup 106; Leiden: Brill, 2003) 349-70.

61. David T. Runia, *Philo in Early Christian Literature* (CRINT 3/3; Assen: Van Gorcum; Minneapolis: Fortress, 1993) 335-42.

62. Runia, *Philo in Early Christian Literature,* 335.

63. Cf. J. N. B. Carleton Paget, "The Christian Exegesis of the Old Testament in the Alexandrian Tradition," in *Hebrew Bible/Old Testament: The History of Its Interpretation*, vol. 1/1: *Antiquity*, ed. Magne Sæbø (Göttingen: Vandenhoeck & Ruprecht, 1996) 478-542.

the concealment is the special meaning of what is told among the Hebrews about the seven circuits around the old temple, and also the equipment on the robe, whose multicolored symbols allude to celestial phenomena, which indicate the agreement from heaven down to earth."[64] This section on the temple is parallel to parts of Philo's interpretation in *Mos.* 2.87-130 (cf. Josephus, *Ant.* 102-23). Clement seems to draw on Philo only at some points, but the general cosmic perspective follows the model of Philo, Josephus, and the author of the Letter to the Hebrews. To Clement the christological application is central: "the robe prophesied the ministry in the flesh by which he [the Logos] was made visible to the world directly" (*Strom.* 5.39:2).[65]

Like Philo, Clement uses the image of body and soul. According to Clement, the interpreter's aim is to advance from the body of Scripture to the soul (*Strom.* 5.90.3).[66] Accordingly, he distinguishes between historical-literal exegesis and the deeper meaning of the text. In eliciting the deeper meaning, Clement, like Philo, makes use of etymologies and numerological speculations. But Clement is less interested in lexical and stylistic details in his exegesis.[67]

As seen above, to Philo the Egyptian servant Hagar represents non-Jewish general education and Sarah represents wisdom. Clement develops a related interpretation in *Strom.* 1.28-32. For Philo, non-Jewish education and philosophy should serve the wisdom revealed in the laws of Moses. For Clement, they represent, together with the Jewish law, the preparatory phase which serves the wisdom that is Christ.[68]

The later Alexandrian and Egyptian fathers such as Didymus and Isidore also had a favorable attitude to Philo's exegesis. Eusebius continued the Alexandrian tradition, but in Palestine. He incorporated a lengthy notice regarding Philo in his *Ecclesiastical History* and gave extensive citations from Philo in his apologetic writings. Among the Cappadocian fathers, Gregory of Nyssa especially drew positively on Philo. In the West, Ambrose and Jerome used Philo's exegesis extensively, and from them Augustine gained knowledge of Philo's exegesis and ideas.

In general, early church writers were interested in Philo's paraphrasing rewritten Bible, his *On the Life of Moses* in particular. This material was used

---

64. Van den Hoek, *Clement of Alexandria and His Use of Philo,* 118; see further *Strom.* 5.32-40.

65. Van den Hoek, *Clement of Alexandria and His Use of Philo,* 140; see further 116-47.

66. Paget, "The Christian Exegesis of the Old Testament," 492.

67. Paget, "The Christian Exegesis of the Old Testament," 498.

68. Van den Hoek, *Clement of Alexandria and His Use of Philo,* 23-47.

in their historical apologetics on the earlier history of Israel. Josephus's writings were utilized by them in the same way. They were also interested in Philo's expository commentaries. They drew on his rules and procedures of exegesis. His literal exegesis was not overlooked, but the main interest was in his allegorical elaborations and its Platonic bent. Runia emphasizes three areas of influence:[69]

> (a) the doctrine of God, with the strong emphasis on unchangeability and essential unknowability; (b) the doctrine of man, created "according to the image" (i.e. the logos), endowed with reason and the capacity to reach out to God and become like unto Him; (c) the doctrine of the virtues or excellences *(aretai),* taken over from Greek philosophy and adapted to the requirements of allegorical expositions and the differing emphases of biblical thought. In this way the church's writers learned from Philo how to mediate between the biblical and philosophical traditions.

The Antiochene school of exegesis in general was critical of Philo. An outstanding representative was Theodore of Mopsuestia, who attacked Philo for his allegorical exegesis. A reaction against Philo grew in the fourth century. He was associated with heretical forms of Christianity, mainly Origenism and Arianism, and direct use of his works diminished, but many Philonic themes were adopted by later authors at second hand through the writings of the early church fathers.

---

69. Runia, *Philo in Early Christian Literature,* 338-39.

Philo and Classical Education

Erkki Koskenniemi

Introduction

Philo of Alexandria does not directly tell about the kind of secular education he had received. Although his works reveal that he was deeply rooted in Greek culture, and several scholars have made good progress toward understanding the issues,[1] still the question has not been investigated thoroughly

1. Alan Mendelson investigated the role of the secular education and briefly showed Philo's appreciation of Greek education but also its limits in his thought; *Secular Education in Philo of Alexandria* (Monographs of the Hebrew Union College 7; Cincinatti: Hebrew Union College Press, 1982). The major study remains Isaak Heinemann's *Philons griechische und jüdische Bildung* (Breslau: Marcus, 1932; repr., Hildesheim: Olms, 1962); and after that, Harry Austryn Wolfson's massive work, *Philo: Foundations of Religious Philosophy in Judaism, Christianity, and Islam* (2 vols.; Cambridge, MA: Harvard University Press, 1948). See also Monique Alexandre, "La culture profane chez Philon," in *Philon d' Alexandrie. Actes du Colloque nationale de Lyon 11-15 Septembre 1996*, ed. Roger Arnaldez, Claude Mondésert, and Jean Poilloux (Paris: CNRS, 1967) 105-30; Naomi G. Cohen, *Philo Judaeus: His Universe of Discourse* (BEATAJ 24; Frankfurt am Main: Lang, 1995) 225-41; Claude Mondésert, "Philo of Alexandria," in *Cambridge History of Judaism*, vol. 3: *The Early Roman Period*, ed. William Horbury, W. D. Davies, and John Sturdy (Cambridge, Cambridge University Press, 1999) 877-900, 893-97. Several scholars have investigated thoroughly how Philo used Plato's works, esp. David T. Runia, *Philo of Alexandria and the Timaeus of Plato* (Philosophia antiqua 44; Leiden: Brill, 1986). I have investigated Philo's classical education in several articles. "Greeks, Egyptians and Jews in the Fragments of Artapanus," *JSP* 13 (2002) 17-31 paved the way for the study. "Moses — A Well-Educated Man: A Look at the Educational Idea in Early Judaism," *JSP* 17 (2008) 281-96 pays attention to the educational ideal as seen in the presentations of Moses' early years. I have listed and analyzed how Philo mentions and uses Greek dramatists and poets in two articles:

enough. This chapter will present what we know of Greek education and what options Jews had and were willing to adopt in Greek Alexandria. Moreover, it will investigate what Philo himself says on the topic and finally address how he uses or mentions Greek philosophers and poets and estimate how well versed he was with secular literature. In seeking to understand Philo's secular training, this article hopes in turn to contribute to our knowledge of Greek education in general.

A scholar asking today how a Jew in Alexandria was educated hears the echo of Heraclitus's phrase: *panta rhei* ("everything flows" or "is in flux"). Recently, the older views on Greek education have been questioned. This is also true concerning its most important institution, the gymnasion. Scholars have not reached agreement on the relation of the gymnasion and the school. We also find opposing views on to what extent non-Greeks were admitted to gymnasions, as well as how many Jews were actually willing to take advantage of doors that might have been open for them. Moreover, the significant sociological role of education and educational systems needs to be given greater attention, as well as the rise of Rome and its impact on the status of Jews in Egypt.[2] All the same, investigating Philo's secular education offers fresh points of view for all of these questions.

Classical Education — A Brief Sketch

The old, aristocratic education is mirrored in Homer's epics: The most important teachers were the elder generation, the main objective was to learn to follow their example, and the education seems to have been rather informal. But the Greek world was changing; colonization made rich people poor and poor people rich, and the Greek *polis* required new skills. The famous Sophists, like Gorgias and Protagoras, fulfilled the needs of new genera-

---

"Philo and Classical Drama," in *Ancient Israel, Judaism, and Christianity in Contemporary Perspective: Essays in Memory of Karl-Johan Illman,* ed. Jacob Neusner et al. (Lanham: University Press of America, 2006) 137-51; "Philo and Greek Poets" *JSJ* 41 (2010) 301-22; see also "Philo and the Sophists," in *Greeks, Jews, and Christians: Historical, Religious and Philological Studies in Honor of Jesús Peláez del Rosal,* ed. Lautaro Roig Lanzillota and Israel Muñoz Gallarte (Estudios de Filología Neotestamentaria 10; Cordoba: Ediciones el Almendro, 2013) 253-80. David Lincicum has recently published an important article, "An Index to Philo's Non-Biblical Citations and Allusions," *SPhAn* 25 (2013) 139-68.

2. Noted esp. by Maren Ruth Niehoff, *Philo on Jewish Identity and Culture* (TSAJ 86; Tübingen: Mohr Siebeck, 2001) 6-8.

tions,[3] and Socrates and philosophical schools followed them. The next decisive turn came with the conquest of Alexander the Great, which created everywhere a new ruling class consisting of Greeks and native aristocrats, who were now learning Greek language and culture.[4]

The main elements of the classical education were developed in classical Greece and were adopted at the time of Alexander, retaining much of the overall tradition throughout the centuries. The history of education in antiquity has frequently been investigated. However, the process of education in the ancient world as presented in older handbooks is no longer appropriate. The classic work of Henri Irénée Marrou *(Histoire de l'éducation dans le antiquité)*[5] should be used with caution, and the deconstruction offered in *Literate Education in the Hellenistic and Roman Worlds* by Teresa Morgan has also prompted criticism.[6] Several shorter works address Greek education.[7]

In the past scholars sought to reconstruct a general pattern of education and to assume a more or less fixed curriculum of studies, advancing from a lower level to the higher.[8] However, they tended to construct an allegedly ancient educational pattern drawing from various regions and nations of the Mediterranean world, sometimes quite freely using sources from different periods.[9] No ancient writer comes close to providing a comprehensive overview

3. See Koskenniemi, "Philo and the Sophists," 255-57.

4. On the number of non-Greeks seeking Greek education, see pp. 108-9 below.

5. First published in French in 1948; the first English edition, trans. George Lamb, was printed in 1956 (repr., Madison: University of Wisconsin Press, 1982).

6. Teresa Morgan, *Literate Education in the Hellenistic and Roman Worlds* (Cambridge: Cambridge University Press, 1998). Some reviewers have treated Morgan's book critically; e.g., Raffaella Cribiore, *Bryn Mawr Classical Review* 1999.05.22. For more or less positive views, see M. B. Trapp, *Classical Review* 50 (2000) 219-20; G. A. Kennedy, *AJP* 121 (2000) 331-34.

7. *Die hellenistische Schule* by Martin P. Nilsson (Munich: Beck, 1955) has not always received the attention it deserves. On Greek education, see also Johannes Christes, "Erziehung," in *DNP* 4 (1996) 110-14.

8. See, e.g., Marrou, *A History of Education,* 150-216, here 160: "There was a special teacher each of the three stages — primary, secondary and higher — of literary education: after the primary-school teacher — the 'grammatist' — γραμματιστής — came the 'grammarian' — γραμματικός — who in his turn was succeeded by the 'rhetor' σοφιστής — or ῥήτωρ." The only reference to sources in this chapter is Strabo, *Geogr.* 14.650.

9. A good example of this kind of research is John T. Townsend's article, "Education (Greco-Roman Period)," in *ABD* 2:312-17: the evidence is collected from very disparate materials — from Gentile and Christian authors, from different regions, and mainly from the elite. This is the major defect of Marrou's book too: he is able even to describe the timetable of classes (*A History of Education,* 148; see his *Nachtrag,* 397-98). The reader misses the discipline of older scholars, carefully listing, e.g., every mention of gymnasions in the inscriptions and then mak-

of education in the Mediterranean world. Sometimes the authors express their educational ideals — what education ought to be. Other sources, especially the approximately four hundred school-papyri,[10] offer a distant glimpse of the actual situation, and brief references in papyri and inscriptions complete the picture. But classical antiquity spanned centuries, and chronological, geographical, and especially sociological factors need to be taken into account. The curriculum of a rich Greek or Roman aristocrat (Cicero, for example) differed even from its initial stages from that of a young man living in an Egyptian rural town. Moreover, the pictures drawn by some scholars, merging, for example, Greek sources with Quintilian's testimony, leave practically no room for the diverse forms of the gymnasion, the principal institution of Greek education. If all sources are investigated critically, a more colorful picture can be drawn, even if it is full of lacunae. This does not mean denying common characteristics, only that educational systems were not consistent in every time and place, and especially that we are not able to define a fixed curriculum or that everyone studied identical subjects, as ἐγκύκλιος παιδεία having all too often been considered an early and clearly defined set of studies.[11] It might be wise to start by briefly discussing the gymnasion, because it is important to consider how many of the Jewish youth may have visited it in Alexandria.

Our knowledge of the Greek gymnasion is based on broad archaeological and literary evidence, and although many questions may remain open, it is easy to present the main points.[12] The glorious military history of the Greeks was based on the units of heavily armed troops operating under strict discipline. This required extensive training, and the roots of the gymnasion are on the large fields outside of the cities, mostly in places with a river or wells for baths. The old phenomenon of ἐφηβεία was closely connected with the gymnasions: recognizing diversity, in the various Greek *poleis* it meant a period in which the youth born in certain year (ἐφήβος was a male between childhood and grown-up status, usually ages twelve to fourteen) were gathered for common training. That in Athens during the classical period free men as old as eighteen

---

ing conclusions based on the evidence (see J. Oehler, "Gymnasium," in PW 7 [1912] 2004-26; "Gymnasiarchos," in PW 7 [1912] 1969-2004). Nilsson was very cautious, writing, e.g.: "Wenn man verallgemeinert, stellt sich die Gefahr ein, eine Einheitlichkeit vorzuspiegeln, die nur eine scheinbare ist" (*Die hellenistische Schule,* 60).

10. On problems involved in the identification and use of the school-papyri, see Morgan, *Literate Education,* 40; and the review by Cribiore (see above, n. 6).

11. See below p. 113.

12. Jean Delorme, "Gymnasium," in *RAC* 13 (1983) 155-75; Ilsetraut Hadot, "Gymnasion," in *DNP* 5 (1998) 19-27.

and nineteen years were ordered to military service is well known.[13] Other cities clearly enlisted their youth earlier and perhaps for a longer period; however, the practice varied greatly geographically as well as chronologically.[14]

The gymnasions did not remain training camps, but became places where people could spend time and hold meetings as needed, and it was there that the early Sophists began teaching youngsters.[15] After the Athenian gymnasions, Academy, Lyceion, and Kynosarges became schools of famous philosophers, gymnasions were no longer merely places where naked men conducted physical training and then washed and relaxed, but were also centers for cultural education — if not schools (see below).

Archaeology shows the flowering of the gymnasions. Basically uniform edifices were built wherever Greeks were in the majority and, after Alexander, wherever those governing non-Greeks were willing to preserve and display their Greek identity.[16] Especially because the cults of Heracles, Hermes, or rulers replaced the original cult of heroes and ancestors, gymnasions were no longer built in association with cemeteries and therefore outside of the cities, but rather inside them, and they became part of the cities' luxurious architecture. According to Pausanias (*Descr.* 10.4.1), a city without a gymnasion should not really be called a *polis*. The typical plan of a gymnasion shows the importance of physical training throughout the centuries.[17] It consisted of *palaestra* with *exedras* and a place (or places) for sports that required considerable room, such as a *stadion* for running, decorated with porticoes and other typical features. The *palaestra* and rooms connected with it[18] were intended for wrestling, boxing, and similar arts, and the *exedra(s)* for baths and culture, including libraries or lecture halls for listening to classical texts *(akroateria)*. Although temples rarely appear in gymnasions, the cult of gods was never absent.[19]

Wealthy benefactors may have built the gymnasions, but they were governed by the cities,[20] which annually appointed gymnasiarchs: the old *quaes-*

13. See, e.g., Aristotle *Politeia* 42.1. On the ephebate, see Nilsson, *Die hellenistische Schule*, 17-29; Hans-Joachim Gehrke, "Ephebeia," in *DNP* 3 (1997) 1072-75.

14. On the scanty sources telling of ἐφηβεία in Alexandria, see below p. 113.

15. On the Sophists, see Koskenniemi, "Philo and the Sophists."

16. On the gymnasions mentioned in the sources, see Hadot, "Gymnasion," 26-27.

17. For plans of the reconstructed gymnasions, see Hadot, "Gymnasion," 19-23.

18. Typically, a *palaestra* was connected with rooms for various training arts, like *konisterion* for wrestling and *sphaeristerion* for boxing; see Delorme, "Gymnasium," 20-23.

19. See the extensive documentation in Nilsson, *Die hellenistiche Schule*, 61-75; see also Delorme, "Gymnasium," 169-70; Hadot, "Gymnasion," 25.

20. According to Morgan, the cities did not try to control education (*Literate Education*, 27). This view is possible only because she, like some other scholars, is not persuaded by the

tio vexata is whether the gymnasiarch ran the gymnasion or only paid the considerable costs, and it is clear now that his — or sometimes her — task varied chronologically and geographically.[21] The gymnasions were built to train young, free men of the cities, and many cities were wealthy enough to offer distinct buildings for different ages: Pergamon, for example, distinguished between παῖδες, ἔφηβοι, and νεοί (i.e., young men after their ephebate).[22] As noted above, Athens enlisted only young adults, here for a period of two years (ages eighteen-nineteen), which meant that all kinds of education were provided earlier. Apparently, the training prior to the ephebate varied and was mostly private during the Hellenistic period.[23]

The gymnasion was a typical Greek institution, and it gained importance when established in the regions where Greeks lived among non-Greeks. It was a part of Greek identity, and for that reason also very traditional, retaining, for example, martial training after mercenaries had taken over the military role of the citizens. Greeks trained for sports in gymnasions, but this segment of the population was too noble to ever make a career as professional athletes.[24] During the early imperial period, the gymnasion slowly started to lose its function when the Roman *thermae* became common throughout the Roman world.

How was the gymnasion associated with schools? Unfortunately, we know very little in general about the ancient Greek school,[25] and consequently can only infer the connection between the school and the gymnasion. Several scholars, Marrou and Martin Nilsson among them, have assumed that the gymnasions were essentially schools[26] where children went

---

evidence that the gymnasions were essentially schools. But at least in some non-Greek areas, private persons appointed the gymnasiarchs; see Victor A. Tcherikover, *CPJ* 1:38

21. Oehler ("Gymnasiarchos," 1969-2004) gives an overview of the geographical and chronological distribution of the office and considers also the old debate on the nature of the office (esp. 1975-86). See also Nilsson, *Die hellenistische Schule*, 53-57. On the named gymnasiarchs in Egypt, see Pieter J. Sijpesteijn, *Nouvelle liste des gymnasiarques des métropoles de l'Égypte Romaine* (Studia Amsteolodamensia ad epigraphicam, ius antiquum et papyrologicam perintentia 28; Zupthen: Terra, 1986).

22. See Nilsson, *Die hellenistische Schule*, 31; W. Dörpfeld, "Die Arbeiten zu Pergamon 1902-1903: Die Bauwerke," *MDAI. Athenische Abteilung* 29 (1904) 121-151.

23. Nilsson, *Die hellenistische Schule*, 40-41.

24. Delorme, "Gymnasium," 161-62.

25. See below, n. 38.

26. Marrou writes of ephebate and gymnasion: "even after it had lost its original military purpose and became an instrument of higher education"; *A History of Education*, 111. See also Nilsson, *Die hellenistische Schule*, 31-32; Tcherikover, *CPJ* 1:38; Townsend, "Education (Greco-

after having privately received an elementary education, but Morgan is skeptical on the evidence.[27] The gymnasions had *akroateria* (i.e., auditoriums) and libraries, and sometimes altars, but this only proves that they were cultural centers, which no scholar doubts. The fact that classical Athens conscripted youth for the two-year ephebate in their eighteenth year clearly shows that the fundamental cultural education was provided earlier, although the ephebate undoubtedly supplemented their learning. A lengthy Athenian inscription dating to 100/99 (SIG[3] 717) clearly shows the rich training the ephebs had received, including instruction from philosophers (καὶ ἐσχόλασαν δι᾽ ὅλου τοῦ ἐνιαουτοῦ τοῖς φιλοσόφοις μετὰ πάσης εὐταξίας).[28] A gymnasiarch was said to have hired a rhetor for "boys, ephebs, and others" in Eretria (τοῖς τε παισὶν καὶ ἐφήβοις καὶ τοῖς ἄλλοις τοῖς βουλομένοις; IG 12.9.234). Several inscriptions quoted by J. Oehler show how the gymnasiarchs sought to train both the mind and the body of the ephebs: music, grammar, and philology are mentioned in these inscriptions.[29] Moreover, the Hellenistic age seems to have placed more emphasis on culture.[30] Although the fragmentary evidence is admittedly slight, it is hard to claim that the gymnasions did not somehow resemble our schools. Johannes Christes's words regarding the ephebate *(Ephebengymnasion)* in the Hellenistic *poleis* may be bold ("It is the first public school"),[31] but they seem to be concordant with the sources we have.

The importance of the gymnasions should be evident now, but what did it mean for non-Greeks in the Hellenistic world? To go to a gymnasion meant adopting Greek identity, but it is not clear to what extent that was actually allowed. Isocrates already in his *Panegyricus* 50 proclaimed that Greeks were no longer a race, but it was possible to be Greek through education. But was this merely an idealistic projection, all too easily believed by Western philhellenes (who especially were willing to become Greeks through education) and subsequently by modern scholars? Char-

---

Roman Period)," 314-15; Henriette Harich-Schwarzbauer, "Erziehung," *RGG*[4] 2 (1999) 1505-9; Lester L. Grabbe, "The Hellenistic City of Jerusalem," in *Jews in the Hellenistic and Roman Cities*, ed. John R. Bartlett (London: Routledge, 2002) 12, calls the gymnasion "a grammar school."

27. Morgan, *Literate Education*, 28-29.

28. On the inscription, see Nilsson, *Die hellenistische Schule*, 21-27.

29. See Oehler, "Gymnasiarchos," 1998-2000; "Gymnasium," 2013-18.

30. See esp. the extensive inscription containing a law on gymnasiarchs (Berea, mid-2nd century B.C.E.; SEG 27.261); Gehrke, "Ephebeia," 1075.

31. Christes, "Erziehung," 114.

acteristically, scholars have held that the elite of non-Greek nations flocked to gymnasions,[32] but again we lack statistics. More recently scholars have claimed that non-Greeks were an exception in the gymnasion, which was a *conditio sine qua non* for further education, if not replaced by other institutions.[33] According to Ilsetraut Hadot, the most important impact of the gymnasions on hellenization was that non-Greeks founded their own institutions in an attempt to model the original.[34] However, we have evidence of many gymnasions among non-Greeks, not only from Athenaeus's report that Poseidonius was unhappy with the comportment of non-Greeks in one of them (Athenaeus *Deipn.* 5.210). Martin Hengel indicates how common gymnasions were in Palestine and how eagerly people participated in games typical of gymnasions.[35] Victor Tcherikover indicates that village gymnasions were numerous in the Ptolemaic period,[36] and because there were no "citizens" in these villages, the gymnasions were certainly accessible for noncitizens. Non-Greeks also functioned as gymnasiarchs, evidence that they were not restricted by ethnicity.[37] However, this should not deny the Greeks' resistance to including the masses; the proportion of non-Greeks certainly varied and in general was not very great.

The gymnasion was thus a significant institution in the Greek world, but it was certainly not identical in every place and time. The duration of the training varied greatly, as did apparently the percentage of non-Greeks involved as well. What preceded the gymnasion also varied, and unfortunately

---

32. The great and influential work of Johann Gustav Droysen, *Geschichte des Hellenismus* (3 vols.; Gotha: Perthes, 1836-43) pictured the Hellenistic world as a *Mischkultur,* attributing to the Hellenes the mission of teaching the barbarians (see, e.g., 3:25). Cf. also Martin Hengel, *Judaism and Hellenism,* trans. John Bowden (Philadelphia: Fortress, 1974) 65-67.

33. Delorme, "Gymnasium," 163-66; Hadot, "Gymnasion," 27. Writing on the early Hellenistic period, Lester L. Grabbe strongly contends: "citizenship and membership of the gymnasium were jealously guarded and were the exclusive privilege of the Greek settlers"; *Judaism from Cyrus to Hadrian* (Minneapolis: Fortress, 1994) 165.

34. On the alternative options non-Greeks offered their youth, see below p. 121.

35. Hengel, *Judaism and Hellenism,* 73, with documentation; Nilsson was a little more cautious; *Die hellenistische Schule,* 84.

36. Tcherikover refers to SB 1106 (οἱ τοῦ γυμνασίου τοῦ Ἡρακλείου Μακεδόνες; Sebennytos), SB 7245 (Samaria; 221/220 B.C.E.), SB 6157 (Theadelphia; 150/149 B.C.E.); *CPJ* 1:38.

37. Tcherikover refers to Thracians (SB 6157-58; 150/149 B.C.E.), Persians (SB 7246; place unknown, 3rd/2nd century B.C.E.), and Arabs (SB 3460); *CPJ* 1:38. Moreover, the two last mentioned served as gymnasiarchs.

we know only little of it. Apparently, education prior to the gymnasion was mostly private, and uniformity among schools belongs to later times.[38] Some Greek education was provided in the gymnasion, some outside of it, and non-Greeks may have imitated the gymnasions if they were excluded from this institution.

It is generally easier to identify the content of the education than where it was presented, although a fixed curriculum, whereby all pupils supposedly received the same initial instruction and with which some then advanced, has often been falsely assumed.[39] The studies of the administrator in a small provincial state in Egypt differed from what a Greek nobleman received from boyhood, not only because the elite continued longer with their education. It is therefore wise to be careful in using terms such as "primary" and "higher," or even "primary," "secondary," and "higher" education," or with speculation over who has or who has not visited "Rhetorhenschulen."[40] At any rate, the initial education involved the elements of literacy, reading and writing, and the instruction was for the most part private.[41] Often girls also acquired skills in these areas, in acknowledgment

38. Several writers mention schools, but provide less information than we would like (Herodotus *Hist.* 6.27; Pausanius *Descr.* 6.9.6). Thucydides reports that all the pupils in the three schools of the Boiotian Mycalessus were killed (*Hist.* 7.29.6); see also Aeschines *c. Timarchum* 200. Moreover, inscriptions in Teos and Miletus tell how the city selected teachers and for what purpose; see SIG³ 577-78 and Marrou, *A History of Education,* 112-14. However, the evidence does not justify Marrou's account: "When the child was seven, school began. Communal education had long been the rule, and in the Hellenistic age it was only the sons of kings who could have private tutors, like Alexander"; *A History of Education,* 143-45. Marrou refers quite freely to, e.g., Plato, Quintilian, Plautus, Terence, and Plutarch, thus combining material from a vast area, both chronologically and geographically. Cf. Nilsson, *Die hellenistische Schule,* 9-10; Morgan, *Literate Education,* 32.

39. See, e.g., Marrou's presentation in *A History of Education,* 150-216; and Townsend's uncritical survey of earlier uncritical works; "Education (Greco-Roman Period)," 312-15.

40. The best example might be the alleged Hellenistic education of the apostle Paul. Scholars used to know more about this than the sources tell. Georg Strecker is a good example of a scholar relying heavily on the curricular model that is now outdated: "Die rhetorische Fertigkeit, die in den echten Paulusbriefen zutage tritt, deutet darauf hin, dass Paulus nicht nur eine hellenistische Elementarschule besucht, sondern das hellenistische Schulsystem in allen Stufen durchlaufen hat"; "Der vorchristliche Paulus: Überlegungen zum biographischen Kontext biblischer Überlieferung — zugleich eine Antwort an Martin Hengel," in *Texts and Contexts: Biblical Texts in Their Textual and Situational Contexts. Essays in Honor of Lars Hartman,* ed. Tord Fornberg and David Hellholm (Oslo: Scandinavian University Press, 1995) 238.

41. See above, p. 107.

of their role as the first teachers of their children,[42] as also did the poor, frequently even slaves.[43]

Instruction began with lectures on classical literature, especially Homer, and lectures on this literature remained a focus throughout the entire process. Students then advanced with reading and writing, and lectures again consisted mainly of Homer and other classical authors, generally the same body of texts, although not as consistently as previously thought.[44] Students were soon introduced to elements of what came to be regarded as a fixed pattern of ἐγκύκλιος παιδεία. We now know that most occurrences of this phrase originate from the first century c.e. or later and that the diverse characterizations do not permit an unambiguous definition of the term.[45] Consequently, ἐγκύκλιος παιδεία can no longer be interpreted as a fixed set of studies in curricular form; it did, however, consist of a number of elements commonly addressed in the Hellenistic period, some of which were given more central place than others. Philo frequently mentions ἐγκύκλια or μέση παιδεία and subjects listed by, for example, Quintilian (*Inst.* 1.10.1): skills for reading and writing, grammar,[46] literature, geometry, astronomy, the principles of music and logic.[47] Content of the studies varied, but the elements Philo calls ἐγκύκλια or μέση παιδεία[48] were studied in every place. The rich could also afford the expenses required by professional teachers or philosophers or send their youth to the great cultural centers, such as Athens, Rhodes — or Alexandria.

---

42. See Morgan, *Literate Education,* 48-49.

43. Cornelius Nepos describes in his *Atticus,* ch. 12, how the Roman aristocrat, undoubtedly following Greek models as evident from the wording, took care that every slave in his house was able to perform public reading.

44. Instead of a fixed curricular model, Morgan suggests a new model: the "core" included what most people learned in the school, i.e., reading and writing and reading Homer and *gnomai,* and the "periphery" was everything outside the core. It does not mean a homogenous material, although some authors (Euripides, Menander) stood nearer to the "core" than others.

45. On ἐγκύκλιος παιδεία, see Harald Fuchs, "Enkyklios Paideia," in *RAC* 5 (1962) 365-98; Marrou, *A History of Education,* 176-85; Morgan, *Literate Education,* 33-39.

46. To Cicero and Philo, grammar still meant studying the texts of the masters. Formal study of grammar is a later phenomenon, and it was apparently used to improve the Greek of those who were able to speak Greek, not to teach foreigners. See Morgan, *Literate Education,* 162-69.

47. Morgan, *Literate Education,* 69-73.

48. See below, p. 120.

Jews and Secular Education in Alexandria

The scattered evidence does not allow an accurate presentation of the education and educational institutions in Greek Egypt in general, and particularly in Alexandria. Scholars disagree on to what extent Egypt differed from the rest of the Greek world. Teachers are named sporadically, and gymnasions or gymnasiarchs have frequently been mentioned in several cities.[49] Few if any of the culture centers of the Mediterranean world could compete with Alexandria. Strabo only mentions "the gymnasion" in Alexandria, but it is inconceivable that such a city would have only one of them, and other sources do mention more.[50] The great city had enjoyed the patronage of enlightened rulers from the very beginning, and the Museion and the Library offered opportunities second to none in the Hellenistic world.[51] Alexandria thus offered all the best options for a Greek free man. The main question is whether or not admission to the gymnasion was open to non-Greeks in general, or for Jews in particular. Moreover, how willing were the Jews to make compromises in the face of the cult of foreign gods?

As all the diadochs, the first Ptolemy met a huge challenge in trying to govern his area. Undoubtedly he could use in his administration cultivated Greeks from all areas of his domain, such as Cyprus and Cyrene. Strict distinction, however, should be made between Greeks and native Egyptians, "the ultimate other," in Philo's view.[52] Papyrologists consider the incredible bureaucracy of Ptolemaic Egypt, which employed the Greek language. It required and hired a great number of officials of all ranks, including people able to use both the native language and Greek.[53] Consequently, there was need for learned people and for those willing to be educated. Education would have been essential for people in towns, for the small elite class, and for administration of the larger provincial cities in Egypt. The school-papyri illuminate the studies of the first group, some

49. See Oehler, "Gymnasium," 2004-26; "Gymnasiarchos," 1969-2004.

50. See P. M. Fraser, *Ptolemaic Alexandria* (Oxford: Clarendon, 1972) 2:93, referring to *P.Teb.* 700.37 (124 B.C.E.): τὰ ἐν Ἀλεξανδρείαι γυμνάσια.

51. On the Museion and the Library, see Andreas Glock, "Museion," *DNP 8* (2000) 507-11.

52. See Niehoff, *Philo on Jewish Identity and Culture,* 45-74.

53. For documentation, see Dorothy J. Thompson, "The Ptolemies and Egypt," in *A Companion to the Hellenistic World,* ed. Andrew Erskine (Oxford: Blackwell, 2003) 111.

literary sources address the second, while the third remains almost completely terra incognita to us.[54]

P. M. Fraser assumes that the gymnasions in Alexandria in the early Ptolemaic period admitted Greek-speaking people regardless of nationality, and certainly boys from the large Greek population who were not citizens.[55] Consequently, some people of Egyptian origin certainly acquired a good, Greek education, but this must have been a small part of the population. We know only a little regarding the ephebate in Egypt, especially in Alexandria. We do have an inscription that is probably a list of ephebs coming to Alexandria. All of these fourteen novices bear genuine Greek names, and so do their fathers.[56] However, we should not forget that the names of Philo and his brother Alexander do not reveal their national identity as does Isidorus the gymnasiarch, hinting to his Egyptian origin. The boys were fourteen years old when they started the ephebate, simultaneously avoiding the tax paid by the Egyptians from this age on, but they or their parents may have applied for admission much earlier. Admission to the ephebate and gymnasion was indeed not free. Applicants went through *eiskrisis,* which purpose was to carefully screen those willing to join the ephebate.[57] In the Roman period, admission was strictly regulated. It was granted by the gymnasiarch, with final decision by the prefect himself.[58] Actually, *Gnomon idios logos* (44), an administrative guide provided by the Romans, rules that if an Egyptian father has registered his son as an epheb, both the father and the son

54. See Morgan, *Literate Education,* 45-46.

55. Fraser, *Ptolemaic Alexandria,* 1:76-77. In lack of statistics, Fraser refers to the nearly five hundred names appearing in early Alexandrian papyri: about half of all persons bear Greek names but are not citizens. There was apparently a marked Greco-Egyptian population in the city ("Persians of the *epigone*"); only eighteen had Egyptian names, and only ten were called "Alexandrians" (1:91-92).

56. CIG 4682; SB 8279. The word μέλλακες is not common, but apparently these were novice ephebs; see Fraser, *Ptolemaic Alexandria,* 2:166.

57. See *CPJ* 150; Ulrich Wilcken and Ludwig Mitteis, *Grundzüge und Chrestomathie des Papyruskunde* (Leipzig: Teubner, 1912) 1:143-47; Nilsson, *Die hellenistische Schule,* 143-47; E. Mary Smallwood, *The Jews under Roman Rule: From Pompey to Diocletian* (2nd ed.; SJLA 20; Leiden: Brill, 1981) 232; Niehoff, *Philo on Jewish Identity and Culture,* 20; and esp. Delia, *Alexandrian Citizenship,* 71-73.

58. Wilcken and Mitteis, *Grundzüge und Chrestomathie der Papyruskunde,* 1:2. Nos. 143-47; P.Oxy 18.2186 (as late as 260 C.E.). Also, Marrou *A History of Education,* 110; Nilsson, *Die hellenistische Schule,* 90-91; Fraser, *Ptolemaic Alexandria,* 2:166. On the ephebate and citizenship, see J. E. G. Whitehorne, "The Ephebate and the Gymnasial Class in Roman Egypt," *Bulletin of the American Society of Papyrologists* 19 (1982) 171-84.

relinquish one-fourth of their property.[59] Egyptians were apparently exceptions, at least in Alexandrian gymnasions at the time.[60]

The available sources do not allow us to define the legal status of the Jews in Alexandria in detail. Josephus claims that the Jews had ἰσοπολιτεία in Alexandria (C. Ap. 2.36; J.W. 2.487), as in several other cities, for example, in Antioch (J.W. 7.44; 7.110). However, it is obvious that his witness is one-sided and even wrong. It is true that Jews were numerous in the city, and they were favored by the Ptolemies, who especially needed loyal mercenaries. The documents show that Jews were able to make a career in the Ptolemaic army, and for historical reasons they held an intermediate position between the Greeks and the native Egyptians.[61] Uprisings in Upper Egypt, led by rebellious native Egyptian pharaohs,[62] certainly enabled Jews to retain this intermediate status. In Alexandria, they had their own *politeuma,* led by their ethnarch, and their history in the city meant a continuous struggle to preserve their loosely defined role and even expand it. The Hellenistic *polis* allowed this, because its administration was complex, apparently based on deme organization, and it was possible for Jews to maintain their own internal local structures.[63] They were never considered Ἀλεχανδρίνοι as a class, although most were equal with the numerous Greeks having no status as citizens.

The Roman takeover presented problems.[64] The complex structures of the great Hellenistic city were made simpler. People either were citizens or were not, and the place for Jewish organizations vanished. The privileges of the Jews had depended on the goodwill of the Ptolemaic rulers, but now they had lost their role in the army and the administration. About the time of

---

59. Text in *Der Gnomon des Idios Logos,* ed. Emil Seckel und Wilhelm Schubart (BGU 5/1; Berlin: Weidmannsche, 1919; repr., Milan: Cisalpino Goliardica, 1973). My interpretation of the paragraph follows the commentary on the text by Woldemar Graf Uxkull-Gyllenband in the second volume (BGU 5/2; Berlin: Weidmansche, 1934; repr., Milan: Cisalpino Goliardica, 1973) 58.

60. According to Hengel, who in general believes that non-Greeks frequently visited gymnasions, Egyptians were banned in Egypt for political reasons, although there were exceptions; *Judaism and Hellenism,* 65-67; see also Fraser, *Ptolemaic Alexandria,* 2:160.

61. In early Ptolemaic Egypt, Jews were often recognized as belonging to "tax-Hellenes"; see Willy Clarysse and Dorothy J. Thompson, *Counting the People in Hellenistic Egypt,* vol. 2: *Historical Studies* (Cambridge: Cambridge University Press, 2006) 147-48.

62. On these pharaohs, see Thompson, "The Ptolemies and Egypt," 115-16.

63. See Richard Alston, "Philo's *In Flaccum:* Ethnicity and Social Space in Roman Alexandria." *Greece & Rome* 44 (1997) 167.

64. See Niehoff, *Philo on Jewish Identity and Culture,* 6-8, 21-22.

Philo, their privileged status began to deteriorate, especially when the Romans started to expand the class of citizens.[65] Augustus apparently replaced the office of ethnarch with γερούσια, and it was a serious blow that the Jews were not, as were the Alexandrian citizens, exempted from the λαογραφία in 24/23 or even 5/4 B.C.E., when a new class paying reduced tax was created.[66] It became evident that Ἰουδαῖος ἀπὸ Ἀλεξανδρείας was not the same as Ἀλεξανδρεύς and that the new bureaucracy drew the limits sharply, as in the case of Helenos, a Jew desperatedly trying to preserve his privileged status.[67]

The pogroms in Alexandria produced a new threat. Several episodes show how the Greek citizens sought to make clear that Jews were not citizens. They coerced Flaccus to proclaim that Jews were aliens and foreigners, and that they must leave the city within days unless a license to live in its bounds was granted (*Flacc.* 53-54). Symbolic of the Jews' worsened status, they were humiliated during the pogroms by flogging with the same instrument as the native Egyptians.[68] Claudius reacted to the riots in dual fashion.[69] Although he punished some of the anti-Jewish agitators, he reminded the Jews that, regardless of permission to live according to their traditional customs (ἀλλὰ ἐῶσιν αὐτοὺς τοῖς ἔθεσιν χρῆσθαι), they did not live in a city of their own and should not expect more privileges than they already had or

---

65. See Fraser, *Ptolemaic Alexandria*, 796.

66. See Smallwood, *The Jews under Roman Rule*, 231-32; John J. Collins, *Between Athens and Jerusalem: Jewish Identity in the Hellenistic Diaspora* (2nd ed.; BRS; Grand Rapids: Eerdmans; Livonia: Dove, 2000) 115-17.

67. See *CPJ* 151 (5/4 B.C.E.). The man claims to be Ἀλεξανδρεύς and son of an Ἀλεξανδρεύς, who had lived all his life in Alexandria and had been trained in the gymnasion. However, the public administrator had not exempted him from the taxes meant for non-Greeks. Moreover, a second hand had flatly changed his title, correcting Ἀλεξανδρέως to Ἰουδαίου τῶν ἀπὸ Ἀλεξανδρε(ίας). The probable reason for the loss of status as citizen was that his Jewish mother lacked citizen status. On this important papyrus, see Tcherikover, *CPJ* 2:29-33; Smallwood, *The Jews under Roman Rule*, 228-29; Niehoff, *Philo on Jewish Identity and Culture*, 21.

68. *Flacc.* 78-80. See also Aryeh Kasher, *The Jews in Hellenistic and Roman Egypt: The Struggle for Equal Rights* (TSAJ 7; Tübingen: Mohr Siebeck, 1985) 240-42; Grabbe, *Judaism from Cyrus to Hadrian*, 405-9; Richard Alston, "Philo's *In Flaccum*," 171; Peder Borgen, *Philo of Alexandria: An Exegete for His Time* (NovTSup 86; Leiden: Brill, 1997) 25.

69. Josephus also quotes an edict of Claudius in *Ant.* 19.280-85. Most scholars have doubted the authenticity of the edict, or claimed that Josephus or his source deliberately edited the version found in *CPJ*. It is not, however, ruled out that Claudius issued several edicts; see Miriam Pucci Ben Zeev, *Jewish Rights in the Roman World: The Greek and Roman Documents Quoted by Josephus Flavius* (TSAJ 74; Tübingen: Mohr Siebeck, 1998) 295-326. Be this as it may, Josephus does not speak here of ephebate or gymnasion.

attempt to take part in games organized by the gymnasiarchs (μηδὲ ἐπισπαίειν[70] γυμνασιαρχικοῖς ἢ κοσμητικοῖς ἀγώσει).[71]

With all of this in mind, it is not easy to determine which doors were open for Jews in Alexandria seeking a secular education. The entire status of the Jews there was changing, and this undoubtedly influenced educational options, precisely in Philo's lifetime.[72] Basically, evidence for his education may point in different directions. What had been possible in his youth was perhaps no longer an option when he wrote his works.

Before turning to Philo's writings, we must consider the evidence of Jews educated in the Greek manner in Alexandria and reexamine Claudius's important letter of 41 c.e.[73] The practice of learned Jews writing in Greek was well established before the time of Philo. Aristobulus and Demetrius were learned scholars, and some Jews were able not only to model Greek literary genres but also to emulate the works of famous poets such as Homer, Phocylides, and the Attic dramatists. Ezekiel the Tragedian skillfully imitated Aeschylus's *Persians* in his *Exagoge*.

As noted, many scholars claim that Jews attended gymnasions, assuming that these were schools. They provide largely indirect evidence,[74] contending that apart from the gymnasions one could not gain knowledge such as that evident, for example, in Philo. But there is also some direct evidence. Dositheos (*CPJ* 3.230 no. 127)[75] was *hypomnematographos* of the Ptolemaic king. Alexander, the brother of Philo, was a Roman citizen and certainly had admission to the gymnasion. His son Tiberius Julius Alexander governed

---

70. On the reading, see Tcherikover, *CPJ* 2:33

71. See *CPJ* 153 and Tcherikover, *CPJ* 2:37-39; Collins, *Between Athens and Jerusalem,* 120-21. An attempt to restrict admission to ephebate to prevent "uncultured and uneducated" people from corrupting the citizen body of Alexandria was made already 20-19 B.C.E., and it apparently threatened the status of the Jews in the city; see *CPJ* 150 and Gregory E. Sterling, "Judaism between Jerusalem and Alexandria," in *Hellenism in the Land of Israel,* ed. John J. Collins and Gregory E. Sterling (Notre Dame: Notre Dame University Press, 2001) 276-77.

72. Philo was born ca. 20-10 B.C.E. His reference in *Anim.* 58 may refer to the horse race mentioned by Pliny (*Nat.* 8.160) in the year 47; Borgen, *Philo of Alexandria,* 14-26; Mondésert, "Philo of Alexandria," 878-79.

73. P. London 1912; *CPJ* 1:11.

74. E.g., Hengel: "The remarkable and probably historically unique fusion of Jewish and Hellenistic culture in Alexandria from the third century is only understandable on the grounds of the unhindered access of Egyptian Jews to the treasures of Greek education. Here the gymnasion became an important point of transition"; *Judaism and Hellenism,* 66. See Erich S. Gruen, "Jews and Greeks," in Erskine, *A Companion to the Hellenistic World,* 275.

75. See Hengel, *Judaism and Hellenism,* 71.

first Thebaid, then Judea, and subsequently Egypt. No doubt Philo's entire family enjoyed the best education in Alexandria. Elsewhere, the list of ephebs in Cyrene contains Jewish names.[76] Helenos, mentioned above, had visited the gymnasion, and according to Claudius, Jews were willing to take part in the games organized by the gymnasiarchs. These were certainly not boys from the streets, but those closely linked to the gymnasion. However, as we know very little of the ephebate in Alexandria, we also know very little of the Jews as ephebs and their association with gymnasions. Does this simply reflect limited sources, or does it indicate that no Jews were involved, or only a few?

If we analyze every word in Claudius's letter, it makes some things very clear, but also causes problems, particularly when we inquire about admission of Jews to gymnasions. The claim that Jews were foreigners, that they had no right to live in the city, was rejected. They could still live in Alexandria "according to their manner," but they still had to remember that this was really not their own city. However, the document clearly states that it was not permissible to persecute Jews or evict them from the city. More puzzling is what Claudius writes regarding the ephebate and games. Scholars generally believe that there was a class of people who had visited the gymnasion but were not citizens.[77] Now Claudius clearly says that everyone who has served as epheb is included in the body of citizens, unless they were of servile origin. But parallel sources, from Alexandria and especially from other cities of Egypt, show how risky it is to base judgments on a single document. On the one hand, some people were citizens, even though they had not visited gymnasions in Alexandria.[78] But on the other hand, youth

---

76. See SEG 20.740-41; Gruen, "Jews and Greeks," 274.

77. Occasionally documents use the phrase οἱ ἀπὸ τοῦ γυμνασίου or οἱ ἐκ τοῦ γυμνασίου, and the meaning is not obvious. Some scholars claim that these were citizens, and that the gymnasion was precisely the boundary separating citizens from noncitizens; Smallwood, *The Jews under Roman Rule,* 231. However, although they constituted a special group, apparently none of them were citizens. The Ptolemies seem not to have recognized everyone as a citizen following the ephebate in the gymnasion. This was a prerequisite for being added to the hereditary body of citizens, but it did not guarantee it, e.g., if the mother was not the daughter of a citizen. Clearly, οἱ ἀπὸ τοῦ γυμνασίου indicated a group distinct from the Greek citizens in Ptolemaic Cyprus (*CPJ* 1:59; J. Drescher, "A New Coptic Month," *JEA* 46 (1960) 111. According to Nilsson, *Die hellenistische Schule,* 92, the phrase originally referred to the ephebs who had recently ended their ephebate, but was later used more loosely, even of children and women, who belonged to the social class that was admitted to the gymnasion.

78. Diana Delia, *Alexandrian Citizenship during the Roman Principate* (American Classical Studies 23; Atlanta: Scholars, 1991) 73-74.

were not admitted to the ephebate, even though both parents were citizens, unless they could trace both paternal and maternal lines to the original membership rolls which were of Augustan date.[79]

The case of Helenos, whose petition was apparently filed in Augustus's time, shows that Jews had already encountered problems decades earlier. Helenos had to realize that a Jew from Alexandria was not an Alexandrinian citizen even if his father had been, and not even if he had visited the gymnasion. The scribe who amended his appeal showed that following the Roman conquest the lines affecting the status of the Jews had been strictly redrawn: there was little room for a middle position. The Romans viewed the gymnasion precisely as a tool for preserving the social classes, using it to distinguish between Greeks and non-Greeks.[80] Helenos, as several Jews before him, had visited the gymnasion and apparently served as epheb. According to Claudius, this should have made Helenos a citizen. It did not, however, apparently because his mother had not been a citizen even though his father was,[81] or simply because he was a Jew. Claudius apparently omitted some details in his letter, and Fraser may be correct in his assumption that the legislations of Claudius and his predecessors were not identical.[82]

At the time of Claudius's letter, there was a group of Jews, and perhaps others as well, who tried to take part in the games arranged by the gymnasiarchs. These individuals probably had some association with the institution but were not fully insiders. The only such group for which we have some evidence consists of people whose citizenship was in doubt. This would seem to be precisely the place of the young Jewish elite in Alexandria in Philo's time. The sources show how difficult their lives were. The gymnasions were hotbeds for pogroms, and it was there that Jews were beaten. The worst agitators were two gymnasiarchs, named Lampon and Isidoros (*Flacc.* 20.128-35; *CPJ* 156). Rioters in 38 C.E. also initiated a pogrom by confining Jews within the gymnasion (*Flacc.* 32-40).[83] This was the heart of the Greek identity, the place for clubs, feasts, and meals.[84] To participate in the gym-

---

79. See Carroll A. Nelson, *Status Declarations in Roman Egypt* (ASP 19; Amsterdam: Hakkert, 1979) 10-25; *FIRA* 2.3.19.

80. Nilsson, *Die hellenistische Schule,* 85.

81. Tcherikover, *CPJ* 2:32.

82. Fraser, *Ptolemaic Alexandria,* 1:76-77.

83. Alston notes how the Greek population started the riots from gymnasion, which was their own space, advanced to the theater and streets that were common, and finally violated the houses of Jews, i.e., their own space; "Philo's *In Flaccum*," 165-72.

84. See Nilsson, *Die hellenistische Schule,* 78-80.

nasial games and elicit the reaction of the spectators required courage and may have sparked violence. Apparently this involved young Jews, because Claudius considered it appropriate to ban them from the games.

This all means that Philo lived in a crucial time when both Jews' desire for and their rights to secular education were redefined. What do his own works reveal?

Philo's Own Witness: Why and When Should a Jew Study the Classical Authors?

The question of secular education was a burning issue in Alexandria, even apart from the legal struggle and before the pogroms. The great city offered the best options for eager students. But how keen was the Jewish community to send their offspring for secular training? It was impossible to obtain office without a good education. However, this education also posed the danger of assimilation.

Philo did not hesitate to rewrite Moses' early years to show that the Legislator had received the best secular education in the world, and totally anachronistically he reported that Moses even had teachers from Greece.[85] However, Philo was also aware of the dangers of this education. He openly expresses his view on the classical education in *De congressu eruditionis gratia*. According to Philo, it is impossible for a man to beget children from "Sarah" (= virtue) if he does not visit her maidservant "Hagar."[86] The maidservant of virtue is the encyclical education (ἐγκύκλιος παιδεία) that allegedly was also given to Moses.[87] Grammar, music, geometry, astronomy,

---

85. On Moses' education, see *Mos.* 1.21-24; also Koskenniemi, "Moses — A Well-Educated Man," 287-90; Niehoff, *Philo on Jewish Identity and Culture,* 69-70.

86. See also *Cher.* 3; 8; *Ebr.* 34, where Philo writes similarly: "And thus we see that Hagar or the lower education, whose sphere is the secular learning of the schools" (*Cher.* 3). See Karl-Gustav Sandelin, "The Danger of Idolatry According to Philo of Alexandria," *Temenos* 27 (1991) 138-43; cf. Mendelson, *Secular Education in Philo,* xxiv.

87. "Arithmetic, geometry, the lore of metre, rhythm and harmony, and the whole subject of music as shown by the use of instruments or in textbooks and treatises of a more special character, were imparted to him by learned Egyptians. These further instructed him in the philosophy conveyed in symbols, as displayed in the so-called holy inscriptions and in the regard paid to animals, to which they even pay divine honors. He had Greeks to teach him the rest of the regular school course, and the inhabitants of the neighboring countries for Assyrian letters and the Chaldean science of the heavenly bodies. This he also acquired from Egyptians, who give special attention to astrology" (*Mos.* 1.21-24; LCL). On the concept and content of

rhetorical education, and other studies are a road leading toward virtue (*Congr.* 1-12). Visiting the maidservant teaches many useful things, but it also instructs one to reject the errors in the works of poets and historians. Solid food is not given to children before they have first received milk, and this milk is the Greek encyclical education (*Congr.* 13-19).[88] A Greek education without the Torah only produces a sophist, and for Philo, "Ishmael" is the worst example of this.[89] As Peder Borgen notes, the treatise is inter alia Philo's warning directed towards the Jewish youth, because secular studies also endangered their religion.[90]

Philo thus recommends exactly the same pathway that his Moses followed. Indeed, it was also his own way, as disclosed in *Congr.* 72-80. The picture is romantic, and unfortunately Philo does not inform his readers where he begat children from Hagar, at least not here. He does not mention the gymnasion, or a school (unlike the translation of F. H. Colson, for example, in *Congr.* 79 [LCL]), only τὰ ἐγκύκλια or ἡ ἐγκυκλική (παιδεία), naming here grammar, geometry, and music as handmaids he used to bring treasures to his real wife.[91] Actually, although Philo very often speaks about education (παιδεία),[92] he uses the word γυμνάσιον remarkably seldom, and not at all in this important treatise. Out of nine appearances in his works, in four the word is clearly used metaphorically, referring to ethical and spiritual training (*Mut.* 172; *Somn.* 2.69, 129; *Prov.* 2.44). He uses the word in the concrete sense five times (*Opif.* 17; *Flacc.* 34, 37, 139; *Legat.* 135), mostly in the context of the pogroms. But all the same, Philo never connects the gymnasion in these few appearances with any kind of education other than physical training, and never speaks of his own past in the gymnasion. However, he does give a clue, although not as clearly as in the LCL translation. Philo writes on the commandment instructing one to honor his parents and praises the merits of the parents as follows:

---

the ἐγκύκλιος παιδεία, see p. 111. On the concept in Philo, see Mendelson, *Secular Education in Philo*, 1-24.

88. Hagar often represents the lower form of education, e.g., in *Cher.* 3.9-10. In *Cong.* 81-86 Philo expresses his view on when to start the different phases of studies: Egypt represents childhood and body and cannot be educated; a man needs to spend ten years in Canaan and then go on to Hagar.

89. See Koskenniemi, "Philo and the Sophists," 266-72.

90. The dangers of the encyclical studies concerned Philo even in *Leg.* 3.167; see Borgen, *Philo of Alexandria*, 162-65.

91. See Niehoff, *Philo on Jewish Identity and Culture*, 181-82.

92. Philo uses the word in two senses, both denoting the educational process and the end result of instruction; see Mendelson, *Secular Education in Philo*, 1-2.

First, they have brought them out of non-existence; then, again, they have held them entitled to nurture and later to education of body and soul, so that they may have not only life, but a good life. They have benefited the body by means of the gymnasion and the training there given (διὰ τῆς γυμναστικῆς καὶ ἀλειπτικῆς), through which it gains muscular vigour and good condition and the power to bear itself and move with an ease marked by gracefulness and elegance. They have done the same for the soul by means of letters and arithmetic and geometry and music and philosophy as a whole which lifts on high the mind lodged within with mortal body and escorts it to the very heaven and shews it the blessed and happy beings that dwell therein, and creates it an eager longing for the unswerving ever-harmonious order which they never forsake because they obey their captain and marshal. (*Spec.* 2.229-30)

To be accurate, Philo does not speak of the gymnasion and the training given there, but *gymnasial* training, which leaves open the place and the institution. When explaining the commandments to his Jewish audience, Philo assumes that the parents have given this kind of education to their children. It is simplest to say that he only refers to the gymnasion. However, if only a small part of the Jewish population was admitted to gymnasions, were they the only ones who received that kind of education? Some scholars, especially Hadot, have hinted of alternatives the non-Greeks developed to replace the Greek secular education, and although Philo's works give little information of such institutions, we cannot rule out that something like that existed in Jewish Alexandria. At any rate, the content and the consequences of his education, not the building or institution, are decisive when tracing Philo's secular education.

Philo and Greek Philosophers and Poets

Both Philo and Josephus often refer to or quote ancient writers. A closer look is needed to recognize the striking difference. In Josephus's works, historians take the lion's share of all quotations and references. He rarely refers to philosophers and poets, and when he does, he reveals his deficient knowledge.[93] Few scholars deny that Josephus was a talented and industrious writer; how-

---

93. See Erkki Koskenniemi, "Josephus and Greek Poets," in *The Intertextuality of the Epistles,* ed. Thomas L. Brodie (Sheffield: Sheffield Phoenix, 2006) 46-60.

ever, contrary to the common modern view, the best education in Jerusalem had not trained him well in Greek literature. But Philo was different. He frequently refers to Greek philosophers and skillfully uses Greek poets. Scholars have thoroughly investigated how Philo employed, for example, some Platonic works and their influence on his thought. Space here allows only a few examples.[94]

The pre-Socratic philosophers were well known to Philo. He mentions the legendary Seven Sages, both as a group (*Prob.* 73)[95] and often individually. Consequently, he refers to Bias (*Prob.* 152), Solon (*Opif.* 104-5), occasionally Pythagoras (*QG* 1.17; 3.349), and often, with deep appreciation, to the "Pythagoreans" of his own time (for example, "the saintly company of the Pythagoreans, τὸν μὲν οὖν τῶν Πυθαγορείων ἱερώτατον θίασον, *Prob.* 2), considering them to be true Pythagoreans as he did the entire classical tradition,[96] and naming men like Philolaus (*Opif.* 100) and Ocellus (*Aet.* 12). Philo says that he had personally read the work of Ocellus.[97] It is less im-

---

94. See also Niehoff, *Philo on Jewish Identity and Culture*, 138-39; David Lincicum, "A Preliminary Index to Philo's Non-Biblical Citations and Allusions," *SPhAn* 25 (2013) 139-67.

95. The tradition of seven legendary sages originated sometime in the sixth or fifth century B.C.E., and Plato refers to them in *Prot.* 343a. Writers knew the "Seven," but disagreed concerning who this included until Demetrius of Faleron, whose list generally gained acceptance. On the seven sages, see Johannes Christes, "Sieben Weise," in *DNP* 11 (2001) 526. On the ancient lists, see Hermann Diels and Walter Kranz, *Die Fragmente der Vorsokratiker* (12th ed.; Dublin: Weidmann, 1966) 1:61-62. Philo's writings are not properly noted in this famous collection. The index in part 3 (p. 619) includes only some of his quotations.

96. The modern view on Pythagoras and Pythagoreans drastically differs from what Philo and his fellow scholars thought. Modern scholars may disagree at crucial points, but agree that historically we only see the shadow of Pythagoras, and that his figure can justly be compared with that of Orpheus or other shadows of the remote times. Rather, the "Pythagoreans" as Philo knew them were no more faithful followers of Pythagoras than many famous philosophers, including Plato and Aristotle, who accepted parts of the Pythagorean tradition and belonged to the philosophic tradition that appreciated doctrines attributed to Pythagoras. A "Pythagorean" renaissance appeared in the first century B.C.E., but this movement had virtually nothing to do with Pythagoras or Pythagoreanism and was mainly a product of Platonist philosophers. This did not prevent ancient tradition from treating the new movement, called Neopythagoreans by most modern scholars, as Pythagoreans. On the Pythagoreans, see Karlheinz Hülser, "Pythagoreer/Pythagoreismus," in *RGG*⁴ 6 (2003) 1846-48. On Philo and Pythagoreans, see Horst Moehring, "Moses and Pythagoras: Arithmology as an Exegetical Tool in Philo," in *Studia Biblica 1978: Sixth International Congress on Biblical Studies, Oxford 3-7 April 1978*, ed. Elizabeth A. Livingstone (JSOTSup 11; Sheffield: Sheffield University Press, 1979) 205-8; Ray Barraclough, "Philo's Politics: Roman Rule and Hellenistic Judaism," *ANRW* 2.21.1 (1984) 443.

97. There is no article on Ocellus in *DNP*. On the work, written probably ca. 150 B.C.E., see Rudolf Beutler, "Okellos," in PW 17/2 (1937) 2361-80.

portant that he, as did the entire ancient tradition, erroneously considered Ocellus a pre-Socratic philosopher and that the work was indeed written much later. The point is that Philo was not merely dependent on handbooks or collections of anecdotes and summaries, of which the work of Diogenes Laertius is the best-known example. That he had personally studied an author so little known as Ocellus certainly implies that he had also thoroughly read famous philosophers, as his acquaintance with Plato shows. At any rate, he knew philosophers such as Zeno the Eleatic (*Prob.* 97, 108, 160), Heraclitus (e.g., *Leg.* 1.108; *QG* 3.5; *Her.* 214), and Anaxagoras (*Contempl.* 14) and was as well aware of their teaching as any Greek writer; moreover, as was typical in his times, he skillfully employed the questionable reputation of the great Sophists like Protagoras and Gorgias toward his own ends.[98]

That Philo was fond of Plato is generally well-known, and the contacts between these two philosophers has been a crucial theme in studies on Philo.[99] Only few words are thus needed here on Plato in Philo's writings. He names Plato fourteen times,[100] but to list these passages would be but a beginning. Philo often uses Platonic concepts to speak for his cause. Often, as in *Leg.* 3.115, he takes the Platonic division of the soul and describes how "some philosophers" have précised the view. No mention of Plato or *Phaedrus* is made when Philo presents the three parts of the soul; for him this was something that required no motivation. And when he says that the mortal body has been "quite properly" called a sepulchre for the human νοῦς, he does not consider it necessary to refer to *Cratylus* (400b) or to *Gorgias* (493a). When Philo presents the structure of heaven (*Decal.* 103-103; *Cher.* 22), he does not mention his source, i.e., *Timaeus* 36. For Philo, Plato represented facts, not opinions, and this means that Plato is omnipresent in his writings. In *Quod omnis probus liber sit*, Philo criticizes people who seek physicians to acquire health but do not care that their soul is sick. He continues:

> But since we have it on the sacred authority of Plato (κατὰ τὸν ἱερώτατον Πλάτωνα) that envy has no place in the divine choir (φθόνος ἔξω θείου

---

98. See Koskenniemi, "Philo and the Sophists," 266-79.

99. For a short presentation of Plato's influence on Philo, see Barraclough, "Philo's Politics," 442. The ideas in *Timaeus* and *Theaetetus* are of crucial importance for Philo's theology, as shown by David T. Runia (esp. *Philo of Alexandria and the Timaeus of Plato* [Philosophia antiqua 44; Leiden: Brill, 1986]); and Wendy E. Helleman, "Philo of Alexandria on Deification and Assimilation to God" (*SPhAn* 2; BJS 226; 1990) 51-71.

100. *Opif.* 119; 133; *Prob.* 13; *Contempl.* 57; 59; *Aet.* 13; 14; 16; 17; 27; 38; 52; 141.

χοροῦ ἵσταται), and wisdom is most divine and most freehanded, she never closes her school of thought but always opens her doors to those who thirst for the sweet water of discourse. (*Prob.* 13)

These words, quoted also in *Spec.* 2.249, are taken from *Phaedrus* 247a, but the main interest lies in the words κατὰ τὸν ἱερώτατον Πλάτωνα. (We should be aware of the textual problem; most manuscripts read λιγυρώτατον instead of ἱερώτατον.) In *Fug.* 63, Philo characterizes Plato as "a man highly esteemed, one of those admired for their wisdom." Plato is praised with words usually reserved only for Moses.

Socrates made a great impression on many young thinkers, not only on Plato. His manner of discussing philosophical themes with his pupils invoked several schools which are called "Socratic," but which took very different paths. Philo knew the Socratic schools well. He knew Aristotle (e.g., *Aet.* 16, 18; *QG* 3.16) and the Peripatetics (Theophrastus,[101] *Aet.* 117; Critolaus,[102] *Aet.* 55, 70, 74), and of course the famous Stoics (Zeno,[103] *Prob.* 53, 57; Chrysippus,[104] *Aet.* 45-51, 91; Cleanthes,[105] *Aet.* 91). As were many Greek writers, he seems to have been fond of the Cynics, particularly because of their ascetic ideals and their manner of fearlessly confronting rulers and tyrants (Antisthenes,[106] *Prob.* 28-29; Aristippus,[107] *Agr.* 151; *Plant.* 151; Diogenes,[108] *Gig.* 34; 157; *Aet.* 77; *Prob.* 121-24). He despised the Epicurean cosmology[109] (*Post.* 2; *Aet.* 8) and ethics.[110]

This brief summary is not meant to serve as a comparison of Philo's ideas

101. On Theophrastus, see William W. Fortenbaugh and Johannes van Opphuijsen, "Theophrastus," in *DNP* 12 (2002) 385-93.

102. On Critolaus, see Robert Sharples, "Kritolaos," in *DNP* 6 (1999) 855.

103. On Zeno, see Walter Ameling, "Zenon von Kition," in *DNP* 12 (2002) 744-48.

104. On Chrysippus, see Brad Inwood, "Chrysippus," in *DNP* 2 (1997) 1177-83.

105. On Cleanthes, see Brad Inwood, "Kleanthes," in *DNP* 6 (1999) 499-500.

106. See esp. *Alleg. Interp.* 3.45 and 3.185, and Erkki Koskenniemi, *The Old Testament Miracle-workers in Early Judaism* (WUNT ser. 2 206; Tubingen: Mohr-Siebeck, 2005) 141; on the literal interpretation, see pp. 125-26.

107. On Aristippus, see Klaus Döring, "Aristippos," in *DNP* 1 (1996) 1103-4.

108. On Diogenes, see Marie Odile Goulet-Cazé, "Diogenes von Sinope," in *DNP* 3 (1997) 598-600.

109. On Philo and Epicureans, see Barraclough, "Philo's Politics," esp. 443-44; A. Peter Booth, "The Voice of the Serpent: Philo's Epicureanism," in *Hellenization Revised: Shaping a Christian Response within the Graeco-Roman World*, ed. Wendy E. Helleman (Lanham: University Press of America, 1994) 159-72.

110. Apparently Philo refers to Epicureans in *Somn.* 2.277, 283, but does not mention the names.

with the entirety of the Greek philosophical tradition. The important point is that Philo mentions almost all of the important earlier philosophers, and if he occasionally makes historically inaccurate judgments, this does not attest lack of education but rather the impact of strong Greek tradition. Philo had a favorite philosopher, Plato, although an actual symposium with the historical Plato would certainly have surprised him. Above all, far from rejecting every philosopher in discordance with the Torah, Philo firmly stood in the philosophical tradition of the imperial era, both Greek and Jewish. On the Greek side, theoretical speculations were less important now, and philosophy meant especially a wise manner of living. For example, Philo could have consistently rejected Diogenes of Sinope,[111] because he despised the skeptics' theory of knowledge. However, he admired Diogenes' disposition before the powerful, and set him as a model for his readers. He could even mention Theodorus, the atheist and hedonist,[112] positively toward that end (*Prob.* 127-28). In imperial times, every great philosopher shared a common heritage, regardless of their controversial doctrines, and Philo here follows the mainstream. As for the Jews, their own scholars had long claimed Moses as the teacher of all Greek writers and philosophers. Every Greek insight thus originated from Judaism, and all shortcomings of Greek philosophy were merely deviations from the Torah.

I have elsewhere given a full account of how Philo quoted or mentioned dramatists and poets, and what follows is only a brief summary. Philo frequently quotes the masters of Greek tragedy.[113] He twice quotes Aeschylus (*Prob.* 143; *Aet.* 49) and once Sophocles (*Prob.* 19), and very often Euripides (e.g., *Prob.* 21-22; *Leg.* 1.7; *Ios.* 78; *Spec.* 4.47), who was the most popular playwright in the Hellenistic world. Moreover, not only had Philo read the plays or listened to them in the lecture halls, but he also twice reports that he had personally visited the theater. In *Ebr.* 177 he describes what he had seen "often" in the theater, and in *Prob.* 152 he vividly describes the impact of the marvelous play on the spectators, including himself. It was impossible to understand anything about classical drama without a thorough knowledge of Greek mythology, but this was not a problem for one such as Philo. He sometimes writes very critically on theater (*Agr.* 35), but it is easy to under-

---

111. See Goulet-Cazé, "Diogenes von Sinope."

112. On Theodorus, see Klaus Döring, "Theodoros aus Kyrene," in *DNP* 12/1 (2001) 326-27.

113. See Erkki Koskenniemi, "Philo and Classical Drama," in *Ancient Israel, Judaism, and Christianity in Contemporary Perspective: Essays in Memory of Karl-Johan Illman*, ed. Jacob Neusner et al. (Lanham: University Press of America 2006) 137-51.

stand that in his time as well as today the ethical level of the plays varied.[114] Understandably, Philo only once quotes Menander, and even then without mentioning the author (Παιδίον in *Her.* 5).

Philo's references to the other poets underscore what was evidenced in his quotations of the dramatists.[115] Philo greatly appreciates Homer, disregarding all the critical words of Plato, his favorite philosopher. For Philo, Homer is *the* poet (*Abr.* 10; see also *Mut.* 179; *Conf.* 4), and he quotes him often and skillfully, with no traces of apology. Although the *Iliad* was foremost in the school-papyri, Philo often refers to the *Odyssey* as well (see, e.g., *Fug.* 31; *Legat.* 80; *Migr.* 195). He also quotes Hesiod (*Ebr.* 149-50; *Aet.* 17-19), Solon (*Opif.* 104), Pindar (*Aet. 121; Virt.* 172), or Theognis (*Prob.* 155), vividly and precisely, apparently citing verses from memory. Of course, he may also write very critically of "poets" and their fiction, equating them with "sophists" (see, e.g., *Opif.* 157). But in general, his attitude is surprisingly positive.

Philo's works thus show that he was undoubtedly a master of Greek literature, acquainted with both philosophers and poets, and employing them as skillfully as would other imperial writers, such as Plutarch, Philostratus, or any learned sophist. It is true that he credits the treasures of Greek literature with certain superiority.[116] Philo was fully aware of the tradition — but where had he learned it?

It is clear that Philo was not alone in knowledge of the Greek writers to whom he referred, but rather stood within a tradition. Alexandrian Jewish scholarship undoubtedly represented the fruit of a long process, wherein a number of their elite were admitted to gymnasions. But Philo's works also suggest how Jewish tradition had developed. Philo did not hesitate to visit the theater and observe Euripides' work, and he was hardly the only Jew in Alexandria doing so. Otherwise it would be strange that he could quote or refer to so many Greek philosophers and poets even in works that were clearly written for a mainly Jewish audience, as in *De specialibus legibus*. Although Philo had certainly memorized poetic passages during his training so that he could spontaneously cite individual verses, the poets hardly be-

---

114. Although chronological factors should not be overlooked, it is perhaps wise to observe that Augustine writes very critically of the theater in general (*Conf.* 1.32; 2.8), but especially on certain performances (*Conf.* 2.4), and that theater with nude women was an abomination to Lactantius (*Epit.* 58.5 [SC 335 (1987) 226]).

115. See Koskenniemi, "Philo and Greek Poets."

116. Niehoff, *Philo on Jewish Identity and Culture,* 139-58. Niehoff also observes Philo's distance from Greek literature; it is true, but only so, that he eclectically takes and leaves what he needs.

longed to his background alone. I have suggested elsewhere that he also had a private library, as did learned Greeks and Romans, and that he would read passages aloud at banquets, as was the Greek model.[117] If we assume that Philo and his fellow scholars had more than just limited contact with the Jewish community — and he had, because he represented them at Gaius's court — the Alexandrian synagogue was indeed a *didaskaleion* (*Mos.* 2.216), where many people were able to access Philo's learned treatises, filled with references to Greek literature.

Conclusion

> The Jewish representation of the city was of separate communities each integral to the whole, a multi-cultural society in which civic space, facilities, and privileges were shared. This view of the urban community was directly contrary to Roman representations.[118]

Richard Alston finely formulates the changes that occurred in Philo's lifetime, especially from the Jewish perspective regarding the native Egyptians, who had been relegated primarily as outsiders from the very beginnings of the city. The Jewish elite of earlier generations undoubtedly had admission to the gymnasions, and Philo apparently enjoyed this tradition that had produced so many learned individuals. He used to visit the theater, and he enjoyed the treasures of Greek poetry, having no difficulty in eagerly quoting it when writing for a Jewish as well as a broader audience. Undoubtedly the synagogue he visited was amply filled with people able to follow his learned treatises. The Jewish community had developed and discussed the ideas they found in the classical texts — probably in their own libraries and banquets. However, Philo's own works as well as other sources show that change was in the works. The Roman rulers considered Alexandria a Greek city, although Jews were permitted to live there. The complex administration of the Hellenistic city with demes and various organizations allowed room for their own *politeuma,* at least as long as the rulers favored them. In the Roman view, however, people either were or were not citizens, and this rapidly eroded the special status of the Jews that had not been clearly defined. At the same time, it was not easy for the Greek population to subordinate themselves to the

117. See Koskenniemi, "Philo and Greek Poets," 304.
118. Alston, "Philo's *In Flaccum,*" 173.

Romans. As elsewhere, Greek nationalistic feelings and particularly Greek institutions gained importance, as the Atticistic ideals clearly attest.[119] The Romans promoted these ideas by supporting the ephebate and gymnasions. After Alexandria had lost its independence, the gymnasions understandably became hotbeds of Greek nationalist sentiment, and consequently difficult places for Jews, especially for those not fully ready to abandon their ancestral religion. Apparently, Philo was one of the last secularly trained Jews in Alexandria. After some decades, the cruel aftermath of the revolts decimated the number of Jews in Egypt and decimated what remained of their flourishing culture.

---

119. On Greek identity during the imperial time, see Erkki Koskenniemi, *Der Philostrateische Apollonios* (CHL 94; Helsinki: Societas Scientiarum Fennica, 1991) 45-57.

"The Jewish Philosophy": Reading Moses via Hellenistic Philosophy according to Philo

Gregory E. Sterling

In his account of the crisis precipitated by Gaius's order for a statue to be erected in Jerusalem, Philo explained why Petronius, the governor of Syria, was favorably disposed toward Jewish resistance to the emperor's wishes. Philo's explanation included Petronius's limited understanding of the Jewish faith. The Alexandrian wrote: "But he himself, so it seems, had some glimmers of the Jewish philosophy and religion" (ἐναύσματα τῆς Ἰουδαϊκῆς φιλοσοφίας ἅμα καὶ εὐσεβείας; *Legat.* 245).[1] Philo more frequently referred to the Jewish system of belief and practices as his "ancestral philosophy" (ἡ πάτριος φιλοσοφία; *Somn.* 2.127; *Mos.* 2.216; *Contempl.* 28; *Legat.* 156), a description shared by the later historian Josephus (*C. Ap.* 2.47; cf. also 1.54). They were not the only authors who presented Judaism as a philosophy: the author of *4 Maccabees* did so as well (*4 Macc.* 5:22).

While there were undoubtedly other Jewish authors who made similar claims, Philo stands apart because he did far more than use philosophy for apologetic reasons as Josephus did[2] or offer an eclectic synthesis of moral

---

1. All translations are my own unless otherwise noted.

2. On Josephus's use of philosophy, see Steve Mason, "Should Any Wish to Enquire Further (*Ant.* 1.25): The Aim and Audience of Josephus's *Judean Antiquities/Life*," in *Understanding Josephus: Seven Perspectives* (JSPSup 32; Sheffield: Sheffield Academic, 1998) 64-103; S. Daniel Breslauer, "Philosophy in Judaism: Two Stances," in *The Blackwell Companion to Judaism*, ed. Jacob Neusner and Alan J. Avery-Peck (Oxford: Blackwell, 2000) 162-80, esp. 166-67, although I would qualify Breslauer's view that for Josephus "Jewish consciousness is basically philosophical" (p. 167). This may have been Josephus's presentation, but it was superficial and would have been perceived as superficial by any professional philosopher in the Roman world.

philosophy without a theoretical base as the author of *4 Maccabees* did.[3] Philo had a much better grasp of Hellenistic philosophy, and it shaped his writings in profound ways. Ancients recognized Philo's intellectual accomplishments and commented on them in different ways. The most common way was to emphasize his great learning. Eusebius described Philo as "a man of the highest distinction not only among us, but among pagans who pursue education" (*Hist. eccl.* 2.4.2).[4] Others also emphasized his learning[5] or wisdom.[6] Some were more specific and noted his learning of philosophy. So Eusebius — in the same text that we have just cited above — went on to describe his contributions to his ancestral faith and then to philosophy: "it is not necessary to say anything about his capacities with respect to his philosophical contributions or his contributions to liberal education in the pagan world since he is reported to have surpassed all his contemporaries, especially in his zeal for the Platonic and Pythagorean ways of life" (*Hist. eccl.* 2.4.2-3). Others made similar observations, although the specifics varied. Josephus wrote simply that Philo "was not without experience in philosophy" (φιλοσοφίας οὐκ ἄπειρος; *Ant.* 18.259), a statement that Eusebius repeated (*Hist. eccl.* 2.5.4). Some simply called him a philosopher[7] or linked him with contemplation;[8] still others — as Eusebius above — linked him with specific philosophical traditions.[9]

While the presence of philosophy in Philo's writings is a given, its importance and role have been the subject of debate. The consensus today is that Philo was first and foremost an exegete of Moses' writings;[10] he was not

3. For an overview of the attempts to situate the philosophical background of *4 Maccabees*, see Robert Renehan, "The Greek Philosophic Background of Fourth Maccabees," *Rheisches Museum für Philologie* 115 (1972) 223-38, esp. 223-26.

4. The testimonia for Philo were collected by Leopold Cohn and conveniently printed in Cohn, Paul Wendland, Siegfried Reiter, and Hans Leisegang, eds., *Philonis Alexandrini opera quae supersunt* (7 vols.; Berlin: Reimer, 1896-1930) 1:lxxxxv-cxiii, hereafter abbreviated PCW. For an analysis of the titles and epithets see David T. Runia, "Philonic Nomenclature," *SPhAn* 6 (1994) 1-27.

5. Jerome, *Jov.* 2.14; *Epist.* 29.7.1; Augustine, *Faust.* 12.39; Cassiodorus, *Inst. Div. Litt.* (PL 70:1117B); Armenian translator, *Praef. In libr. Philonis De prov.* vii; John of Damascus, *Prol. in Sac. Par.* (PG 95:1040B); and the Armenian translator of Eusebius, *Chron.* p. 213. Cf. also Eusebius, *Praep. ev.* 13.18.12.

6. Pseudo-Justin, *Cohortatio ad Gentiles* 9.2; 13.4; Pseudo-Chrysostom, *In sanctum Pascha sermo* 7.2; and the *Chronicon Paschale* (PG 92:69A).

7. Anastasius Sinaita, *Viae dux* 13.10.1; Anastasius incertus, *In hexaemeron* 7 (PG 89:961); Anonymous, *Exegesis Psalmorum* 29.1; *Souda*, s.v. Ἀβραάμ.

8. Isidore of Pelusium, *Ep.* 3.19; Arethas, *Comm. in Apoc.* 1 (PG 106:504).

9. For the references, see the discussion under "An Eclectic Thinker" below.

10. This is an *opinio communis*. The most important works that have pointed out Philo's

a philosopher in the same way that Philodemus (ca. 110-40/35 B.C.E.) was in the Epicurean tradition, or Eudorus (*fl.* ca. 25 B.C.E.) was in the Platonic tradition, or Seneca (ca. 4 B.C.E./1 C.E.–65 C.E.) and Epictetus (ca. 50–second century C.E.) were in the Stoic tradition. Philosophy did, however, matter to him. It is impossible to read his works without some understanding of his relationship to Hellenistic philosophical traditions. This essay attempts to sketch some of the most important aspects of the larger concerns that someone must keep in mind when reading Philo.

Philo's Predecessors

Philo's accomplishment was not singular: previous generations of Jews in Alexandria had learned to use Hellenistic philosophy to explain their Scriptures. He inherited their insights and expanded them. While he may have been without peer in the execution of his work, he could not have accomplished what he did without earlier colleagues.[11]

Aristobulus

The first known Jewish author to use Hellenistic philosophy was the second-century B.C.E. exegete Aristobulus.[12] Unfortunately, we only have five frag-

---

fundamental task as an exegete are Valentin Nikiprowetzky, *Le Commentarie de l'écriture chez Philon d'Alexandrie* (ALGHJ 11; Leiden: Brill, 1977); and Peder Borgen, *Philo of Alexandria: An Exegete for His Time* (NovTSup 86; Leiden: Brill, 1997). For recent treatments of his work as an exegete, see David Instone Brewer, *Techniques and Assumptions in Jewish Exegesis before 70 C.E.* (TSAJ 30; Tübingen: Mohr Siebeck, 1992) 198-213; Folker Siegert, "Early Jewish Interpretation in a Hellenistic Style," in *Hebrew Bible/Old Testament: The History of Its Interpretation,* vol. 1/1: *Antiquity,* ed. Magne Sæbø (Göttingen: Vandenhoeck & Ruprecht, 1996) 162-88; Adam Kamesar, "Biblical Interpretation in Philo," in *The Cambridge Companion to Philo* (Cambridge: Cambridge University Press, 2009) 65-91; Gregory E. Sterling, "The Interpreter of Moses: Philo of Alexandria and the Biblical Text," in *A Companion to Biblical Interpretation in Early Judaism,* ed. Matthias Henze (Grand Rapids: Eerdmans, 2012) 415-35.

11. On the tradition, see my overview, "Philosophy as the Handmaid of Wisdom: Philosophy in the Exegetical Traditions of Alexandrian Jews," in *Religiöse Philosophie und philosophische Religion der frühen Kaiserzeit,* ed. Rainer Hirsch-Luipold, Herwig Görgemanns, and Michael von Albrecht (STAC 51; Tübingen: Mohr Siebeck, 2009) 67-98.

12. The standard critical edition is Carl R. Holladay, *Fragments from Hellenistic Jewish Authors,* vol. 3: *Aristobulus* (SBLTT 39; SBLPS 13; Atlanta: Scholars, 1995). The work of Nikolaus

ments of his work preserved for us: fragment 1 positions the Passover cosmologically by placing it in the intersection of the sun's vernal equinox and the moon's autumnal equinox; fragments 2 and 4 argue that the anthropomorphisms applied to God in the LXX are allegorical expressions denoting divine qualities; fragment 3 makes the theft-of-philosophy argument, i.e., the Greeks stole philosophy from the Jews; and fragments 4 and 5 explain creation.

Aristobulus was explicit about his point of orientation: "I want to urge you to accept the interpretations according to a philosophical rationale (φυσικῶς) and not to fall into a mythical and all too human frame of reference" (frag. 2). Can we be any more specific about his "philosophical rationale"?[13] According to ancient sources, Aristobulus was associated with the Peripatetic school.[14] There is some evidence for this in the fragments. In frag. 4, Aristobulus cited a pseudo-Orphic poem that drew a distinction between God's being (οὐσία) and power (δύναμις). This is the same distinction drawn in the pseudo-Aristotelian treatise *On the Heavens (De mundo)*. Aristobulus used it to explain how God could be transcendent and yet immanent: God was transcendent in being but immanent in power. The distinction allowed him to explain anthropomorphic expressions in the LXX as expressions of God's power, not God's being (frag. 2).[15] It would, however, be a mistake to consider Aristobulus a Peripatetic or to have exclusive allegiance to Aristotle and his school. Aristobulus also knew and used Stoic concepts such as the definition of philosophy or wisdom (frag. 5.12).[16] He appears to have used what suited his purposes, although the distinction that he drew between the divine being and power suggests that he was comfortable operating within the conceptual framework of Peripatetic thought.

Walter, *Der Thoraausleger Aristobulus: Untersuchungen zu seinen Fragmenten und zu pseudepigraphischen Resten der jüdisch hellenistischen Literatur* (TUGAL 86; Berlin: Akademie, 1964), remains fundamental to the study of Aristobulus.

13. On the meaning of φυσικῶς see Steven DiMattei, "Moses' *Physiologia* and the Meaning and Use of *Physikos* in Philo of Alexandria's Exegetical Method," *SPhAn* 18 (2006) 3-32.

14. Holladay, *Aristobulus,* Test. 2, 4, 8, 8a, 8b, 12, 13, 14, 14a, 15 and frags. 2, 3.

15. Cf. also the statement in frag. 4: "All philosophers acknowledge that it is necessary to hold devout views about God which our school prescribes exceptionally well."

16. See his citation of Aratus in frag. 4.6.

Pseudo-Aristeas

The next known example is the pseudonymous author of *The Letter of Aristeas.*[17] The letter was purportedly written by an official of the Egyptian court; however, his knowledge of Judaism and sympathy for the Jews suggests that Aristeas was a pseudonym for a Jewish writer.[18] While the date of the letter is not certain, it was probably composed in the later part of the second century B.C.E.[19] The letter relates the legend of the translation of the Hebrew Scriptures into Greek so that they could be included in the Alexandrian library.

The philosophical orientation of the letter is evident in Demetrius of Phalerum's (the head of the Alexandrian library) explanation of why the Jewish Scriptures should be included in the library. He wrote to Ptolemy II Philadelphus: "These writings must also be included in your library in an accurate version because the legislation is very philosophical (φιλοσοφωτέρον) and authentic, since it is divine" (*Let. Aris.* 31). The philosophical orientation of the Jewish people and Scriptures are highlighted in two ways. The first takes place when Aristeas quotes Eleazar's (the Jewish high priest) explanations of the Jewish laws: "For in general everything is similarly constituted in relation to philosophical reasoning (πρὸς φυσικὸν λόγον)" (*Let. Aris.* 143). Aristeas ended his preface to the laws with the statement to his brother, the ostensible recipient of the letter: "I have been led by your love of learning, Philocrates, to set out clearly for you the solemnity and philosophical mindset of the law (φυσικὴν διάνοιαν τοῦ νόμου)" (*Let. Aris.* 171). Eleazar unpacked the philosophical orientation of the laws through allegorical explanations. So, for example, "parting the hoof" denotes the ability to discriminate between good and evil, while "chewing the cud" signifies memory. Interestingly, Philo knew the same traditions.[20] The second indicator of the philosophical orientation of Pseudo-Aristeas occurs in a series

17. I have used the edition of André Pelletier, *Lettre d'Aristée à Philocrate* (SC 89; Paris: Cerf, 1962).

18. The name Aristeas appears three times in the text: *Let. Aris.* 18, 40, 43.

19. The two termini are Ptolemy II Philadelphus (285-247 B.C.E.) and Josephus, who cited the work at the end of the first century C.E. in *Ant.* 12.11-118. On Josephus's use of *The Letter of Aristeas*, see André Pelletier, *Flavius Josèphe, adaptateur de la Lettre d'Aristée: Une reaction atticisante contre la* Koiné (Paris: Kincksieck, 1962). The most helpful discussions of the date are Moses Hadas, ed. and trans, *Aristeas to Philocrates* (New York: Ktav, 1973) 18-53; Albert-Marie Denis, *Introduction à la littérature religieuse Judéo-Hellénistique: Pseudépigraphes de l'Ancient Testament* (2 vols.; Turnhout: Brepols, 2000) 2:935-41.

20. Cf. *Let. Aris.* 150-52 and Philo, *Agr.* 131-45; *Spec.* 4.106-9, esp. 108, for "parting the hoof" and *Let. Aris.* 153-60 and Philo, *Agr.* 131-45; *Spec.* 4.106-9 for "chewing the cud." Both draw from Lev 11:1-8; Deut 14:4-8.

of symposia that the king held over a period of seven days for the Jewish translators who came to Egypt. The Jewish sages engaged in exchanges with the king — each translator responded to a question during the symposia. The narrator could not resist making the point of the translators' role in the symposia explicit: "they (the Jewish translators) were far more advanced than the philosophers (in Ptolemy's court) since they took their starting point from God" (*Let. Aris.* 235). While this has a different nuance than Aristobulus's theft-of-philosophy argument, the spirit is the same: the Jewish philosophy is superior.

The Allegorists

These are the only two independent documents that precede Philo and have significant philosophical elements. They do not, however, represent his only predecessors. Philo frequently referred both to a group of allegorical exegetes[21] and to a group of literalists.[22] While his heart lay with the former, he insisted on the value of both perspectives. In a famous description of the allegorists, he wrote: "There are some who, understanding the literal laws as symbols of intelligible realities, are extremely scrupulous about the latter but carelessly neglect the former whom I fault for their neglect" (*Migr.* 89). He concluded his description with a comparison of the Scriptures to a human being — a formulation that anticipated the more famous statements of Clement and Origen several centuries later: "it is necessary to consider these things (the literal meanings) to be like a body, and the deeper sense like the soul. Therefore, just as it is necessary to provide for the body since it is the house of the soul, so it is necessary to take care of the literal laws" (*Migr.* 93).[23] While some have attempted to identify the allegorists with a specific group,[24] it is preferable to leave them anonymous just as Philo did.

There is another line of evidence that confirms the presence of other interpreters. If "consistency is the hobgoblin of little minds" — as Emerson

21. David M. Hay, "Philo's References to Other Allegorists," *SPhilo* 6 (1979-80) 41-75, collected seventy-four references in the Philonic corpus.

22. Montgomery J. Shroyer, "Alexandrian Jewish Literalists," *JBL* 55 (1936) 261-84; David M. Hay, "References to Other Exegetes," in *Both Literal and Allegorical: Studies in Philo of Alexandria's Questions and Answers on Genesis and Exodus* (BJS 232; Atlanta: Scholars, 1991) 81-97.

23. Cf. Clement, *Strom.* 6.132.3; Origen, *Princ.* 4.2.4.

24. E.g., Joan E. Taylor, *Jewish Women Philosophers of First-Century Alexandria: Philo's "Therapeutae" Reconsidered* (Oxford: Oxford University Press, 2003) 126-53, identified them with the Therapeutae.

suggested[25] — Philo was a genius. Anyone who has read his commentaries has encountered inconsistencies within them. While numerous factors contributed to the presence of tensions within his writings — especially the constraints of the biblical text on which he was commenting — one factor was Philo's preservation of earlier interpretations.[26] The most famous example of this is the presence of two lines that demarcate the intelligible world from the sense-perceptible world in the interpretation of Genesis 1 and 2. Philo first argued that the use of the cardinal number "one" in "day one" versus the ordinal numbers used in the "second" through the "sixth" days signaled the divide between the two (*Opif.* 15-35, esp. 15-16, 35). Later when he came to Genesis 2, he appears to have made the two creation accounts the divide (*Opif.* 129-30). How do we explain this? While there are multiple possibilities, the best explanation in my judgment is that there were multiple Platonizing interpreters who had found two different lines of demarcation between the two worlds.[27] Philo incorporated both since his concern was the metaphysical dependence of the sense-perceptible world on the intelligible world, not the specifics of where the line between the two worlds was drawn.

Summary

The recognition that Philo stood within a line of philosophically oriented interpreters — and some not philosophically inclined — requires us to

---

25. Ralph Waldo Emerson, *Essays,* first series: *Self-Reliance* (Boston: Munroe, 1841): "A foolish consistency is the hobgoblin of little minds, adored by little statesmen and philosophers and divines."

26. This insight was the basis for the establishment of the Philo Institute and the launching of the *SPhilo*. See Robert G. Hamerton-Kelly, "Sources and Traditions in Philo Judaeus: Prolegomena to an Analysis of His Writings," *SPhilo* 1 (1972) 3-26; Burton L. Mack, "Exegetical Traditions in Alexandrian Judaism: A Program for the Analysis of the Philonic Corpus," *SPhilo* 3 (1974-75) 71-112; "Philo Judaeus and Exegetical Traditions in Alexandria," in *ANRW* 2.21.1 (1984) 227-71. Unfortunately, the project never materialized. The most important publication along the lines envisioned by the original founders of the Philo Institute is Thomas H. Tobin, *The Creation of Man: Philo and the History of Interpretation* (CBQMS 14; Washington: Catholic Biblical Association of America, 1983).

27. See the treatment of Tobin, *The Creation of Man,* 123-24, for the view above. David T. Runia, *Philo of Alexandria and the* Timaeus *of Plato* (Philosophia antiqua 44; Leiden: Brill, 1986) 556-58; *Philo of Alexandria: On the Creation of the Cosmos according to Moses: Introduction, Translation and Commentary* (PACS 1; Leiden: Brill, 2001) 19-20, offers a critique with other possibilities.

think of his work within a tradition rather than as a singular expression. Philo did not write his massive corpus de novo, but as an heir to a tradition. Nor was he alone. He had a roughly contemporary figure who wrote under the pseudonym of Solomon who also worked within the framework of Stoicism and, more especially, Platonism to think through the Jewish faith.[28] Unfortunately, we cannot sketch the contours of this tradition with confidence. There have been notable attempts to do so. Thomas Tobin gathered the traditions about the creation of humanity together and posited a genealogical tree that connected specific exegetical forms and positions within a group of texts to larger philosophical traditions in an effort to sketch the evolution of Philo's predecessors.[29] While the associations of texts with specific philosophical traditions is clear, the genealogical character of his scheme has been less widely embraced. Richard Goulet argued in the opposite direction: he contended that Philo corrupted an earlier, magisterial commentary on the entire Pentateuch; however, it is not possible — in my judgment — to identify a single strand of sustained commentary within Philo.[30] More recently, Maren Niehoff has attempted to reconstruct the evolution of Jewish exegesis against the background of the Homeric scholia by assessing its acceptance or rejection of Alexandrian scholarship, although her reconstruction makes several assumptions that I am not willing to make.[31] In spite of the limited nature of our knowledge of the development of the tradition, the presence of the tradition and its importance for Philo should not be minimized.

---

28. On the Wisdom of Solomon, see Chrysostome Larcher, *Études sur le Livre de la Sagasse* (EBib; Paris: Gabalda, 1969); James M. Reese, *Hellenistic Influence on the Book of Wisdom and Its Consequences* (AnBib 41; Rome: Biblical Institute Press, 1970); David Winston, *The Wisdom of Solomon* (AB 43; Garden City: Doubleday, 1979); Hans Hübner, *Die Weisheit Salomos im Horizont biblischer Theologie* (Biblisch-theologische Studien 22; Neukirchen-Vluyn: Neukirchener, 1993) 55-81; John J. Collins, *Jewish Wisdom in the Hellenistic Age* (OTL; Louisville: Westminster John Knox, 1997) 196-232.

29. Tobin, *The Creation of Man*.

30. Richard Goulet, *La philosophie de Moïse: Essai de reconstitution d'un commentaire philosophique préphilonien de Pentateuque* (Histoire des doctrines de l'Antiquité classique 11; Paris: Vrin, 1987). For a critique, see David T. Runia, review of *La philosophie de Moïse*, *JTS* 40 (1989) 590-602.

31. Maren Ruth Niehoff, *Jewish Exegesis and Homeric Scholarship in Alexandria* (Cambridge: Cambridge University Press, 2011). For a critique, see my review, *JECS* 21 (2013) 139-40.

An Eclectic Thinker

There is another factor that also contributes to our difficulty in forming a clear assessment of Philo's use of philosophy. Like many Hellenistic and early Roman thinkers, Philo was eclectic in his use of philosophy. I do not mean that he was intellectually indiscriminate and randomly drew from one school of thought and then another as it struck his fancy; rather, he drew what he considered to be the best from each tradition and incorporated it into his own thought.[32] This means that he did not treat all philosophical traditions as equals, but measured them against his own understanding of reality and incorporated them appropriately.[33]

Platonism

The most important philosophical tradition for Philo was Platonism. This was not an option for his predecessors until the rise of Middle Platonsim (80 B.C.E.–220 C.E.) in the first part of the first century B.C.E.[34] Antiochus of Ascalon (b. ca. 130 B.C.E.) broke with the skeptical mindset of the New Academy (267-80 B.C.E.) and turned back to a more dogmatic reading of select Platonic treatises with much the same spirit that had characterized the Old Academy (347-267). However, he did more than turn to the past: he incorporated Aristotle and the Peripatetics back into the tradition and claimed the Stoics as heirs of the Old Academy.[35] The result was that Middle Pla-

---

32. John M. Dillon and Anthony A. Long, eds., *The Question of "Eclecticism": Studies in Later Greek Philosophy* (Hellenistic Culture and Society 3; Berkeley: University of California Press, 1988), esp. the editors' introduction on pp. 1-13.

33. There is a great deal of literature on the relationship between Philo and philosophy. Two of the more important recent works are the essays in a special section of the *SPhAn* 5 (1993): Gregory E. Sterling, "Platonizing Moses: Philo and Middle Platonism," 96-111; David T. Runia, "Was Philo a Middle Platonist? A Difficult Question Revisited," 112-40; David Winston, "Response to Runia and Sterling," 141-46; Thomas H. Tobin, "Was Philo a Middle Platonist? Some Suggestions," 147-50; John Dillon, "A Response to Runia and Sterling," 151-55, as well as the more recent and helpful collection of Francesca Alesse, ed., *Philo of Alexandria and Post-Aristotelian Philosophy* (Studies in Philo of Alexandria 5; Leiden: Brill, 2008).

34. The standard treatment is John M. Dillon, *The Middle Platonists, 80 B.C. to A.D. 220* (rev. ed.; Ithaca: Cornell University Press, 1996).

35. For a detailed treatment of Antiochus, see John Glucker, *Antiochus and the Late Academy* (Hypomnemata 56; Göttingen: Vandenhoeck & Ruprecht, 1978). See also David Sedley, ed., *The Philosophy of Antiochus* (Cambridge: Cambridge University Press, 2012).

tonism was heavily influenced by both the Peripatetics and the Stoics. One of the key figures of the new movement worked in Alexandria: Eudorus (*fl.* ca. 25 B.C.E.).[36] Eudorus, like other Middle Platonists, elevated the first principle in Plato to a position of transcendence. In order to bridge the gap between the first principle and humanity, Eudorus and other Middle Platonists posited an intermediary figure. Plato had already posited a second principle, although he called the second principle by various names: the Good in *Republic* 6, the One in the *Parmenides,* the Demiurge or World Soul in the *Timaeus,* and the principles of the unlimited or indeterminate potentiality and limit or precise numbers in the *Philebus.* Middle Platonists drew from Plato's precedent and developed the second principle. They called the second principle "the Idea,"[37] "the heavenly Mind,"[38] "the demiurgic God,"[39] and the "Logos."[40] The goal of humanity according to Eudorus was to be like God.[41]

It is not hard to see why Philo and his immediate Jewish predecessors or contemporary Jewish colleagues found Middle Platonism attractive: the transcendence of God and the dependence of the visible world on the unseen world aligned with their basic Jewish theology. Philo referred to Plato by name eleven times as he introduced a reference to a statement of the Athenian (*Opif.* 119, 133; *Prob.* 13; *Contempl.* 57; *Aet.* 13, 14, 16, 27, 38, 52, 141). In one case, he referred to him as "the most sacred Plato" (κατὰ τὸν ἱερώτατον Πλάτωνα; *Prob.* 13)[42] and in another as "the great Plato" (*Aet.* 52). He cited or paraphrased Plato in the following places:

Plato	Philo
Erx. 397	*Plant.* 171
Menex. 238a	*Opif.* 133
Phaedr. 60b-c	*Ebr.* 8; *QG* 4.159
Phaedr. 245a	*Prov.* 2.43

36. For a recent treatment see Mauro Bonazzi, "Towards Transcendence: Philo and the Renewal of Platonism in the Early Imperial Age," in Alesse, *Philo of Alexandria and Post-Aristotelian Philosophy,* 233-51.

37. Timaeus of Locri, *On the Nature of the World and the Soul* 7.

38. Alcinous, *Didaskalikos* 10.3.

39. Numenius, frag. 12 ll. 1-3.

40. Antiochus of Ascalon (in Cicero, *Acad. post.* 28-29); Eudorus (if Philo was influenced by him); Plutarch, *Mor.* 369, who limited the role of the Logos to the immanent relationship between the Logos and humanity but not the transcendent relationship between the Logos and the first principle.

41. Based on Plato, *Theaet.* 176a-b.

42. This is the reading of M. Other mss read λιγύρωτατον ("most clear-toned").

Phaedr. 246e	*QG* 3.3
Phaedr. 247a	*Spec.* 2.249; *Prob.* 13; cf. also *Leg.* 1.61; 3.7;
	Fug. 62, 74
Phaedr. 259c	*Prob.* 8; *Contempl.* 35
Resp. 473c-d	*Mos.* 2.2
Soph. 226e	*Migr.* 220
Theaet. 176a-b	*Fug.* 63
Theaet. 176b-c	*Fug.* 82
Theaet. 191c-d	*Her.* 181
Tim. 22b-23c	*Aet.* 146-49
Tim. 24e, 25c-d	*Aet.* 141
Tim. 28b-c	*Prov.* 1.21
Tim. 28c	*Opif.* 21
Tim. 29a	*Plant.* 131
Tim. 29b	*Prov.* 1.21
Tim. 29e	*Opif.* 21; *QG* 1.6
Tim. 32c-33b	*Aet.* 25-26
Tim. 33c-d	*Aet.* 38
Tim. 35b	*Num.* (frag.)
Tim. 37e, 39c	*Aet.* 52; see also *Spec.* 1.90
Tim. 38b	*Prov.* 1.20
Tim. 41a-b	*Aet.* 13
Tim. 75d-e	*Opif.* 119; *QE* 2.118
Tim. 90a	*Plant.* 17

Philo appears to have cited ca. twenty-seven Platonic texts, drawn from eight of the Athenian's works.[43] This, however, hardly exhausts Philo's indebtedness to Plato. He drew extensively from select treatises without citing them directly. As the above list of citations suggests but does not capture, Philo was heavily indebted to Plato's *Timaeus* for his account of creation;[44] he re-

43. On Philo's citations of Plato, see David T. Runia, "The Text of the Platonic Citations in Philo of Alexandria," in *Studies in Plato and the Platonic Tradition: Essays Presented to John Whittaker,* ed. Mark Joyal (Aldershot: Hampshire; Brookfield: Ashgate, 1997) 261-91. I have included the references in the Armenian texts as well as several others that lack explicit introductory phrases but contain clear citations. I have dropped some of the texts listed in Runia, which he also considers problematic, e.g., Plato, *Tim.* 49a, 50d, 51a, 52d, 88d in Philo, *Ebr.* 161. I prefer to think of this as an example of Philo's indebtedness to the basic contents of the *Timaeus.*

44. Philo named the work multiple times: *Aet.* 13, 25, 141. For an analysis of Philo's use of

peatedly drew from the *Phaedrus,* especially the myth of the charioteer;[45] he followed the lead of Eudorus in making the statement in the *Theaetetus* ("likeness to God") the goal of philosophy;[46] and explicitly referred to the *Symposium* in *On the Contemplative Life.*[47] He probably knew basic handbooks such as we later find in Alcinous's *Didaskalikos.* There can be little doubt that Philo knew Platonic philosophy and had not only read but also digested some of Plato's treatises.

His knowledge of Plato's thought and sympathy with it did not make him a Platonist in the sense that he belonged to the Platonic *hairesis.*[48] However, Platonism — as it was formulated by Middle Platonists — did exercise a profound influence on Philo. As we have already seen, he understood the cosmos via the Platonic divide between the intelligible world and the sense-perceptible world. This divide shaped his understanding not only of reality but also of the way in which reality is grasped. Like Plato, he privileged sight as the source for philosophy (Plato, *Tim.* 47a-d; Philo, *Opif.* 54).[49] In short, Philo was Platonic in his metaphysics and epistemology. His basic orientation toward Platonism is why the aphorisms that connected Philo or Philo's understanding of Moses with Plato make good sense. The second-century- C.E. Numenius, who probably knew Philo's works, asked: "What is Plato but Moses speaking in Attic?" (frag. 8).[50] The aphorism first attested in Jerome is more direct: "either Plato philonizes or Philo platonizes" (*Vir. ill.* 11). Jerome went even further in another statement when he called Philo "another or a Jewish Plato" (*Ep.* 70.3.3; cf. also *Ep.* 22.35.8). Isidore of Pelusium thought that

---

the *Timaeus,* see Runia, *Philo of Alexandria and the* Timaeus *of Plato; Philo of Alexandria: On the Creation of the Cosmos.*

45. See esp. *QG* 3.3; *Leg.* 2.99-104; *Agr.* 67-94. For detailed treatments of Philo's use of the Platonic myth, see Anita Méasson, *Du char ailé de Zeus à l'Arche d'Alliance: Images et mythes platoniciens chez Philon d'Alexandrie* (Paris: Études Augustiniennes, 1986); Elisabetta Villari, *Il morso e il cavaliere: Una metafora della termperanza e del dominio di sé* (Genova: Il melangolo, 2001).

46. Plato, *Theaet.* 176a-b in Philo, *Fug.* 63. See also *Spec.* 4.188. Philo followed the lead of Eudorus. See Dillon, *The Middle Platonists,* 145-46.

47. See Philo, *Contempl.* 57-63, esp. 57 and 59, where he mentions Plato's account of the famous symposium explicitly.

48. On the concept of a *hairesis,* see David T. Runia, "Philo of Alexandria and the Greek *Hairesis*-model," *VC* 53 (1999) 117-47.

49. On Philo's use of the Platonic privilege of sight, see Runia, *Philo of Alexandria and the* Timaeus *of Plato,* 270-76. See also "Philo and Hellenistic Doxography," in Alesse, *Philo of Alexandria and Post-Aristotelian Philosophy,* 22-24.

50. Édouard des Places, *Numénius Fragments: Texte établi et traduit* (Collection des universités de France; Paris: Les Belles Lettres, 1973)=Eusebius, *Praep. ev.* 11.10.14.

Philo was either "a student or an instructor of Plato" (*Ep.* 3.81). All of these early Christians were right in recognizing the strong connection between Plato and Philo, even if they overstated it: Philo devoted his life to understanding Moses, but he understood Moses through the lens of Platonism.

Stoicism

When Antiochus broke with his teacher, Philo of Larissa (159/158-84/83 B.C.E.), and returned to the dogmatic approach of the Old Academy, he made room for the Stoics as heirs of the Old Academy. The result was that Middle Platonism became Stoicized Platonism. While there are serious and significant differences between the two on metaphysical and epistemological grounds, Stoic ethics and categories heavily influenced Middle Platonists.[51]

Philo was no exception. He referred to the Stoics throughout *On the Eternity of the World* (*Aet.* 4, 8, 18, 54, 78, 102); mentioned the Stoa twice (*Aet.* 8, 89); labeled concepts Stoic twice (*Post.* 133; *Aet.* 76); and referred to a number of Stoic philosophers by name, including Zeno (335-263 B.C.E.; *Prob.* 53, 57, 97, 160),[52] Cleanthes (331-232; *Aet.* 90), Chrysippus (ca. 280-207; *Aet.* 48, 90, 94), Diogenes of Babylon (240-152; *Aet.* 77), Boethus of Sidon (*fl.* 2nd century B.C.E.; *Aet.* 76, 78), and Panaetius (ca. 185-109; *Aet.* 76). He also knew the more radical wing of this post-Socratic movement: the Cynics. He mentioned Diogenes (*Plant.* 151; *Prob.* 121-24; 157) and the Cynics as a group (*Plant.* 151). The latter were not, however, important figures for him. The Stoics were far more important: he included Stoic views throughout his writings. It is well known that we lack any full works for the Stoics prior to the so-called Late Stoa or the works of Seneca (4 B.C.E./1 C.E.–65 C.E.), Musonius Rufus (before 30-before 101/102 C.E.), Epictetus (mid-first century–mid-second century C.E.), and Marcus Aurelius (121-80 C.E.). We have only fragments for the Early and Middle periods. Philo is a significant witness to the views of the Stoa. There are only three authors whom Ioannes von Arnim cited more frequently than Philo when he compiled *Stoicorum veterum fragmenta*: Cicero, Galen, and Plutarch.[53] He cited Philo 198 times, slightly more than he cited the fifth-century C.E. anthology of Stobaeus! Von Arnim's use of Philo has been criticized in recent

---

51. See Dillon, *The Middle Platonists*, p. 52 and passim.

52. The last two texts use the adjectival form of the name.

53. Hans Friedrich August von Arnim, *Stoicorum veterum fragmenta* (4 vols.; Leipzig: Teubner, 1903-24).

years: von Arnim would have done better to draw more heavily from Cicero and Seneca and less from Philo. Certainly, more recent works have drawn less on Philo. For example, Anthony A. Long and David N. Sedley in *The Hellenistic Philosophers* only cite Philo ten times, and seven of these deal with Stoic physics.[54] While it is fair to argue that von Arnim was too generous in his use of Philo, it is a mistake to dismiss him entirely. The fact that von Arnim could draw on Philo so extensively for the reconstruction of the Early Stoa indicates the significant influence that the Stoa had on Philo, whether Philo preserved the views of the early Stoa as accurately as others or not.

Philo's relationship with Stoicism was complex. He knew and used Stoic categories, but this was almost unavoidable for those who drew on philosophy in the period. He was most influenced by Stoic thought in his ethics and in his psychology. This does not mean that Philo adapted Stoic ethics or understanding of the human being wholesale: Philo did not share some of the basic metaphysical/ontological presuppositions upon which Stoic ethics and psychology were constructed as systems. The differences, however, did not keep Philo from using Stoic categories when they suited his exegetical needs or contributed to his own moral or psychological thought. It is not responsible to read Philo without noting his use or adaptation of Stoic thought.[55]

Aristotle and the Peripatetics

Another group that the Middle Platonists made some effort to reincorporate was Plato's most famous pupil and his followers.[56] Philo certainly knew the

---

54. Anthony A. Long and David N. Sedley, *The Hellenistic Philosophers* (2 vols.; Cambridge: Cambridge University Press, 1987). The seven that deal with Stoic physics are 46M, 46P, 47R, 47P, 47Q, 52A, 53P. The other three are 28P, 59H, and 67N. For a critique of von Arnim see Anthony A. Long, "Philo on Stoic Physics," in Alesse, *Philo of Alexandria ad Post-Aristotelian Philosophy,* 121-40.

55. For some excellent treatments of the complexity of Philo and Stoic thought, see the relevant essays in Alesse, *Philo of Alexandria and Post-Aristotelian Philosophy:* Long, "Philo on Stoic Physics," 121-40, a rather severe critique of von Arnim; Roberto Radice, "Philo and Stoic Ethics: Reflections on the Idea of Freedom," 141-68, who provides some excellent coverage on ethics; Gretchen Reydams-Schils, "Philo of Alexandria on Stoic and Platonist Psycho-Physiology: The Socratic Higher Ground," 169-95, who covers the psychological dimensions in a sophisticated and informative study; Margaret Graver, "Philo of Alexandria and the Origins of the Stoic ΠΡΟΠΑΘΕΙΑΙ," 197-221, who contributes to the moral dimension.

56. Dillon, *The Middle Platonists,* 51, points out the importance of the Peripatetics for Middle Platonists.

school and some of the basic tenets. In his doxographical treatment of views given in *On the Eternity of the World,* he mentioned Aristotle (384-322 B.C.E.) by name four times (*Aet.* 10, 12, 16, 18), Theophrastus (372-71 or 371/370-288/287 or 287/286) once (*Aet.* 117-19), and Critolaus (*fl.* 2nd century B.C.E.) three times (*Aet.* 55-75, esp. 55, 70, 74). There is little controversy whether Philo knew some of the works of the Stagirite and his students. The extent to which Peripatetic thought influenced Philo is more open to debate.[57] There are some striking features that touch on central tenets to Philo, including an understanding of God as the highest or first cause (*Conf.* 123-24).[58] As was true for Aristobulus, the most striking agreements are in the pseudo-Aristotelian piece mentioned above, *De mundo.*[59] Philo may have drawn from Aristotelian traditions to draw the distinction between God's being and God's power that is so important in his own thought.

Neopythagoreans

Other groups also had significant influence on Philo. One of the most important was the Neopythagoreans. The Pythagorean tradition is known in the early period through several sources; however, in the Hellenistic world, our only real sources of information are the pseudonymous Pythagorean letters.[60] The movement reemerges in the first century B.C.E. and first century C.E., when a number of identifiable figures appear: Nigidius Figulus (d. 45 B.C.E.), Apollonius of Tyana (*fl.* first century C.E.), Moderatus of Gades (ca. 50-100), and Nicomachus of Gerasa (*fl.* ca. 100). The Neopythagoreans

---

57. The most important advocate of Aristotle's influence is Abraham P. Bos, "Philo of Alexandria: A Platonist in the Image and Likeness of Aristotle," *SPhAn* 10 (1998) 66-86. Carlos Lévy, "L'aristotélisme, parent pauvre de la pensée philonienne?" in *Plato, Aristotle, or Both? Dialogues between Platonism and Aristoteliansim in Antiquity,* ed. Thomas Bénatouïl, Emanuele Maffi, and Franco Trabattoni (Hildesheim: Olms, 2011) 17-33, provides a more balanced assessment.

58. See Pierre Boyancé, "Le Dieu très haut chez Philon," in *Mélanges d'historie des religions offerts à Henri-Charles Puech* (Paris: Presse universitaires de France, 1974) 139-49.

59. The most important treatment is Roberto Radice, *La filosofia di Aristobulo e i suoi nessi con il De Mundo attribuito ad Aristotele* (Pubblicazioni del Centro di Ricerche di Metfisica: Collana Temi metafisici e problem del pensiuero antico. Studi e Testi 33; Milan: Via e pensiere, 1994). See also Bos, "Philo of Alexandria," 74-75.

60. On this material, see Holger Thesleff, *An Introduction to the Pythagorean Writings of the Hellenistic Period* (Åbo: Åbo Akademi, 1961); *The Pythagorean Texts of the Hellenistic Period* (Åbo: Åbo Akademi, 1965).

were widely known for their views on the transmigration of the soul (metempsychosis), their arithmologies, and their community life.

Philo mentioned that he had read the treatise of Ocellus, *On the Nature of the Universe*. Iamblichus later identified Ocellus as a Pythagorean (*VP* 36), but the treatise that Philo read was probably a pseudonymous second-century B.C.E. work (*Aet.* 12). He referred to the Pythagoreans as a group at least eight times in his corpus[61] and cited Philolaus (ca. 470-390 B.C.E.), the first Pythagorean to write a book, once (*Opif.* 100). We have already noted above that Eusebius praised Philo's zeal for the Platonic and Pythagorean ways of life (*Hist. eccl.* 2.4.3). Philo's affinities for things Pythagorean were evident enough to Clement of Alexandria (*Strom.* 1.72.4; 2.100.3) and the later ecclesiastical historian Sozomen (*Hist. eccl.* 1.12.9) that they called Philo a Pythagorean.

What was the basis for this identification? The most obvious connection between Philo and the Neopythagoreans is his use of arithmologies. Philo shared the Neopythagorean conviction that numbers reflected the order in the cosmos and drew from this tradition.[62] Anyone who has read his long excursus on the number seven in *De opificio mundi* knows how fascinated he was by numbers and the order they represent.[63] He also knew the same type of literary tradition that Iamblichus later preserved in which a religious-philosophical group was held out as a moral ideal, i.e., in the case of Iamblichus the Neopythagorean communities (*VP* 96-100). Philo held the Essenes (*Prob.* 75-91; *Hypoth.* 8.11.1-18 [in Eusebius *Praep ev.* 8.11.1-18])[64] and Therapeutae *(Contempl.)* out as Jewish exemplars. The presence of numerous such examples — Philo mentioned the Gymnosophists in his writings (*Somn.* 2.556; *Abr.* 182; *Prob.* 43, 74, 93-96)[65] — indicates that it would be a mistake

---

61. Philo used Πυθαγόρειος seven times (*Opif.* 100; *Leg.* 1.14; *Prob.* 2; *Aet.* 12; *QG* 1.17b; 2.12a; 4.8b) and Πυθαγορικός once (*QG* 3.49a).

62. E.g., *Opif.* 89-128; *Leg.* 1.8-15. On Philo's arithmology, see Horst Moehring, "Arithmology as an Exegetical Tool in the Writings of Philo of Alexandria," in *The School of Moses: Studies in Philo and Hellenistic Religion in Memory of Horst R. Moehring,* ed. John Peter Kenney (BJS 304; SPhilo Monograph 1; Atlanta: Scholars, 1987) 141-76.

63. For a detailed treatment, see David T. Runia, "Philo's Longest Arithmological Passage: *De opificio mundi* 89-128," in *De Jérusalem à Rome: Mélanges offerts à Jean Riaud,* ed. Lucian-Jean Bord and David Hamidovic (Paris: Guethner, 2000) 155-74; *Philo of Alexandria: On the Creation of the Cosmos,* 260-308.

64. Philo wrote a third account that has been lost, but was likely a full treatise. See *Contempl.* 1.

65. The last text mentions the famous Calanus. On the Gymnosophists, see also Philostratus, *Vit. Apoll.* 6.6.

to narrow his portraits of the Essenes and Therapeutae to Pythagorean influence.[66]

It is also important to recognize that the line between the Platonic and the Pythagorean tradition was not entirely clear. This is due, in part, to the fact that the philosophers themselves blurred the line. For example, Moderatus argued that Plato's metaphysics were derived from Pythagorean teaching. Later Neoplatonists such as Porphyry and his student Iamblichus each wrote a *Life of Pythagorus*. The result is that it is not always easy to make clear distinctions; e.g., scholars debate whether to consider the second-century c.e. philosopher Numenius a Pythagorean or a Middle Platonist.[67] There is little doubt that Philo was influenced by Neopythagorean thought, but the complexities of its relationship with the Platonic tradition should be kept in mind.

Other Influential Philosophers

There were others who also exercised an influence on Philo. Philo certainly knew who Socrates was and held him in enough esteem that he once compared him to Terah, the father of Abraham (*Somn.* 1.58).[68] One of the authors whom Philo mentions most frequently by name and whom he cites the most is the pre-Socratic philosopher Heraclitus. He mentioned him by name six times.[69] He was even more expansive in his use of Heraclitus. The following chart represents occasions when Philo appears to be drawing from Heraclitus.[70]

---

66. This connection was noted by A. J. Festugière, "Sur une nouvelle édition du 'De Vita Pythagorica' de Jamblique," *REG* 50 (1937) 476-78. For a broader assessment, see Gregory E. Sterling, "'Athletes of Virtue': An Analysis of the Summaries in Acts (2:41-47; 4:32-35; 5:12-16)," *JBL* 113 (1994) 679-96, esp. 688-96.

67. Dillon, *The Middle Platonists*, 378, called the form of philosophy he represents "Pythagorizing Platonism."

68. See also *Deus* 146, 147; *Plant.* 65; *Somn.* 1.55-58; *Contempl.* 57; *Prov.* 2.21 for references to Socrates.

69. Philo used the proper name five times (*Leg.* 1.108; *Her.* 214; *Aet.* 111; *Prov.* 2.67; *QG* 2.5a) and the adjective once (*Leg.* 3.7).

70. The following is based on the index in Miroslav Marcovich, *Heraclitus: Greek Text with a Short Commentary* (Mérida: Los Andes University Press, 1967) 646. I have only considered texts that Marcovich printed as witnesses to the fragments. He has additional references to parallels or allusions. There is now a full study of the relationship between Philo and Heraclitus: see Lucia Saudelli, *Eraclito ad Alessandria: Studi e ricerche instorno all a testimonianza di Filone* (Monothéismes et Philosophie 16; Turnhout: Brepols, 2012).

Heraclitus	Philo
Frag. 8	*Fug.* 179; *Mut.* 60; *Somn.* 1.6; *Spec.* 4.51; *QG* 4.1
Frag. 26	*Leg.* 3.7; *Spec.* 1.208
Frag. 33	*Somn.* 1.153-56; *Mos.* 1.31; *Aet.* 109-10
Frag. 35	*Her.* 208-14; cf. also *QG* 3.5
Frag. 36	*Spec. leg,* 1.148
Frag. 47	*Leg.* 1.107-8; *Fug.* 55; *QG* 4.152
Frag. 54	*Leg.* 3.7; *Aet.* 109
Frag. 55	*Leg.* 3.7; *Spec.* 1.208
Frag. 66	*Aet.* 109-11
Frag. 68	*Prov.* 2.66-67
Frag. 76	*Fug.* 61
Frag. 93	*Mos.* 1.31; *Aet.* 42
Frag. 108	*QG* 2.5
Frag. 114	*Spec.* 1.10

The most important point on which he relied on Heraclitus was the concept of the death of the soul.[71] Philo knew about other pre-Socratics such as Anaxagoras (ca. 500-428 B.C.E.),[72] Democritus (born ca. 460/457),[73] Zeno of Elea (*fl.* early fifth century),[74] and Democritus's later adherent Anaxarchus (*fl.* fourth century),[75] but they did not influence his thought in an appreciable way.

Opponents

Philo knew other philosophical groups, including those he opposed. He knew and cited the standard "Tropes for the Suspension of Judgment"

71. See esp. frag. 47. This has received attention in recent years. See Dieter Zeller, "The Life and Death of the Soul in Philo of Alexandria," *SPhAn* 7 (1995) 19-55; Emma Wasserman, *The Death of the Soul in Romans 7* (WUNT ser. 2, 256; Tübingen: Mohr Siebeck, 2008); John T. Conroy Jr., "Philo's 'Death of the Soul': Is This Only a Metaphor?" *SPhAn* 23 (2011) 23-40.

72. *Contempl.* 14 mentions the famous story that he abandoned his farm to pursue the philosophical life. *Aet.* 4 relates the story in which Anaxagoras explained why he spent the night in the open — he wanted to contemplate the heavens.

73. *Contempl.* 14 and 15 mention the famous story about Democritus's decision to leave his farm to pursue philosophy. *Aet.* 8 summarizes his position that there are many worlds.

74. *Prob.* 106-9 relates his heroic death. Cf. also Diogenes Laertius, *Vit. phil.* 9.27.

75. *Prob.* 106-9 relates the heroic death of Anaxarchus. Cf. also Diogenes Laertius, *Vit. phil.* 9.59.

(Τρόποι τῆς ἐποχῆς) formulated by Aenesidemus (*fl.* first century B.C.E.; see *Ebr.* 166-205)[76] and mentioned the Skeptics as a group once (*Congr.* 52), but did not embrace their orientation. He was more open in his criticisms of Epicurus and his school. He mentioned Epicurus (341-270) by name (*Post.* 2; *Aet.* 8), but expressly rejected his views as "impious." So he asked in his critique of anthropomorphic expressions: "For if the Being has a face and someone wants to escape the divine face can easily relocate elsewhere, why should we reject Epicurean godlessness (τὴν Ἐπικούρειον ἀσέβειαν) or the atheism of the Egyptians or the mythical themes of which life is full?" (*Post.* 2). However, his standard target was the sophists. Bruce Winter has made the case based on the references in Philo that the Second Sophistic was in full swing in the first century C.E.[77] However, it is not clear that Philo actually refers to a distinct tradition, but uses sophist as a category for any who place rhetoric over reason. Even if Winter is right, it only indicates that Philo opposed the group.

Summary

It is clear that Philo knew a good deal about Hellenistic philosophy, considerably more than all but a handful of scholars today. How did he learn his philosophy? Unfortunately, we do not know. He may have attended lectures[78] — perhaps he even attended the lectures of Eudorus — or have hired tutors[79] or both. He undoubtedly gained some of it on his own, but must have had assistance. He knew the traditions in various ways. In some cases, he read treatises directly and thought about them carefully, e.g., Plato's *Timaeus*. In other cases he probably studied handbooks that set out the views of a tradition, e.g., equivalents of the later handbook of Alcinous. In still other in-

---

76. See also Sextus Empiricus, *P.* 1.145-63 and Diogenes Laertius, *Vit. phil.* 9.83-84. On Philo's use of Aenesidemus, see the treatments of Karel Janácek, "Philon von Alexandreia und skeptische Tropen," *Eirene* 19 (1982) 83-97; Carlos Lévy, "Deux problèmes doxographicques chez Philon d'Alexandrie: Posidonius et Enésidème," in *Philosophy and Doxography in the Imperial Age*, ed. Aldo Brancacci (Accademia Toscana di scienze e lettere. La Colombaria Studi 228; Florence: Olschki, 2005) 79-102; Runia, "Philo and Hellenistic Doxography," 29-31.

77. Bruce W. Winter, *Philo and Paul among the Sophists: Alexandrian and Corinthian Responses to a Julio-Claudian Movement* (2nd ed.; Grand Rapids: Eerdmans, 2002).

78. So John Dillon, "Preface," in *Philo of Alexandria: The Contemplative Life; The Giants; and Selections*, trans. David Winston (Classics of Western Spirituality; New York: Paulist, 1981) xiii.

79. So Runia, *Philo of Alexandria and the Timaeus of Plato*, 36.

stances, he had access to doxographical sources or collections of varying philosophical views on a topic or selection of topics, e.g., Aëtius's (*fl.* late first century C.E.) *Placita*.[80] What is clear is that he knew Hellenistic philosophy. It is also clear that he subsumed it to a larger purpose. It is to this purpose that we now turn.

The Value of Philosophy

Philo is one of the most prolific authors in Greek whose works have come down to us. We have roughly two-thirds of more than seventy treatises that we know he wrote. His corpus includes three large commentary series plus a significant number of other treatises. The three commentary series are Philonic in origin: Philo wrote each series as a self-standing and unified work.[81] The other treatises lack authorial grouping(s) and are open to modern reconstructions. I prefer to place them in two groups: the apologetic treatises that were largely set around the crisis of 38-41 C.E. and the philosophical treatises.[82] We will take up the role of philosophy in the commentaries and in the philosophical treatises.

The Commentaries

We suggested at the outset of this survey that Philo was primarily an exegete, not a philosopher. This is clear from a cursory glance at his *oeuvre*. He wrote three major commentaries on the Pentateuch: twelve scrolls titled *Questions and Answers on Genesis and Exodus* which have come to us in fragmentary form arranged in six books,[83] the *Allegorical Commentary* which originally

---

80. On Philo's use of the doxographical tradition, see the important essay of Runia, "Philo and Hellenistic Doxography." On the tradition more broadly, see Jaap Mansfeld and David T. Runia, *Aëtiana: The Method and Intellectual Context of a Doxographer* (3 vols.; Philosophia antiqua 73, 114, 118; Leiden: Brill, 1997-2010).

81. See my " 'Prolific in Expression and Broad in Thought': Internal References to Philo's Allegorical Commentary and Exposition of the Law," *Euphrosyne* 40 (2012) 55-76, for a detailed treatment of the two largest series.

82. For discussions of Philo's works, see Jenny Morris, "The Jewish Philosopher Philo," in Emil Schürer, *The History of the Jewish People in the Age of Jesus Christ (175 B.C.–A.D. 135),* rev. and ed. Geza Vermes and Fergus Millar (3 vols.; Edinburgh: T. & T. Clark, 1973-87) 3/2: 819-70; James R. Royse, "The Works of Philo," in Kamesar, *The Cambridge Companion to Philo,* 32-64.

83. The transmission of QG and QE is complicated: we have fragments in Greek (Françoise

had at least thirty-two treatises, of which nineteen have come down to us[84] and a fragment of another,[85] and the *Exposition of the Laws of Moses* for which we have twelve of the original fifteen treatises.[86] This means that fifty-nine of the approximately seventy or more treatises were commentaries. We cannot forget that commenting on Moses' Pentateuch was Philo's life's work.

The three commentary series are different in content, form, and function. They differ in content by scope: the *Questions and Answers* explore Gen 2:4–28:9 and Exod 12:2–28:24, respectively; the *Allegorical Commentary* provides a running commentary on Gen 2:4–18:2 plus some additional material in Genesis; the *Exposition of the Laws* is a systematic explanation of the entire

---

Petit, *Quaestiones in Genesim et in Exodum: Fragmenta graeca* [Les Œuvres de Philon d'Alexandrie 33; Paris: Cerf, 1978], which must be supplemented with James R. Royse, "Further Greek Fragments of Philo's *Quaestiones,*" in *Nourished with Peace: Studies in Hellenistic Judaism in Memory of Samuel Sandmel,* ed. Frederick E. Greenspahn, Earle Hilgert, and Burton L. Mack [Homage Series 9; Chico: Scholars, 1984] 143-53; "Philo's *Quaestiones in Exodum 1.6,*" in Hay, *Both Literal and Allegorical,* 17-27; "Philo of Alexandria *Quaestiones in Exodum 2.62-68:* Critical Edition," *SPhAn* 24 [2012] 1-68); a very partial Latin translation from the fourth century (Françoise Petit, *L'ancienne version latine des Questions sur la Genèse de Philon d'Alexandrie* [2 vols.; TUGAL 113-14; Berlin: Akademie, 1973]); and a rather literal and still partial Armenian translation from the sixth century (J. B. Aucher, *Philonis Judaei paralipomena Armena: Libri videlicet quottuor* In Genesin, *libri duo* In Exodum, *sermo unus* De Sampsone, *alter* De Jona, *tertius* De tribus angelis Abraamo apparentibus [Venice: Lazarus, 1826]). The number of original volumes is disputed, esp. for Exodus. Eusebius says that there were five books in *QE* (*Hist. eccl.* 2.18.5). On the original structure, I have followed the lead of Enzo Lucchesi, "La division en six livres des *Quaestiones in Genesim* de Philon d'Alexandrie," *Mus* 89 (1976) 383-95; James R. Royse, "The Original Structure of Philo's Quaestiones," *SPhilo* 4 (1976-77) 41-78; "Philo's Division of His Works into Books," *SPhAn* 13 (2001) 76-85.

84. *Leg.* 1 (= existing *Leg.* 1-2), 3 (*Leg.* 2 and 4 are missing); *Cher., Sacr., Det., Post., Gig.* and *Deus* (originally one treatise but now two), *Agr., Plant., Ebr.* 1 (2 is missing [see Eusebius, *Hist. Eccl.* 2.18.2 and Philo, *Sobr.* 1]); *Sobr., Conf., Migr., Her., Congr., Fug., Mut., Somn.* 2 and 3 (= our 1 and 2; 1, 4, and 5 are missing). Philo mentioned a number of works that were not preserved (e.g., *Sobr.* 52, mentions a work on Shem; *Mut.* 53 [cf. also Eusebius, *Hist. eccl.* 2.18.3] refers to two scrolls on the covenants; *Her.* 1 suggests that there was once a work on rewards). Still others may be postulated based on lacunae in the series (e.g., Gen 1:1-31 is missing; see Thomas H. Tobin, "The Beginning of Philo's *Legum Allegoriae,*" *SPhAn* 12 [2000] 29-43).

85. *De Deo* is only extant in an Armenian fragment. See Folker Siegert, *Philon von Alexandrien: Über die Gottesbezeichnung "wohltätig verzehrendes Feuer" (De Deo): Rückübersetzung des Fragments aus dem Armenischen, deutsche Übersetzung und Kommentar* (WUNT 46; Tübingen: Mohr Siebeck, 1988); "The Philonian Fragment De Deo: First English Translation," *SPhAn* 10 (1998) 1-13.

86. *Mos.* 1-2, *Opif., Abr., Jos., Decal., Spec.* 1-4, *Virt.,* and *Praem.* We are missing *De Isaaco* and *De Jacobo* (*Jos.* 1) as well as a treatise on the passions (*Leg.* 3.139).

Pentateuch.[87] They differ significantly in form: the *Questions and Answers* are an example of a zetematic work or what medieval scribes called *erotapokriseis* — they pose questions on the biblical text and then provide answers which, in this case, offer both literal and allegorical readings; the *Allegorical Commentary* cites the biblical text and works carefully through it lemma by lemma, adding secondary and tertiary biblical texts in expansive allegorical treatments; the *Exposition* often offers a paraphrase as a literal reading and expands the treatment with allegorical readings. The implied audience and corresponding function for each commentary series are also different: the *Questions and Answers* appear to be a preliminary commentary for those beginning to learn the Pentateuch; the *Allegorical Commentary* is for the initiated who are adept with the text and have some philosophical background; the *Exposition* was likely for any interested reader and may have even targeted pagans — at least as part of the implied audience.

This means that the role of philosophy is different in the three series: it is present in all three, but is most important in the allegorical treatments. Philo routinely read the text philosophically by means of allegory. He was not alone: there were a number of intellectuals who read Eastern texts through the lens of Hellenistic philosophy by means of allegory.[88] One of the most important was another Alexandrian who was a political opponent of Philo: Chaeremon, an Egyptian priest who is also identified with the Stoics.[89] Chaeremon used allegory to interpret Egyptian myths as references to the physical world. He was joined by the Middle Platonist Plutarch, who interpreted the same myths but with a different philosophical frame of reference in his *De Iside et Osiride*. Plutarch explained his orientation in these words: "One must not use the myths as if they were entirely factual, but take what is fitting from each as it accords with truth." The basis for determining what "accords with truth" was philosophy: "For this reason it is necessary that especially with regard to these matters we should take the reason that comes from philosophy as our guide and piously reflect on each of the things that are said or done" (*Is. Os.* 378a). Chaeremon and Plutarch did for Egyptian religion what Philo accomplished for Judaism. Numenius broadened the scope to include numerous religions from the East rather than a single

---

87. Philo offered slightly different explanations of the plan in three texts: *Abr.* 2-5; *Mos.* 2.45-47; *Praem.* 1-3. For details, see Sterling, "'Prolific in Expression and Broad in Thought.'"

88. For an analysis, see Sterling, "Platonizing Moses."

89. On Chaeremon, see Pieter Willem van der Horst, *Chaeremon: Egyptian Priest and Stoic Philosopher* (EPRO 101; Leiden: Brill, 1984); Michael Frede, "Chaeremon der Stoiker," in *ANRW* 2.36.3 (1989) 2067-2103.

tradition. According to Eusebius, he held the following: "After having spoken to this point and sealing it with the testimonies of Plato, it will be necessary to return and connect it to the teachings of Pythagoras" — a clear coupling of the Platonic and Pythagorean traditions we noted above — "and to summon the most reputable nations, introducing their rites and doctrines, and the setting up of temples, all carried out in agreement with Plato, whatever the Brahmans, Jews, Magi, and Egyptians have determined" (frag. 1a).[90]

Philosophy was the key for all of these authors that unlocked the real message of the Middle Eastern traditions that they explained. We might be tempted to smile and call them naive as interpreters. While they did not work with our categories, they were not naive. Philo was fully aware that people might accuse him of reading Plato into Moses. He made the point explicitly when he set out his understanding of the intelligible world or cosmos: "If someone wanted to use clearer words, he would say that the intelligible cosmos is nothing other than the Logos of God in the act of creating the cosmos." He explained what he meant: "For the intelligible city is nothing other than the reasoning capacity of the architect who is in the process of thinking through the founding of the intelligible city." In case someone objected that this was good Platonic philosophy but not scriptural exegesis, he injected: "This teaching comes from Moses; it is not mine. For as he describes the creation of the human being, he expressly acknowledges in the following statements that he was cast *in the image of God*" (*Opif.* 24-25). Philo understood the Logos to be the Image of God and human beings to be created in the image of the Image (*Opif.* 25; see also *Leg.* 3.96; *Her.* 230-331). In this way he had a three-tiered universe: God, the Logos, humanity or God, the intelligible world, and the sense-perceptible world. But why apply the language of Gen 1:27 to the creation of the intelligible world? His reasoning is opaque until we remember that Plato said: "If these arguments hold, then it is completely necessary that this cosmos is an image of another (τόν δε τὸν κόσμον εἰκόνα τινὸς εἶναι)" (*Tim.* 29b). Philo associated the language of Plato with the language of Gen 1:27.

The same connection between Platonic thought and the biblical text appears in the account of the tabernacle. Four texts in the LXX state that Moses made the tabernacle on the basis of the model that he saw on the mount (Exod. 25:8 [MT 9]; 25:40; 26:30; 27:8). In the *Questions and Answers on Exodus,* Philo cited three of these and argued that the incorporeal pattern that Moses saw of the tabernacle was the Platonic "idea" or pattern that was

---

90. The standard edition is des Places, *Numénius Fragments.*

used to create the sense-perceptible tabernacle (Exod 25:8 in *QE* 2.52; Exod 24:40 in *QE* 2.82; Exod 26:30 in *QE* 2.90). The point of the text was not so much about the tabernacle as it was about the relationship between the intelligible and sense-perceptible worlds. He brought the first two passages from Exodus together in the account in *De vita Mosis:* "He (Moses) saw within his soul the incorporeal ideas of the corporeal objects that were about to be made. It was necessary that the sense-perceptible copies be shaped according to these, as if from an archetypal picture and noetic patterns (νοητῶν παραδειγμάτων)" (*Mos.* 2.74). The final phrase is an echo of Exod 25:8: "You will make (it) for me according to everything that I show you on the mount: the pattern of the tent (τὸ παράδειγμα τῆς σκηνῆς) and the pattern of all the furnishings (τὸ παράδειγμα πάντων τῶν σκευῶν αὐτῆς)." The Alexandrian concluded by including the language of Exod 25:40 — "See that you make it according to the type (κατὰ τὸν τύπον) that has been shown to you on the mount" — when he wrote: "Therefore the shape of the pattern (ὁ τύπος τοῦ παραδείγματος) was stamped on the mind of the prophet, painted and molded invisibly without any matter by unseen forms. He fashioned the final product according to the shape (πρὸς τὸν τύπον)" (*Mos.* 2.76). The point for Philo was that the Platonic ideas were embedded in the biblical text. He simply read Moses and saw the reality expressed by Plato.[91]

The Philosophical Treatises

This conviction meant that Philo had no qualms about the values of Hellenistic philosophy. He even ventured directly into the domain of philosophy in a series of treatises that are philosophical in nature. Unfortunately, time has not been kind to these: out of eight known treatises, we have three in Armenian (*Prov.* 1, 2; *Anim.*) with some parallel Greek fragments for one of these (*Prov.* 2 in Eusebius, *Praep. ev.* 7.21; 8.14), two in Greek (*Prob.*; *Aet.* 1), and one fragment of another in Armenian (*Num.*); the other two are completely lost.[92] Unlike the biblical commentaries, these texts do not cite or paraphrase Scripture; rather, they engage authors from the larger Greco-Roman world. Some are doxographic in nature and set out the views of

---

91. For a fuller treatment of these texts, see Gregory E. Sterling, "Ontology versus Eschatology: Tensions between Author and Community in Hebrews," *SPhAn* 13 (2001) 200-201. The author of Hebrews made the same Platonic distinction based on Exod 25:40. See Heb 8:1-5, esp. vv. 4-5.

92. *Prob.* 1 mentions a counterpart and *Aet.* 1.150 anticipates a second treatise.

various philosophical traditions. They are not cast in the form of a commentary, but use the genres that circulated widely in the philosophical schools: two are dialogues that remind us of Cicero's dialogues *(De providentia* and *De animalibus),*[93] one is a thesis that argues a case by setting out the arguments and counterarguments *(De aeternitate mundi),*[94] two are discourses that argue a thesis, which in this case is a paradox *(Quod probus liber sit* and the lost *Quod omnis improbus servus sit),* and the fragment is an arithmology *(De numeribus).*

Summary

How did all of these texts function? There are different possibilities. We should not assume that all had the same function. Some have thought that Philo taught in a house of prayer, a very distinct possibility. I have argued that he had a private school much like we know that philosophers and physicians operated, e.g., Philodemus, Epictetus, Galen, or Plotinus.[95] The school setting would explain not only the *Questions and Answers* as well as the *Allegorical Commentary,* but the philosophical treatises as well. The *Exposition* may have had a broader setting, as did the apologetic treatises. If this is correct, beginning students would have used the *Questions and Answers,* while advanced students would have used the *Allegorical Commentary* and the philosophical treatises.

Conclusions

What was the final purpose behind this massive effort? Why did Philo interpret Moses through the lens of Hellenistic philosophy? Why did he defend some of his basic positions in philosophical treatises? Philo believed that Hellenistic philosophy — at least the traditions he accepted — and the Jewish

93. On Philo's dialogues, see Abraham Terian, "A Critical Introduction to Philo's Dialogues," in *ANRW* 2.21.1 (1984) 272-94.

94. On the genre, see David T. Runia, "Philo's *De aeternitate mundi:* The Problem of Its Interpretation," *VC* 35 (1981) 105-51.

95. Gregory E. Sterling, "'The School of Sacred Laws': The Social Setting of Philo's Treatises," *VC* 53 (1999): 148-64; "Philo's School: The Social Setting of Ancient Commentaries," in *Sophisten in Hellenismus und Kaiserzeit: Orte, Methoden und Personnen der Bildungsvermittlung,* ed. Beatrice Wyss (STAC; Tübingen: Mohr Siebeck, forthcoming).

faith came together at the most important juncture: the understanding of the divine.[96] Philo put it this way in his treatments of virtues that conclude his discussion of Mosaic legislation: "For what comes to the adherents of the most esteemed philosophy, comes to the Jews through their laws and customs, namely the knowledge of the highest and most ancient Cause of all and the rejection of the deception of created gods" (*Virt.* 65; cf. Clement of Alexandria, *Strom.* 1.5.28). Plutarch expressed a similar thought in a famous passage: "There is nothing to be alarmed about if, in the first place, they preserve the gods in common with us and neither make them the gods of the Egyptians alone nor understand by these names the Nile and only the land the Nile waters nor claim that the marshes and lotus-flowers are the only work of the gods," reasoning, "since this would deprive other people who do not have a Nile or Buto or Memphis of great gods." He concluded: "But all have and know Isis and the gods with her, even though some only recently learned to address them by Egyptian names; they have known and honored the power of each from the beginning" (*Is. Os.* 377c-d.; cf. also 351c-e, 354b-c, 355b-c, 369b-d, 376a).

These two citations represent an intersection that transformed the thought of the late Hellenistic and early to late Roman worlds. Hellenistic philosophy turned toward a form of monotheism.[97] While there were variations in how different thinkers understood the ultimate principle or God, there was a movement to recognize a transcendent being or power. Philo recognized the possibilities that existed in Hellenistic philosophy. He developed an allegory of the soul that sought to bring about the union of a human with the divine. While Moses was the ultimate authority, he did not hesitate to use the philosophical thought of his day to articulate the ascent of the soul to the divine. In this sense, it is fair for someone like Numenius, who had probably read Philo, to ask, "What is Plato but Moses speaking in Attic?" (frag. 8).

---

96. On the place of God in Philo, see my "The First Theologian: The Originality of Philo of Alexandria," in *Renewing the Tradition: Festschrift for James Thompson*, ed. Mark Hamilton, Thomas H. Olbricht, and Jeffrey Patterson (Eugene: Wipf & Stock, 2006) 145-62.

97. See Polymnia Athanassiadi and Michael Frede, *Pagan Monotheism in Late Antiquity* (Oxford: Clarendon, 1999); Stephen Mitchell and Peter Van Nuffelen, eds., *Monotheism between Pagans and Christians in Late Antiquity* (Leuven: Peeters, 2010).

Why and How to Study Philo

Why Study Philo? How?

Torrey Seland

Why Study Philo?

The question might be taken as rhetorical: Why study Philo? But it might be good to reflect on it from time to time and make up one's mind concerning why Philo is important. In fact, the present book might be read from beginning to end as an endeavor to demonstrate to the reader that Philo is indeed important. Others have been even more emphatic in their arguments for the relevance of Philo: Gregory E. Sterling has written an article with the provocative title "Philo Has Not Been Used Half Enough."[1] In this article he states frankly, concerning the importance of Philo in studying early Christianity: "I think that the Philonic corpus is the single most important body of material from Second Temple Judaism for our understanding of the development of Christianity in the first and second centuries. . . . I am convinced, that the Philonic corpus helps us to understand the dynamics of early Christianity more adequately than any other corpus."[2] In another study he has called Philo "the first theologian."[3] And Abraham Terian has suggested in an article in which he reflects upon the question "What if the works of Philo

---

1. Gregory E. Sterling, "'Philo Has Not Been Used Half Enough': The Significance of Philo of Alexandria for the Study of the New Testament," *PRSt* 30 (2003) 251-69.

2. Sterling, "'Philo Has not Been Used Half Enough,'" 252.

3. Gregory E. Sterling, "The First Theologian: The Originality of Philo of Alexandria," in *Renewing the Tradition: Festschrift for James Thompson,* ed. Mark Hamilton, Thomas H. Olbricht, and Jeffrey Patterson (Eugene: Wipf & Stock, 2006) 145-62.

had been newly discovered?"[4] that then they might have received an interest comparable to what the Qumran scrolls received fifty years ago.

It is not the purpose of the present chapter to provide a collection of all the arguments that have been offered in support of the relevance of studying Philo. Today hardly any scholar of Second Temple Judaism, early Christianity, or Greek philosophy of that period sees any great imperative in arguing for his relevance. It should be taken for granted.

Philo of Alexandria (ca. 20 B.C.E.–50 C.E.), or Philo Judaeus as he is also called, was a Jewish scholar, philosopher, politician, and author who lived in Alexandria all his life and who has had a tremendous influence through his many books. His literary production is impressive, greater than that of any other Jew we know from that century. He wrote at least seventy treatises, of which about fifty are still extant, in whole or in part. His works are considered to be of tremendous value for students of the Judaism of his time, for students of the early Christian traditions that found their way into the New Testament, and of both the social life and theology of the early churches in the Diaspora. Therefore, there are many reasons for studying him.

Up until the seventeenth century, many scholars believed that Philo had some knowledge of, and possibly even some relationship to, early Egyptian or even Roman Christians. Some thought he referred to early Egyptian Christian groups in his writings when he wrote about the Therapeutae (cf. *De vita contemplativa*) or that he had met Peter, the apostle, during his stay in Rome in the late thirties. Some ancient Christian sources even consider him to have been a Christian himself, some even a bishop.[5] But as far as we know today, Philo never met any Christians, nor does he tell anything about any Christians, nor did any of the New Testament writers know him. It is nevertheless a remarkable fact that during many centuries after his death his works were preserved, not by the Jews, but by Christians who came to cherish them and to adopt many of the ideas inherent in his works. Today any scholar interested in first-century Judaism or early Christianity, with regard to both theology and the social world of the Diaspora Jews or early Christians, should be somewhat familiar with Philo's works. During the last century or so, we have come to realize that his literary remains contain evidence of various relevant traditions about Jewish life and theology, various ways of

---

4. Abraham Terian, "Had the Works of Philo Been Newly Discovered," *BA* 57 (1994) 86-97.

5. David T. Runia, *Philo in Early Christian Literature: A Survey* (CRINT 3/3; Assen: Van Gorcum; Minneapolis: Fortress, 1993) 3-7.

interpreting the Jewish Scriptures as well as information about the life of the Jews as minority groups in the Greco-Roman world of the first century C.E. For this reason, they are of tremendous importance too for studying the Judaism of his time. And philosophers and historians of ancient philosophy are considering him important as a witness of philosophical trajectories of his time, but are often almost bewildered by the many philosophical traditions present in his works. So he is also important for the study of ancient Greco-Roman philosophy.

Methodological Issues in Studying Philo

One might ask, however: Is Philo representative? Is he representative of the Judaism of the Diaspora in his times? Is he, probably a wealthy Jew, a member of the elite Jewish segments of the city of Alexandria, representative of the Diaspora Judaism of his time in general? The question should not receive a clear-cut yes or no; it contains too many unknowns to be handled quite so simply. Philo was probably indeed wealthy and part of an elite family, and we gain fairly good knowledge of his own Judaism, that is, his religion as set forth through his interpretations of the Torah. But how much do we know about other fairly contemporary persons' conceptions of their own religion? We have no similar amount of knowledge for any comparable Jewish person from the Diaspora at this time. If, for instance, we consider the Jewish historian Josephus, we must realize that he too wrote extensively; he too lived several decades in the Diaspora (Rome); but he was not a Diaspora Jew in the same sense as Philo, as he grew up and became an adult while living in Judea and Galilee. We have, admittedly, other writings or partial writings from some other Diaspora writers, but their literary remains are not comparable to that of Philo, neither in extent nor content.[6] For this reason, Philo has been considered by some as a singular scholar. To some extent, that issue is still debated. Philo himself was well aware of having both previous and

6. For a review of these writers and their works, see, e.g., John J. Collins, *Between Athens and Jerusalem: Jewish Identity in the Hellenistic Diaspora* (2nd ed.; BRS; Grand Rapids: Eerdmans; Livonia: Dove, 2000); Gregory E. Sterling, "Recluse or Representative? Philo and Greek-Speaking Judaism Beyond Alexandria," in *Society of Biblical Literature 1995 Seminar Papers,* ed. Eugene H. Lovering Jr. (Atlanta: Scholars, 1995) 595-616. For the texts, see the volumes edited by Carl R. Holladay, *Fragments from Hellenistic Jewish Authors,* vol. 1: *Historians* (SBLTT 20; SBLPS 10; Chico: Scholars, 1983); vol. 2: *Poets* (SBLTT 30; SBLPS 12; Atlanta: Scholars, 1989); vol. 3: *Aristobulus* (SBLTT 39; SBLPS 13; Atlanta: Scholars, 1995).

contemporary rivals as expositors of Scripture.[7] Admittedly, considering Philo's economic position and status, he was not very representative of his Alexandria. However, taking into account Philo's own conceptions of himself and his "Judaism," he in many ways considers himself a mainstream Jew in his relationship to and interpretations of the Torah, the foundational writings of the Jewish synagogue communities in the Diaspora (*Migr.* 89-93). He was most probably not an outsider, considering his relation to the synagogue. And for that reason alone, Philo is worthy of extensive study. In addition, considering the role his works and ideas played among the emergent groups propagating belief in Jesus of Nazareth as the promised Messiah, and especially in the development of their ideology and theology, Philo again cannot be neglected.[8] In the same way, as demonstrated by the articles of Karl-Gustav Sandelin and Ellen Birnbaum in the present volume, Philo is quite valuable for understanding the Jewish groups of his time, not only in Alexandria or in the Diaspora at large, but also in Palestine. Let us proceed, then, on how to approach the study of Philo.

How Study Philo?

In the following we will first reflect briefly on how to study Philo, but then our main focus will be on presenting a practical guide concerning the kind of auxiliary means and resources we have available when trying to get into his works and his thought world, that is, his social and symbolic universe.

How To Read His Texts

For a student, coming to the works of Philo for the first or even second time, the pivotal question might be: Where should I start? Considering the twelve volumes of the Loeb edition, which he or she probably will be advised to use, it is not the smartest thing to begin with volume one, *De Opificio* and the *Legum allegoriae*, even though it might be interesting to look at Philo's ex-

---

7. See the references from Philo's works as presented in David M. Hay, "Philo's References to Other Allegorists," *SPhilo* 6 (1979-80) 41-75; Montgomery J. Shroyer, "Alexandrian Jewish Literalists," *JBL* 55 (1936) 261-84. On Aristobulus as a predecessor, see Peder Borgen, "Aristobulus — A Jewish Exegete from Alexandria," in *Paul Preaches Circumcision and Pleases Men* (Relieff 8; Trondheim: Tapir, 1983) 179-90.

8. See here Runia, *Philo in Early Christian Literature.*

positions of the creation. Admittedly, there might be several ways to start. However, one of the scholars who spent his lifetime studying Philo, Erwin R. Goodenough, has written a small *Introduction to Philo* in which he suggests a reading list for the beginner.[9] I myself have found this list really valuable and helpful, so I present it here as one of the best ways of approaching Philo's texts themselves.

1. The first work(s) to read, according to Goodenough, are the treatises *Against Flaccus (In Flaccum)* and *On the Embassy to Gaius (Legatio ad Gaium).* These are Philo's more historical treatises. They are not his first writings — they might actually be among his very latest — but they demonstrate how Philo considered the situation of the Jews in the Diaspora as well as the role of Israel in that world.

2. Next comes *On the Contemplative Life (De vita contemplativa).* This is a fragmentary work, but it was probably a part of an apology for the Jews, addressed to Gentiles. This work should be followed by the remainder of what is now called the *Hypothetica,* a work also to be categorized as apologetical, according to Goodenough, written for a Gentile audience. The first of these works describes the enigmatic group of the Therapeutae, which lived in seclusion in the desert. Philo seems to admire these people, and they might represent for him something of an ideal community.[10]

3. The student should next read Philo's two books *On the Life of Moses (De vita Mosis* I-II). As in ancient times, Goodenough surmises, reading these books will probably make the reader eager to get to know more about the Jewish traditions. This can be gained by reading further in Philo's works, proceeding with:

4. *The Exposition of the Laws of Moses.* This is a not a label created by Philo, but by scholars in recent times, constituting a comprehensive category that comprises several treatises among Philo's expositions of the Torah. Ac-

9. See Erwin R. Goodenough, *An Introduction to Philo Judaeus* (2nd ed.; Oxford: Blackwell, 1962; repr., Brown Classics in Judaica; Lanham: University Press of America, 1986) 30-51.

10. There has been some discussion whether the Therapeutae represent a real community or not; see, e.g., Troels Engberg-Pedersen, "Philo's *De vita Contemplativa* as a Philosopher's Dream," *JSJ* 30 (1999) 40-64; and contra David M. Hay, "Foils for the Therapeutae: References to Other Texts and Persons in Philo's *'De Vita Contemplativa,'"* in *Neotestamentica et Philonica: Studies in Honor of Peder Borgen,* ed. David E Aune, Torrey Seland, and Jarl Henning Ulrichsen (NovTSup 106; Leiden: Brill, 2003) 330-48. But such questions should be left out at the beginning of a first reading. For further studies on the Therapeutae, see Joan Taylor, *Jewish Women Philosophers of First-Century Alexandria: Philo's "Therapeutae" Reconsidered* (Oxford: Oxford University Press, 2003). A commentary is forthcoming, written by David M. Hay (†) and Joan Taylor.

cording to Goodenough, they are written for the Gentiles. Others will disagree. In this group, the reader will be dealing with *On the Creation of the World (De opificio mundi); On the Life of Abraham (De Abrahamo); On the Life of Joseph (De Iosepho); On the Decalogue (De decalogue); On the Special Laws 1-4 (De specialibus legibus I-IV); On the Virtues (De virtutibus);* and *On Rewards and Punishments (De praemis et poenis).* Goodenough states: "The reader who has followed Philo to this point has had a very good introduction to the man, and stands at the threshold of his deeper thought."[11]

5. The next group of writings to be read is suggested by many scholars to have been written for more informed readers. It is as if Philo here wants to lead his readers further into his intellectual world. These works contain much more allegorical expositions; according to Goodenough, they were written for the Jews, for the insiders. Not all scholars today completely agree with Goodenough in dividing the intended readers as Gentile and Jewish, but most would probably agree that these treatises are for more advanced readers. At any rate, a reader today will probably be much better off if she or he reads the *Exposition* before digging into these.

The Allegorical Commentary, as these writings are labeled today, consists of eighteen titles and twenty-one books; they begin with specific biblical texts, but often digress in a way sometimes quite frustrating to the uninformed reader. Goodenough suggests that "Philo meant these works to be read by initiates who knew the main parts of his doctrines, and who would read them as books of devotion."[12] Be that as it may, these books take their points of departure in some specific biblical texts. I list them here according to the biblical texts they deal with: *Allegorical Interpretation 1-3 (Legum allegoriae I-III;* on Gen 2:1-17; 2:18–3:1a; 3:8b-19); *On the Cherubim (De cherubim;* Gen 3:24–4:1); *On the Sacrifices of Cain and Abel (De sacrificiis Abelis et Caini;* Gen 4:2-4); *That the Worse Attacks the Better (Quod deterius potiori insidari soleat;* Gen 4:8-15); *On the Posterity and Exile of Cain (De posteritate Caini;* Gen 4:16-25); *On Giants (De gigantibus;* Gen 6:1-4a); *That God Is Unchangeable (Quod Deus sit immutabilis;* Gen 6:4b-12); *On Agriculture (De agricultura;* Gen 9:20-21); *On Noah's Work as a Planter (De plantatione;* Gen 9:20-21 continued); *On Drunkeness (De ebrietate;* Gen 9:20-21 continued); *On Sobriety (De sobrietate;* Gen 9:20-21 continued); *On the Confusion of Tongues (De confusione linguarum;* Gen 11:1-9); *On the Migration of Abraham (De migratione Abrahami;* Gen 12:1-6); *Who Is the Heir of Divine Things?*

11. Goodenough, *An Introduction to Philo Judaeus,* 45.
12. Goodenough, *An Introduction to Philo Judaeus,* 47.

(*Quis rerum divinarum heres;* Gen 15:2-18); *On the Preliminary Studies* (*De congressu quaerendae eruditionis gratia;* Gen 16:1-6); *On Flight and Finding* (*De fuga et inventione;* Gen 16:6b-14); *On the Change of Names* (*De mutatione nominum;* Gen 17:1-5, 16-22); *On God* (*De Deo;* Gen 18); *On Dreams 1* (*De somniis* I; Gen 28:10-22 + 31:10-13); *On Dreams 2* (*De somniis* II; Gen 37:8-11; 40:9-11, 16-17; 41:17-24).

6. The student having explored the *Allegorical Commentary,* there remain only a few works: *Questions and Answers on Genesis* and *Questions and Answers on Exodus.* These are a type of commentary on two biblical books, but in the form of questions and answers. They might very well have originated in some setting of Philo's teaching and are interesting as examples of how he could deal with particular texts.

The rest belong to the more philosophical works of Philo. Some of these also demonstrate that parts are missing, or in some cases only one of a two-volume set is preserved. Those who manage to read through the above-mentioned works of Philo will surely want to read these as well, and in this way they will have a great impression of how variegated the authorship of Philo is: *On the Eternity of the World (De aeternitate mundi); That Every Good Person Is Free (Quod omnis probus liber sit); On Providence and Alexander (De providentia)* or *Whether Animals Have Reason (De animalibus).*[13]

For those thus having been initiated into the world of Philo and who want to study a particular topic or issue in these works in a more comprehensive way, she or he might choose a somewhat different procedure. Whether reading Philo on a computer or on paper, the procedures should be adapted to the texts. In the present handbook, there is an informative chapter by Adele Reinhartz[14] on how to read Philo if searching for social issues. If the purpose is to investigate some other matters, whether aspects of his philosophy, theology, or concrete exegesis, the procedure might be somewhat different.

Today a new reader, whether an M.A. or Ph.D. student or not, might be tempted to use the computer and some of the programs dealt with later in

---

13. The reader should, however, be aware that Philo's authorship of some of these works is disputed. See, e.g., Roald Skarsten, *Forfatterproblemet ved De aeternitate mundi i corpus philonicum* (Bergen: Universitetet i Bergen, 1987); Kåre Fuglseth, "The Reception of Aristotelian Features in Philo and the Authorship Problem of Philo's De Aeternitate Mundi," in *Beyond Reception: Mutual Influences Between Antique Religion, Judaism, and Early Christianity,* ed. David Brakke, Anders-Christian Jacobsen, and Jörg Ulrich (Bern: Lang, 2006) 57-67; Maren Ruth Niehoff, "Philo's Contribution to Contemporary Alexandrian Metaphysics," in Brakke, Jacobsen, and Ulrich, *Beyond Reception,* 35-55.

14. See below, pp. 180-99.

this section that contain the texts of Philo and simply search for certain terms and expressions without actually reading his books. This might be a helpful procedure in some cases, but it should not deter anyone from a thorough reading of the texts themselves in their (con)textual settings. I have seen too many dissertations that have applied a delimiting method of selecting Philo's texts and which have come up with too meager results, in some cases even with somewhat skewed results.

In an article entitled "How to Read Philo," David T. Runia[15] comes up with four good recommendations, which I endorse and reproduce here:[16]

1. When pursuing a particular topic in Philo, always aim at taking into account all the relevant passages. This might be seen to be stating the obvious. But Philo's oeuvre is vast. Not all parts are equally accessible (note especially the Armenian works), yet any subject can turn up virtually anywhere.

2. When examining a particular passage, special attention must be paid to the context, which in Philo's case nearly always means the exegetical context. It is necessary, before all else, to locate the biblical texts which form the basis of the passage.

3. Next we should attempt to establish the exegetical problem which has impelled Philo to develop the passage under discussion.

4. The final step draws us away from the immediate concerns of contextuality. Since Philo regarded it as his task to expound Mosaic thought in relation to accepted Greek scientific, philosophical, and theological ideas, it will accordingly be the task of his interpreter to reconstruct this process in reverse.

As can been seen from these four recommended procedures, Philo is not easy reading, and he can be approached from a variety of perspectives and with very different goals in mind. Taking Runia's four steps seriously, putting them into practice will prove immensely rewarding and also safeguard a person from making mistakes by building one's case on too meager a basis.

In the next sections we will deal with some of the texts and various resources available for a serious study of Philo's works.

---

15. David T. Runia, "How to Read Philo," in *Exegesis and Philosophy: Studies on Philo of Alexandria* (Aldershot: Variorum, 1990) 185-98. This article is also available at http://torreys .org/philo-art/howtoreadphilo.html.
16. Runia, "How to Read Philo," 193.

Text Editions

The most authoritative text is still the old edition provided by Leopold Cohn, Paul Wendland, Siegfried Reiter, and Hans Leisegang, eds., *Philonis Alexandrini opera quae supersunt* (7 vols.; Berlin: Reimer, 1896-1930; repr., Berlin: de Gruyter, 1962-63).

But the version most often used today, and probably also the most available and easiest to use, is the bilingual volumes in the Loeb Classical Library: F. H. Colson and G. H. Whitaker, *Philo, with an English Translation* (10 vols.; London: Heineman; Cambridge, MA: Harvard University Press, 1929-62) and two supplementary volumes containing *Questions and Answers in Genesis and Exodus,* translated from Armenian by Ralph Marcus (Cambridge, MA: Harvard University Press, 1953). Some of Philo's works, however, are extant only in an Armenian translation; the Greek texts of these are completely lost.[17] Abraham Terian has provided us with valuable tools in his translation of some of these; see especially *Philonis Alexandrini De animalibus: The Armenian Text with an Introduction, Translation, and Commentary* (Chico: Scholars, 1981); *Alexander, e versione armeniaca;* and *Quaestiones et Solutiones in Exodum, e versione armeniaca et fragmenta graeca.* The latter two were published in *Les œuvres de Philon d'Alexandrie,* vols. 36 and 34c (Paris: Cerf, 1988, 1992). There have, of course, been other editions of Philo's works, but these remain the main editions for us today.[18]

Translations

Happily, we are in the situation of having several translations available, and more are probably to come. Some of these editions are bilingual, containing both the Greek text and a modern translation. Here is a sample of what might be considered the most relevant for M.A. and Ph.D. students:

English First of all, we have the edition of Colson et al. in the Loeb Classical Library, mentioned above, containing the Greek text and an English trans-

17. On the Armenian texts, see C. Mercier, *Quaestiones et Solutiones en Genesim I et II e Versione Armeniaca* (Les œuvres de Philon d'Alexandrie 34a; Paris: Cerf, 1979); *Quaestiones et Solutiones en Genesim III-IV-V-VI e Versione Armeniaca* (Les œuvres de Philon d'Alexandrie 34b; Paris: Cerf, 1984). On these Armenian texts in general, see also Sara Mancini Lombardi and Paola Pontani, eds., *Studies on the Ancient Armenian Version of Philo's Works* (Studies in Philo of Alexandria 6; Leiden: Brill, 2011).

18. On these and other critical editions, see Roberto Radice and David T. Runia, *Philo of Alexandria: An Annotated Bibliography 1937-1986* (VCSup 8; Leiden: Brill, 1988) 10-19.

lation. The Greek text is that of Cohn-Wendland, but with some different text-critical suggestions and emendations.

An older English translation is still in use, originally published in 1854-55, reprinted as late as 1993: *The Works of Philo: Complete and Unabridged,* trans. C. D. Yonge (Peabody: Hendrickson, 1993). This is the translation used in the computer programs presented below and also the main one available on the Internet. It should not, however, be considered adequate for use in scholarly works, for reasons most succinctly stated by Runia.[19]

German *Philo von Alexandria, Die Werke in deutscher Übersetzung,* ed. Leopold Cohn, Isaak Heinemann, Maximilian Adler, and Willy Theiler (7 vols.; Breslau: Marcus, 1909-38; repr., Berlin: de Gruyter, 1962-64). This is still the only comprehensive German translation available. In the bibliography by Radice and Runia it is characterized as being of "mainly a historical and retrospective value."[20]

French Roger Arnaldez, Jean Pouilloux, and Claude Mondésert, eds., *Les Oeuvres de Philon d'Alexandrie* (36 vols.; Paris: Cerf, 1961-92). These volumes contain introductions and notes on the Greek texts, but of various lengths and quality. The Greek text is that of Cohn-Wendland (see above), and the later volumes have much longer and better notes than the first published volumes.

---

19. Runia notes the following aspects as pivotal:

(1) Various careless errors were discovered. This is no doubt due to the great speed with which the translation was prepared. (2) On a number of occasions Yonge's use of an inferior text leads to a less meaningful rendering (but note also that at least twice he is saved from unnecessary emendations). (3) Rather often Philo's meaning is not as clearly and exactly rendered as one would like (the result of the tendency to smooth over difficulties in the text). For the most part, however, the translation manages to give a reasonable indication of the contents of Philo's text. It is clear enough for a first orientation, but is quite insufficient to guarantee a precise idea of what Philo meant to say when he wrote his works. In short, it would be most unwise to base a serious discussion on Yonge's translation without reference to the Greek text or to other translations.

See his review at Ioudaios Review: ftp://ftp.lehigh.edu/pub/listserv/ioudaios-review/4.1994/philo.runia.009. A more extensive review is given by Runia in *SPhilo* 6 (1994): 171-82.

20. See Radice and Runia, *Philo of Alexandria: An Annotated Bibliography 1937-1986,* 19-20: "The Translation is, for the most part, amply annotated and of a high standard, particularly in view of the time in which it was produced. It is, however, not without inaccuracies and obscurities, so that today we today, on the whole, say that it remains mainly a historical and retrospective value, having been superseded in clarity and precision by the Loeb English translation."

Spanish *Obras completas de Filón de Alejandría,* trans. José Maria Triviño (4 vols.; Colección Valores en el tiempo; Buenos Aires: Acervo Cultural, 1975-76). This is the first complete translation of the works of Philo into Spanish. It is now superseded by another Spanish edition in five volumes, of which the first volume was published in 2009: *Filón de Alejandría obras completas,* ed. José Pablo Martín; trans. Martín, Francisco Lisi, Marta Alesso (Madrid: Editorial Trotta).[21]

In addition to these comprehensive sets of translations, there are several other translations available of individual volumes of Philo's works. For an overview of these volumes, see the bibliographies listed below.

Indexes and Lexica

While there are several indexes to Philo's works, there is no specific Philonic Greek lexicon. Actually, there is not much need for one. The two most used lexica, the BDAG and Liddell-Scott et al., are also immensely relevant for a student of Philo's Greek.

> William Arndt, Frederick W. Danker, and Walter Bauer, *A Greek-English Lexicon of the New Testament and Other Early Christian Literature* (3rd ed.; Chicago: University of Chicago Press, 2000). Often abbreviated as BDAG.
>
> In addition to being a lexicon of the New Testament and early Christian literature, it also refers to the texts of Philo and Josephus as well as those of the Apocrypha and Pseudepigrapha.

> Henry George Liddell, Robert Scott, Henry Stuart Jones, and Roderick McKenzie, *A Greek-English Lexicon* (revised and augmented throughout; Oxford: Clarendon; New York: Oxford University Press, 1996).
>
> Probably the best and most-used lexicon of Greek literature available. A must for any serious student. It comprises Greek texts from the elev-

---

21. Also available (per 2012) are José Pablo Martín, ed., *Filón de Alejandría obras completas,* vol. 5 (Madrid: Editorial Trotta, 2009), comprising *De vita Mosis, De vita contemplativa, In Flaccum,* and *Legatio ad Gaium;* vol. 2 (2010), containing *De cherubim; De sacrificiis; Quod deterius; De posteritate Caini; De gigantibus; Quod Deus sit immutabilis; De agricultura; De plantatione; De ebrietate;* and *De sobrietate;* and vol. 3 (2012) which includes *De confusione linguarum, De migratione Abrahami, Quis rerum divinarum heres sit, De congressu eruditionis gratia, De fuga et inventione, De mutatione nominum,* and *De Deo.*

enth century B.C.E. to the Byzantine period, including the Septuagint and the New Testament.

Gerhard Kittel and Gerhard Friedrich, *Theological Dictionary of the New Testament,* trans. Geoffrey W. Bromiley (10 vols.; Grand Rapids: Eerdmans, 1964-76).

Though being primarily a New Testament dictionary, and by now somewhat dated, it also includes extensive sections on the uses of specific terms in the works of Philo.

With regard to indexes, there are several available. The following are probably the most relevant for any M.A. and Ph.D. student investigating Philo:

Günter Mayer, *Index Philoneus* (Berlin: de Gruyter, 1974).

This index uses the text of Cohn-Wendland-Reiter and contains all the references for the terms given. A somewhat strange aspect is that each book of Philo is given a number, which is used in the references instead of the (abbreviated) names of the books. It takes some time to get used to that feature.

Peder Borgen, Kåre Fuglseth, and Roald Skarsten, *The Philo Index: A Complete Greek Word Index to The Writings of Philo of Alexandria* (Grand Rapids: Eerdmans; Leiden: Brill, 2000).

This Index was first published in a preliminary edition in 1997 in Trondheim, Norway.[22]

Roald Skarsten, Peder Borgen, and Kåre Fuglseth, *The Complete Works of Philo of Alexandria: A Key-Word-In-Context Concordance* (8 vols.; Piscataway: Gorgias, 2005).

This work is almost a curiosity, as everyone having Philo's text available in one of the computer programs mentioned below would be able to compile such a concordance in no time. The price also limits its availability for the average person ($2,405). For those who do have access,

---

22. Peder Borgen, Kåre Fuglseth, and Roald Skarsten, *The Philo Index: A Complete Greek Word Index to the Writings of Philo of Alexandria Lemmatised and Computer Generated* (UniRel Studieserie 25; Trondheim: Religionsvitenskapelig Institutt NTNU, 1997).

the concordance makes it easy to see the specific Philonic terms in their immediate context.

Biblia Patristica Supplément: Philon d'Alexandrie (Paris: Editions du Centre National de la recherche scientifique, 1982).

This volume provides a listing of Philo's references to the text segments in the Old Testament and is very useful when looking for where Philo deals with a particular verse or section from the Old Testament.

Reading Philo in the Computer Age

Recent decades have seen an almost revolutionary development in the production and use of personal computers. Modern PCs, laptops, reading devices such as iPad™ and even smartphones have been developed to prove great auxiliary means for every student. Modern strong processors, Internet access, and the huge storage possibilities have made them excellent means for handling great amounts of texts.

The work of making a digitalized version of Philo's texts was carried out in Norway, beginning as early as in the late 1960s. Professor Peder Borgen, then at the University of Bergen, initiated the project, and in the years of 1970-73 a machine-readable text of Philo's writings was established and a *Key-Word-in-Context* (KWIC) concordance was produced by Roald Skarsten. The work was based on the text in the Cohn and Wendland edition. This concordance was not, however, published. Only two copies were made; one was kept by Professor Borgen, and I was able to make use of it as a Ph.D. student in the 1980s at the University of Trondheim, where Borgen had then moved and worked as a professor since 1976.

In the years 1990 to 1993, more money had been raised, making it possible to engage Kåre Fuglseth to complete the project of tagging the texts and adding still others. A preliminary edition of the index was published in Trondheim in 1997, and the final edition by Eerdmans in 2000. It is this grammatically tagged text version that is the basis for the texts of Philo now available in several computer programs to be mentioned below.

Philo on the Computer

The profit of searching and reading digitalized texts will be well known to most readers of this book. Suffice here to mention the great ease of searching for various terms, even down to precise grammatical forms or lemma, searching for clusters of terms, making KWIC lists and boolean searches like "and-or" or "and-not," etc. In addition, advanced programs like those mentioned below also include lexica, translations, and other ancient texts relevant for studying Philo. Some even contain commentaries and other relevant expository material. Some of these computer programs can be used on smartphones like the Apple iPhone™ or iPad™ or Android phones and might have additional extensive web pages available. The list below, given in alphabetical order, mentions the most relevant programs at the time of writing this review (2011). In most cases, you can start by buying just a few books, or you can buy specialized and comprehensive packages.

> *Accordance*™ (http://www.accordancebible.com) is a program for Macintosh™ machines. Accordance 10.4 for Windows™ became available in 2014. Applets are also available for iPad™ and iPhone™. Philo's texts can be bought as an add-on or included in a larger package.

> *BibleWorks*™ (http://bibleworks.com/) is for Windows PCs; Mac users require additional virtualization software. This claims to be "a tightly integrated collection of Bible software tools designed specifically for scholarly analysis of the Bible text." Philo's texts are included in the base package from version 8 on.

> *Logos Bible Software*™ (http://www.logos.com) was made for Windows PCs, but a Mac version is also now available. Those who buy a package will also have included the works available on iPad™ and iPhone™ and via a web version. In addition, in 2011 Logos also started Vyrso™, a reader accessory for iPad™, iPod Touch™, and iPhone™ for Logos Bible Software desktop application users. Logos is probably the program having the widest range of literature available in their packages.

Another digital library that should be mentioned is TLG™, the *Thesaurus Linguae Graecae* (see http://www.tlg.uci.edu/), which can be of great help to Philo scholars. It can, according to their website, be characterized thus: "Founded in 1972 the TLG has collected and digitized most literary texts written in Greek from Homer to the fall of Byzantium in AD 1453. Its goal is to create a comprehensive digital library of Greek literature from antiquity to the present era." The TLG texts first became available to the scholarly community on magnetic tapes and later in CD-ROM format. Having this CD, an additional program was necessary to read it. In 2001 they developed a website and started focusing their resources on web dissemination, and since 2004 they are no longer licensing the texts in CD-ROM format. Users have to subscribe, either as a private person or through their institution, in order to have full access to these texts. An abridged version (http://www.tlg.uci.edu/demo/fontsel) is open to the general public. TLG is a tremendous resource. When searching for terms or expressions, one can search not only the works of Philo but all the other ancient Greek texts at the same time. There are extensive abilities to limit and refine one's searches, whether to authors or to time periods.

Internet Resources

The emergence of the Internet and its general availability today, to many if still not to all, has provided both challenges and prospects for the scholarly world. When it first came into being, it did not take long before scholars saw the advantage of the Internet both as a medium for connecting to and communicating with colleagues, but also as a means for transmitting and presenting scholarly studies to a more general public. Especially as the graphic interface of Windows™ and the World Wide Web came into being (1993), the use of the Internet "exploded." First came extensive professional and private websites, then blogs, and in more recent years social media like Facebook and Twitter. Also came reading devices like Kindle™ and iPad™, and what used to be a simple cellphone developed into smartphones, small computers with astonishing possibilities. And the software companies started to produce software capable of communicating with these various devices or platforms, making it possible to use them all from desktop computers to the phone in your pocket.

Those who grew up before all these resources became not only available, but also indispensable — that is, before the present generation of what have been called the digital natives[23] — have seen a technological development of communication devices hardly comparable to anything before.

For some years now, there have been a couple of web pages devoted to Philo studies. The *Studia Philonica Annual* has its own website (http://divinity.yale.edu/philo-alexandria), and another site gathering and offering links to Philo studies is also available (http://torreys.org/bible). The latter provides links to articles, reviews, and other material related to Philo studies present on the Internet.

23. John Palfrey and Urs Gasser, *Born Digital: Understanding the First Generation of Digital Natives* (New York: Basic Books, 2008).

Google started out as a simple search engine, but has since developed multiple services and products for using the Internet. For Philo studies, two in particular are relevant: Google Books (http://books.google.com/) and Google Scholar (http://scholar.google.com/). The former is useful both for searching *for* and for searching *in* books. Google usually does not show all the contents of a particular book, but by using the search facilities, one can get a fair enough impression to decide if the item is relevant or not. Google Scholar is useful when searching for references and quotations from particular scholars, Scripture, and books.

The Greek text of Philo's works is available on the Internet at various sites (cf. http://torreys.org/bible/resource_page_3-1/), and Harvard University Press has announced publication of the entire Loeb Classical Library for fall 2014. Several of the computer programs mentioned above are also planning to integrate a digitized version of the Loeb edition in their setups. In addition, Perseus Digital Library (http://www.perseus.tufts.edu/hopper/) represents a great collection of other texts that might also be relevant for Philo studies.

Bibliographies, Reviews, and Other Handbooks

One of the most urgent questions a scholar may ask when beginning study of a particular topic is whether relevant bibliographies are available. In the case of Philo, we are blessed with several bibliographies, and each year new reviews of published works are issued in the *Studia Philonica Annual.*

Bibliographies

There is hardly another person from antiquity for whom we have available such extensive bibliographic works as Philo of Alexandria. These are like goldmines for researchers on any topic dealt with in the Philonic works and research. The following are the most relevant.[24]

> Erwin R. Goodenough, *The Politics of Philo Judaeus: Theory and Practice* (New Haven: Yale University Press, 1938).
>
> This volume contains as a second part "A General Bibliography of Philo" (pp. 124-321), which is an impressive resource collected by How-

---

24. For a more comprehensive list of older bibliographies, see Radice and Runia, *Philo of Alexandria: An Annotated Bibliography 1937-1986*, 3-10.

ard L. Goodhart and Goodenough, covering manuscripts of Philo, editions and translations, bibliographies, general studies, studies of individual treatises, works on various doctrines of Philo, and much more. Some of these are annotated, and in some cases reviews are also mentioned. The lists are arranged chronologically under each heading.

Earle Hilgert, "Bibliographia Philoniana 1935-1981," in *ANRW* 2.21.1 (1984) 47-97.

Roberto Radice, *Filone di Alessandria: bibliografia generale 1937-1982* (Elenchos 8; Naples: Bibliopolis, 1983).

Roberto Radice and David T. Runia, *Philo of Alexandria: An Annotated Bibliography, 1937-1986* (VCSup 8; Leiden: Brill, 1988).

This work originated as an English translation of the above-mentioned Italian work of Roberto Radice. In addition, a team of scholars was engaged in compiling supplementary material to make it as comprehensive as possible.

David T. Runia, ed., *Philo of Alexandria: An Annotated Bibliography, 1987-1996* (VCSup 57; Leiden: Brill, 2000).

This volume is a continuation of the 1988 volume by Radice and Runia (2nd ed. 1992). Prepared by the editor with the collaboration of the members of the International Philo Bibliography Project, it contains an almost complete listing of all scholarly writings on Philo in most languages for the period 1987 to 1996. Part one lists texts, translations, commentaries, etc. (seventy-five items). Part two contains critical studies (880 items). Part three presents additional works for 1937-86 (170 items). A brief description of the contents is provided for each.

David T. Runia, ed., *Philo of Alexandria: An Annotated Bibliography, 1997-2006* (VCSup 109; Leiden: Brill, 2012).

A further compilation by Runia in collaboration with the International Philo Bibliography Project: E. Birnbaum, K. A. Fox, A. C. Geljon, M. R. J. Hofstede, H. M. Keizer, J. P. Martín, M. S. Niehoff, R. Radice, J. Riaud, K.-G. Sandelin, D. Satran, G. Schimanowski, T. Seland, and

D. Zeller. Part one lists texts, translations, commentaries, etc. (58 items). Part two contains critical studies (1024 items). Part three includes additional works for 1987-96 (42 items). In all cases a brief description of the contents is given.

The International Philo Bibliography Project continues to publish extensive annotated bibliographies each year in *Studia Philonica Annual,* for example:

D. T. Runia, K. Bertholet, E. Birnbaum, A. C. Geljon, H. M. Keizer, J. Leonhardt-Balzer, J. P. Martín, M. R. Niehoff, and T. Seland, "Philo of Alexandria: An Annotated Bibliography 2007. Supplement: A Provisional Bibliography 2008-2010," *SPhAn* 22 (Atlanta: Society of Biblical Literature, 2010) 209-68.

Thus comprehensive bibliographies to Philo are available, and using the current issues of *Studia Philonica,* one will be able to keep up to date year by year. The bibliographic reviews in *Studia Philonica,* however, focus on works published two years back (e.g., the 2011 issue comments on items published in 2009). For more recent reviews of relevant Philo studies, one might consider other bibliographic resources, including:

New Testament Abstracts (see also http://catholicbiblical.org/publications/nta.).

Published three times a year, the focus is reviews of studies related to the New Testament. As it contains sections on the Jewish world and Greco-Roman world, it also covers Philo studies relevant to the New Testament literature. *NTA* is now also available to institutions in an online format from EBSCO publishing. The current version includes all abstracts and book notices published from 1985 through 2006 (*NTA* 29-50; see http://www .ebscohost .com/academic/new-testament -abstracts-online).

Introductions

Reading introductions to Philo is profitable not only for getting to know Philo better, but also for seeing the orientations and emphases of various scholars. Accordingly, I list some of the most relevant here. A student will surely benefit from reading more than one.

Four comprehensive articles should be mentioned first:

Peder Borgen, "Philo of Alexandria: A Critical and Synthetical Survey of Research since World War II," in *ANRW* 2.21.1 (1984) 98-154.

Peder Borgen, "Philo of Alexandria," in *Jewish Writings of the Second Temple Period,* ed. Michael E. Stone (CRINT 2/2; Assen: Van Gorcum; Minneapolis: Fortress, 1985) 233-82.

Ellen Birnbaum, "Two Millennia Later: General Resources and Particular Perspectives on Philo the Jew," *Currents in Biblical Research* 4 (2006) 241-76.

David T. Runia, "Philon d'Alexandrie," in *Dictionnaire des philosophes antiques,* ed. Richard Goulet (Paris: Editions du Centre national de la recherche scientifique, 2011) 5:362-90.

These four articles provide a fairly good review of the relevant discussions concerning Philo in recent decades without being ridden by some specific theories adopted by the authors. The next two works are interesting, both because the introduction by Goodenough gives a brief presentation of Philo from the perspective of the author, a very prolific writer whose works took a very specific profile, and because, in reading Sandmel, we enter into the thoughts and adaptations by a Jewish pupil of Goodenough.

Erwin R. Goodenough, *An Introduction to Philo Judaeus* (2nd ed.; Oxford: Blackwell, 1962; repr., Brown Classics in Judaica; Lanham: University Press of America, 1986; originally published 1940).

Samuel Sandmel, *Philo of Alexandria: An Introduction* (Oxford: Oxford University Press, 1979).

The most recently published introductions are:

Kenneth Schenck, *A Brief Guide to Philo* (Louisville: Westminster John Knox, 2005).

Written by a New Testament scholar who provides interesting insights for the use of Philo in New Testament studies, this is probably the one to be read first, if possible.

Adam Kamesar, ed., *The Cambridge Companion to Philo* (Cambridge: Cambridge University Press, 2009).

An anthology of nine articles, written by as many renowned Philo scholars, this volume contains many good introductions to Philo's life and writings, his thought, and his influence and significance.

Mireille Hadas-Lebel, *Philo of Alexandria: A Thinker in the Jewish Diaspora*, trans. Robyn Frechet (Studies in Philo of Alexandria 7; Leiden: Brill, 2012).

This comprehensive introduction is a recent translation of a volume published in French in 2003.

For an introduction at a more advanced level, this work by Peder Borgen is certainly to be recommended:

Peder Borgen, *Philo of Alexandria: An Exegete for His Time* (NovTSup 86; Leiden: Brill, 1997).

Commentaries

Over the past several decades only a few commentaries proper have been published,[25] and no general commentary series was available until the beginning of this millennium. Now, with the launching of the Philo of Alexandria Commentary Series (PACS) in 1991, there has been a change in this situation.[26] The first volume was published in 2001, and by 2013 three more were available.[27] The first volume of PACS is on *De Opificio*:

25. Of the few older commentaries published, one might mention especially Herbert Box, ed., *Philonis Alexandrini In Flaccum* (London: Oxford University Press, 1939); E. Mary Smallwood, ed., *Philonis Alexandrini Legatio Ad Gaium* (2nd ed.; Leiden: Brill, 1970). See further the remarks in Radice and Runia, *Philo of Alexandria: An Annotated Bibliography 1937-1986*, 46-47; David T. Runia, ed., *Philo of Alexandria: An Annotated Bibliography, 1987-1996* (VCSup 57; Leiden: Brill, 2000) 19-20.

26. On this series, see http://divinity.yale.edu/philo-alexandria.

27. Pieter Willem van der Horst, *Philo's Flaccus: The First Pogrom: Introduction, Translation, and Commentary* (PACS 2; Leiden: Brill, 2003); Walter T. Wilson, *Philo of Alexandria: On Virtues: Introduction, Translation, and Commentary* (PACS 3; Leiden: Brill, 2011); Albert C Geljon and David T. Runia, *Philo of Alexandria: On Cultivation* (PACS 4; Leiden: Brill, 2013).

David T. Runia, *Philo of Alexandria: On the Creation of the Cosmos according to Moses: Introduction, Translation, and Commentary* (PACS 1; Leiden: Brill, 2001).

At this point in our review of helpful tools for studying Philo, we have in many ways come to the end of a journey. Now it is time to turn to a study of the works of Philo himself, and we end this survey with a few brief comments on how scholars perceive Philo's possible own sources as an expositor of the Scriptures.

Philo as an Expositor: Using Sources and Exegetical Traditions

Scholars have long sought Philo's sources and the traditions he inherited as a background for understanding his expositions of the Scriptures. At present, this quest has not provided many answers. When writing on the life of Moses, Philo himself states:

> I will . . . tell the story of Moses as I have learned it, both from the sacred books, the wonderful monuments of his wisdom which he left behind him, and from some of the elders of the nation; for I always interwove what I was told with what I read, and thus believed myself to have a closer knowledge than others of his life's history. (*Mosis* 1.4)

Here Philo clearly admits that he is using sources.[28] His primary source is the Pentateuch. There are surprisingly few references in his works to parts of the Scriptures outside the Pentateuch. Naomi Cohen finds no more than forty-six references to the Prophets and the Writings.[29] The program set forth by Robert G. Hamerton-Kelly in 1972[30] concerning the source analysis of Philo's writings has not been followed up by many other scholars.[31] This is

---

28. See also *Spec.* 1.8 concerning circumcision: "These are the explanations handed down to us from the ancient studies of divinely gifted men who made deep researches into the writings of Moses. To these I would add that I consider. . . ." Cf. *Spec.* 3.178.

29. Cf. Naomi Cohen, *Philo's Scriptures: Citations from the Prophets and Writings: Evidence for a Haftarah Cycle in Second Temple Judaism*, JSJSup 123 (Leiden: Brill, 2007). See my review available at http://bookreviews.org/bookdetail.asp?TitleId=6391&CodePage=6391.

30. Robert G. Hamerton-Kelly, "Sources and Traditions in Philo Judaeus: Prolegomena to an Analysis of His Writings," *SPhilo* 1 (1972) 3-26.

31. See Thomas H. Tobin, *The Creation of Man: Philo and the History of Interpretation*

to a great extent due to the nature of Philo's writings: they take the form of expositions. As expositions "they consist of exegetical paraphrases of words and phrases from the Pentateuchal texts together with other words and phrases."[32] Thus in Philo's expositions can be found Old Testament words and phrases interwoven with comments that reflect various ideas and traditions. Hence, the interest in recent research has shifted to a search for exegetical traditions in Philo's works. The supposition in this research, as Burton L. Mack once stated it in a programmatic essay,[33] is that

> Philo used traditional exegetical methods and materials. These materials are diverse and may reflect stages of exegetical history or "schools" of exegesis which are in debate with one another. Philo employed these traditions with varying degrees of acceptance, and he reworked them with varying degrees of consistency.

In fact, this assessment concurs with Philo's own statement in *De vita Mosis* 1.4 quoted above. It is obvious that he had predecessors. Aristobulus is one of the more prominent.[34] In addition, we see from Philo's works that there were several other scholars at work in Alexandria at his time, and that he had to cope with their writings and thus with their interpretations. In recent research there have been some efforts to describe and characterize these, but no one has come closer to their real identity than to characterize two groups as the literalists and the allegorists.[35] So by studying Philo, one must draw upon what scholars have learned about his social world, his texts and textual contexts, but also, hopefully, gain an impression of the range of his views, his works, and his influence, not least through his later "history of consequences."

(CBQMS 14; Washington: Catholic Biblical Association of America, 1983). Peder Borgen, on the other hand, states in "Philo of Alexandria: A Critical and Synthetical Survey of Research since World War II," in *ANRW* 2.21.1 (1984) 132, that "Hamerton-Kelly is too optimistic when he maintains that the methods of source analysis as traditionally employed still can be used."

32. Borgen, "Philo of Alexandria: A Critical and Synthetical Survey," 132.

33. Burton L. Mack, "Exegetical Traditions in Alexandrian Judaism," *SPhilo* 3 (1974-75) 71-112, here 75.

34. On Aristobulus, see Nikolaus Walter, "Hellenistische Diaspora-Juden an der Wiege Des Urchristentums," in *The New Testament and Hellenistic Judaism,* ed. Peder Borgen and Søren Giversen (Aarhus: Aarhus University Press, 1995; Peabody: Hendrickson, 1997) 37-58; Borgen, "Aristobulus — A Jewish Exegete from Alexandria."

35. See Shroyer, "Alexandrian Jewish Literalists"; Hay, "Philo's References to Other Allegorists."

Summary and Outlook

Any M.A. or Ph.D. student working on Philo should become aware of the impressive range of tools that are available concerning this important figure from the ancient Greco-Roman world. Many of his texts survive in Greek and some in Armenian. We have various translations, lexica, indexes, several introductions written by foremost experts, impressive bibliographies, and a commentary series now appearing with the publication of volumes on the individual treatises of Philo. And as all his texts become digitalized, we will have impressive computer programs available to search his texts in a way that scholars only a few decades ago could hardly imagine. But whatever tools might be presented, it is Philo's own texts that should be the primary focus.

Philo's *Exposition of the Law* and Social History: Methodological Considerations

Adele Reinhartz

The various Philonic treatises grouped under the heading *Exposition of the Law* constitute a relatively orderly and literal (as opposed to allegorical) commentary on the "Holy Scriptures." These treatises have been mined for information about Philo's philosophical and intellectual background, such as his knowledge of Greek cosmology, Roman law, and rabbinic oral tradition, as well as for insight into the political organization and aspirations of the Alexandrian Jewish community.[1] The homiletical tone of the commentary and the frequent rhetorical use of the second person form of address, however, suggest that these treatises may also provide insight into other, more private issues and concerns of Philo's community, at least as he perceived them. Explicit discussions of parent-child relationships, divorce, inheritance, and other aspects of family life raise the rather tantalizing possibility of using Philo's *Exposition* as a source for social history in general, and the history of the family in particular.[2]

---

1. Cf. David T. Runia, *Philo of Alexandria and the Timaeus of Plato* (Philosophia antiqua 44; Leiden: Brill, 1986); Erwin R. Goodenoough, *The Jurisprudence of the Jewish Courts in Egypt* (1929; repr., Amsterdam: Philo, 1968); Samual Belkin, *Philo and the Oral Law* (Cambridge, MA: Harvard University Press, 1940); Aryeh Kasher, *The Jews in Hellenistic and Roman Egypt: The Struggle for Equal Rights* (TSAJ 7; Tübingen: Mohr Siebeck, 1985).

2. Social history may be defined as the study of "people's relationships with each other in families, kinship groupings, status groupings, villages, urban neighbourhoods, regions and polities"; Sheldon J. Watts, *A Social History of Western Europe, 1450-1720* (London: Hutchinson University Library, 1984) 1. "Families in former times," as one such work is titled, have become a subject of great interest on the part of historians in recent years, as indicated by the growing

This chapter is a preliminary attempt to address the question of whether it may be possible to draw social-historical data from Philo's exegetical discussions in the *Exposition*. We will consider, first, the rather formidable methodological obstacles which block the way to such an approach and, second, the differing assumptions that would either prevent or facilitate this enterprise. Finally, we will look at some examples of scriptural exposition related to family issues. These will be drawn from *On the Special Laws (Spec.)*, with occasional forays into *On the Decalogue (Decal.)* and *On the Virtues (Virt.)*.

Methodological Problems

The *Exposition* is an exegetical work, the structure and content of which for the most part are based directly on the Pentateuch as Philo read it. This is evident not only from its contents but also from explicit Philonic statements to that effect. In *On the Life of Abraham (Abr.)* 3, Philo describes his task in the *Exposition* as the "examination of the law in regular sequence."[3] In *Decal.* 1, he proposes "to give full descriptions of the written laws," while in *On the Special Laws* he focuses on "the particular ordinances" which he considers to be grouped under the ten headings provided by the Decalogue (*Spec.* 1.1).[4]

It is its exegetical genre that is at the root of the methodological difficulties in tapping the *Exposition* for data pertaining to Jewish family life in Philo's Alexandria.[5] Three problems may be singled out. First, Philo makes

---

numbers or articles and monographs in this area. See Jean Louis Flandrin, *Families in Former Times* (Cambridge: Cambridge University Press, 1972); Thomas E. J. Wiedemann, *Adults and Children in the Roman Empire* (London: Routledge; New Haven: Yale University Press, 1989); Mark Golden, *Children and Childhood in Classical Athens* (Baltimore: Johns Hopkins University Press, 1990); Shaye J. D. Cohen, ed., *The Jewish Family in Antiquity* (BJS; Atlanta: Scholars, 1993).

3. All citations and quotations from Philo are from *Philo*, trans. F. H. Colson and G. H. Whitaker (10 vols.; LCL; London: Heinemann; Cambridge, MA: Harvard University Press, 1929-62).

4. Cf. Richard D. Hecht, "Preliminary Issues in the Analysis of Philo's *De Specialibus Legibus*," *SPhilo* 5 (1978) 1-56.

5. On the importance of recognizing exegesis as Philo's primary activity in the *Exposition*, see David T. Runia, "How To Read Philo," in *Exegesis and Philosophy: Studies on Philo of Alexandria* (Aldershot: Variorum, 1990) 191; Thomas H. Tobin, *The Creation of Man: Philo and the History of Interpretation* (CBQMS 14; Washington: Catholic Biblical Association of America,

no attempt to provide a comprehensive discussion of "the Jewish family"; any insights into his views on family-related issues must be gleaned from the various places where these topics arise in his tenfold classification of Jewish law. So, for example, the laws pertaining to forbidden marriages, incest, and intermarriage are discussed under the category of the sixth commandment, which forbids adultery (*Spec.* 3.8, 22-29). Many other issues, such as child mortality, average ages of betrothal and marriage, and belief and practices related to fertility and infertility are mentioned only briefly, if at all.

Second, it is clear that his discussions of family issues often, though not always, arise when and where they do simply because they appear in the biblical text upon which he happens to be commenting. Hence we cannot determine with any certainty whether his discussion of a specific topic simply represents his thoughts on a particular biblical discussion or whether it also reflects a concern with some aspect of contemporary life. For example, Philo's vivid condemnation of women who grab the genitals of men during a public brawl (*Spec.* 3.175) might give rise to speculation concerning the pugnacious behavior of women in the marketplace. But because this specific case is described in the text he is explicating (Deut 25:11-12), we cannot conclude that he is reflecting on the situation in his own community.

Third, while Philo's attitudes on particular issues are often crystal clear, it is very difficult to discern the presence or nature of any *realia* pertaining to such issues. For example, Philo is very explicit about his abhorrence of homosexual practices (*Spec.* 2.50; 3.37-42). Yet it is virtually impossible to determine from his vitriolic outbursts whether or to what degree homosexuality was practiced in his community. Nor can we say whether his negative views were a reflection or a critique of Jewish popular opinion and/or practice.

A further problem is posed by the paucity and unreliability of external data concerning the Jewish family in first-century Alexandria. Our social-historical endeavor would be on more solid ground if we could correlate Philo's comments with extra-Philonic evidence. While there are a number of papyri from Alexandria, only a few have any relevance for the history of the Jewish family. Notable among these are a deed of divorce,[6] a contract with a wet nurse, and the annulment of such a contract.[7] While these provide

---

1983) 2-5; Burton L. Mack, "Philo Judaeus and Exegetical Traditions in Alexandria," in *ANRW* 2.21.2 (1984) 228.

6. *CPJ* 144 (*CPJ* 2:10-12).

7. *CPJ* 146-47 (*CPJ* 2:15-20).

interesting social-historical data, they do not correlate with any Philonic discussions and hence are of limited value for the present task.

Somewhat more relevant are Jewish inscriptions from Greco-Roman Egypt, some of which make reference to family relationships. Of special interest are tombstone inscriptions that speak of the love of parents for their children or the sadness of young women who died childless or during pregnancy or childbirth.[8] These reflect family values which are also expressed throughout Philo's *Exposition*. Philo too waxes eloquent on the ties of affection in the family, particularly on the part of parents toward their children,[9] and attributes to women in general a strong desire for children.[10] Hence these inscriptions provide general corroboration for claims that Philo, at least in these two respects, is consistent with popular attitudes. They offer little, however, in the way of specific confirmation of other issues discussed in the *Exposition*.

More numerous and detailed are references to the Jewish family in the works of non-Jewish Greek and Roman authors. Such references are often ambiguous or incorrect and hence must be used with caution. Nor do they always reflect the situation in Alexandria. According to Strabo (first century, Pontus), Jews, like Egyptians, "excise" female children (*Geogr.* 17.2, 5). Tacitus (first century, Rome) claims that while Jews abstain from intercourse with foreign women, among themselves nothing is unlawful (*Hist.* 5.5), a statement which ignores Jewish laws against incest (Lev 18:6-18) as well as the laws governing sexual intercourse between husband and wife (Lev 15:19-52; 18:19).

While these statements are clearly incorrect, others have been given more credence. A notable example is the assertion, made by the above-mentioned writers, that Jews rear all their children. Because infanticide and the exposure of infants are also discussed by Philo (*Spec.* 3.110-19; *Virt.* 151-53), scholars have

8. See William Horbury and David Noy, eds., *Jewish Inscriptions of Graeco-Roman Egypt* (Cambridge: Cambridge University Press, 1992) 38. 61, 70, 90, 103, 114.

9. See *Abr.* 195; *Ios.* 4; *Spec.* 2.129, 239-40. It may be claimed that what Philo and his contemporaries actually meant by "love and affection" differed significantly from our own understanding of this affective bond. But see Golden (*Children and Childhood*, 81ff.), who affirms that, contrary to what many scholars have argued, Athenian parents did love their children in the ways that modern parents do, despite the high mortality rate and the practice of infanticide in Classical Greece.

10. See *Mos.* 1.13-14, where Philo attributes the eagerness of Pharaoh's daughter to adopt the infant Moses to her depression over the failure to conceive a child, "though she naturally desired one, particularly of the male sex."

taken these comments along with Philo's condemnation of these practices as evidence that Jews did not engage in them.[11] As we shall see below, however, the audience and intent of Philo's comments in this regard are open to question; furthermore, the assertions of Strabo and Tacitus appear in the same passages as the errors noted above. Although the presence of some errors does not mean that all comments are mistaken, it does highlight the need for caution in using Greco-Roman literature to illuminate Jewish life in Alexandria.

These considerations return us once again to the task of finding a way to extract social-historical data from the *Exposition* itself. Yet, as we have seen, the exegetical focus of these treatises renders this endeavor difficult indeed.

Scholarly Assumptions

The connection between Philo's scriptural expositions and the actual attitudes, activities, and practices of the Jewish community in first-century Alexandria has received little detailed treatment in Philonic scholarship. Studies of Philo's legal commentary have tended to focus on the question of its sources in Greek and Roman law and philosophy on the one hand, and/or Tannaitic or pre-Tannaitic oral tradition and halakah on the other. Erwin R. Goodenough, for example, argued that many passages in *Spec.* reflect the legal practices of Philo's community.[12] What Philo has done in *On the Special Laws,* suggests Goodenough, is to "rebuild the keyhole structure of Jewish law upon a foundation of Greek, Roman, and Alexandrine jurisprudence."[13] Samuel Belkin, while accepting that Philo's legal discussions are based on the decisions of local Jewish courts, argues that most of the laws described in the *Exposition* agree with the principles of Tannaitic law.[14] More recently, scholars have focused on the issue of Philo's dependence on or independence from Palestinian and/or Hellenistic Jewish exegetical traditions,[15] setting aside the question of Philo's own intellectual contribution[16] or the possibility that he may be reacting to or reflecting on real social issues.

---

11. Cf. p. 187 below.

12. Goodenough, *The Jurisprudence of the Jewish Courts,* 10 and passim.

13. Goodenough, *The Jurisprudence of the Jewish Courts,* 14.

14. Belkin, *Philo and the Oral Law,* 5-6, 19.

15. See Burton L. Mack, "Exegetical Traditions in Alexandrian Judaism: A Program for the Analysis of the Philonic Corpus," *SPhilo* 3 (1974-75) 106; Jacques Cazeaux, "Système implicite dons l'exégèse de Philon," *SPhilo* 6 (1979-80) 5; Yehoshua Amir, "Philo and the Bible," *SPhilo* 2 (1978) 1.

16. Mack, "Exegetical Traditions in Alexandrian Judaism," 108.

These trends in Philonic scholarship on the *Exposition* point to assumptions regarding Philo's involvement in the Jewish community. Many scholars consider Philo to be more concerned with Scripture, philosophy, and law than with contemporary social and communal issues per se. Samuel Sandmel, for example, describes Philo as "an ivory tower figure, rather than a man engaged in committee work in the community," a description he infers from Philo's prodigious literary output.[17] Others, however, find this description inadequate, arguing that while Philo's concern with exegesis and philosophy is clearly paramount, his involvement in and concern for Jewish community life is not to be dismissed. Peder Borgen's Philo lives squarely "in the double context of the Jewish community and the Alexandrian Greek community"[18] and is concerned to make the Pentateuch interpret Jewish community life.[19] Borgen concludes that "Philo was an exegete who interpreted the Pentateuch and Jewish exegetical traditions into his contemporary situation, without cutting off their historical basis in the Biblical events."[20]

David T. Runia, Aryeh Kasher, and Scot McKnight assume that certain sections of Philo's work describe the history,[21] institutions,[22] or attitudes[23] of his own city and community. Such assumptions are also basic to Goodenough's discussion of Philo's politics[24] and legal rulings[25] and are expressed explicitly by Belkin, who asserts that "The general view prevalent among scholars that Philo had interest in communal affairs and was, as is sometimes said, an 'individualist' by nature is open to doubt."[26]

A second set of assumptions concerns the nature of the Jewish family in antiquity, an issue closely related to that of the relationship of the Diaspora Jewish community to its non-Jewish social environment. Are we to picture the

---

17. Samuel Sandmel, "Philo Judaeus: An Introduction to the Man, His Writings, and His Significance," in *ANRW* 2.21.1 (1984) 5.

18. Peder Borgen, "Philo of Alexandria: A Critical and Synthetical Survey of Research since World War II," in *ANRW* 11.21.1, 119.

19. Borgen, "Philo of Alexandria: A Critical and Synthetical Survey," 138.

20. Borgen, "Philo of Alexandria: A Critical and Synthetical Survey," 150.

21. Runia, "Polis and Megalopolis: Philo and the Founding of Alexandria," in *Exegesis and Philosophy*, 398.

22. Kasher, *The Jews in Hellenistic and Roman Egypt*, 206, 256.

23. Scot McKnight, "*De Vita Mosis* 1.147: Lion Proselytes in Philo?" *SPhAn* 1 (Atlanta: Scholars, 1989) 58-62.

24. Erwin R. Goodenough, *The Politics of Philo Judaeus: Practice and Theory* (New Haven: Yale University Press, 1938).

25. Goodenough, *The Jurisprudence of the Jewish Courts*.

26. Belkin, *Philo and the Oral Law*, 6.

Jewish family as isolated, insular, and therefore in some sense inoculated against the problems of the Gentile family in Alexandria? Or should we assume that Jewish family relationships may have been similar to and even influenced by those of non-Jews, even when in contravention of what we perceive to be Jewish ideals? Scholars' answers to these questions may reflect not only their academic evaluations of Jewish political and social status in the Diaspora but also more personal issues, such as the tendency to idealize the Jewish family in antiquity. Such idealization is clearly expressed in modern Jewish popular writings intended to reinforce "traditional" Jewish family values. A book titled *Love, Marriage, and Family in Jewish Law and Tradition* declares that

> in the past, virtually impervious to degenerative influences from the outside world, the Jewish home was universally respected as a model of stability, wholesomeness, and integrity. This is no longer the case [in assimilated, twentieth-century Jewish life].[27]

The assumption of a pure, strong, stable family life, while not stated explicitly in scholarship on Jews in antiquity, may be lurking behind the conclusion that certain Gentile practices were unknown among Diaspora Jews. This may explain the readiness of scholars to take the testimony of Strabo et al. that Jews rear all their children, at face value. Menahem Stern, for example, states emphatically that "the Jews' religious duty to rear all their children and their view that the exposure of new-born children is tantamount to murder offer a striking contrast to the Greek habit of killing . . . infants, a constant feature of Greek life."[28]

Historians and social scientists who study the history of the Jewish family suggest that the perfect, uncorrupted Jewish family in antiquity is a myth.[29] David Kraemer introduces a volume of essays on the Jewish family by stating that

> If we understand the dynamism of earlier social conditions, we will appreciate the fact that contemporary experience represents less of a break with the past than we might have believed.

27. Michael Kaufman, *Love, Marriage, and Family in Jewish Law and Tradition* (Northvale: Aronson, 1992) x.

28. Menahem Stern, ed., *Greek and Latin Authors on Jews and Judaism*, vol. 1: *From Herodotus to Plutarch* (Jerusalem: Israel Academy of Sciences and Humanities, 1974) 33.

29. Gerald B. Bubis, *Saving the Jewish Family: Myths and Realties in the Diaspora* (Lanham: University Press of America, 1987) x.

What emerges from this volume, he continues,

> is a picture of immense variety and the realization that down through the ages the Jewish family has adapted almost "organically" to the many and varied environments within which it has had to survive.[30]

This picture is apparently shared by scholars such as John Boswell, who suggests that the Jewish family might not have differed substantially from its Gentile counterpart, even with respect to something as difficult as abandonment of children.[31]

Assumptions regarding the nature of the Jewish family — pure or assimilated — may generate further, more specific assumptions concerning the relevance of Philo's *Exposition* for the history of the Jewish family in antiquity. Perhaps the most important issue of this sort concerns the relationship between legal prohibition and community practice. Does Philo's assertion that a particular act was forbidden by Mosaic law mean that it was in fact foreign to the experience of the Jewish community? Philo himself does not assume this to be the case. For example, he suggests that the laws penalizing men who falsely accuse their wives of infidelity are aimed at those persons "who show fickleness in their relations to women" (*Spec.* 3.79). His discussion of the laws about murder assumes the existence of murderers in the community (e.g., *Spec.* 3.83ff.). Similarly, he is of the conviction that such penalties serve as a deterrent, "as a considerable check on those who are eager to practice the like" (*Spec.* 3.42).

These passages would suggest that Philo's strong condemnation of certain behaviors and his assertions that they are prohibited by Mosaic law point to activities which he perceived to be practiced in his community. This would undermine Léonie Archer's conclusion that the fact that Philo, Josephus, and the *Sibylline Oracles* declare infanticide and exposure to be contrary to Jewish law means that "the practice of exposing unwanted infants . . . was not found among the Jews of the Greco-Roman period."[32]

Implicit in the above discussion is yet another assumption, namely, the

---

30. David Kraemer, ed., *The Jewish Family: Metaphor and Memory* (New York: Oxford University Press, 1989) 5.

31. John Boswell, *The Kindness of Strangers* (New York: Pantheon, 1988) 139-52.

32. Léonie J. Archer, *Her Price Is Beyond Rubies: The Jewish Woman in Graeco-Roman Palestine* (JSOTSup 60; Sheffield: Sheffield Academic, 1990) 28. Cf. also Lawrence E. Stager, "Eroticism and Infanticide at Ashkelon," *BAR* 17/4 (1991) 46.

issue of intended audience. Three possibilities may be suggested. If the intended audience of the *Exposition* is Gentile, as Goodenough argued, then passages condemning practices such as infanticide and homosexuality may not reflect Jewish practice at all, but may rather be directed at activities of the Gentile readership which are amply documented elsewhere.[33] Or, if the audience is also composed of Jews "on the threshold of apostasy," as Sandmel suggested, Philo may be exhorting his Jewish readers not to adopt the immoral practices of their Gentile neighbors.[34] Many scholars, however, consider the *Exposition* to be addressed to the Jewish community as a whole.[35] This view is supported by Philo's assertion that the law, while universally applicable, is addressed in the first place to Jews and proselytes (*Spec.* 4.100, 219; *Virt.* 102).

A priori views of Philo as removed from community life, of the Jewish community in Alexandria as insulated and isolated, of Philo's declarations about Mosaic law as descriptive of Alexandrian reality, and of Philo's *Exposition* as addressed to a Gentile audience work against the use of this poetical composition as a source for the history of the Jewish family. The contrary assumptions — of Philo as involved in community life, of the potential influence of Gentile practices on Jewish family life, of legal prohibitions as directed against actual practice, and of a Jewish audience for the *Exposition* — provide a basis for considering these treatises as a source for social history and, as we have suggested, may be equally plausible.[36]

---

33. See, e.g., Boswell, *The Kindness of Strangers,* 53-137; Donald Engels, "The Problem of Female Infanticide in the Greco-Roman World," *CP* 75 (1980) 112-30; William V. Harris, "The Theoretical Possibility of Extensive Infanticide in the Graeco-Roman World," *CQ* 32 (1982) 114-16; Mark Golden, "Demography and the Exposure of Girls at Athens," *Phoenix* 85 (1951) 316-31; Sarah B. Pomeroy, "Infanticide in Hellenistic Greece," in *Images of Women in Antiquity,* ed. Averil Cameron and Amélie Kuhrt (Detroit: Wayne State University Press, 1983) 207-22.

34. Samuel Sandmel, *Philo of Alexandria: An Introduction* (Oxford: Oxford University Press, 1979) 47.

35. Victor Tcherikover, "Jewish Apologetic Literature Reconsidered," *Eos* 48 (1956) 178-79.

36. This is not to say, of course, that these assumptions are incorrect or that those scholars who refrain from discussing family issues hold to all or even any of these assumptions. For most scholars, their work on Philo simply reflects other legitimate research interests as well as the incontrovertible fact that Philo's *Exposition* is above all an exegetical work and not an analysis of public and private policy and practice.

Scriptural Exposition and Social History

Support for the second set of assumptions is provided by a brief examination of Philo's exegetical strategies in the *Exposition* and the hermeneutical presuppositions which these strategies imply. Philo's exegetical method in the *Exposition* has been considered primarily from three perspectives: his use of sources, whether Greco-Roman, Palestinian, or Alexandrian; his allegorical interpretation; and his grouping of the particular laws according to the ten "headings" of the Decalogue.[37] For the purposes of detecting social-historical information between the lines of exegesis, our focus shall be on the specific moves Philo makes with respect to the biblical text he is expounding.

Several different types of moves may be noticed.

1. In almost every passage, Philo provides a rationale for the biblical law where none is provided by the biblical text itself. In the course of doing so, he often also explains Scripture's silence on issues that in his view might well have been included in biblical legislation.
2. Philo will often extend the laws explicitly discussed in Scripture to cover other situations that seem to him to be analogous to or implicit in biblical law.
3. He reinterprets laws that reflect social conditions that are no longer operative in his place and time.
4. He provides specific instructions and more precise definitions in cases where biblical law provides only a general formulation.

These exegetical moves imply Philo's hermeneutical presuppositions vis-à-vis Mosaic laws as set out literally in Scripture. First, the law is divinely given and applicable to every era and to all Jews. Second, the law covers, either explicitly or implicitly, all aspects of private, family, communal, and ritual life. In doing so, it implies an absolute set of values that can be abstracted from the text and applied to many situations. Third, the law as set out in Scripture requires explanation and interpretation in order that Jews may understand and therefore be able to follow it. Fourth, the law must therefore be explained in ways that will be meaningful to its contemporary audience. Finally, the law should be practiced in its literal sense by all Jews, including those in Philo's community, a view expressed explicitly by Philo in *Migr.* 89-93.

37. Cf. Hecht, "Preliminary Issues."

These hermeneutical presuppositions tend to support the idea that Philo's commentary does reflect his concerns for his own community and addresses those issues in some way. The way that he does so may reflect only his own views and perceptions, but it is also possible that at certain points his work reflects practices and attitudes present in his own community, not only in what he says in a positive way but also in what his legal argumentation critiques. This in turn implies that we can look at his exegesis for hints regarding the texture of family life in his community. We will illustrate this possibility by looking briefly at examples of each of the strategies we outlined above.

Rationalization

The topics of many of Philo's discussions pertinent to family issues are generated by the text itself. His discussions of the widowed or divorced, childless daughter of a priest, who returns to live with her father (*Spec.* 1.129-30; cf. Lev 22:13); of the requirement to redeem one's firstborn, if a son (*Spec.* 1.134-40; cf. Exod 13:2; 22:29; Num 18:15-16); and of the laws of inheritance, according to which "the heirs of parents are to be sons, or failing sons daughters" (*Spec.* 2.124-30; cf. Num 27:8-11), are only a few examples among many of discussions the topics of which are derived directly from biblical law.

Rationalization of biblical law

The rationales that Philo provides for these laws, however, do not necessarily find their explicit source in the biblical text. For example, the biblical commandment to redeem the firstborn son appears in the context of the law concerning the sacrificial offering of firstborn animals. No reason is given in Exodus or Numbers for the requirement to redeem the firstborn son with a financial redemption fee. Philo fills this gap by describing this redemption as "a thank-offering for the blessings of parenthood realized in the present and the hopes of fruitful increase in the future" (*Spec.* 1.138). The "consecration of a fixed sum of money" is intended to prevent the separation of parents from their children and vice versa and to assign equal value to the birth of a child to poor parents as to rich (*Spec.* 1.139-40). This argument places a positive value on procreation and on preserving the integrity of the nuclear family, values expressed in other Philonic discussions.[38]

38. See, e.g., *Virt.* 131-33.

A second example of Philo's rationalization of biblical law concerns the laws of inheritance. The fact that sons take precedence over daughters in matters of inheritance is considered by Philo to be analogous to the law of nature: "just as in nature men take precedence of women, so too in the scale of relationships they should take the first place in succeeding to the property and filling the position of the departed" (*Spec.* 2.124). The biblical text makes no such deduction, though one may infer that according to the biblical view "men take precedence of women" in many legal matters.[39] Philo uses his own thoroughgoing patriarchal worldview to provide the rationale for this biblical law.[40]

Rationalization of omissions from biblical law

In other passages, Philo provides a rationale for the silence of the biblical text. In *Spec.* 2.129-32, for example, he considers a question raised "by some inquirers," namely, "Why . . . does the Law when dealing with the regulations of inheritance mention kinsmen of every degree . . . but leaves parents unmentioned who would naturally inherit from the children as the children do from them?" (2.129). Philo reads into this biblical silence the law's desire to refrain from "sinister thoughts": the distressing possibility that parents might be predeceased by their children, a circumstance "out of tune with and discordant to the harmony and concord which prevails throughout the cosmic order" (2.130). This rationale, like that of the laws of redemption of the firstborn, assumes the affection of parents toward their children, a theme which appears frequently in Philo's discussion of parent-child relations.[41]

Use of contemporary examples

In the course of these rationalizations, Philo often makes use of contemporary examples, drawing on customs, experiences, or events with which his

39. See Judith Romney Wegner, "Leviticus," in *The Women's Bible Commentary*, ed. Carol A. Newsom and Sharon H. Ringe (Louisville: Westminster John Knox, 1992) 36-44.

40. Philo was of course not unique among Greco-Roman writers in his patriarchal worldview. See Mary R. Lefkowitz and Maureen B. Fant, eds., *Women in Greece and Rome* (Toronto: Stevens, 1977); Sarah B. Pomeroy, *Goddesses, Whores, Wives, and Slaves* (New York: Schocken, 1995); Eva Cantarella, *Pandora's Daughters* (Baltimore: Johns Hopkins University Press, 1987).

41. For a survey of Philo's views on this issue, see my "Parents and Children: A Philonic Perspective," in *Jewish Families in Antiquity*, ed. Sha e D. Cohen (BJS 289; Atlanta: Scholars, 1993) 61-87.

readers may be familiar. For example, in *Spec.* 3.159-62, Philo illustrates the unjustified cruelty of some people with the example of a tax collector "a little time ago in our own district." In *Spec.* 1.123-28, Philo seems to be speaking directly of the experience of himself and others of his class when he describes the relationships between masters and slaves:

> Our domestics are always with us and share our lives. They prepare the ordinary food and drink and additional dishes for their masters, stand by the table and carry out the remains. Whether we wish it or not, they will even if they do not take them openly, pilfer them on the sly.

Similarly, Philo attributes the misdeeds such as the taking of bribes to the way in which the offender was raised by the women of the household:

> Now the principal cause of such misdeeds is familiarity with falsehood which grows up with the children right from their birth and from the cradle, the work of nurses and mothers and the rest of the company, slaves and free, who belong to the household. (*Spec.* 4.68)

Implications for the study of the Jewish family in Alexandria

One may speculate that the various ways in which Philo provides a rationale for what is present in or omitted from biblical law reflects his own views, regardless of whether these are paralleled in other Jewish or non-Jewish sources. The brief examples of family law that we have considered demonstrate his patriarchal worldview and his conviction concerning the similarity between Mosaic law and natural law, which justifies the general principle that "men take precedence over women" and that parents should predecease their children. Also evident are the positive evaluation of procreation and familial togetherness, in recognition of which the law, as Philo sees it, makes every effort not to separate parents and children. Finally, Philo's disparaging description of childbearing in *Spec.* 4.68 implies the image of a household as being composed of many people of different classes and roles (slaves, nurses, mothers). This passage may also be indirect testimony to the important role of women in addition to the mother in the raising of children, at least among the higher classes with whom Philo, as suggested by his description of the master-servant relationship, may have been acquainted.

Extension of Biblical Topics

In addition to providing a rationale for biblical laws or the omissions thereof, Philo extends them to cover analogous situations not explicitly described in the biblical text. In doing so, he does not perceive himself as creating new laws, but rather as drawing out and making explicit various laws that are already implicit in the biblical formulation. This strategy is expressed in his comment that "in the fifth commandment on honoring parents we have a suggestion of many necessary laws drawn up to deal wish the relations old to young, rulers to subjects, benefactors to benefited, slaves to masters."

Extension of the law to cover cases similar to but not explicitly mentioned in the biblical text

An example of this strategy is to be found in his extension of the biblical laws concerning rape to include sexual assault of widowed and divorced women, cases which are not discussed in the biblical text itself (*Spec.* 3.64).[42] A second example is to be found in Philo's discussion of inheritance, in which he extends the biblical law by claiming that girls who do not have dowries inherit from the father even when there are sons (*Spec.* 2.125).

This strategy, like the rationale of omissions above (p. 191), demonstrates Philo's perception of a gap in the literary text of the Pentateuch. In these cases, however, rather than rationalizing the gap, he eliminates it by inserting explanations of the laws that are unarticulated in the biblical text. Do these insertions point to issues of concern regarding his own community, or is Philo simply engaged in a theoretical exercise? While this question is difficult to answer in any definitive way, some clues might be provided by the length and tone of each individual discussion. Because it is short and theoretical in its tone, it may be argued that the extension of rape law to include the case of the formerly married woman is based on Philo's perception that the biblical law has omitted one possible situation from its presentation. The case of unmarried daughters left fatherless, however, is explained in much more detail, with provision made for how, where, and by whom a husband is to be

---

42. Cf. Deut 22:22-29. Colson (*Philo*, 7:514-15) notes the difficulty of determining whether "what he says reflects the practice of his time . . . or merely what he feels would be right." Goodenough (*The Jurisprudence of the Jewish Courts*, 90-91) suggests that this was an independent tradition of the Alexandrian courts.

found for such girls. This may point to a situation which actually occurred frequently enough in Philo's community to warrant the development of precise procedures.

Extensions which cover cases only tangentially related to the biblical law under discussion

In *Spec.* 3.34-36, Philo sharply criticizes those "who plough the hard and stony land," namely, men who marry women known to be infertile. Although this discussion would seem to have no connection to any biblical verse,[43] it in fact is an elaboration of the preceding discussion of the laws pertaining to menstruation and intercourse (*Spec.* 3.32-33; cf. Lev 18:19). Philo's main point in the latter discussion is "that generative seed should not be wasted fruitlessly for the sake of a gross and untimely pleasure" (3.32). The theme that seed should not be wasted is also prominent in his discussion of the former point: in mating with barren women, men are "in quest of mere licentious pleasure like the most lecherous of men," a quest which entails the purposeful destruction of "the procreative germs" (*Spec.* 3.34). The tone and length of the discussion conveys Philo's strong disapproval of a situation that no doubt was known to him from the community and expresses his firm belief that the only legitimate purpose of marriage and marital intercourse is procreation.

Spec. 4.203 provides another example of this strategy. In this passage Philo links the biblical prohibition of the mixing of different species of animals with the prohibition of adultery, which is not mentioned in the biblical passage under discussion (Lev 19:19; Deut 22:9-11): "For by prohibiting the crossing of irrational animals with different species he [Moses] appears to be indirectly working towards the prevention of adultery." Like the previous example, this extension expresses the disapproval of a practice, namely adultery, that was the subject of his extreme disapproval in many other passages in the *Special Laws* and, we may reasonably assume, was not totally foreign to Philo's community.[44]

Philo's impassioned arguments against infanticide also fall into this category.[45] *Spec.* 3.110-19 is a comment on Exod 21:22, which discusses the penalties for feticide. *Virt.* 131-33 is part of his discussion of Lev 22:27, which stipulates

43. So Colson, *Philo*, 7:497, 633-34. For an analysis of the rabbinic views on this issue, see Jeremy Cohen, *Be Fertile and Increase, Fill the Earth and Master It: The Ancient and Medieval Career of a Biblical Text* (Ithaca: Cornell University Press, 1989) 135-40.

44. See *Spec.* 3.52-63; *Virt.* 37.

45. For detailed discussion of this issue, see my "Philo on Infanticide," *SPhAn* 4 (Leiden: Brill, 1992) 42-58.

that a newborn ox, sheep, or goat must stay seven days with its mother before being offered by fire to the Lord. Neither of these biblical passages refers to infanticide or exposure of infants, yet they provide Philo with the framework and vocabulary for his condemnation of these practices. Hence he declares that if the law is concerned about the life of an unborn child, how much more must this be true about the life of a newly born child (*Spec.* 3.111). And if "even in the case of irrational animals, the offspring could not be separated from their mother," how much more so is this true of human beings (*Virt.* 135).

As we have already noted, most scholars consider Philo's arguments, together with the statements of non-Jewish Greco-Roman writers, to be evidence that Jews did not kill or expose their newborn children. It may be suggested, however, that the fact that Philo introduces this topic, not once but twice, into exegetical discussions of verses to which it is only tangentially related should make us suspect that he was indeed concerned with the actual or potential recourse to these methods of population control in his own community.[46] The length of his arguments, the rhetorical use of the second person form of address, and the general tone of his discussion point in the same direction. It may be argued that what he is objecting to so strongly is the Gentile practice of exposure or infanticide. It must be noted, however, that his critique of "other nations" refers to their failure to condemn this "sacrilegious practice" (*Spec.* 3.110). Hence the contrast he is making is not between Gentiles who engage in this practice and Jews who do not, but between Gentile law which regards this practice complacently and Mosaic law, which condemns it most strongly.

Implications for the study of the Jewish family in Alexandria

The above comments suggest that the directions in which Philo extends biblical laws, together with the length to which and the rhetorical tone in which he does so, may point to topics of particular concern to him. These topics express his point of view on these issues, as well as the principles which undergird his perspective. They may also, however, hint at actual practices and concerns of the Jewish community, including the ways in which that community dealt with orphaned unmarried girls, and the possibility that some members of the community resorted to infanticide or the exposure of infants.

---

46. A third reference to exposure is to be found in *Mos.* 1.10-11, in Philo's description of the birth and rescue of the infant Moses.

Contemporization of an Obsolete Law

Example of contemporization

In some passages, Philo reinterprets a law that is no longer applicable to his time in such a way as to make it applicable. For example, *Spec.* 2.135-39 is a discussion of Deut 22:15-17, pertaining to matters of inheritance in a situation in which a man has two wives, one loved and the other unloved. Biblical law stipulates that the son of the disliked woman inherits twice what the son of the beloved wife inherits. At a time when bigamy and formal concubinage were apparently no longer practiced in the Jewish community, Philo applies this law to a situation in which a man, legally married to a wife who has borne a son, is engaged in an adulterous relationship which has also resulted in a son. He likens the legal wife to the hated wife of the biblical passage and argues that her son receives twice the portion of the other son, on the grounds that the son of the legal wife has suffered by being abandoned by his father. This law, according to Philo, "shews mercy and pity for the victims of injustice" and equalizes the situation of the two families (*Spec.* 2.138-59). This discussion expresses Philo's abhorrence of adultery, which he criticizes severely elsewhere (cf. also *Spec.* 3.79-83). It also indicates that his condemnation of adultery is based not only on the licentiousness of the act, but also on the fact it has severe social consequences affecting the legal family.

Implications for the study of the Jewish family in Alexandria

Philo's condemnation of adultery expresses his disapproval of licentiousness and passion, which run counter to his views of ideal human behavior. His discussion may also be taken as evidence for the social norm of monogamy in his community and also, plausibly, as a reflection of a contemporary social issue which the Alexandrian community had to address.

Specification of a General Biblical Law

Example of specification

A good example of this procedure is to be found in Philo's treatment of the fifth commandment. The biblical law simply enjoins people to honor their mothers and fathers, without specifying precisely what it means to do so. Philo provides two precise definitions of this commandment. In *Decal.* 111-19, he defines honoring as taking care of one's parents in their old age, a topos common to Greek philosophy.[47] The length and eloquence of his discussions suggests that this was an area of immediate concern to Philo and/or his community.

A similar strategy is evident in *Spec.* 2.228-41. In this section, Philo defines honoring one's parents as "trying both to be good and to seem good, to be good seeking virtue simple and unfeigned, to seem good by seeking it accompanied by a reputation for worth and the praise of those around you" (2.235). Evident in this section is Philo's concern to define the role and authority of parents, though this is not at all the subject of the biblical text of the fifth commandment.

To this latter definition is attached a discussion of the biblical law specifying the death penalty for a rebellious son (Deut 21:18-21). Philo's discussion is considered by some scholars to have been influenced by Roman laws regarding *patria potestas,* according to which the father had the power of life and death over the numbers of his household. This raises the interesting possibility that these laws, or a variation of them, were also operative in family relationships in the Jewish community. Whether or not that is the case, Philo's discussion does not necessarily mean that rebellious sons were actually executed, since this topic is generated by the biblical text itself. It does emphasize, however, the importance to Philo of the preservation of hierarchical relationships within the family and, in particular, of the authority of the father over his children. Recourse to execution is only the most extreme form of asserting such authority; it is an option only after the failure of other disciplinary actions such as upbraiding and admonishing him severely, beating and degrading him, and putting him in bonds. Also to be considered is the possibility of disinheritance. None of these are mentioned in the biblical text about the rebellious son, suggesting that they may derive from Greco-Roman law and/or the actual practice in the community.[48]

Implications for the study of the Jewish family in Alexandria

The fact that Philo spends so much time on this topic implies that the discipline of children, particularly male children, was a problematic issue for him

---

47. Aristotle, *Eth. nic.* 1165a21-27.

48. See Goodenough, *The Jurisprudence of the Jewish Courts,* 70-76; Colson, *Philo,* 7:629; Isaak Heinemann, ed., *Die Werke Philos von Alexandria* (Breslau: Marcus, 1910) 2:173; *Philons griechische und jüdische Bildung* (Breslau: Marcus, 1932) 234.

(*Spec.* 2.232, 234, 240-48). Philo himself blames the permissiveness of parents in allowing their children every luxury with the result that "they run to waste both in body and soul" (2.240).

Conclusions

Our sampling of Philonic exegesis has yielded one certain result: it is much easier to reconstruct Philo's Jewish family values than it is to discern the actual contours of Jewish family life in first-century Alexandria. If one is willing to live with uncertain conclusions, however, several points may be made. First, careful attention to the relationship between biblical legislation and Philonic exegesis thereof may help to identify the issues about which Philo was most concerned. On the assumption that his concerns may be based on the realities of Jewish family life in his community, some exegetical discussions may yield social-historical results. Most significant for this purpose are the passages in which Philo extends the scope of a biblical law to cover areas not mentioned in the biblical formulation of that law. Also significant may be those passages which he reinterprets in the light of changing social relationships. Second, impressions based on Philo's exegetical strategies must be supplemented by considering the tone, length, and content of a particular comment. A lengthy, detailed, and vehement discussion of a topic related only tangentially to a biblical "tag" may be evidence of a significant issue in Philo's community. Third, "throwaway" comments and references to contemporary events, which often appear in Philo's rationalizations, may provide hints regarding household structures and social norms. On the basis of these considerations, it seems reasonable to conclude that situations like adultery, the death of fathers of unmarried daughters, the "rebelliousness" of male children, and the killing or exposure of infants were not unknown within this community and required the development of particular legislative or community policy decisions and procedures.

This preliminary study supports the cautious use of Philo's *Exposition* as a source for data on the Jewish family in Alexandria. These exegetical treatises cannot, however, be our sole source. Rather, they must be supplemented and, where feasible, corroborated or corrected by relevant material in the rest of the Philonic corpus, other Jewish and non-Jewish writings of the time,[49] in-

---

49. E.g., Pseudo-Phocylides. For this text and discussion of its dating and provenance,

scriptions, and papyri. Finally, the entire enterprise must be informed by a healthy but disciplined historical imagination.

One cannot ignore the methodological pitfalls of a social-historical approach to Philo's *Exposition,* nor those that pertain to the other types of material relevant to the Jewish family in the Diaspora. Despite its inherent uncertainty, however, the endeavor is both interesting and worthwhile. It promises to enhance our knowledge of Jewish life in antiquity as well as contribute to the growing field devoted to the social history of the family.

---

see P. W. van der Horst, *The Sentences of Pseudo-Phocylides* (SVTP 4; Leiden: Brill, 1978); "Pseudo-Phocylides Revisited," *JSP* 3 (1988) 15.

Philo's Relevance for the Study of Jews and Judaism in Antiquity

Ellen Birnbaum

In recent decades, a much-debated question — especially in relation to antiquity — is whether we can speak of a "common Judaism," with a core set of characteristics, or only of a plurality of "Judaisms," represented by discrete groups, each with its own distinctive outlook and mode of life.[1] To inform one's approach to this debate, one can draw amply from the writings of Philo of Alexandria. As a Jew living before the destruction of the temple in 70 C.E., Philo offers an abundance of precious evidence about his Jewish contemporaries and their beliefs and practices. Because he came from a wealthy, influential family and was well-educated and thoroughly steeped in Greek philosophy, Philo himself was not typical of most or probably even of many

1. For differing positions, see, e.g., E. P. Sanders, *Judaism: Practice and Belief, 63 BCE–66 CE* (London: SCM; Philadelphia: Trinity Press International, 1994); Wayne O. McCready and Adele Reinhartz, eds., *Common Judaism: Explorations in Second-Temple Judaism* (Minneapolis: Fortress, 2008); Alan Mendelson, "'Did Philo Say the Shema?' and Other Reflections on E. P. Sanders' *Judaism: Practice and Belief,*" *SPhAn* 6 (1994) 160-70; Jacob Neusner, *Judaism and Its Social Metaphors: Israel in the History of Jewish Thought* (Cambridge: Cambridge University Press, 1989); *The Way of Torah: An Introduction to Judaism* (6th ed.; Belmont: Wadsworth, 1997); Jonathan Z. Smith, "Fences and Neighbors: Some Contours of Early Judaism," in *Imagining Religion: From Babylon to Jonestown* (Chicago: University of Chicago Press, 1982) 1-18; Michael L. Satlow, "Defining Judaism: Accounting for 'Religions' in the Study of Religion," *JAAR* 74 (2006) 837-60; *Creating Judaism: History, Tradition, Practice* (New York: Columbia University Press, 2006). See also n. 10 below. For a learned and insightful overview of the debate, see Seth Schwartz, "How Many Judaisms Were There? A Critique of Neusner and Smith on Definition and Mason and Boyarin on Categorization," *Journal of Ancient Judaism* 2 (2011) 208-38. I am grateful to Professor Schwartz for sharing an advance copy of his paper with me.

Jews in antiquity. Nonetheless, his voluminous writings — used wisely — can shed light on both the commonality and the diversity among these Jews. In this chapter, we shall explore seven areas (a nice Philonic number!) in which Philo contributes valuable information. These areas include (1) Jewish practices, (2) beliefs and ideas, (3) community institutions, (4) the Bible and biblical exegesis, (5) Jews and Jewish identity, (6) Jews' attitudes toward non-Jews and their culture, and (7) historical events pertaining to Jews.

Before turning to these areas, however, we would do well to reflect on what it means to use the Philonic evidence wisely. As a first step, it is essential simply to read what Philo has to say on particular subjects, such as those discussed further below. Passages on most subjects, like Passover or the divine powers, will be obvious to locate, either because one can perform a word search and/or consult other scholarly treatments for guidance. In reading through Philo's works for specific topics, however, researchers should also be alert to information that he conveys in passing. Describing the oppression of the Alexandrian Jews in 38 C.E., for example, Philo mentions the names of three members of the *gerousia,* or council of elders, and thereby contributes to our knowledge of Greek-Jewish names of his day.[2] It is also essential to take into account Philo's aims and possible audience(s), since he may present topics differently to his own elite circle and to outsiders, some of whom may be hostile toward Jews and their mode of life.[3] Reading Philo in this way will provide a "baseline" regarding details and impressions that he conveys or wishes to convey about specific topics. This information is valuable in itself as it expresses the experience and perspective of one Jew in antiquity. The information may also, however, represent the experiences and perspectives of an even broader group or groups of Jews in Alexandria, the Diaspora, or "the whole habitable world" (*oikoumenē; Flacc.* 44; *Legat.* 214).

To determine just how widely representative the Philonic evidence is requires us to use it in relation to other sources. Although Philo lived in the

---

2. *Flacc.* 76; see also n. 36 below. Another interesting piece of information that Philo mentions in passing is the posture maintained by the Therapeutae during their meetings (*Contempl.* 30; see also 77), which resembles the posture of Jews described in another context (*Somn.* 2.126). One wonders what significance this posture held.

3. For this and other methodological considerations, see Ellen Birnbaum, "What Does Philo Mean by 'Seeing God'? Some Methodological Considerations," in *Society of Biblical Literature 1995 Seminar Papers,* ed. Eugene H. Lovering Jr. (Atlanta: Scholars, 1995) 535-52; David T. Runia, "How To Read Philo," *NedTT* 40 (1986) 185-98; repr. in *Exegesis and Philosophy: Studies on Philo of Alexandria* (Aldershot: Variorum, 1990) Study II.

first century C.E., his writings may also shed light on sources both earlier and later, and these, in turn, may illuminate his works as well. A particularly controversial question has been the extent to which Philo can and should be read in connection with rabbinic literature. It seems to me, however, that no sources should be excluded. Despite the many methodological challenges, fruitful comparisons have been made between Philo and the rabbis, and the value of any comparison will rest on the strength of the evidence and the arguments of the researcher.[4] As is generally the case, two related guiding principles are that one should distinguish between fact and speculation and avoid making assertions that go beyond the evidence.

At the most basic level of comparison, it is necessary to ask in what way the Philonic evidence is similar to other sources and in what way it is different. The answers to these questions will hopefully suggest factors that should be emphasized, possible paths of influence, the strengths and limitations of the comparison, and the extent to which commonalities and differences are significant indicators about Jews and Judaism in antiquity as a whole. This last issue may at times prove too difficult to evaluate. In that case, the Philonic evidence will serve to raise questions about the larger picture, and this raising of questions is in itself worthwhile! Finally, in comparing Philo to other sources, one should also pay attention to what he does not mention. Although arguments from silence do not constitute proof, one can consider whether Philo's silence on particular issues is significant and, if so, why and how.[5]

What, then, are the sources to which Philo can or should be compared? These encompass a wide range of literary works, documents, inscriptions, and other archaeological evidence from the Second Temple and rabbinic

4. For an overview of the debate, see Ellen Birnbaum, "Two Millennia Later: General Resources and Particular Perspectives on Philo the Jew," *Currents in Biblical Research* 4 (2006) 252-53. See also David Winston, "Philo and Rabbinic Literature," in *The Cambridge Companion to Philo,* ed. Adam Kamesar (Cambridge: Cambridge University Press, 2009) 231-53; Richard D. Hecht, "Preliminary Issues in the Analysis of Philo's *De Specialibus Legibus,*" SPhilo 5 (1978) 1-55; Samuel Belkin, *Philo and the Oral Law: The Philonic Interpretation of Biblical Law in Relation to the Palestinian Halakah* (Cambridge, MA: Harvard University Press, 1940); *The Midrash of Philo,* vol. 1, ed. Elazar Hurvitz (New York: Yeshiva University Press, 1989) (Hebrew); Naomi G. Cohen, *Philo Judaeus: His Universe of Discourse* (BEATAJ 24; Frankfurt am Main: Lang, 1995). For a worthwhile caution on the limits of drawing parallels, see Samuel Sandmel, "Parallelomania," *JBL* 81 (1962) 1-13.

5. See, e.g., references to the question of an Alexandrian Jewish *politeuma,* the temple at Leontopolis, non-Jewish intellectuals in Alexandria, and the *laographia* mentioned below on pp. 210, 212, 222, and 224. See also nn. 27, 37, 67, and 70 below.

periods.[6] Thus literature alone encompasses the Hebrew Bible; the Greek Bible, which includes the Apocrypha; Pseudepigrapha; Dead Sea Scrolls; Josephus; other Jewish literature written in Greek, like the fragments of Aristobulus and Artapanus; Greek and Roman literature; early Christian writings, including the New Testament; and rabbinic works. Documentary, inscriptional, and archaeological sources are rather too diffuse to name, but the evidence is available in various compilations.[7]

The question of Philo's relationship to other expressions of Judaism in antiquity has long been debated. In the mid-twentieth century, Erwin R. Goodenough considered Philo in connection with various literary sources and archaeological evidence and concluded that he represented a distinctive, hellenized kind of Judaism that contrasted strongly with what some have called "normative Judaism."[8] Both of these terms are now used much

6. I understand the Second Temple period to begin with the return from exile and the rebuilding of the temple in the late sixth century B.C.E. and the rabbinic period to end with the redaction of the Babylonian Talmud in the early sixth century C.E. Although this time period, to which I refer loosely as "antiquity," probably yields the most productive comparisons, depending on the issue, comparisons with materials both later and earlier can also be useful. Because Philo's writings are so focused on biblical interpretation, for example, I am including the entire Hebrew Bible, even though the Pentateuch, on which he concentrates most, dates from a much earlier period and even though he himself relied on the Greek translation. For useful comparisons with later Jewish sources, see David Winston, "Philo's *Nachleben* in Judaism," *SPhAn* 6 (1994) 103-10; Elliot R. Wolfson, "Traces of Philonic Doctrine in Medieval Jewish Mysticism: A Preliminary Note," *SPhAn* 8 (1996) 99-106.

7. Two important compilations of documentary evidence and inscriptions, e.g., are Victor A. Tcherikover, Alexander Fuks, and Menahem Stern, eds., *CPJ* (3 vols.; Cambridge, MA: Harvard University Press, 1957-64); and William Horbury and David Noy, eds., *Jewish Inscriptions of Graeco-Roman Egypt* (Cambridge: Cambridge University Press, 1992). Exemplary book-length studies that have used wide-ranging evidence include John M. G. Barclay, *Jews in the Mediterranean Diaspora: From Alexander to Trajan (323 BCE–117 CE)* Edinburgh: T. & T. Clark, 1996); Terence L. Donaldson, *Judaism and the Gentiles: Jewish Patterns of Universalism (to 135 CE)* (Waco: Baylor University Press, 2007); Anders Runesson, Donald D. Binder, and Birger Olsson, *The Ancient Synagogue from Its Origins to 200 C.E.: A Source Book* (Leiden: Brill, 2008). See also Gregory E. Sterling, "'Thus Are Israel': Jewish Self-Definition in Alexandria," *SPhAn* 7 (1995) 1-18.

8. E.g., Erwin R. Goodenough, *By Light, Light: The Mystic Gospel of Hellenistic Judaism* (1935; repr., Amsterdam: Philo, 1969); *Jewish Symbols in the Greco-Roman Period* (13 vols.; New York: Pantheon, 1953-68). For "normative" Judaism, see, e.g., George Foot Moore, *Judaism in the First Centuries of the Christian Era* (2 vols.; New York: Schocken, 1971). For a comparative study between Philo and other Jewish sources, including rabbinic, see Samuel Sandmel, *Philo's Place in Judaism: A Study of Conceptions of Abraham in Jewish Literature* (augmented ed.; New York: Ktav, 1971); see also Satlow, *Creating Judaism*, 2-4.

less frequently, however, in part because "normativity" has proved too difficult to define and because Hellenistic influences can be found even in so-called normative Judaism — i.e., of the homeland and also of the rabbis.[9]

To be sure, the attempt to characterize Judaism in antiquity altogether has been beset by challenges. Some scholars, for example, have tried to understand Jewish life during this period by coining the term "Middle Judaism." Instead of addressing the normative-Hellenistic divide, this coinage responds to a different problem, namely, allusions to Judaism of this era as either early or late.[10] The latter designation, rarely in use today, was adopted by scholars who viewed Judaism of the time to have been replaced by early Christianity and thus to have been in its last stages. Apart from the adjective — be it Hellenistic, normative, early, middle, or late — the usefulness of the very term *Judaism* itself has also been questioned as inadequate to what it is meant to describe.[11]

Although we are duly aware of the various complexities involved in trying to characterize Jews and their beliefs and practices in antiquity, the above-mentioned debates will not be our foremost concern. Instead, regardless of the terminology or periodization one prefers, we shall be primarily interested in recognizing commonality and diversity among these Jews and continuities and discontinuities among their beliefs and practices. Such an approach will allow us to focus on Philo's relevance for our understanding of the Jewish past and beyond.

Under the categories below, we shall consider the ways in which Philo's works have been and/or can be used to inform the study of Jews and Judaism in antiquity. These discussions are necessarily brief, but I hope that they will be both illustrative about past research and suggestive for the future.

---

9. See, e.g., Martin Hengel, *Judaism and Hellenism: Studies in Their Encounter in Palestine during the Early Hellenistic Period,* trans. John Bowden (2 vols.; London: SCM; Philadelphia: Fortress, 1974; repr. in 1 vol. 1981); John J. Collins and Gregory E. Sterling, eds., *Hellenism in the Land of Israel* (Notre Dame: University of Notre Dame Press, 2001); Saul Lieberman, *Greek in Jewish Palestine; Hellenism in Jewish Palestine* (New York: Jewish Theological Seminary of America, 1994). See also Birnbaum, "Two Millennia Later," 262.

10. Gabriele Boccaccini, *Middle Judaism: Jewish Thought, 300 B.C.E. to 200 C.E.* (Minneapolis: Fortress, 1991). See also Martin Goodman, "Early Judaism," in *Judaism in the Roman World: Collected Essays* (Leiden: Brill, 2007) 1-19; Martin S. Jaffee, *Early Judaism* (Upper Saddle River: Prentice Hall, 1997); Lawrence H. Schiffman, *Understanding Second Temple and Rabbinic Judaism* (Jersey City: Ktav, 2003).

11. Satlow, "Defining Judaism"; *Creating Judaism.*

Practices

In his four treatises devoted to "the special laws" and in various other passages throughout his works, Philo gives considerable attention to such Jewish practices as circumcision; the Sabbath; festivals, including the Fast (or Day of Atonement) and the annual celebration on Pharos of the Greek Bible translation; sacrifices; dietary laws; and other pertinent topics. Most of these practices are recognizable as part of a larger Jewish tradition, whereas others, such as the Pharos celebration, may be unique to Alexandria. Focusing on individual subjects or covering a broader range, scholars have informed our understanding of Jewish practices in Philo's day from his own perspective and that of other sources.[12] Nonetheless, much remains to be done.

The Passover festival — in Greek, *pascha* — offers a striking example. Philo's treatment of this festival suggests both continuities and discontinuities with what we know from other sources. According to both the Hebrew and Greek Bibles, for instance, the Passover sacrifice commemorates the Lord's passing over or protecting the houses of the Israelites when he smote the Egyptian firstborn.[13] Philo, however, does not mention this basis of the holiday. For him, the festival instead commemorates Israel's crossing through the sea away from the land of Egypt; indeed, Philo regularly refers to the festival with words that pertain to "crossing," e.g., *diabasis* or *diabatēria*.[14]

12. See, e.g., Alan Mendelson, *Philo's Jewish Identity* (BJS 161; Atlanta: Scholars, 1988); Jutta Leonhardt, *Jewish Worship in Philo of Alexandria* (TSAJ 84; Tübingen: Mohr Siebeck, 2001); Lutz Doering, *Schabbat: Sabbathalacha und -praxis im antiken Judentum und Urchristentum* (TSAJ 78; Tübingen: Mohr Siebeck, 1999); Herold Weiss, *A Day of Gladness: The Sabbath among Jews and Christians in Antiquity* (Columbia: University of South Carolina Press, 2003); Ellen Birnbaum, "Who Celebrated on Pharos with the Jews? Conflicting Philonic Currents and Their Implications," in *Philon d'Alexandrie: un penseur à l'intersection des cultures gréco-romaine, orientale, juive et chrétienne*, ed. Sabrina Inowlocki-Meister and Baudouin Decharneux (Turnhout: Brepols, 2011) 63-82; see also Birnbaum, "Two Millennia Later," 248-49.

13. Exod 12:27; the Hebrew has the added verbal similarity between the verb *pasach* ("protect"; often translated too as "pass over") and the noun *pesach* (the Paschal sacrifice); see also Bernard M. Levinson, *Deuteronomy and the Hermeneutics of Legal Innovation* (Oxford: Oxford University Press, 1997) 58.

14. See, e.g., *Migr.* 25; *Spec.* 2.145. Philo's explanation in *Spec.* 2.146 that "the festival is a reminder and thank-offering for that great migration from Egypt" accords with the explanation for the sacrifice in Deut 16:1. (Unless otherwise noted, all translations of Philo's works are taken from F. H. Colson, G. H. Whitaker, and Ralph Marcus, trans., *Philo* [10 vols.; London: Heinemann; Cambridge, MA: Harvard University Press, 1929-62].) See also Colson, *Philo*, 7:394, n. a and 627, note on *Spec.* 2.145. On the complex development and transformation of the holiday

Symbolically, moreover, the crossing-feast signifies the leaving behind by the soul, represented by Israel, of passions and concerns of the body, represented by Egypt, the land of the body.

After reading the relevant passages about Philo's understanding of this festival, we might well ask how widely representative it is. Is Philo speaking only for himself, his own circle of associates, a broader group of Jews in Alexandria, or an even wider population? To my knowledge, Philo's symbolic understanding of the festival is not mentioned in other Jewish sources. Philo does speak, however, of a group known as the Therapeutae, who lived near Alexandria and who periodically enacted the thanksgiving song on the model of Moses and the Israelites after their crossing of the sea. Might Philo's symbolic understanding of the Passover be in any way connected to this practice? Because our evidence is limited, any such connection must unfortunately remain merely a suggestion. Nonetheless, Philo describes the group's allegorical approach to Scripture, and, to be sure, the Therapeutae may have ascribed to Israel's crossing of the sea a significance not unlike his interpretation of the Passover festival.[15]

Other aspects of Philo's account of the Passover holiday invite similar exploration. In *Spec.* 2.148, for example, he speaks of a banquet at which guests, having been "cleansed by purificatory lustrations," gather "to fulfill with prayers and hymns the custom handed down by their fathers." Do we have here an example of some sort of "proto-Seder," later developed by the rabbis, at which participants recited Psalms from a liturgical grouping that we now call Hallel?[16] Again, the evidence is unfortunately too scanty to allow a positive answer. Philo's description of this observance, however, makes a valuable contribution to our understanding of Jewish practices in antiquity.

---

within the Bible, see Levinson, *Deuteronomy and the Hermeneutics of Legal Innovation,* 53-97, esp. 77-78. See also Leonhardt, *Jewish Worship,* 29-38 (as in the Bible, Philo deals with the Festival of the Unleavened Bread as separate but connected to the Passover); Sarah J. K. Pearce, *The Land of the Body: Studies in Philo's Representation of Egypt* (WUNT 208; Tübingen: Mohr Siebeck, 2007) 124-26; Nicholas de Lange, "The Celebration of the Passover in Graeco-Roman Alexandria," in *Manières de penser dans l'Antiquité méditerranéenne et orientale,* ed. Christophe Batsch and Mădălina Vârtejanu-Joubert (JSJSup 134; Leiden: Brill, 2009) 157-66.

15. *Contempl.* 83-89. Although the choirs of the Therapeutae enacted the thanksgiving song, Philo does not mention (and we therefore do not know) whether they celebrated Passover. On the Therapeutae, see below, pp. 214, 219, and n. 59.

16. Leonhardt, *Jewish Worship,* 30, 35-36. See also Baruch M. Bokser, *The Origins of the Seder: The Passover Rite and Early Rabbinic Judaism* (Berkeley: University of California Press, 1984).

One further detail in Philo's discussion also merits our attention. In the same passage (*Spec.* 2.148), he writes, "On this day every dwelling-house is invested with the outward semblance and dignity of a temple. The victim is then slaughtered and dressed for the festal meal which befits the occasion." Based on this description and other Philonic references, much debate has centered on whether or not the paschal sacrifice was carried out in Alexandria and at other locales away from the temple.[17] Although the matter remains inconclusive, such questions bring to life the situation of Jews celebrating the Passover festival while the temple was still standing.

The kinds of issues we have raised and briefly explored here in relation to Passover can be and have been similarly applied to other practices that Philo discusses. As we have seen, the Philonic evidence imparts at a minimum the impressions, experience, and understanding of one Jew in first-century c.e. Alexandria. It also contributes, however, to a larger portrait of Jewish life in antiquity and suggests areas of commonality and difference, be they ritual practices, interpretation of these practices, or both.[18]

Beliefs and Ideas

Philonic beliefs and ideas encompass such topics as the Logos, divine powers, various notions about God and humanity, ethics and virtue, the law of nature, the role of the Jews in relation to humanity, reward and punishment, homeland and Diaspora, and visions of an ideal future. Indeed, we have no dearth of studies devoted to these topics.[19] Our present concern, however,

17. Mendelson, "'Did Philo Say the Shema?'" 163-64; Leonhardt, *Jewish Worship*, 31-33; Nils Martola, "Eating the Passover Lamb in House-temples at Alexandria: Some Notes on Passover in Philo," in *Jewish Studies in a New Europe: Proceedings of the Fifth Congress of Jewish Studies in Copenhagen 1994*, ed. Ulf Haxen, Hanne Trautner-Kromann, and Karen Lisa Goldschmidt-Salamon (Copenhagen: Reitzel, 1998) 521-31; de Lange, "The Celebration of the Passover."

18. In his critique of Jonathan Z. Smith, Schwartz astutely distinguishes between what he calls ritual difference and theological difference, the latter referring to explanations of the ritual ("How Many Judaisms Were There?" 221).

19. See, e.g., the following chapters in Kamesar, *Cambridge Companion to Philo*: Cristina Termini, "Philo's Thought within the Context of Middle Judaism," 95-123; Roberto Radice, "Philo's Theology and Theory of Creation," 124-45; Carlos Lévy, "Philo's Ethics," 146-71. See also Jenny Morris, "Philo's Philosophical Thought," in Emil Schürer, *The History of the Jewish People in the Age of Jesus Christ (175 b.c.–a.d. 135)*, ed. Geza Vermes, Fergus Millar, and Martin Goodman (rev. ed.; Edinburgh: T. & T. Clark, 1987) 3/2:871-89; Harry Austryn Wolfson, *Philo:*

is not to describe Philo's beliefs and ideas but rather to explore their relevance for the study of Jews and Judaism in antiquity. Because Philo was so influenced by Greek philosophy, many of his beliefs and ideas may at first appear rather different from those in other Jewish sources that were not similarly influenced. Occasionally, however, we can indeed find some important continuities.

Philo's doctrine of divine powers serves as an instructive example. Philo speaks of these powers as a way of expressing God's interaction with humanity and the world. In different passages the number of these powers varies, but in one thread Philo speaks of the two names of God *(kyrios* and *theos)* as signifying his royal and creative powers, respectively. These in turn correspond further to God's punitive and beneficial powers. Because Philo explains the correspondence between God's names and his powers on the basis of the Greek,[20] one might initially characterize this belief as remote from other Jewish traditions in Hebrew or Aramaic. Interestingly, however, the rabbis also correlate God's two names with his two *middot,* or measures, the merciful and the punitive. Even more striking, the rabbis' correlation of God's names and his powers is the opposite of Philo's correlation! Regardless, however, some studies have shown some possible links between the two approaches.[21] Philo's doctrine of divine powers, then, may be distinct from what we find in other sources, but aspects of this doctrine may also share some commonalities with rabbinic beliefs.

Another area that exemplifies what we can learn from studying Philo in relation to other sources is the topic of the covenant (Hebrew *berit;* Greek *diathēkē*). Philo's understanding of this concept is shaped by the Greek *diathēkē,* which denotes a testament or a will. In many biblical passages, the covenant serves as an important expression of the relationship between God and Israel.[22] Rather than an agreement between two parties, which the He-

---

Foundations of Religious Philosophy in Judaism, Christianity, and Islam (2 vols.; Cambridge, MA: Harvard University Press, 1948); David Winston, "Philo's Ethical Theory," in *ANRW* 2.21.1 (1984) 372-416; see also Birnbaum, "Two Millennia Later," 260-61.

20. *Conf.* 137; *Mut.* 29; *Abr.* 121; *Mos.* 2.99. See also Colson and Whitaker, *Philo,* 4:556, note on *Conf.* 137; and Colson, *Philo,* 6:63, note on *Abr.* 121.

21. Cristina Termini, *Le potenze di Dio: Sudio su* dunamis *in Filone di Alessandria* (Rome: Institutum Patristicum Augustinianum, 2000) 92-96; N. A. Dahl and Alan F. Segal, "Philo and the Rabbis on the Names of God," *JSJ* 9 (1978) 1-28; Arthur Marmorstein, "Philo and the Names of God," *JQR* 22 (1932) 295-306; *The Old Rabbinic Doctrine of God,* vol. 1: *The Names and Attributes of God* (1927; repr., New York: Ktav, 1968) esp. 41-53.

22. E.g., Exod 19–24, esp. 19:5-6; Lev 26:3-13; Deut 9:5; see also Deut 7:6-8; 26:16-19.

brew signifies, however, the covenant, according to Philo, instead indicates God's free bestowal of a gift (as in a will). Thus, in the four instances in which Philo refers to the covenant between God and Israel he does not affirm the sense of an agreement, and in two instances he assigns to the term an allegorical meaning.[23] The concept of covenant may indeed have held special significance for Philo because he devoted two treatises to the topic (*Mut.* 53; cf. *QE* 2.34), but unfortunately these are no longer extant. Even though he does not affirm the biblical sense of the covenant in the relationship between God and Israel, however, Philo nonetheless does believe that the Jews have a special relationship with God and that they serve as his priestly nation.[24]

For some other sources in antiquity, the notion of covenant as an agreement between two parties is indeed important, especially for the Dead Sea community, which saw itself as those with whom God had forged a new covenant.[25] The notion is not, however, centrally important for all sources, which, like Philo, may conceptualize a special relationship between God and Israel but in different terms. Josephus, for example, does not refer to the covenant between God and Israel at all but instead highlights the theme of divine *pronoia* ("providence") for the nation.[26] Thus Philo is but one source

---

23. *Sacr.* 57; *Det.* 67; *QE* 2.34, 106. The first and last references include allegorical interpretations. See Ellen Birnbaum, *The Place of Judaism in Philo's Thought: Israel, Jews, and Proselytes* (BJS 290; SPhilo Monographs 2; Atlanta: Scholars, 1996) 128-59.

24. Birnbaum, *The Place of Judaism*, 160-92.

25. Annie Jaubert, *La notion d'alliance dans le judaïsme aux abords de l'ère chrétienne* (Paris: Éditions du Seuil, 1963) 116-249. On the covenant idea in the Dead Sea community, see also the following chapters in Stanley E. Porter and Jacqueline C. R. de Roo, eds., *The Concept of the Covenant in the Second Temple Period* (JSJSup 71; Leiden: Brill, 2003): Craig A. Evans, "Covenant in the Qumran Literature," 55-80; Martin G. Abegg, "The Covenant of the Qumran Sectarians," 81-97; Michael O. Wise, "The Concept of a New Covenant in the Teacher Hymns from Qumran (1QH^a x-xvii)," 99-128; Stephen A. Reed, "The Role of Food as Related to Covenant in Qumran Literature," 129-64.

26. Harold W. Attridge, *The Interpretation of Biblical History in the* Antiquitates Judaicae *of Flavius Josephus* (HDR 7; Missoula: Scholars, 1976); Lester L. Grabbe, "Did All Jews Think Alike? 'Covenant' in Philo and Josephus in the Context of Second Temple Judaic Religion," in Porter and de Roo, *The Concept of the Covenant*, 251-66; D. A. Carson, Peter T. O'Brien, and Mark A. Seifrid, eds., *Justification and Variegated Nomism*, vol. 1: *The Complexities of Second Temple Judaism* (Tübingen: Mohr Siebeck; Grand Rapids: Baker, 2001). On the notion of the covenant in the ancient Jewish Diaspora in Egypt, see Anna Maria Schwemer, "Zum Verhältnis von Diatheke und Nomos in den Schriften der jüdischen Diaspora Ägyptens in hellenistisch-römischer Zeit," in *Bund und Tora: Zur theologischen Begriffsgeschichte in alttestamentlicher, frühjüdischer und urchristlicher Tradition,* ed. Friedrich Avemarie und Hermann Lichtenberger (WUNT 92; Tübingen: Mohr, 1996) 67-109.

among others that do not emphasize the covenant and instead conceptualize the relationship between God and Israel within a different framework. His writings, then, help to fill out the larger picture of Jewish commonality and diversity of his time.

Community Institutions

Three particularly important community institutions to which Philo refers are the temple, the synagogue (which he speaks of primarily as the *proseuchē*), and the *gerousia*. Because scholars have debated whether the Alexandrian Jews of his day constituted a *politeuma*, or community of foreigners with certain rights within a Greek city,[27] it is noteworthy that Philo does not refer to such an organization.

With regard to the temple, Philo speaks at length about its symbolic meaning, the high priest, his vestments, and various sacrifices. As C. T. R. Hayward writes of Philo's portrayal, "Most important is his conviction that the Temple in some manner represents the universe, the high priest a figure mediating between earth and heaven, and the public sacrifices of the Temple representing in a fashion the homage not only of Jews, but of the whole human race to God."[28] That other Jews in antiquity shared this attitude can be seen in similar discussions elsewhere. To take but one example, Philo's elaborate allegorization of the priestly garments as representative of the universe has a parallel in Josephus, and the same approach is suggested in the Wisdom of Solomon.[29]

---

27. Victor A. Tcherikover, *Hellenistic Civilization and the Jews,* trans. Shimon Applebaum (New York: Atheneum, 1975) 296-332; Aryeh Kasher, *The Jews in Hellenistic and Roman Egypt: The Struggle for Equal Rights* (TSAJ 7; Tübingen: Mohr Siebeck, 1985); Barclay, *Jews in the Mediterranean Diaspora,* 25 n. 18, 60-71; Constantine Zuckerman, "Hellenistic *politeumata* and the Jews: A Reconsideration," *Scripta Classica Israelica* 8/9 (1985-88) 171-85; Gert Lüderitz, "What Is the Politeuma?" in *Studies in Early Jewish Epigraphy,* ed. Jan Willem van Henten and Pieter Willem van der Horst (AGJU 21; Leiden: Brill, 1994) 183-225; Erich S. Gruen, *Diaspora: Jews amidst Greeks and Romans* (Cambridge, MA: Harvard University Press, 2002) 74-75.

28. C. T. R. Hayward, ed., *The Jewish Temple: A Non-biblical Sourcebook* (London: Routledge, 1996) 109.

29. *Mos.* 2.109-35; *Spec.* 1.84-97; Josephus, *Ant.* 3.159-87; Wis 18:24. See also Natalio Fernández Marcos, "Rewritten Bible or *Imitatio?* The Vestments of the High-Priest," in *Studies in the Hebrew Bible, Qumran, and the Septuagint Presented to Eugene Ulrich,* ed. Peter W. Flint, Emanuel Tov, and James C. VanderKam (VTSup 101; Leiden: Brill, 2006) 321-36; David Winston, ed., *The Wisdom of Solomon* (AB 43; Garden City: Doubleday, 1979) 321-22.

Philo also conveys the significance of the temple in a rather different, nonexegetical context, namely, when he and his delegation in Rome discover that Caligula intends to install a statue inside the temple. Comparing the local Alexandrian houses of prayer *(proseuchai)* to the Jewish temple, Philo despairs of pleading about the defiled Alexandrian *proseuchai* before the emperor: "For clearly to houses less conspicuous and held in lower esteem no regard would be paid by one who insults that most notable and illustrious shrine whose beams like the sun's reach every whither, beheld with awe both by east and west" (*Legat.* 191; see also 194). He later refers to Jews' practice of sending envoys on difficult journeys to the temple and of their "unprecedented dedication" to it (*Legat.* 216-17). In his emotional narrative Philo attests to the great importance of the temple for all Jews, even one like himself, who was so well-established in the Diaspora.

As for the local houses of prayer just mentioned, as Lee Levine has observed, "The writings of Philo are of inestimable importance as a source for Alexandrian Jewry generally and for the synagogue in particular."[30] Indeed, in a recent sourcebook entitled *The Ancient Synagogue from Its Origins to 200 C.E.*, the evidence from Philo figures prominently.[31] In a related study, Donald Binder offers a succinct summary and evaluation of this evidence. He notes that in the exegetical works, Philo occasionally offers personal asides that contain relevant passages. Especially significant, however, are Philo's references to prayer houses in his treatises *Against Flaccus* and *On the Embassy to Gaius,* which pertain to life and events contemporary to Philo's time. Binder cautions that Philo may present information from other regions through the lens of what he himself was familiar with in Alexandria, and the apologetic nature of some of his works may have colored his presentation. In addition, Levine believes that Philo's depictions may represent only an elite group.[32]

Despite these cautions, Philo's references to prayer houses in such locations as Alexandria, Asia, Rome, and Judea are invaluable. Moreover, his

---

30. Lee I. Levine, *The Ancient Synagogue: The First Thousand Years* (2nd ed.; New Haven: Yale University Press, 2005) 89.

31. Runesson, Binder, and Olsson, *The Ancient Synagogue,* 322 (see under "Philo"); see also Stephen K. Catto, *Reconstructing the First-Century Synagogue: A Critical Analysis of Current Research* (LNTS 363; London: T. & T. Clark, 2007) 17-27.

32. Donald D. Binder, *Into the Temple Courts: The Place of the Synagogues in the Second Temple Period* (SBLDS 169; Atlanta: Society of Biblical Literature, 1999) 46-49; unfortunately, Binder does not give examples of Philo's personal asides. See also Levine, *The Ancient Synagogue,* 89-90.

allusions to such activities as assembling, reading and expounding the law, and honoring rulers highlights the question of what Jews did in these gathering places. In their aforementioned sourcebook, Anders Runesson, Donald Binder, and Birger Olsson outline four broad areas of research in the burgeoning field of synagogue studies. These areas include physical aspects of the structure; liturgical aspects; social, or nonliturgical, aspects; and issues related to synagogue leadership and operations.[33] Used in conjunction with other sources, Philo's references contribute significantly to what we know about this ancient institution. Other sources in turn can add to our knowledge about Alexandria. Some rabbinic passages, for example, offer a fascinating description of the physical structure and congregational seating arrangement of Alexandria's largest synagogue as well as a custom there related to reading the Torah, but whether these passages refer to the same large synagogue that Philo mentions in *Legat.* 134 remains uncertain.[34]

Regarding the *gerousia,* Philo provides valuable information when he writes that "our council of elders had been appointed to manage Jewish affairs, after the death of the genarch, by our savior and benefactor Augustus, orders to that effect having been given to Magius Maximus just before the latter began to govern the city on Egypt's border and the country."[35] Scholars have used this statement in connection with evidence from Strabo, Josephus, and rabbinic sources to try to ascertain the nature and history of this governing body among the Alexandrian Jews.[36]

This brief overview highlights Philo's importance in contributing to our knowledge of ancient Jewish communal institutions and, it is hoped, suggests further areas of investigation. To be sure, Philo's writings are important for their references to the Jewish temple. They are also notable, however, for their lack of mention of the temple established centuries earlier at Leontopolis in the nome of Heliopolis.[37] What does this silence signify? We also

33. Runesson, Binder, and Olson, *The Ancient Synagogue,* 7-13.

34. Levine, *The Ancient Synagogue,* 91-96; Rivka Ulmer, *Egyptian Cultural Icons in Midrash* (SJ 52; Berlin: de Gruyter, 2009) 174-78.

35. *Flacc.* 74. The translation here is that of Pieter W. van der Horst, *Philo's Flaccus: The First Pogrom* (PACS 2; Leiden: Brill, 2003) 67; see also notes on this passage, pp. 168-70.

36. Philo refers to the council in passing in his description of the violence against Jews in Alexandria. As noted earlier, he also provides the names of three members of this council: Euodus, Trypho, and Andro (*Flacc.* 76); see van der Horst, *Philo's Flaccus,* 168-72, esp. 171. See also Victor Tcherikover, "Prolegomena," in *CPJ* 57 n. 22.

37. Runesson, Binder, and Olson, *The Ancient Synagogue,* 282-85; see also Ulmer, *Egyptian Cultural Icons in Midrash,* 207-12.

know that Philo visited the Jerusalem temple at least once (*Prov.* 2.64). How easy was it for Egyptian Jews to travel to the temple, and how frequently did they go? As for the synagogue, the four areas of research mentioned earlier are rich with possibilities.[38] Finally, we have much yet to learn about the makeup and functions of the *gerousia,* issues that one would expect to be important for our understanding of the political and social status of Jews in Philo's Alexandria.[39]

The Bible and Biblical Interpretation

Since the bulk of Philo's writings is devoted to biblical exegesis, it is hardly surprising that these writings are a treasure trove of information about the Greek Bible and, more widely, biblical interpretation.[40] In *Mos.* 2.25-44, Philo describes the translation of the Mosaic legislation into Greek in an account that parallels the one in the *Letter of Aristeas,* but with important differences. Most fundamentally, where the *Letter* presents the translation as the outcome of committee consultations, Philo believes that each member of this committee worked separately and, through inspiration, all came up with precisely the same translation. This element of inspiration places the translation on the same footing as the Hebrew — indeed, Philo claims that the two sets of writings are regarded as "sisters" (*Mos.* 2.40) — and thus his account implicitly authorizes exegetical activity based on the translation.[41] Like the *Letter*

38. For an interesting but speculative study about the practice of reading *haftarot* in the synagogues of Alexandria, for example, see Naomi G. Cohen, *Philo's Scriptures: Citations from the Prophets and Writings: Evidence for a* Haftarah *Cycle in Second Temple Judaism* (JSJSup 123; Leiden: Brill, 2007), also discussed on p. 214 below.

39. Possibly related to the topic of community institutions is the question of whether the Alexandrian Jewish community "took the law into its own hands" in punishing certain transgressions of the Mosaic laws; see, e.g., Torrey Seland, *Establishment Violence in Philo and Luke: A Study of Non-Conformity to the Torah and Jewish Vigilante Reactions* (Biblical Interpretation 15; Leiden: Brill, 1995).

40. Recent scholarly debates have focused on whether one can properly use the term "Bible"; for expediency, I am using this term here. See, e.g., the program for the conference titled "What Is Bible?" (May 30–June 2, 2010), sponsored by the University of Koblenz-Landau and University of Vienna (http://www.sbl-site.org/meetings/programunits_resources.aspx and http://www.sbl-site.org/assets/pdfs/Whatisbibleprogram.pdf).

41. Philo stops short of saying explicitly that the inspiration came from God, but this is implicit (see, e.g., *Mos.* 2.36). For comparisons between Philo's account and that of the *Letter of Aristeas,* see Abraham Wasserstein and David J. Wasserstein, *The Legend of the Septuagint:*

of Aristeas, then, Philo reinforces that the translation of the Hebrew Scriptures into Greek played a central role for the Greek-speaking Jewish Diaspora.

Philo also provides additional information about the holy writings. He himself focuses primarily on the Pentateuch, which he speaks of often as the teachings or the law(s) of Moses.[42] Nonetheless, it is clear that for him, the holy writings encompassed more. Describing the life of the Therapeutae, for example, he relates that its members, closeting themselves apart to be "initiated into the mysteries of the sanctified life," took with them nothing "but laws and oracles delivered through the mouth of prophets, and psalms and anything else which fosters and perfects knowledge and piety" (*Contempl.* 25). It has been suggested that Philo may be referring here to the traditional Jewish division of Scripture into Torah, Prophets, and Writings.[43] Naomi Cohen has recently published an informative and suggestive work titled *Philo's Scriptures,* in which she discusses his way of referring to the pentateuchal books and his use of passages outside the Pentateuch. Among her many fascinating observations is that Philo ascribes quotations of non-pentateuchal verses to students and followers of Moses.[44] Philo's use of designations for the followers of Moses and his view of their relationship (and that of Moses himself) to the holy writings beyond the Pentateuch is but one of many potentially fruitful areas of investigation. Another is how Philo's biblical text compares with what we know of the Greek translation. Scholars have devoted much detailed work to this issue, and much remains to be done.[45]

From *Classical Antiquity to Today* (Cambridge: Cambridge University Press, 2006) 35-45; Jennifer M. Dines, *The Septuagint* (London: T. & T. Clark, 2004) 65-67.

42. E.g., *Opif.* 1-3; *Spec.* 3.6; *Contempl.* 64. See also Yehoshua Amir, "Authority and Interpretation of Scripture in the Writings of Philo," in *Mikra: Text, Translation, Reading and Interpretation of the Hebrew Bible in Ancient Judaism and Early Christianity,* ed. Martin Jan Mulder and Harry Sysling (CRINT 2/1; Assen: Van Gorcum; Minneapolis: Fortress, 1990), esp. 433-40; Hindy Najman, *Seconding Sinai: The Development of Mosaic Discourse in Second Temple Judaism* (JSJSup 77; Leiden: Brill, 2003).

43. Colson, *Philo,* 9:520, note on *Contempl.* 25; see also Josephus, *Ag. Ap.* 1.38-40.

44. Cohen, *Philo's Scriptures,* 175-97. Though I disagree with her interpretation of these references, she has called attention to an intriguing issue; see Ellen Birnbaum, review of Naomi G. Cohen, *Philo's Scriptures, JJS* 60 (2009) 331-34.

45. See, e.g., Herbert E. Ryle, *Philo and Holy Scripture, or the Quotations of Philo from the Books of the Old Testament* (London: Macmillan, 1895); Peter Katz, *Philo's Bible: The Aberrant Text of Bible Quotations in Some Philonic Writings and Its Place in the Textual History of the Greek Bible* (Cambridge: Cambridge University Press, 1950); James R. Royse, "Some Observa-

Moving from the biblical text to its interpretation, we find in Philo's works a field rich with engaging questions, of which many have been explored while others await investigation. One can begin, for example, with a straight-forward examination of an exegetical theme, like Egypt or Israel, or a biblical verse or couple of verses, like Gen 1:27 and 2:7 on the creation of humanity or Exod 16:4 on manna as bread from heaven, to see how Philo deals with it (or them) throughout his works.[46] One will generally find, however, that such investigations quickly lead into other paths — an exploration of Philo's philosophical ideas; his social situation in Alexandria; his identity as a Jew; his awareness of other approaches to Scripture, both literal and allegorical; his familiarity with Greek forms of writing and Homeric exegesis; and his knowledge of and relationship to broader Jewish traditions — whether from earlier or contemporary sources from Alexandria, Judea, or elsewhere. Examination of such exegetical topics can also lead to and benefit from exploration of the themes or passages in later rabbinic and Christian sources.[47]

Philonic scholarship abounds with splendid studies in all these areas. Again and again, they reveal Philo as a complex interpreter of enormous breadth, who shares exegetical methods, questions, and traditions with other Jewish sources but who also incorporates Greek forms of writing, philosophical ideas, and allegorizations of myths *not* found in other Jewish sources. Indeed, of all the areas that we have been examining, Philo's biblical exegesis perhaps best illustrates that he shows marked continuities with other Jews in antiquity but in some ways also remains notably distinct from them.

Two of Philo's interpretations of Abraham aptly illustrate this observa-

---

tions on the Biblical Text in Philo's *De Agricultura,*" *SPhAn* 22 (2010) 111-29; Robert Kraft, "Philo's Bible Revisited: The 'Aberrant Texts' and their Quotations of Moses," in *Interpreting Translation: Studies on the LXX and Ezekiel in Honour of Johan Lust,* ed. Florentino García Martínez and Marc Vervenne (BETL 192; Leuven: Peeters, 2005) 237-53.

46. See, e.g., Pearce, *The Land of the Body;* Birnbaum, *The Place of Judaism in Philo's Thought;* Thomas H. Tobin, *The Creation of Man: Philo and the History of Interpretation* (CBQMS 14; Washington: Catholic Biblical Association of America, 1983); Peder Borgen, *Bread from Heaven: An Exegetical Study of the Concept of Manna in the Gospel of John and the Writings of Philo* (NovTSup 10; Leiden: Brill, 1965).

47. For different perspectives on Philo as an exegete, see, e.g., Peder Borgen, *Philo of Alexandria: An Exegete for His Time* (NovTSup 86; Leiden: Brill, 1997); Cohen, *Philo Judaeus;* James L. Kugel, *Traditions of the Bible: A Guide to the Bible As It Was at the Start of the Common Era* (Cambridge, MA: Harvard University Press, 1998); Louis H. Feldman, *Philo's Portrayal of Moses in the Context of Ancient Judaism* (Notre Dame: University of Notre Dame Press, 2007); Maren Ruth Niehoff, *Jewish Exegesis and Homeric Scholarship in Alexandria* (Cambridge: Cambridge University Press, 2011).

tion. Even though Gen 11:31–12:5 does not elaborate on Abraham's background in Chaldea, Philo understands the patriarch's departure as his leaving behind the false Chaldean creed of astrology and the equation of creation with God and as his becoming aware of God's existence as pilot and charioteer of the universe (e.g., *Abr.* 60-80, esp. 69-70). Similar views of Abraham's departure from Chaldea and his discovery of God are found in such other Jewish sources as *Jubilees,* Josephus, and *Genesis Rabbah,* and these similar approaches suggest the existence of a broader, common tradition.[48]

By contrast, in another interpretation Philo understands Abraham's mating with Hagar before he can conceive a child with Sarah as signifying the mind's pursuit of the encyclical studies (a Greek school curriculum of different disciplines) before it can successfully unite with virtue. In this allegorization, Hagar symbolizes the encyclical studies; Sarah, virtue; and Abraham, the mind (*Congr.* 11-12). To my knowledge, this interpretation is not found in any other Jewish sources. Instead, it appears to be influenced by an analogy, based on Homer's *Odyssey,* in which the suitors of Penelope who mate with her handmaids are likened to students who remain at the level of the encyclical studies without advancing to the study of philosophy.[49] Just as Philo can exhibit commonality with other Jewish traditions, then, so too can he demonstrate distinctiveness from them.

Jews and Jewish Identity

Philo's valuable contributions to our understanding of Jews in antiquity range from information about individual Jews — most notably, himself — to

---

48. *Jub.* 12:16-21; Josephus, *Ant.* 1.154-56; *Gen. Rab.* 39:1; see also Kugel, *Traditions of the Bible,* 243-51, 259-61.

49. John Dillon, "Ganymede as the Logos: Traces of a Forgotten Allegorization in Philo," *SPhilo* 6 (1979-80) 37; Yehoshua Amir, "The Transference of Greek Allegories to Biblical Motifs in Philo," in *Nourished with Peace: Studies in Hellenistic Judaism in Memory of Samuel Sandmel,* ed. Frederick E. Greenspahn, Earle Hilgert, and Burton L. Mack (Homage Series 9; Chico: Scholars, 1984) 15-18; Monique Alexandre, *De congressu eruditionis gratia,* vol. 16 of Roger Arnaldez, Claude Mondésert, and Jean Pouilloux, eds., *Les oeuvres de Philon d'Alexandrie* (Paris: Cerf, 1967) 29-72. For an example of how Philo may blend both interpretations of Abraham mentioned here into a larger tradition that appears to be uniquely Alexandrian, see Ellen Birnbaum, "Exegetical Building Blocks in Philo's Interpretation of the Patriarchs," in *From Judaism to Christianity: Tradition and Transition: A Festschrift for Thomas H. Tobin, S.J., on the Occasion of His Sixty-fifth Birthday,* ed. Patricia Walters (NovTSup 136; Leiden: Brill, 2010) 69-92.

the entire Jewish nation. Interestingly, Josephus provides more specific information about Philo's family and standing in the community than Philo does himself.[50] Nonetheless, in a few first person asides, Philo expresses his enjoyment of sports (e.g., *Prob.* 26; *Prov.* 2.58) and theater (*Ebr.* 177; *Prob.* 141), moments of inspiration or lack thereof (e.g., *Cher.* 27; *Migr.* 34-35), and weariness with public responsibilities (*Spec.* 3.1-6). Based on his apparently very wealthy family background and broad education in both Greek and Jewish learning, it would appear that Philo belonged to an economic and intellectual elite. It is therefore striking and puzzling that in a passing remark he speaks of "we poor people" (*Spec.* 2.20).

Besides Philo's self-referential comments, he mentions, as we have seen, three members of the *gerousia* who were oppressed and flogged during the anti-Jewish violence in Alexandria. In his account of this violence, he provides many other useful details about the Alexandrian Jewish community, such as where they lived and how they earned a living (*Flacc.* 55, 57). Elsewhere he alludes to a family that suffered the indignities inflicted by an overzealous tax collector.[51] Besides details about these specific individuals, it might also be possible to glean information about Jewish women, children, and families from Philo's writings, but only with careful attention to the challenging methodological issues.[52]

Philo's works also offer clues about the ways in which various Jews identified or practiced as Jews. In *Migr.* 89-93, for example, he addresses a group, presumably in or near Alexandria, who ignored the literal sense of the law in favor of its allegorical meaning. As mentioned in the previous section, Philo also refers to other biblical interpreters, who included both literalists

---

50. *Ant.* 18.259; see also Daniel R. Schwartz, "Philo, His Family, and His Times," in Kamesar, *The Cambridge Companion to Philo*, 9-31; Ellen Birnbaum, "A Leader with Vision in the Ancient Jewish Diaspora: Philo of Alexandria," in *Jewish Religious Leadership: Image and Reality*, ed. Jack Wertheimer (New York: Jewish Theological Seminary of America Press, 2004) 1:57-90.

51. *Spec.* 3.159-62. Philo does not specify that this family was Jewish, but the context suggests that this was the case.

52. See, esp., the previous chapter by Adele Reinhartz. See also Reinhartz, "Parents and Children: A Philonic Perspective," in *The Jewish Family in Antiquity*, ed. Shaye J. D. Cohen (BJS 298; Atlanta: Scholars, 1993) 61-88; "Philo on Infanticide," *SPhAn* 4 (1992) 42-58; Maren Ruth Niehoff, *Philo on Jewish Identity and Culture* (TSAJ 86; Tübingen: Mohr Siebeck, 2001) 161-87; Daniel R. Schwartz, "Did the Jews Practice Infant Exposure and Infanticide in Antiquity?" *SPhAn* 16 (2004) 61-95; Niehoff, "Response to Daniel R. Schwartz," *SPhAn* 17 (2005) 99-101; Dorothy Sly, *Philo's Perception of Women* (BJS 209; Atlanta: Scholars, 1990).

and allegorists.[53] In a passage that has surprising resonance these two millennia later, Philo reports that the Fast (his name for the Day of Atonement) "is carefully observed not only by the zealous for piety and holiness but also by those who never act religiously in the rest of their life. For all stand in awe, overcome by the sanctity of the day, and for the moment the worse vie with the better in self-denial and virtue" (*Spec.* 1.186). Beyond these "once-a-year" Jews, Philo speaks of those who actually abandoned their ancestral traditions — motivated by the desire for more sensual freedom, by social ambition, or by intellectual alienation. Indeed, some have observed that Alexandria, with its remarkably varied range of Jews, calls to mind the similarly diverse Jewish population of a modern American city like New York, albeit twenty centuries later.[54]

Philo's discussion of Jews in antiquity, however, goes well beyond the Alexandrian community alone. Despite religious differences within the community, in many of his works Philo speaks of the entire "Jewish nation" as if it were a united entity.[55] All or most of these works were likely aimed at a mixed audience of Jews and non-Jews and may have had the purpose of presenting the Jews in the best possible light.[56] Here Philo often emphasizes

53. See, e.g., Niehoff, *Jewish Exegesis and Homeric Scholarship;* Montgomery J. Shroyer, "Alexandrian Jewish Literalists," *JBL* 55 (1936) 261-84; David M. Hay, "Philo's References to Other Allegorists," *SPhilo* 6 (1979-80) 41-75; "References to Other Exegetes," in *Both Literal and Allegorical: Studies in Philo of Alexandria's* Questions and Answers on Genesis and Exodus (BJS 232; Atlanta: Scholars, 1991) 81-97; Wolfson, *Philo,* 1:55-73.

54. See, e.g., Wolfson, *Philo,* 1:55-86; Barclay, *Jews in the Mediterranean Diaspora,* 103-24. See also Shaye J. D. Cohen, Foreword to Joseph Mélèze Modrzejewski, *The Jews of Egypt: From Rameses II to Emperor Hadrian,* trans. Robert Cornman (Edinburgh: T. & T. Clark; Philadelphia: Jewish Publication Society, 1995) xi-xv; Gershon Shaked, "Alexandria: On Jews and Judaism in America," *Jerusalem Quarterly* 49 (1989) 47-84. Ironically, Philo's own nephew left behind Jewish ancestral practices and served in different capacities as a Roman official. We know of these details not from Philo himself, however, but from Josephus and other sources (see, e.g., *J. W.* 2.220, 223, 309, 492-93, 497; 4.616-18; 5.45, 510; *Ant.* 20.100). See also E. G. Turner, "Tiberius Iulius Alexander," *JRS* 44 (1954) 54-64.

55. Presumably there were also economic, political, and other differences among Jews, but it is difficult to identify these on the basis of Philo alone. See, e.g., Shimon Applebaum, "The Social and Economic Status of the Jews in the Diaspora," in *The Jewish People in the First Century: Historical Geography, Political History, Social, Cultural, and Religious Life and Institutions,* ed. Shemuel Safrai and Menahem Stern (CRINT 1/2; Assen: Van Gorcum; Philadelphia: Fortress, 1976) 701-27; Barclay, *Jews in the Mediterranean Diaspora,* 41-47, 158-63, 231-319; Tcherikover, "Prolegomena," esp. 48-93; Miriam Pucci ben Zeev, "New Perspectives on the Jewish-Greek Hostilities in Alexandria During the Reign of Emperor Caligula," *JSJ* 21 (1990) 227-35.

56. Birnbaum, "Two Millennia Later," 255-57.

the spiritual role of the Jews in relation to God,[57] but he also provides some practical information. Thus he reports that "there were no less than a million Jews resident in Alexandria and the country from the slope of Libya to the boundaries of Ethiopia." He adds that "so populous are the Jews that no one country can hold them, and therefore they settle in very many of the most prosperous countries in Europe and Asia both in the islands and on the mainland" (*Flacc.* 43, 45). In addition, he refers to specific Jewish communities in Rome, Syria, and Asia. One must, of course, take into account the likely overstatement of some of Philo's observations, but his reports of the large Jewish population in antiquity are probably based in reality.[58]

Beyond Jewish communities in different locales around the world, Philo describes two specific communities defined primarily by their distinctive beliefs and practices: the Essenes in "Palestinian Syria" (or "Judaea"; *Prob.* 75-91; *Hypoth.* 11.1-18) and the Therapuetae of the Lake Mareotis region near Alexandria *(Contempl.).* Because Philo is a key source about the Essenes, scholars, especially in Qumran studies, must reckon with his discussion of this community and consider it in relation to the other scanty references to this group. By contrast, Philo is our *only* source about the Therapeutae. Because we must rely totally on him, some scholars have questioned whether the latter group even existed, while others have given ample credence to his account.[59]

---

57. Borgen, *Philo of Alexandria: An Exegete for His Time,* esp. 206-24; Birnbaum, *The Place of Judaism,* 160-92.

58. On Jews in Rome, Syria, and Asia, see e.g., *Legat.* 155-61, 281-84, 311-15. For how Philo might be used in connection with other sources to shed light on Jews in the Mediterranean Diaspora, one can consult the impressive volume on this subject (and with this title) by Barclay, *Jews in the Mediterranean Diaspora;* see also Brian McGing, "Population and Proselytism: How Many Jews Were There in the Ancient World?" in *Jews in the Hellenistic and Roman Cities,* ed. John R. Bartlett (London: Routledge, 2002) 88-106; Walter Scheidel, "Creating a Metropolis: A Comparative Demographic Perspective," in *Ancient Alexandria between Egypt and Greece,* ed. William V. Harris and Giovanni Ruffini (Leiden: Brill, 2004) 1-31.

59. For different approaches, see, e.g., Joan E. Taylor and Philip R. Davies, "The So-Called Therapeutae of *De Vita Contemplativa:* Identity and Character," *HTR* 91 (1998) 3-24; Taylor, *Jewish Women Philosophers of First-Century Alexandria: Philo's 'Therapeutae' Reconsidered* (Oxford: Oxford University Press, 2003); Troels Engberg-Pedersen, "Philo's *De Vita Contemplativa* as a Philosopher's Dream," *JSJ* 30 (1999) 40-64; David M. Hay, "The Veiled Thoughts of the Therapeutae," in *Mediators of the Divine: Horizons of Prophecy, Divination, Dreams, and Theurgy in Mediterranean Antiquity,* ed. Robert M. Berchman (Atlanta: Scholars, 1998) 167-84; Shari Goldberg, "The Two Choruses Become One: The Absence/Presence of Women in Philo's *On the Contemplative Life,*" *JSJ* 39 (2008) 459-70. Attitudes toward Philo's account have also been shaped by Eusebius's discussion of the Therapeutae, which is dependent on that of Philo;

Besides all the individuals, groups, and communities described so far, Philo speaks of yet another group of Jews, namely, proselytes. Unfortunately, he neglects to report such practical details such as what was required of these individuals to become Jews. Moreover, we have no concrete evidence of proselytes from Alexandria at this time. Despite these regrettable lacunae, however, Philo's discussions offer important insights into the way that he understands these figures. Describing them in several passages as persons who leave behind their social and religious backgrounds to join the Jews in their belief in and worship of the one true God, Philo contributes significantly to our understanding of Jewish proselytes in antiquity.[60]

Jews' Interactions with and Attitudes toward Non-Jews and Their Culture

References to non-Jews and their culture permeate Philo's works. As with several other areas that we have discussed, it can be difficult to discern the extent to which Philo's attitudes are representative of other Jews. One must, of course, keep in mind his background and position as one of the elite in the Alexandrian Jewish community. Regardless of how typical or atypical his own views are, however, they are nonetheless instructive, informative, and thought-provoking. In his treatises *Against Flaccus* and *On the Embassy to Gaius,* Philo provides ample information about his attitudes toward contemporary Roman rulers, including Flaccus, the prefect of Egypt; Gaius Caligula, the emperor; and a host of other figures like Augustus; Tiberius; Sejanus; Petronius; Pontius Pilate; Capito; Macro; Julia Augusta, wife of Augustus; and an unnamed local official, who may or may not have been Jewish.[61] In these treatises and elsewhere, he also refers to the Ptolemies.

---

see, e.g., David T. Runia, *Philo in Early Christian Literature: A Survey* (CRINT 3/3; Assen: Van Gorcum; Minneapolis: Fortress, 1993) 212-31.

60. Donaldson, *Judaism and the Gentiles,* 217-78; Borgen, *Philo of Alexandria: An Exegete for His Time,* 206-24; Birnbaum, *The Place of Judaism,* 193-219; Shaye J. D. Cohen, *The Beginnings of Jewishness: Boundaries, Varieties, Uncertainties* (Berkeley: University of California Press, 1999) 140-74; Michael F. Bird, *Crossing Over Sea and Land: Jewish Missionary Activity in the Second Temple Period* (Peabody: Hendrickson, 2010).

61. It has been suggested that the last reference, found in *Somn.* 2.123-32, may even have been to Philo's nephew, Tiberius Julius Alexander; see, e.g., Daniel R. Schwartz, "Philonic Anonyms of the Roman and Nazi Periods: Two Suggestions," *SPhilo* 1 (1989) 63-69; Robert A. Kraft, "Philo and the Sabbath Crisis: Alexandrian Jewish Politics and the Dating of Philo's Works," in *The Future of Early Christianity: Essays in Honor of Helmut Koester,* ed. Birger A.

Beyond the ruling classes, Philo mentions other specific non-Jewish Alexandrians and Egyptians like Isidorus, Dionysius, Lampo, Carabbas, and Helicon. Philonic references to individual non-Jews also include such Greek cultural figures as Plato, Aristotle, Homer, Euripides, Zeno, Anaxarchus, and Xenophon. In addition to these individuals, he speaks more broadly of Greeks, Alexandrians, and Egyptians, as well as other groups like the Persian Magi and the gymnosophists of India.

We are fortunate to have many studies of Philo's discussion of and attitudes toward non-Jews.[62] These present a very mixed picture: Philo expresses great admiration for many of the Greek cultural personages mentioned above and for others like the Persian Magi and Indian gymnosophists. He can also be quite positive about certain Romans like Augustus, Tiberius, and Julia Augusta. By contrast, he does not hold back his disdain for Flaccus and Gaius. He is also generally hostile toward all Egyptians and most Alexandrians (the Ptolemies are an exception). Indeed, Philo's overall attitude toward his non-Jewish neighbors is quite negative, and he also portrays these neighbors as hostile to the Jews. In light of this rather bleak depiction, Philo's account of admiring non-Jews joining the Jewish celebration on Pharos to honor the translation of the Hebrew Bible into Greek appears nothing short of paradoxical![63] Elsewhere Philo makes a passing reference to "our friends of yesterday" (*Flacc.* 62). To be sure, he may be using sarcasm here, but one wonders whether in fact relations between Jews and non-Jews had at one

---

Pearson (Minneapolis: Fortress, 1991) 131-41. Philo mentions some of the Roman figures listed in the text in his report of Agrippa's letter to Gaius (*Legat.* 276-329); on this letter, see Daniel R. Schwartz, *Agrippa I: The Last King of Judaea* (TSAJ 23; Tübingen: Mohr Siebeck, 1990) 200-202.

62. See, e.g., Ray Barraclough, "Philo's Politics: Roman Rule and Hellenistic Judaism," in *ANRW* 2.21.1 (1984) 436-86; Niehoff, *Philo on Jewish Identity and Culture,* esp. 45-74, 111-58; Mendelson, *Philo's Jewish Identity,* 115-28; Peder Borgen, "Philo and the Jews in Alexandria," in *Ethnicity in Hellenistic Egypt,* ed. Per Bilde et al. (Aarhus: Aarhus University Press, 1992) 122-38; Koen Goudriaan, "Ethnical Strategies in Graeco-Roman Egypt," in Bilde et al., *Ethnicity in Hellenistic Egypt,* 74-99; Ellen Birnbaum, "Philo on the Greeks: A Jewish Perspective on Culture and Society in First-Century Alexandria," in *In the Spirit of Faith: Studies in Philo and Early Christianity in Honor of David Hay,* ed. David T. Runia and Gregory E. Sterling (SPhAn 18; BJS 332; 2001) 37-58; "Portrayals of the Wise and Virtuous in Alexandrian Jewish Works: Jews' Perceptions of Themselves and Others," in Harris and Ruffini, *Ancient Alexandria between Egypt and Greece,* 125-60, esp. 147-60; Pearce, *The Land of the Body;* John Bruce Burke, "Philo and Alexandrian Judaism" (Ph.D. diss., Syracuse University, 1963) 136-39. Philo's writings also yield information relevant to non-Jews' attitudes toward Jews; see, e.g., n. 71 below.

63. *Mos.* 2.41-44; Birnbaum, "Who Celebrated on Pharos?"

time been better. For the fullest and most informed understanding, Philo's writings must be considered together with all the available evidence.

A related topic concerns Jews' involvement with and attitudes toward non-Jewish culture. Here again, Philo presents a considerably complex picture. On one hand, he himself is thoroughly steeped in Greek philosophy and learning, and he may have been educated in the gymnasium.[64] He speaks as well of his attendance at Greek sports events and the theater. On the other hand, Philo also presents the Jewish way of life as superior to Greek cultural values. Faith in the one, true God, who is also the God of the Jews, for example, trumps the ideals of beauty expressed in Greek artistic creations like paintings and sculpture (*Abr.* 262-69). The modest banquets of the Jewish Therapeutae far outshine the sensuous and luxurious banquets of the Greeks and Italians.[65] Regarding Egyptian culture, Philo is almost completely negative. He focuses in particular on the false worship of the Egyptians, which includes veneration of the Nile and of animals. As Sarah Pearce has shown, Philo associates this false worship with the Egyptian character, which he understands to be marked primarily by the inability to see God.[66]

The extent to which Jews interacted with non-Jews and their culture and the attitudes Jews held toward their neighbors and their ways thus offer yet another potentially promising avenue of research. It is especially interesting, for example, that Alexandria at this time was well-known as a center of learning and philosophy, yet Philo mentions no contemporary intellectual figures and never refers to the famous Library and/or Museum.[67] With re-

64. See, e.g., Alan Mendelson, *Secular Education in Philo of Alexandria* (Monographs of the Hebrew Union College 7; Cincinnati: Hebrew Union College Press) 28-33; Tcherikover, "Prolegomena," 37-39.

65. *Contempl.* 40-63. For additional examples, see, e.g., Birnbaum, "Philo on the Greeks," 45-48.

66. Pearce, *The Land of the Body,* 241-308.

67. On the Alexandrian Library, see, e.g., Mostafa El-Abbadi, *Life and Fate of the Ancient Library of Alexandria* (2nd ed.; Paris: UNESCO/UNDP, 1992). On Philo's contemporaries, see, e.g., John M. G. Barclay, *Flavius Josephus: Against Apion* (Translation and Commentary 10; Leiden: Brill, 2007) 170-71 n. 7; 153 n. 973; 158-59 n. 1018 (for Apion, Chaeremon, and Lysimachus, respectively). On Jews' involvement (or noninvolvement) with non-Jewish culture, see, e.g., Peder Borgen, " 'Yes,' 'No,' 'How Far'? The Participation of Jews and Christians in Pagan Cults," in *Paul in His Hellenistic Context,* ed. Troels Engberg-Pedersen (Edinburgh: T. & T. Clark; Minneapolis: Fortress, 1995) 30-59; Torrey Seland, "Philo and the Clubs and Associations of Alexandria," in *Voluntary Associations in the Graeco-Roman World,* ed. John S. Kloppenborg and Stephen G. Wilson (London: Routledge, 1996) 110-27. Maren Niehoff has recently suggested a link between Homeric scholarship and Jewish exegesis in Alexandria; see *Jewish Exegesis and Homeric Scholarship.*

searchers continuing to probe and archaeologists continuing to excavate, one hopes that further progress can be made toward understanding the ancient Alexandrian milieu.

Although Philo is best placed to provide information about Alexandria, he also refers fleetingly, as mentioned earlier, to Jewish communities from other parts of the world. Especially if new evidence appears or research breakthroughs occur, his accounts can help to shed additional light on relations between Jews and non-Jews elsewhere in the *oikoumenē* as well. Finally, comparison with other writings like the fragments of Artapanus, the Wisdom of Solomon, and Josephus will further help to place Philo's discussions of non-Jews and their culture in perspective.[68]

Historical Events That Pertain to Jews

If not for Philo's two treatises *Against Flaccus* and *On the Embassy to Gaius,* we would have only a passing reference in Josephus's *Antiquities* (18.257-60) to the outbreak of violence against the Alexandrian Jews, an episode that some have called "the first pogrom." Moreover, except for the occasional asides in Philo's exegetical works that allude to less than tranquil circumstances in his environment,[69] one would hardly guess that Alexandria was the scene of this great hostility. In Philo's accounts of this event, he imparts many valuable details: these include references to Agrippa's visit to Alexandria; practices surrounding the mourning for Drusilla, Gaius's sister; the letter sent by the Jews to congratulate Gaius upon his becoming emperor; and the eventual appearance by Philo and other Jewish delegates before this emperor. He also describes the leadership of both Flaccus and Gaius, including the initial promising periods when each first took office and the factors that led — at least in Philo's eyes — to these rulers' subsequent decline. Finally, he provides information about Alexandria itself — its population, some of its personalities, the nature of its public life, and some of its physical

---

68. The fragments of Artapanus and the Wisdom of Solomon exemplify very different attitudes toward Egyptian worship; see, e.g., Barclay, *Jews in the Mediterranean Diaspora,* 127-32, 181-91. On Josephus's attitudes toward different ethnic groups, see Tessa Rajak, "Ethnic Identities in Josephus," in *The Jewish Dialogue with Greece and Rome: Studies in Cultural and Social Interaction* (Leiden: Brill, 2002) 137-46; John M. G. Barclay, "The Politics of Contempt: Judaeans and Egyptians in Josephus's *Against Apion,*" in *Negotiating Diaspora: Jewish Strategies in the Roman Empire* (LSTS 45; London: T. & T. Clark, 2004) 109-27.

69. *Somn.* 2.123-32, *Spec.* 3.1-6, 159-62. See also nn. 51 and 61 above.

features and institutions, including quarters of the city, its synagogues, theater, gymnasium, hippodrome, and beach. Interestingly, he does not mention the *laographia*, or poll tax, which some have considered an important contributing factor to the Alexandrian tensions.[70]

Philo's reports are not without their complications. Indeed, his two versions of the Alexandrian uprising are not entirely consistent, and each account has its own rhetorical purposes. To fill out the picture even more, we are fortunate to have some precious documentary evidence both from the opponents of the Jews in Alexandria and from Gaius's successor, Claudius, who addressed the two adversarial groups in his famous letter. Many scholars have attempted to sort out just what was at stake in this conflict. To be sure, the more angles that we consider, the more we can understand this episode and such related issues as the complex makeup of the Jewish and non-Jewish Alexandrian populations and the nature of Roman rule.[71]

In addition to the violence in Alexandria and related details, Philo recounts other episodes elsewhere that had a bearing upon or involved the Jews: the construction of an altar in Jamnia to honor Gaius and the Jews' tearing it down; Gaius's subsequent order to place a statue in the Jerusalem temple; the reaction of Petronius; the appeal of the Jews to Petronius; Agrippa's letter to Gaius in Rome, which itself contains many useful references; and Gaius's reaction to this appeal (*Legat.* 184-348). Other sources like Jose-

70. For helpful commentaries on *Flacc.* and *Legat.*, see, e.g., van der Horst, *Philo's Flaccus*; Herbert Box, *Philonis Alexandrini: In Flaccum* (London: Oxford University Press, 1939); E. Mary Smallwood, ed., *Philonis Alexandrini Legatio ad Gaium* (2nd ed.; Leiden: Brill, 1970). On the *laographia*, see, e.g., Tcherikover, "Prolegomena," 60-68; Gruen, *Diaspora*, 75-77.

71. Herbert A. Musurillo, ed., *The Acts of the Pagan Martyrs: Acta Alexandrinorum* (Oxford: Clarendon, 1954) 4-26, 93-140; Tcherikover and Fuks, *CPJ* 2:55-81. For the letter of Claudius, see *CPJ* 2:36-55; H. Idris Bell, *Jews and Christians in Egypt* (Oxford: Oxford University Press, 1924) 1-37. See also Barclay, *Jews in the Mediterranean Diaspora*, 48-71; Gruen, *Diaspora*, 54-83; Peter Schäfer, *Judeophobia: Attitudes toward the Jews in the Ancient World* (Cambridge, MA: Harvard University Press, 1997) 136-60; Andrew Harker, *Loyalty and Dissidence in Roman Egypt: The Case of the* Acta Alexandrinorum (Cambridge: Cambridge University Press, 2008) 1-47; Sandra Gambetti, *The Alexandrian Riots of 38 C.E. and the Persecution of the Jews: A Historical Reconstruction* (Leiden: Brill, 2009); Pucci ben Zeev, "New Perspectives on the Jewish-Greek Hostilities." Allen Kerkeslager has written a series of articles on the events in Alexandria in 38 C.E.; see, e.g., "Agrippa I and the Judeans of Alexandria in the Wake of the Violence in 38 CE," *REJ* 168 (2009) 1-49; "Agrippa and the Mourning Rites for Drusilla in Alexandria," *JSJ* 37 (2006) 367-400; "The Absence of Dionysios, Lampo, and Isidoros from the Violence in Alexandria in 38 CE," *SPhAn* 17 (2005) 49-94. Daniel R. Schwartz compares accounts of Philo and Josephus in "Philo and Josephus on the Violence in Alexandria in 38 CE," *SPhAn* 24 (2012) 149-66.

phus and Tacitus also contribute to the record of what took place. As with all the other areas discussed here, scholars must remember to take into account Philo's own biases as well as those of other sources.[72] Used cautiously, however, Philo contributes amply to our awareness of past events, particularly those to which he was witness or in which he himself participated.

Conclusion

Philo's exegetical and nonexegetical works can be and have been mined for their wealth of information about Jews and Judaism in antiquity. These areas include Jewish practices, beliefs and ideas, community institutions, holy writings and their interpretation, Jews and Jewish identity, Jews' involvement with and attitudes toward non-Jews and their culture, and historical events. Philo occasionally shows strong commonalities with what we know about other Jews, but he also displays important differences and distinctive features. Rather than attempting to characterize Philo generally as representative or not representative of Jews and Judaism in antiquity, it is best to consider individual issues in all their complexity.

Scholars have produced many exemplary studies in all the above areas to advance our knowledge of the past. Many topics, however, remain unexplored or await further clarification and insight. As with any source, one must always be aware of how Philo's own biases, aims, and interests may shape his presentations. While some topics — like the anti-Jewish violence in Alexandria — may pertain especially to Philo's own day, others — like observance of the Sabbath and other holidays — may shed light on both earlier and later periods. Philo's relevance for the study of Jews and Judaism, then, need not be confined to a particular century. Indeed, the astute and careful researcher may find meaningful continuities and discontinuities between Philo and other Jews from the distant past to our very own day.

---

72. See, e.g., Josephus, *J. W.* 2.184-203; *Ant.* 18.261-309; Tacitus, *Hist.* 5.9. See also Smallwood, *Philonis Alexandrini Legatio ad Gaium*, 31-36; Daniel Schwartz, *Agrippa I*, 18-23, 77-89. Erich S. Gruen addresses aspects of these events in "Caligula, the Imperial Cult, and Philo's Legatio," *SPhAn* 24 (2012) 135-47.

Philo's Relevance for the Study of the New Testament

Per Jarle Bekken

Introduction

Philo of Alexandria is a representative of Diaspora Judaism and of Judaism as such in the late Second Temple period. His writings have also been used to illuminate the background and the wider context of the New Testament and the early church.[1] It is easy to forget that substantial parts of the New Testament are dependent on their relationship to the Jewish Diaspora. Either the New Testament was written by Jews *in* the Jewish Diapora or *to* members and communities living in a Jewish Diaspora context. In light of this fact, Philo's writings are not only a major representative of such a Hellenistic Judaism, but also, perhaps, *the* most important body of material to inform about the world of Diaspora Judaism that formed the background for the New Testament writings.

My task is to give the reader a glimpse of the way Philo's writings, written during the first half of the first century c.e., can illuminate aspects of the New Testament, written during the second half of the same century.

An attempt to cover all the New Testament books would be too repetitive for the reader and definitively extend beyond the limits of the present chapter.

---

1. See, e.g., David Runia, "Philo and the Early Christian Fathers," in *The Cambridge Companion to Philo*, ed. Adam Kamesar (Cambridge: Cambridge University Press, 2009) 210-30. See also the collected essays in Roland Deines und Karl-Wilhelm Niebuhr, eds., *Philo und das Neue Testament: Wechselseitige Wahrnehmungen: I. Internationales Symposium zum Corpus Judaeo-Hellenisticum 1.-4. Mai 2003, Eisenach/Jena* (WUNT 171; Tübingen: Mohr Siebeck, 2004).

Instead, a thematic approach will be provided,[2] surveying representative topics and texts which might show Philo's relevance for the study of the New Testament. We will consider the following categories, within which Philo can shed light on various aspects of the New Testament: (1) Scripture and exegesis; (2) beliefs, motifs, and metaphors; (3) Jews' relation to non-Jews and pagan society; (4) inner-Jewish conflicts and punishments; (5) historical information.

The following comparison of Philo with New Testament writings is based on the assumption that no direct relationship or influence is plausible, and that as such the Philonic writings represent a rich collection of data providing useful illustration of the Jewish and Greco-Roman background of the New Testament.

Scripture and Exegesis

As an exegete for his time, Philo testifies to a variegated approach to Scripture, including the use of exegetical traditions, structures, and techniques, and various ways of rewriting the Bible.[3] As we shall see, the New Testament writings display many parallels to such an exegetical use of Scripture.

Exegetical Traditions

By "exegetical tradition" we mean expositions that go beyond the scriptural texts interpreted and which might be documented by other independent sources. Philo provides illustrations of such traditions in the exposition of the Hebrew Bible in the New Testament. Examples are taken from Paul's Letter to the Romans, the Gospel of John, and the Letter to the Hebrews.

In Gen 17:17, we read about Abraham's reaction to the promise given him by God: "Then Abraham fell on his face and laughed, and said to himself, 'Can a child be born to a man who is a hundred years old? Can Sarah, who is ninety years old, bear a child?'"

Philo, Paul, and the Gospel of John seem to follow a Jewish exegetical tradition based on Gen 17:17. The parenthetical references inserted in the

---

2. Folker Siegert has recently tried to combine a thematic and more "canonical" approach in "Philo and the New Testament," in Kamesar, *The Cambridge Companion to Philo*, 175-209.

3. See Peder Borgen, *Philo of Alexandria: An Exegete for His Time* (NovTSup 86; Leiden: Brill, 1997).

Philonic text which follows refer to motifs that resemble Paul's reasoning in Romans 4 and point to an underlying common exegetical tradition based on Gen 17:17:

> Rightly did he laugh in his joy over the promise, being filled with great hope (cf. Rom 4:18) and in the expectation that it would be fulfilled, and because he had clearly received a vision, through which he knew more certainly Him who always stands firm (cf. Rom 4:16), and him who naturally bends and falls. But to God all things are possible (cf. Rom 4:21), even to change old age into youth, and to bring one who has no seed or fruit into the begetting and fruitfulness (cf. Rom 4:17, 19). And so, if a centenarian and a woman of ninety years produce children, the element of ordinary events is removed, and only the divine power (cf. Rom 4:20 about God's power visible in man's life) and grace clearly appear. (*QG* 3.55-56)[4]

An exposition of Gen 17:17 lies also most probably behind the motifs of Abraham's joy and vision referred to by Jesus according to John 8:56: "Your ancestor Abraham rejoiced that he would see my day; he saw it and was glad." Thus, it is likely that both John 8:56 and *QG* 3.55 share the same exegetical tradition based on Gen 17:17.[5] Although Genesis does not mention Abraham's joy or gladness, the descriptions of joy or rejoicing in Philo (*Mut.* 177-78; *Leg.* 3.217-18) and other Jewish literature (e.g., *Jub.* 15:17, *Tg. Onq.* on Gen 17:17) prior to and contemporary with John are reinterpretations of Abraham's "laughter" in Gen 17:17. Both Philo and John associate the joy with the vision in which the promise was revealed. In John the vision and promise have been interpreted and transferred to Abraham's vision of Jesus as a person who lived prior to and contemporary with Abraham (cf. John 8:57).[6]

In both *Leg.* 3.88 and Rom 9:10-12, 20-23, the idea illustrated is God's foreknowledge and election of two contrasting persons, Jacob and Esau, even before their birth. Moreover, in both cases God is pictured as a maker of clay pots. These agreements make it probable that Philo and Paul draw here on a common tradition of exposition of Gen 25:23.[7]

---

4. Cf. Halvor Moxnes, *Theology in Conflict: Studies in Paul's Understanding of God in Romans* (NovTSup 53; Leiden: Brill, 1980) 194-206.

5. Moxnes, *Theology in Conflict*, 198.

6. Cf. Tineke de Lange, *Abraham in John 8,31-59: His Significance in the Conflict between Johannine Christianity and Its Jewish Environment* (Amsterdam: Amphora, 2008) 131-34.

7. Per Jarle Bekken, *The Word Is Near You: A Study of Deuteronomy 30:12-14 in Paul's Letter to the Romans in a Jewish Context* (BZNW 144; Berlin: de Gruyter, 2007) 211.

The motif that God swore an oath in his promise to Abraham according to Gen 22:16 occurs in several passages in Philo's writings (*Leg.* 3.203-8; *Sacr.* 91-96; *Abr.* 73). In the first two texts Philo refers to the interpretation of others, which might imply that here he is involved in an exegetical exchange with other exegetes. The issue, which offended both Philo and the other exegetes, regards the use of anthropomorphic language about God. Thus they protested against the thought that God was said to swear an oath. However, on the basis that God is unlike humans, Philo defended that only God could bear witness to himself, since God alone has exact knowledge of divine matters. These passages have been compared to Heb 6:13-20 and John 5:31-40; 8:12-20.[8] Heb 6:13-20, which also quotes Gen 22:16, shares several commonalities in terminology and motifs, pointing to an underlying common exegetical tradition. The main message implied by this exegetical tradition was that the promise of God to Abraham was guaranteed by his oath, indicating that it is impossible that God would prove false. When God swears there is no longer any room for doubt.[9] Thus, both Philo and the author of the Letter to Hebrews agree that the purpose of divine swearing was to sustain faith and to provide a foundation of hope (cf. Heb 6:12, 18).[10]

The parallel material in Philo, *Leg.* 3.205-8 also provides documentation for the view that the controversy on self-witness reflected in John 5:31-40 and 8:12-20 is a specifically "Christian" version of a discussion which most probably also existed among Jews in Alexandria. In particular, the view represented by Philo, that only God was capable of giving a self-authenticating testimony, may illuminate the Jewish background of the point made by the Evangelist that Jesus could testify in his own case because of his divine origin.[11]

Both Philo and John give witness to a widespread exegetical debate on Gen 2:2-3, that God rested on the seventh day. The problem was the convic-

---

8. Cf. Moxnes, *Theology in Conflict*, 141-45.

9. Helmut Koester, "Die Auslegung der Abraham-Verheissung in Hebräer 6," in *Studien zur Theologie der alttestamentlichen Überlieferungen*, ed. Rolf Rendtorff und Klaus Koch (Neukirchen: Neukirchener, 1961) 95-109.

10. Cf. also Sidney G. Sowers, *The Hermeneutics of Philo and Hebrews: A Comparison of the Interpretation of the Old Testament in Philo Judaeus and the Epistle to the Hebrews* (Basel Studies of Theology 1; Zurich: EVZ; Richmond: John Knox, 1965) 70-71.

11. See Per Jarle Bekken, "The Controversy on Self-Testimony according to John 5:31-40; 8:12-20 and Philo, *Legum Allegoriae* III.205-208," in *Identity Formation in the New Testament: Papers from the Nordic New Testament Conference in Lund, August 2007*, ed. Bengt Holmberg and Mikael Winninge (WUNT 227; Tübingen: Mohr Siebeck, 2008) 19-42.

tion that God cannot stop working in the upholding of the world. Consequently, the notion of God's Sabbath rest, as recorded in Genesis (God rested on the seventh day), stands in tension with this working. Evidence for such exegetical debate on the Sabbath rest is found as early as the second century B.C.E., from the Jewish Alexandrian exegete Aristobulus,[12] and more material is found in Philo and in rabbinic writings.[13] Philo, relying on the Septuagint rendering, reads Gen 2:2-3 to mean that God "caused to rest," as distinct from "rested": "for He causes to rest that which, though actually not in operation, is apparently making, but He himself never ceases making" (*Leg.* 1.5-6). Thus, for Philo the meaning of the seventh day is that God, who has no origin, is always active: "He is not a mere artificer, but also Father of the things that are coming into being" (*Leg.* 1.18). All created beings are dependent and truly inactive in all their doings: "the Seventh Day is meant to teach the power of the Unorginate and the non-action of created beings" (*Migr.* 91).

An interpretation of Gen 2:2-3 similar to that of Philo seems to be presupposed in John 5:1-18. The Son of God brings the Father's upholding and providential activity to bear upon the case of the healing of a person on the Sabbath. And the healed person is dependent and inactive, even in the carrying of the mat on the Sabbath, because the Son of God told him to do so. The rationale for this is stated in John 5:17: "My Father is working still, and I am working." It is immediately apparent to the "Jews" that Jesus not only robs God of his divine prerogative, but also in this way increases the breaking of the Sabbath. This is brought out both from the charge against Jesus for making himself equal to God and from their violent reaction against Jesus according to John 5:18: "For this reason the Jews were seeking all the more to kill him, because he not only broke the Sabbath but was also calling God his own father."

---

12. Nikolaus Walter, *Der Thoraausleger Aristobulus* (TUGAL 86; Berlin: Akademie, 1964) 170-71; Peder Borgen, "Philo of Alexandria," in *The Literature of the Jewish People, in the Period of the Second Temple and the Talmud*, vol. 2: *Jewish Writings of the Second Temple Period: Apocrypha, Pseudepigrapha, Qumran Sectarian Writings, Philo, Josephus*, ed. Michael Stone (CRINT 2/2; Assen: Van Gorcum; Philadelphia: Fortress, 1984) 277; *Paul Preaches Circumcision and Pleases Men and Other Essays on Christian Origins* (Relieff 8; Trondheim: Tapir, 1983) 180, 184-5; *Philo, John, and Paul* (BJS 131; Atlanta: Scholars, 1987) 12.

13. According to rabbinic exegesis, the Sabbath commandment does not forbid one to carry something about in one's house on the Sabbath. God's homestead is the upper and lower worlds. He may thus be active within it without coming into conflict with the Sabbath (*Gen. Rab.* 30:6).

Problem-Solving Exegesis

The method of "question and answer" is a common feature both to Philo, John, and Paul. According to John, Jesus' public teaching in the form of a dialogue with his interlocutors often took place in the synagogue or the temple (cf. John 6:59; 7:14, 28; 18:20). Philo's writings in general make evident that John's use of such a form is appropriate when reporting activities in a learned setting within Judaism such as the synagogue or the temple.[14] Thus, Philo testifies to the use of questions and answers and problem-solving exegesis as part of the teaching activity in the synagogue, as suggested by his report on expository activity among the Therapeutae: "the President of the company . . . *discusses* some questions arising in the Holy Scriptures or solves one that has been propounded by someone else" (*Contempl.* 75).

The same verbs for *"to discuss"* are used elsewhere in Philo's writings when an exegetical question is raised and answers and solutions are given.[15] Against the background of the teaching activity in learned Jewish settings, authors such as Philo and Paul would themselves probably draw on the "questions-and-answer" form as a rhetorical or literary device in their discourses.[16] The following examples will illustrate this.

The exegetical problem of order and rank in the pentateuchal account can be addressed and solved. This exegetical feature is common to Philo, rabbinic literature, and Paul. Philo and the rabbinic literature sometimes even draw on the same exegetical traditions. For example, the question of why Adam was created last is asked several times in rabbinic writings (e.g., *Gen. Rab.* 8:1; *Lev. Rab.* 14:1; *t. Sanh.* 8:7). Particularly interesting is the parallel in structure and content between *Opif.* 77: (a) "One should ask the reason why man comes last in the world's creation, for, as the sacred writings show (b) he was the last whom the Father and Maker fashioned" and *t. Sanh.* 8:7 and 9: (b) "Man was created last. (a) And why was he created last?"

Both texts raise the question in point (a), while point (b) states the fact that man according to the biblical text was created last. The reason why man came last in the order of creation although he was higher in rank is stated in both texts: As a giver of a banquet does not summon to supper before the meal is prepared, the Ruler and King of all creation has prepared all things for man before he was created. At this point an exegetical tradition is shared

---

14. Cf. *Spec.* 1.214; *Legat.* 1.33, 48, 91; 2.103; *QG* 1.62.

15. See, Borgen, *Philo of Alexandria: An Exegete for His Time,* 100-101.

16. Cf. Bekken, "The Controversy on Self-Testimony," 31-32.

between the two texts (*Opif.* 78; *t. Sanh.* 8:9), in which the picture of a banquet is employed to provide the answer, thus beyond the text of Genesis 1.[17] The basic principle which is presupposed in such discussions of order and rank is that the last in an order is inferior and of subordinate rank relative to the first in the order. This idea is implicitly mentioned and presupposed in *Opif.* 87: "The fact of having been the last to come into existence does not involve an inferiority corresponding to his place in the series."

Paul's writings contain two examples of a similar means of reasoning for solving an exegetical problem of order and rank in the pentateuchal story. In Rom 4:3 Paul quotes Gen 15:6: "Abraham believed God, and it was reckoned to him as righteousness." On this basis Paul asked in Rom 4:10: "How then was it reckoned to him?" This "how?" refers not to the process of how this happened, but to its "when": "Was it *before* or *after* he had been circumcised?" The answer was: "It was not *after*, but *before* he was circumcised. He received the sign of circumcision as a seal of the righteousness that he had by faith while he was still uncircumcised" (Rom 4:10-11). Thus, in Rom 4:12 Paul maintained that the basic and superior principle which had priority for Jews and Gentiles alike was righteousness by faith. Thus, the law of Moses regarding circumcision had an inferior and subordinate place relative to the principle of righteousness of faith and was meant primarily as a judicial approval ("seal") for those Jews who followed the example of Abraham and believed. The purpose of this order and rank between the principles of faith and the law of circumcision was that Abraham was meant to be the father of both Jews and Gentiles who believed, without distinction.

A similar kind of problem-solving reasoning is also to be found in Galatians 3. In this chapter Paul applies the rhetorical device of questions and answers in order to explain from Scripture the Galatians' experience of having received the Spirit on the basis of faith independent of and outside the realm of the law of Moses. In Paul's reasoning, the point made in Gal 3:15-18 was that the law of Moses had a subordinate specific function which contributed to the purpose of implementing God's promise to Abraham on the basis of righteousness by faith. In this regard Paul argues from the pentateuchal account of order and rank, implying that the law which came *later* was subordinate and unable to make invalid the promise *previously* given by God: "My point is this: the law, which came four hundred and thirty years *later*, does not annul a covenant *previously* ratified by God, so as to nullify the promise" (Gal 3:17).

---

17. See Borgen, *Philo of Alexandria: An Exegete for His Time*, 87-89.

The Method of Contrast

Besides question and answer, many other exegetical methods are used. One such method was the way of confirming, correcting, and expanding a certain reading of a biblical text by means of the contrast form "not-but."

A contrast may be used to confirm a certain reading of the text over against an alternative one.[18] Thus, in *Migr.* 1 and 43, the contrast indicates a confirmation of the reading of the text of Gen 12:1: "into the land that I will show you": "He says not 'which I am shewing,' but 'which I will shew thee.'" Such a philological confirmation of one particular reading of a text is also used in rabbinic exegesis, as in *Mek.* on Exod. 15:11: "Doing wonders: It is not written here 'Who did wonders,' but 'who does wonders,' that is, in the future." Paul offers another example of the same method in Gal 3:16: "'and to his offspring': It does not say 'and to offsprings,' as referring to many, but, referring to one, 'and to your offspring,' which is Christ."

The contrast may also serve to correct a given reading, as, for example, to be found to be the case in *Det.* 47-48: "Cain rose up against Abel his brother and slew him" (Gen 4:8) [. . .] It must be read in this way, 'Cain rose up and slew himself,' not someone else." *Mek.* on Exod. 16:15 offers a rabbinic parallel: "Man did eat the bread of strong horses (Ps 78:25); Do not read 'of strong horses,' but 'of the limbs,' that is, 'bread' that is absorbed by the 'limbs.'"

When the Greek verb is translated back into Hebrew, John 6:31-32 is also to be seen as an example of this way of correcting a certain reading: "Jesus then said to them: 'It was not Moses who *gave* (Hebrew: *nātan*) you the bread from heaven; my Father *gives* (Hebrew: *nōtēn*) you the true bread from heaven.'" Here words from the quotation of the Hebrew Bible (italicized) are woven together with other words in an exegetical paraphrase. Moreover, the different tenses used in *gave* and *gives* are due to different vocalizations of the Hebrew word behind the Greek text, *nātan* ("gave") and *nōtēn* ("gives").[19]

In his expositions Philo might use the contrast form "not only — but also" to include more than one reading of a text. *Spec.* 4.149-50 can be rendered as an example: "thou shalt not remove thy neighbor's landmarks which thy forerunners have set up. Now this law, we may consider, applies *not only*

---

18. For the following, see Peder Borgen, *Bread from Heaven: An Exegetical Study of the Concept of Manna in the Gospel of John and the Writings of Philo* (NovTSup 10; Leiden: Brill, 1965) 62-65.

19. Cf. Borgen, *Bread from Heaven,* 63-64.

to allotments and boundaries of land . . . *but also* to the safeguarding of ancient customs."

In Rom 4:12, Paul makes use of a similar "inclusive mode of contrast" in his exposition of Gen 15:6 to express that Abraham is father to the circumcised "who are *not only* circumcised *but also* follow the example of faith which our father Abraham had before he was circumcised."

In Rom 9:24-26, the same mode of contrast clarifies that God acts in the same way in the present as he has acted in the history of Israel, "including us whom he has called *not only* within Israel, as he calls Jews, *but also* by calling the Gentiles (Rom 9:24). Such a comprehension is derived from Hos 2:23 LXX and Hos 1:9 LXX, which Paul quotes in Rom 9:25-26.

Exegetical Paraphrase

Philo, Paul, and John follow a common method of exegetical paraphrase as to the way the wording of biblical texts is rendered and interpreted, including the practice of selective citation, omissions, and rephrasing of words, phrases, and sentences from Scripture, which are either repeated or replaced with interpretative terms and supplemented with other qualifying terms.

Both Philo's and Paul's use of Deut 30:12-14 follow the method of an exegetical paraphrase.[20] The following exegetical structures and features have been observed for Rom 10:6-17 with parallels in *Virt.* 183-84 and *Praem.* 80-81:

1. The structure of a scriptural citation followed by an exposition introduced by an exegetical phrase ("that is") is repeated three times in Rom 10:6-8.

2. A quotation from the Hebrew Bible (Deut 30:14 in Rom 10:8) is followed by an exegetical paraphrase throughout the unit of Rom 10:8-17. The exposition is demarcated by an inclusio, with agreements in terminology between Rom 10:8 and Rom 10:17.

3. Rom 10:8-10 displays this exegetical form: (a) Words from the Hebrew Bible (Deut 30:12-14) are quoted or alluded to. (b) The allusion/quotation is given an exposition which is signaled and introduced by an exegetical expression ("that is"). (c) Then follows a sequence, introduced by a conjunction, which gives the rationale and expands the exposition.

---

20. For the expository use of Deut 30:12-14 in Rom 10:6-10, cf. Bekken, *The Word Is Near You*, 54-69.

4. Moreover, in Rom 10:8-9 we have the structure of a quotation (Deut 30:14) followed by an exposition, in which the exposition refers to and repeats words from the biblical quotation and a causal proposition is added as a rationale.

Although the exposition in John 6:31-58 consists of dialogue including scholarly exchanges, there are several unifying threads which demonstrate that the passage is composed as a whole: The statement "our fathers ate manna in the wilderness," v. 31, is repeated in v. 49 and v. 58. Throughout the section the words "bread from heaven he gave them" (v. 31b) are built into the formulations, and from 6:49 to 6:58 the remaining word in the biblical quotation in v. 31, "to eat," is added. Philo offers many examples of exegetical paraphrase in which a quotation from the Hebrew Bible is interpreted in such a systematic way, for exampale, in *Leg.* 3.162-68, which may be taken as a close parallel to John 6:31-58. Here Exod 16:4 is cited: (a) "Behold I rain upon you bread out of heaven, (b) and the people shall go out and they shall gather the days portion for a day, (c) that I may prove them whether they will walk by my law or not."

In the exposition, the first phrase of the quotation, (a) "Behold I rain upon you bread out of heaven," is paraphrased and discussed in *Leg.* 3.162. The second phrase, (b) "and the people shall go out and they shall gather the days portion for a day," follows in the exegetical paraphrase in *Leg.* 3.163-67a. Finally, the third phrase, (c) "that I may prove them whether they will walk by my law or not," is repeated verbatim as part of the exposition of *Leg.* 3.167b-68.[21]

Individuals as Symbolic Embodiments of Character Traits

In Philo's *Exposition of the Laws of Moses*, specific persons are seen as embodiments of general virtues and vices or of other properties. Thus, some of the character traits associated with Abraham, Moses, and Cain can serve as examples. By the notion of character trait, I here think of a disposition to act in a particular way, a virtue or a vice.[22]

In the writings of Philo, Abraham emerges as a paradigmatic figure. In Philo's view, Abraham's story has been recorded because it provides models

21. Cf. Borgen, *Bread from Heaven*, 61-69.
22. For this definition, see Hindy Najman, "Cain and Abel as Character Traits: A Study in the Allegorical Typology of Philo of Alexandria," in *Eve's Children: The Biblical Stories Retold and Interpreted in Jewish and Christian Traditions,* ed. Gerald P. Luttikhuizen (Leiden: Brill, 2003) 107-18.

for readers to emulate. Abraham is a model because of his "zeal for piety," "the highest and greatest of virtues" (*Abr.* 60). One of those virtues was his faith in God. Because of his conversion to the one God, he became the father and the model for both Jews and Jewish proselytes (*Mut.* 16; *Virt.* 212-20). In the New Testament, texts such as Jas 2:20-24; Rom 4:1-25; and Gal 3:6–4:31 point out various aspects of Abraham's exemplarity of faith in God for both Jews and Gentiles and need to be understood against such a Jewish background.[23]

In Philo's writings, Moses is often associated with the idea of heavenly ascent. According to *Sacr.* 8, God advanced Moses to a place beside himself, saying to him, "stand here with me" (Deut 5:31). Moses even participated in God's nature to the extent that he was not "added" at his death (*Sacr.* 8-10). Then in §9 Philo writes:

> When he [God] after having lent him to the earthly things, permitted him to associate with them, he endowed him not at all with some ordinary virtue of a ruler or a king, with which forcibly to rule the soul's passions, but he appointed him to be god, having declared the whole bodily realm and its leader, the mind, [to be his] subjects and slaves "For I give you," he says, "as god to Pharaoh" [Exod 7:1].

Correspondingly, according to the Gospel of John, Jesus was a divine person who, having been with God (John 1:1; 17:5), and having been given power over all flesh (John 17:2), dwelled among human beings on earth (John 1:14; 17:1). While Moses was adopted into his role, Jesus had been with the Father prior to the world being made (John 17:5; cf. 1:1).[24] In different ways both Philo and John solved the problem of ditheism by emphasizing that Moses and Jesus, respectively, were dependent on God. Thus, in *Det.* 160-61 Philo makes clear that Moses was passive when he appeared and functioned as god, as seen from the scriptural formulation that God *gave* him as god to Pharaoh (Exod 7:1). In a similar way, John emphasized the functional union with God. Thus, according to John 10:31-36, Jesus was accused for blasphemy because he, being a man, made himself God. Jesus answers in John 10:37-38 that his works are done in union with his Father: "If I am not doing the works of my Father, then do not believe in me; but if I do them . . . , believe the

23. Cf. Leander E. Keck, *Romans* (ANTC; Nashville: Abingdon, 2005) 125-26.

24. Moses is here seen as sharing in God's nature, so that at his death he is not "added" like others. He is translated (Deut 34:5) through that Word by which the whole cosmos was formed. In this way, Moses is the prototype of the Wise Man (*Sacr.* 8, 10).

works, that you may know and understand that the Father is in me and I am in the Father." Thus, Jesus did nothing by himself (cf. John 8:28).[25]

According to Philo, the archetype of evil is Cain, so that every selfish person may be associated with the vices of Cain: lying, wickedness, godlessness, greed, and murder. Philo's interest in Cain is evident from the fact that three treatises are devoted to an interpretation of Genesis 4.[26] The Gospel and the First Epistle of John seem to presuppose Jewish haggadic traditions based on Genesis 4 related to such a description of Cain. Accordingly, John 8:44 and 8:47 indicate that Jews who are searching for the possibility of killing Jesus are called murderers and liars, with character traits belonging to those associated with Cain. However, unlike the Gospel of John, the murder of Cain is explicitly referred to in 1 John 3:12. Apparently, the negative example of Cain fit well with the description the author of 1 John wanted to communicate to his audience regarding their common opponents and their attitudes.[27]

Scripture as Witness

In John 5:39, the witness of the Scriptures is mentioned: "You search the Scriptures because you think that in them you have eternal life; and it is they that bear witness to me." In the literary context of chapters 5–6, John 5:39 functions as a hermeneutical principle with a parallel formulated in 5:46: "If you believed Moses, you would believe me, for he wrote of me." The phrase "search" in 5:39 is a Greek equivalent for the technical term for performing midrashic exegesis. The Scripture quoted in 6:31 and its midrashic exposition in the subsequent vv. 31-58 can be seen to serve as an illustration of the searching of the Scriptures and their witness to Jesus mentioned in 5:39.[28] Thus, for example, on the basis of the hermeneutical key formulated in John 5:39, the pronouncement in 6:35a, "I am *the bread* of life," renders the precise meaning of the central term in the scriptural quotation in 6:31b: "*bread* from

---

25. Cf. Peder Borgen, "The Gospel of John and Philo of Alexandria," in *Light in a Spotless Mirror: Reflections on Wisdom Traditions in Judaism and Early Christianity*, ed. James H. Charlesworth and Michael A. Daise (Harrisburg: Trinity Press International, 2003) 45-76.

26. See Najman, "Cain and Abel as Character Traits."

27. See Maarten J. J. Menken, "The Image of Cain in 1 John 3,12," in *Miracles and Imagery in Luke and John: Festschrift Ulrich Busse*, ed. Jozef Verheyden, Gilbert Van der Belle, and Jan G. Van der Watt (BETL 218; Leuven: Peeters, 2008) 195-211.

28. Cf. Peder Borgen, *Early Christianity and Hellenistic Judaism* (Edinburgh: T. & T. Clark, 1998) 217.

heaven he gave them to eat." Thus, the Hebrew Bible quoted in John 6:31b and its exposition in v. 35a bear witness to Jesus.

Likewise, Paul affirmed that while righteousness of God has been disclosed apart from the law (through Christ), it is nevertheless attested by the Law and Prophets as judicial documents and foundation (Rom 3:21-22).

Again, Philo in *Leg.* 3.207-8 provides an analogy to the conception of the "Scriptures" accredited to humans as divine witness. Using the exegetical method of confirming one reading of the biblical text against an alternative one,[29] Philo makes a distinction between God's own testimony and the witness of the divine word, which in the context of *Leg.* 3.207 is characterized as "the searching word," accredited to human beings:

> Moses too, let us observe, filled with wonder at the transcendence of the Uncreated, says, "and thou shalt swear by his name" [Deut 6:13], not "by him," for it is enough for the created being that he should be accredited and have witness borne to him by the Divine word; but let God be his own most sure guarantee and evidence.[30]

Moreover, in *Leg.* 3.162 we have a close parallel to John 5:39. There we find the transitional formulation with the verb *martyreō* as the key word: "That the food of the soul is not earthly but heavenly, we shall find abundant witness in the Sacred Word." Thus, we find here a correspondence to the idea in John 5:39 that the "Scriptures" bear witness to Jesus, who, according to 6:31-58, is "the bread of life" which came down from heaven.

Beliefs, Motifs, and Metaphors

The following examples of Philo's beliefs and metaphors may be fruitful for comparison with New Testament passages.

Eschatology

Both Philo and Paul presupposed a future hope of eschatological blessings relative to obedience to the law of Moses. Whereas Philo in *Praem.* 79-82

---

29. Cf. Borgen, *Philo of Alexandria: An Exegete for His Time,* 155.
30. See Bekken, "The Controversy on Self-Testimony," 39-40.

interpreted Deut 30:11-14 in continuity with the claim of Deut 28:1 LXX about actions in obedience to the law as a condition for the fulfillment of the eschatological blessings, in Rom 10:5-10 Paul sets actions in obedience to the laws of Moses as prescribed by Lev 18:5 in an adversative relationship to Deut 30:12-14. Accordingly, the inauguration of the eschaton and participation in eschatological salvation was no longer conditional on obedience to the law, in terms of regulations and "works" according to the law of Moses, but in terms of faith in Christ. According to Paul, this reinterpretation of the law of Moses in an eschatological perspective was a consequence of the Christ-event. By the inauguration of the eschatological age, the law was abolished by Christ. In this sense, Christ was the "end" of the law (Rom 10:4).[31]

In Philo's "eschatology," the motif of a Jewish sovereign, holding universal claim on the nations, formed an integral part of his thought. On this basis, Philo reckons with a future victory for the Hebrew nation, if necessary by means of a future "man" who would be king of all nations and bring to full realization the universal charge of the Hebrew nation as rulers of all nations. The scriptural basis for this future expectation in Philo's writings is Num 24:7 LXX. Its application in various accounts in the Septuagint version of this text proves that it represented a living tradition.[32] In *Mos.* 1.290, Philo elaborates on this text when he depicts a Hebrew "emperor" who would one day come forth from Israel and rule over the nations: "There shall come forth from you one day a man and he shall rule over many nations, and his kingdom spreading every day shall be exalted on high." In *Praem.* 95, Philo again refers to Num 24:7 LXX and contends that the future victory over the nations will take place at the hand of a "man" who will lead the Hebrew army as a warrior king: "For 'there shall come forth a man,' says the oracle, and leading his host to war he will subdue great and populous nations."[33]

Similar to Philo, Paul has a scriptural basis for his expectation of a Jewish sovereign who would come to rule the nations. Whereas Philo's idea of a

31. See Bekken, *The Word Is Near You*, 187-92.

32. See Martin Hengel, "Messianische Hoffnung und politischer 'Radikalismus' in der 'jüdischen Diaspora,'" in *Apocalypticism in the Mediterranean World and the Near East: Proceedings of the International Colloquium on Apocalypticism, Uppsala, August 12-17, 1979,* ed. David Hellholm (2nd ed.; Tübingen: Mohr Siebeck, 1989) 655-86.

33. For recent discussions of Philo's eschatology, see Katell Berthelot, "Philo's Perception of the Roman Empire," *JSJ* 42 (2011) 166-87, esp. 184-86; Bekken, *The Word Is Near You,* 117-37.

future king was warranted by the Pentateuch, Paul's scriptural basis of "messiah" was mainly the predictions in the Former and Latter Prophets and the Psalms of a Davidic messiah.[34] In Rom 15:12 we find eschatological expectations regarding the future king and the age to come similar to those of Philo in *Mos.* 1.290 and *Praem.* 95. Paul sees Isa 11:10 as the scriptural basis for the expectation of a future king who will rule the nations: "The Root of Jesse shall come, he who rises to rule the Gentiles; in him shall the Gentiles hope." Paul understands Jesus as the anointed king, the Messiah, welcoming Jews and Gentiles alike. Thus, Jesus Christ, sprung from the root of Jesse, has become the source of hope for both Jews and the nations.

A common trait of several Philonic texts is to contrast the Jews who in one way or another betrayed their Jewish religion with the proselytes.[35] In *Praem.* 152, the proselyte, securing for himself a place in heaven,[36] is further contrasted to the disobedient Jew, who has falsified the sterling of his high lineage and is dragged down to hell, to Tartarus.[37] We should note that the passage in *Praem.* 152 belongs to the section of curses, *Praem.* 127-61, which describes the resulting consequences of disobedience of the law in eschatological perspective. This means that Philo reckons on an exchange between proselytes and the disobedient Jew as an "eschatological" possibility in the future. In *Praem.* 152, the idea of disregard for descent is expressed in the metaphorical language applied to the proselyte. Here Philo speaks of the virtue of the proselyte as the moral quality that merits the prize of heaven. This virtue, coming from ignoble birth, is compared to a full-grown stem bearing fruit, which has been cultivated from being a wild weed. Thus the origin of descent is in turn pictured as the root. Philo applies this example to the proselyte in contrast to the disobedient Jew, including this metaphor-

---

34. Cf. Nils A. Dahl, "Messianic Ideas and the Crucifixion of Jesus," in *The Messiah: Developments in Earliest Judaism and Christianity,* ed. James H. Charlesworth (Minneapolis: Fortress, 1992) 382-403.

35. Examples of such texts are *Spec.* 1.51ff.; *Virt.* 183.

36. Cf. the use of the same proselyte motif in Eph 2:6, which states how the Christian (Gentile) has been seated with Christ in heaven.

37. Cf., e.g., *Leg.* 3.162-68. With regard to the theme of the heavenly quality of the Jewish nation in Philo, see Borgen, *Bread from Heaven,* 133-45. The basis for the contrast here between the proselyte and the apostate relative to the law is found in Philo's view of the laws of Moses as a manifestation of the cosmic laws and principles. Accordingly, the heavenly reality and the cosmic and ethical principles are the foundation of the Jewish nation in its relationship to the rest of the world. This combination of universalism and particularism is formulated in *Mos.* 2.52: "Thus whoever will carefully examine the nature of the particular enactments will find that they seek to attain to the harmony of the universe."

ical language, as a lesson for all humans to learn that God welcomes virtue irrespective of descent.[38]

There are close agreements between *Praem.* 152 and Rom 11:17-24. If we replace Philo's proselytes with Paul's Gentile Christian "proselytes" and Philo's "virtue" with Paul's "faith," we will recognize a similar pattern of thought and even some similarities in the metaphorical language.[39] The agreements make it probable that both Philo and Paul elaborate on motifs applied to proselytes in contemporary Judaism.[40] Like Philo, Paul reckons in Rom 11:17-24 with an exchange of roles between unbelieving Jews and incoming Christian "proselytes," however not as a possibility in the future, but as a report of events which have already taken place. In a similar way to Philo, the Christian "proselytes" are pictured as wild branches which God has grafted onto the domesticated olive tree. According to Paul, the removal of the natural branches has happened in order to make place for other branches to be grafted in: "You will say, 'Branches were broken off so that I might be grafted in.' That is true. They were broken off because of their unbelief, but you stand fast only through faith" (Rom 11:19-20). This language has a close parallel in *Praem.* 152, where similar metaphors are applied to the coming in of proselytes in contrast to some of Israel, who were excluded from the history of God's blessing and promise because of disobedience to the laws of Moses. In a way similar to Philo, Paul uses the image of the olive tree to illustrate God's impartiality and sovereign freedom independent of origin and descent. Paul emphasizes that the Christian "proselytes" stand in the tree because of faith and that they are supported by the root: "do not boast over the branches. If you do boast, remember it is not you that support the root, but the root that supports you" (Rom 11:18). Like Philo, Paul here elaborates on the image of the root as the origin of descent. The metaphor of the root here probably refers to Abraham.[41] The unbelieving Jews are pictured as branches which naturally belong to the

---

38. Rabbinic literature too uses the language of "Einsenken eines Schösslings in Abraham" about proselytes converting to Judaism; e.g., *b. Yebam.* 63a, according to Str-B 3:292.

39. Cf. the remark by Heikki Räisänen, who takes it for granted that the Gentiles in Rom 11:17-24 are seen as proselytes: "In this allegory, ethnic Israel is seen as God's people, and Gentiles are viewed as proselytes"; "Paul, God and Israel: Romans 9-11 in Recent Research," in *The Social World of Formative Christianity and Judaism: Essays in Tribute to Howard Clark Kee,* ed. Jacob Neusner et al. (Philadelphia: Fortress, 1988) 178-206, here 187.

40. Cf. Klaus Haacker, *The Theology of Paul's Letter to the Romans* (Cambridge: Cambridge University Press, 2003) 105-6.

41. In Judaism, the root of the planting of Israel can be thought of as Abraham; cf. *1 En.* 93:5, 8; Philo, *Her.* 279.

tree, but which have been removed. Paul stresses that their exclusion was a result of their lack of faith (Rom 11:23). As in Israel's history, so now God deals sovereignly with God's chosen people in disregard of physical descent, which has come to expression in God's exclusion of some Jews and the inclusion of Christian "proselytes" (cf. Rom 9:6-33). Thus, Paul's use of the olive tree is consistent with this line of thought in Romans 9, and serves as another explanation of the exchange of roles between Jews and incoming "proselytes" because of their reaction to the gospel.

The universal perspective and the dichotomy of the relationship between Israel and the nations also remain in the eschatological perspective throughout Romans 11. The present rejection of the gospel by the Jews is here interpreted by Paul as a phase which will lead eventually to the salvation of "all Israel." On this point too, Philo's eschatological perspective in *On Rewards and Punishments* provides a parallel. In *Praem.* 162-72, Philo deals with the future hope of rewards for the Jewish nation. The content of *Praem.* 162-72 may be summarized: If those in the Diaspora who have strayed away from the ancestral teaching reproach themselves for going astray by confessing their sin, they will find favor with God (*Praem.* 162-63). Here Philo comments that the curses which have befallen them (cf. Deut 28:15-68) serve as a disciplinary warning; they are not intended to destroy them.[42] This conversion to virtue will strike awe into their masters, who will set them free, ashamed to rule over men better than themselves (*Praem.* 164). Like a return from exile, they will rally "with one impulse to the one appointed place, guided in their pilgrimage by a vision divine and superhuman" (*Praem.* 165).[43] According to Philo, three factors make "the reconciliation with the Father" (God) possible: (1) the clemency and kindness of God; (2) the intercession of the holy founders of the race (the immortal patriarchs), who "cease not to make supplications for their sons and daughters" (*Praem.* 166); and (3) "the reformation working in those who are being brought to make a covenant of peace" (*Praem.* 167). In *Praem.* 168, Philo envisages the return of the exiled people to their homeland, in which the ruined cities will be rebuilt,[44] the barren land will become fruitful once again, and prosperity will exceed that of the ancestors, thanks to the abundant riches God will pour out upon them. In *Praem.* 169-72, Philo describes the grand reversal of fortunes. Those who

42. Cf. 2 Macc 6:12; Wis 3:5; 12:22; *Pss. Sol.* 13:6-10; 18:4.
43. "The one appointed place" for the ingathering of the last days probably refers here to Jerusalem; see Bar 4:36–5:9; *Pss. Sol.* 11; Tob 13:8-18; 14:5-7; 1 *En.* 26:1; *Jub.* 8:19; *Sib. Or.* 5:250.
44. Cf. the motif of a rebuilding of Jerusalem in Tob 13:16-7; 14:5; 1 *En.* 90:28-29; *Sib. Or.* 5:249-52, 420-27; 2 *Apoc. Bar.* 32:2-4.

have mocked and persecuted the Jewish nation "will reap the rewards of their cruelty" (*Praem.* 171). Finally, "new growths will shoot up" from the root of the Jewish nation. The conditions of the restoration are underscored in *Praem.* 172 by the emphasis placed on devotion to virtue.

It is interesting that many of the motifs associated with the restoration of Israel in *Praem.* 162-72 can also be detected in Romans 11. Thus, to justify his hope of Israel's restoration, Paul appeals to the following motifs: (a) God's mercy (Rom 11:32; cf. 9:16): "For God has consigned all men to disobedience, that he may have mercy upon all; (b) grace (Rom 11:29): "For the gifts and the call of God are irrevocable"; (c) the ancestral fathers (reflected in Rom 11:28; cf. 9:5; 11:16): "but as regards election they are beloved for the sake of their forefathers." These motifs are similar to those Philo described in *Praem.* 166-67 as "intercessors," which the disobedient Jews were to hope for in order to be reconciled with God. In addition, it can be noted that these motifs in *Praem.* 162-72 and Rom 11:26 seem to emphasize the trust of the final restoration of Israel, which will take place geographically away from Jerusalem/ Zion (cf. Rom 9:26): "and so all Israel will be saved; as it is written, 'The Deliverer will come from Zion, he will banish ungodliness from Jacob.'" Moreover, Philo's way of describing Israel's restoration by means of the picture of the new growths which will shoot up from the root of the Jewish nation has a parallel in Paul's use of the picture of the branches which will be "grafted back into their own olive tree" to illustrate the final salvation of all Israel (Rom 11:24-32). These observations indicate that Philo and Paul share motifs belonging to a common eschatology dealing with the hope of a future restoration of the Jewish nation.

Human and Divine Agency

Philo applies ideas of agency both to human envoys and on the spiritual and divine level. On a human level, Philo illustrates how the halakic principles of agency reflect the conventions of agency and diplomacy in the Greco-Roman world.[45] Thus, as the leader of the delegation representing the Alexandrian Jewry to Emperor Gaius Caligula, he states in general the relation

---

45. For the correspondence between Greco-Roman conventions on diplomacy and envoys and halakhic principles of agency, see Margaret M. Mitchell, "New Testament Envoys in the Context of Greco-Roman Diplomatic and Epistolary Conventions: The Example of Timothy and Titus," *JBL* 111 (1992) 641-62.

between the envoys and those who have sent them in the following way: "the suffering of envoys recoils on those who have sent him" (*Legat.* 369). In this connection he uses Greek technical terms for the human "envoys." The term for "envoy" is used in the paragraph which follows in *On the Embassy to Gaius:* "Surely it was a cruel situation that the fate of all the Jews everywhere should rest precariously on us five envoys" (§ 370).[46]

On the divine level, Philo applies the idea of an "envoy" to the Logos as ambassador from the heavenly God and King to the human beings on earth. The Logos acts as a mediator between the human race and God and as envoy of the ruler, God, to his subjects: "This same Logos both pleads with the immortal as suppliant for afflicted mortality and acts as ambassador of the ruler to the subject" (*Her.* 205). The term "envoy" is furthermore used by Philo for angels who are envoys back and forth between humans and God (*Gig.* 16). Angels are "the servitors and lieutenants of the primal God whom he employs as ambassadors to announce the predictions which he wills to make to our [Jewish] race" (*Abr.* 115).

A frequently used characterization of Jesus in the Gospel of John is "the one who is sent by the Father" and of God as "the one who sent me," and similar phrases. In such passages John applies ideas of agency and diplomacy to christology. Moreover, Philo exemplifies a Jewish environment that might serve as a background for the suggestion that in passages such as John 1:10-11; 8:39-40; 10:35 the author alludes to the appearance of the *Logos Asarkos,* revealed to Abraham and to Israel on Sinai prior to the incarnation as an agent and mediator of God.

Temple and Priesthood

At times Philo personifies the Jerusalem temple by transferring it to the religious life of persons. Thus the external temple and the actual city of Jerusalem seem to be pointing beyond the literal and material meaning:

> do not seek for the city of the Existent among the regions of the earth, since it is not wrought of wood and stone, but in a soul in which there is no war-

---

46. Cf. also *Flacc.* 97, 98; *Legat.* 182. Cf. Borgen, *Philo, John, and Paul,* 171-84. See now also Borgen, "The Gospel of John and Hellenism," in *Exploring the Gospel of John: In Honor of D. Moody Smith,* ed. R. Alan Culpepper and C. Clifton Black (Louisville: Westminster John Knox, 1996) 98-123.

ring. . . . For what grander or holier house could we find for God in the whole range of existence than the vision-seeking mind. (*Somn.* 2.250-51)

In *Cher.* 98-107 it is stated that the house prepared for God the King of Kings, the Lord of all, is not made of stone and timber, but it is the soul that is fitted to him. In the invisible soul the invisible God has his earthly dwelling place. To this temple belong teaching, virtues, and noble actions.[47]

Philo does not in this way ignore the earthly temple made by hands; however, the spiritual and personal appropriation is seen as basic. Accordingly, he warns the spiritualists in *Migr.* 92 that "we shall be ignoring the sanctity of the temple and a thousand other things, if we are going to pay heed to nothing except what is shown us by the inner meaning of things." At least once Philo himself had visited the temple "to offer up prayers and sacrifices" (*Prov.* 2.64). He also admires the splendor (*Legat.* 198) and beauty (*Spec.* 1.72) of the temple of Jerusalem and gives detailed information of its size and composition (*Spec.* 1.71-73).

There is also a personification of the temple in John's Gospel, applied to Jesus Christ. Jesus is the divine tabernacle (John 1:14). His person in life, death, and resurrection is the temple (2:21). His appearances and teaching activity take place in the temple and often during the feasts, such as Sabbath, Passover, Tabernacles, and Dedication. In this way the true temple and its divine presence have been transferred to Jesus Christ. Thus, the Johannine community went beyond those whom Philo criticizes in *Migr.* 92. There they were warned not to go beyond the boundary of practices connected to the temple, while the Johannine community seems to have experienced a separation away from it.

Corresponding to Philo's application of the temple institution, he retains the institutional and literal sense of the priesthood of the Jerusalem temple, while at the same time he transfers it to encompass the Jewish people as such. The Jewish people are to be conceived as a priesthood in their relation to the world, offering sacrifices and prayers on behalf of all (cf., e.g., *Mos.* 2.224; *Spec.* 2.145, 162). Thus, there is evidence for a kind of "common priesthood" in the writings of Philo.

This Philonic idea of a "common priesthood" of the Jewish people of God seems to be reflected in 1 Pet 2:5-9. However, here it is reinterpreted and

---

47. Philo can also interpret the temple cosmologically. The heavenly temple is the highest and truly holy temple. The spiritual and the cosmic realities have constitutive significance; *Spec.* 1.66-67.

transferred to the role of the "Christians" among Jews and Gentiles as the people and spiritual temple of God, with Jesus Christ as its new foundation.[48]

Divine Birth

Philo gives basis for locating John's thought of rebirth within a Jewish context. Thus, Philo says in *QE* 2.46 that Moses' ascent at Sinai was a second birth, different from the first. Philo interprets Exod 24:16 about God calling Moses above on the seventh day:

> But the calling above of the prophet is a second birth better than the first. For the latter is mixed with a body and had corruptible parents, while the former is an unmixed and simple soul of the sovereign, being changed from a productive to an unproductive form, which has no mother, but only a father, who is (the Father) of all. Wherefore, the "calling above" or, as we have said, the divine birth happened to come about for him in accordance with the ever-virginal nature of the hebdomad. For he "is called on the seventh day," in this (respect) differing from the earthborn first molded man, for the latter came into being from the earth and with a body, while the former (came) from ether and without a body. Wherefore the most appropriate number, six, was assigned to the earthborn man, while the one differently born [was assigned] the higher nature of the hebdomad.

There are several agreements between the Philonic passage and John 3:3-10 and 1:13:[49] (1) The idea of birth (John 3:5; 1:13). (2) This birth is from above (3:3). (3) It is a birth with God as father, without a mother (1:13). (4) It is a second birth, different from the birth from a woman (3:3-10). (5) There is correspondence between John's distinction of flesh-spirit and Philo's flesh-mind.

It is important to note that Philo bases his conception of Moses' rebirth on an interpretation of the Sinai event by drawing on Jewish exegetical

---

48. See Torrey Seland, *Strangers in the Light: Philonic Perspectives on Christian Identity in 1 Peter* (Biblical Interpretation 76; Leiden: Brill, 2005) 79-115.

49. See Peder Borgen, *"Logos Was the True Light" and Other Essays on the Gospel of John* (Trondheim: Tapir, 1983) 133-48.

traditions. This understanding is supported by the fact that the experience of the burning bush and the revelation at Sinai are interpreted as birth in rabbinic traditions.[50] *Song Rab.* 8:2 might serve as an example to be quoted: "'I would lead Thee, and bring Thee': I would lead Thee from the upper world to the lower. 'I would bring Thee into my mother's house': this is Sinai. R. Berekiah said: Why is Sinai called 'my mother's house'? Because there Israel became like a newborn child."[51] R. Berekiah's word about Israel as "a newborn child" was an interpretation of the "mother" mentioned in *Song Rab.* 8:2, and it is therefore evident that the picture of birth is meant here. Other parallels exist, such as in *Exod. Rab.* 30:5, where the idea is expressed that the Torah conceived Israel at Sinai. The rabbinic passages corroborate that Philo relies on Jewish exegesis as the basis for his understanding of the Sinaitic ascent as rebirth, and Philo supports the hypothesis that the core of the rabbinic passages goes back to the beginning of the first century or earlier.

This exegetical tradition of a divine rebirth of Israel at Sinai has then been transferred in the Gospel of John to mean the birth of the people of God who believed in Jesus as the Son of God.

The Law, Wisdom, and Manna

In John 6:31-58, Jesus identifies himself with the bread from heaven, which like the law of Moses gives life to the world,[52] and like Wisdom satisfies the thirst and hunger of those who come:

> Jesus then said to them, "Truly, truly, I say to you, it was not Moses who gave you the bread from heaven; my Father gives you the true bread from heaven. For the bread of God is that which comes down from heaven and gives life to the world." They said to him, "Lord, give us this bread always." Jesus said to them, "I am the bread of life; he who comes to me shall not hunger, and he who believes in me shall never thirst." (John 6:32-35)

---

50. Edmund Stein, "Der Begriff der Palingenesie im talmudischen Schrifttum," *MGWJ* n.s. 47 (1939) 194-205; Erik Sjöberg, "Wiedergeburt und Neuschöpfung im palästinischen Judentum," *ST* 4 (1950) 44-85.

51. Translation in Harry Freedman and Maurice Simon, *Midrash Rabbah*, vol. 9: *Song of Songs* (London: Soncino, 1961) 303.

52. See *Tanh. Shemoth* 25; *Mek.* on Exod 15:26; *Exod. Rab.* 29:9.

In a corresponding way Philo combines wisdom, the law, and the manna in *Mut.* 253-63, where it is said that the manna that rains down from heaven is the heavenly Sophia, which is in particular sent from above on the seventh day, on the Sabbath, when the laws of Moses are read and expounded.[53]

Jews' Relation to Non-Jews and Pagan Society

Jewish Proselyte Characterizations[54]

In *Virt.* 175-82, Philo describes the various aspects of conversion needed when a Gentile converts to Judaism. It is made clear here that the conversion of Gentiles entails a religious, social/national as well as ethical change of lifestyle. In the following, some of the main aspects will be described, with parallels in the New Testament.

From many gods to the one God

The conversion from polytheism to Jewish monotheism was central when Gentiles became proselytes. *Virt.* 179 may illustrate this theme:

> So therefore all these who did not at the first acknowledge their duty to reverence the Founder and Father of all, yet afterwards embraced the creed of one instead of a multiplicity of sovereigns, must be held to be our dearest friends and closest kinsmen.

A corresponding formulation in Philo is found in *Virt.* 102-4:

> the incomers . . . abandoning . . . the temples and images of their gods . . . have taken the journey to a better home, from idle fables to the clear vision of truth and the worship of the one and truly existing God.

The issue of transition from polytheism to monotheism is elsewhere described by Philo by means of the model proselytes Abraham and Tamar.

---

53. The manna is identified with the law also in *Mek.* on Exod 13:17. See further Borgen, *Bread from Heaven*, 148-50.

54. For the following, see Borgen, *Philo, John, and Paul*, 207-16; Seland, *Strangers in the Light*, 68-77.

Abraham is described as a son of an astrologer. Realizing that this could prevent his progression to the One God, Abraham broke up from his native country "knowing that if he stayed the delusions of the polytheistic creeds would stay within him and render it impossible to discover the One" (*Virt.* 214). Abraham is thus the first person spoken of as believing in God and a model of those "abandoning the ignobility of strange laws and monstrous customs which assigned divine honours to sticks and stones and soulless things in general" (*Virt.* 219). Likewise, Philo describes Tamar as a model proselyte who "became schooled in the knowledge of the monarchical principle by which the world is governed" (*Virt.* 220).

In the New Testament and other Christian writings this motif is also a basic element in the conversion of the polytheists: Gal 4:8-9; 1 Thess 1:9; Acts 15:19; 1 Pet 4:3-4.

From pagan immorality to Jewish morality

In passages about proselytes, Philo describes the ethical change from pagan vices to the Jewish virtues, which immediately follows the worship of the One God, as a life in accordance with the laws of Moses. Philo's explicit reference in *Virt.* 180-82 to the passing of the convert into "the government/ way of life under the best laws" documents this:

> but a man should convert, . . . but also in the other fundamental things of life, by passing, as it were from mob-rule, which is the vilest of misgovernments, into democracy, the government/way of life under the best laws. . . . For it is excellent and profitable to desert without a backward glance to the ranks of virtue and abandon vice, that malignant distress; and where honor is rendered to the God who is, the whole company of the other virtues must follow in its train as surely as in the sunshine the shadow follows the body. The proselytes become at once temperate, content, modest, gentle, kind, humane, serious, just, high-minded, truth-lovers, superior to the desire for money and pleasure.

In a corresponding way, Paul uses a catalog of (vices and) virtues to describe the new life of the Christian converts: "But the fruit of the Spirit is love, joy, peace, patience, kindness, goodness, faithfulness, gentleness, self-control" (Gal 5:22-23).

From other ethnic groups to the Jewish politeia

A conversion to Judaism involved a change of social and ethnic identity. Becoming a Jew was tantamount to repudiating one's national affiliation and taking on a Jewish ethnic identity. The proselyte, Philo says, has fled from his country (cf. *Praem.* 17; *Virt.* 214; *Spec.* 1.52). The model of the proselytes is Abraham, moving from his own country to a new one:

> He is the standard of nobility for all proselytes, who, abandoning the ignobility of strange laws and monstrous customs which assigned divine honors to stocks and stones and soulless things in general, have come to settle in a better land, in a commonwealth full of true life and vitality, with truth as its director and president. (*Virt.* 219)[55]

In *Virt.* 102, Philo says that the proselytes have left their family, their country, and their customs: "abandoning their kinsfolk by blood, their country, their customs, and the temples and images of their gods. . . ." Leaving the context of family and kinfolk could imply the risk of their lives.

> they have taken the journey to a better home, from idle fables to the clear vision of truth and the worship of the one and truly existing God. He commands all members of the nation to love the incomers, not only as friends and kinsfolk, but as themselves both in body and soul.

New Testament writings draw on such proselyte traditions in their description of the "Christian" proselytes. Thus, for example, in Eph 2:11-22, in accordance with the proselyte pattern of contrast, the present situation of the Christian converts is characterized against the pagan background, when they were uncircumcised Gentiles, alienated from the commonwealth of Israel, strangers and foreigners, while they now are fellow citizens and members of the household. The "Christian" use of such proselyte motifs breaks away from the Jewish notion, as the Christians are not to make an ethnic and legal break away from their families, country, and nation. Instead of becoming citizens of the Jewish nation of the law of Moses, the Christians are included in the one people of God among Jews and Gentiles (Eph 2:11-13; cf. Rom 4:12). The motif that proselytes became enemies of families and

55. Cf. *Abr.* 62.

friends at the risk of persecution and of their own lives might lie behind passages in the Letter of 1 Peter (cf. 2:12; 4:4, 12-16).

In *Virt.* 102, the commandment of Lev 19:34 is applied to characterize the nature of the loving community into which the proselytes enter. According to Paul, the same commandment should describe the community life into which the Christians have arrived (Gal 5:13-14). The issues of love, friendship, and goodwill toward the proselytes on the part of the loving community have parallels in the characterization of Christian converts in 1 Peter as well (cf. 1:22; 2:17; 4:9; 5:9).

Participation in Pagan Cults

As for the problem of how Jews should interact with their pagan surroundings and participate in pagan society, there existed a varied spectrum of views and practices within both the synagogue and the early church. One problem area was the relationship to pagan cults. Jews held a variety of views regarding this issue. Accordingly, there were Jews and Christians who took part in pagan cults to such an extent that they became apostates or were regarded as apostates by other Jews (*Spec.* 1.315-16) and Christians (Rev 2:14). Philo seems to have followed the approach that practiced a limited integration with society at large and interpreted idolatry as participation in pagan cults. Although Philo accepted the participation of a Jew in club life with the focus on prudence, he also pointed to the dangerous possibility that such activity could lead to irregularities and actual participation in idolatry (*Ebr.* 20-29, 95). Similarly, Paul also limits the definition of idolatry to sacrificial acts of a pagan cult. Thus, in 1 Cor 8-10 Paul permits Christians to eat food used in pagan practice (1 Cor 8:1, 4), while it is evident that some other Christians in Corinth regarded this as participation in sacrificial pagan worship (1 Cor 10:1-22).[56]

The attitude toward sacrificial food was only one part of the eating practices which could serve as a barrier between Jews, Christians, and others. One other question was how far one could go regarding dining with Gentiles. According to *Ios.* 202, Joseph held a combined dinner for Egyptians and Jews by dealing with each group according to their ancestral tradition by observ-

---

56. See Karl-Gustav Sandelin, "Drawing the Line: Paul on Idol Food and Idolatry in 1 Cor 8,1–11,1," in *Neotestamentica et Philonica: Studies in Honor of Peder Borgen*, ed. David E. Aune, Torrey Seland, and Jarl Henning Ulrichsen (NovTSup 106; Leiden: Brill, 2003) 108-25.

ing a form of selective eating. Philo himself seems to have adopted this practice by following the Jewish dietary laws when taking part in meals with Gentiles (cf. *Leg.* 3.156). The case reported by Paul in Gal 2:11-14 might represent a parallel to this kind of separated dining within the same location. Here Paul reports without details that "some who came from James" argued for separation between Jews and Gentiles during the meals so that Jews could eat according to their own customs. It is possible that those Jews who advocated such a view at the same time proposed that Jews and Gentiles were to have different meals in the same room in accordance with Philo's description of the banquet arranged by Joseph.[57]

The Challenge of the Roman Emperor

Despite how integrated the Jews and Christians were within the Greco-Roman culture, the religious and cultic claims of the Roman emperor represented a challenge to both Jewish and Christian beliefs. A common ground between Philo and New Testament authors is the imperial ideology they had to face in their encounter with Roman emperor worship.[58] Both regarded the imperial claim to divinity of the Roman emperor as blasphemy over against the legitimate and proper right to divinity of Moses and Jesus, respectively.[59] As an illustration of this, we can cite the image of Moses depicted as the ideal king and "god" in *On the Life of Moses* 1 and the position of Jesus as Sovereign in the New Testament, which to some extent might be understood against the background of Emperor Gaius seen as a caricature of a counterfeit God. Here three motifs common to Philo, John the Seer, and Paul shall be outlined.[60]

---

57. Cf. Borgen, *Early Christianity and Hellenistic Judaism*, 28.

58. See Hans-Georg Gradl, "Kaisertum und Kaiserkult: Ein Vergleich zwischen Philos *Legatio ad Gaium* und der *Offenbarung des Johannes*," NTS 56 (2009) 116-38.

59. On this subject, see Samuel Vollenweider, "Der 'Raub' der Gottgleichheit: Ein Religionsgeschichtlicher Vorschlag zu Phil 2,6(-11)," NTS 45 (1999) 413-33.

60. For the following comparison of Philo, the Gospel of John, and Revelation, see Wayne A. Meeks, "The Divine Agent and His Counterfeit in Philo and the Fourth Gospel," in *Aspects of Religious Propaganda in Judaism and Early Christianity*, ed. Elisabeth Schüssler Fiorenza (Notre Dame: University of Notre Dame Press, 1976) 43-67; Borgen, *Early Christianity and Hellenistici Judaism*, 293-307. To the observations from the Gospel of John and Revelation, we have added data from Philippians.

The illegitimate usurpation and proper ascent to the divine realm

In *Plant.* 67-68, Philo contrasts kings who receive God as their portion with kings who have extended their kingship to the divine realm. The latter Philo describes as kings "who have acquired royal and imperial sway, . . . made themselves masters of all earth's regions to its fullest bounds, all nations, Greek and barbarian alike, all rivers, and seas unlimited in number and extent. For even had they, besides controlling these, extended their empire, an idea which it were impious to utter, to the realm of the upper air, alone of all the things made by the Creator" (§68). As already noted above, Gaius Caligula was a historical example of such a ruler who illegitimately went beyond the limits of humans and invaded the divine realm: "he no longer considered it worthy of him to abide within the bounds of human nature but overstepped them in his eagerness to be thought a god" (*Legat.* 75).

According to Philo, Petronius, who was Gaius's viceroy in Syria, described his superior in this manner: "a despot who is young and judges that whatever he wishes is beneficial and that what he has once decreed is as good as accomplished, be it ever so unprofitable and charged with contentiousness and arrogance. For having soared above man, he is already enrolling himself among gods" (*Legat.* 218). According to Philo, Moses is seen as an example of one who makes a legitimate extension of his kingship to the divine realm. Thus, Philo contrasts Moses and those "who thrust themselves into positions of power by means of arms and engines of war and strength of infantry, cavalry, and navy" (*Mos.* 1.148). Moreover, in contrast to his counterpart Gaius, Moses was called god and entered the divine realm (*Mos.* 1.158).

As stages leading to the claim of being a god, Gaius won three contests: "Two of these, the Senate and the Equestrian Order, concerned his relations to his Capital; the third was his family life" (*Legat.* 74). At every stage he won by getting people killed; then "he no longer considered it worthy of him to abide within the bounds of human nature but overstepped them in his eagerness to be thought a god" (*Legat.* 75). Gaius at first compared himself to the so-called demigods, Dionysos, Heracles, and the Dioscuri (*Legat.* 78). Then he worked up from them to the great gods, Hermes, Apollo, and Ares (*Legat.* 93, 114).

The section of *Mos.* 1.149-62 is an excursus which differs from the Pentateuch narrative. Philo reports on Moses becoming a divine king and achieving the status as "god" in three stages: (a) At the outset, Moses had the status of lordship of Egypt as son of the daughter of the then-reigning king.

Moses gave up and renounced completely his expected inheritance from the kinsfolk of his adaption. (b) For this reason, God bestowed on him the kingship and "thought it good to requite him with the kingship of a nation more populous and mightier, a nation to be consecrated above all others" (1.149). (c) Philo states that, having received this position, Moses did not exploit the situation, "like some, take pains to exalt his own house, and promote his sons, of whom he had two, to great power and make them his consorts for the present and his successors for the hereafter" (1.150). (d) Due to virtuous life and behavior toward others, God rewarded him by installing him as universal king and god: "Again, was not the joy of his partnership with the Father and Maker of all magnified also by the honor of being deemed worthy to bear the same title? For he was named god and king of the whole nation" (1.158).

Correspondingly, Jesus went through stages as part of his ascent to his heavenly role and charge, but in the opposite direction to the counterpart Gaius, Jesus descended as in the form of God, by becoming humanlike and by being put to death and crucifixion, as the reascent to his enthronement as a divine being, according to John the Seer in Rev 5:6, 12, and Paul in Phil 2:7-8.

The acquiring of divine titles as God and ruler of the world

Gaius usurped and adopted the divine titles of God and the name of Zeus when he took initiative to convert the Jerusalem temple "into a temple of his own to bear the name of 'Gaius, the New Zeus Epiphanes'" (*Legat.* 346). Correspondingly, Jesus is called by the name of God, *Kyrios,* as an affirmation of his divinity and divine charge of the world (Phil 2:9, 11).

According to Philo, acts of *proskynēsis* were part of the worship of the emperor (*Legat.* 134-36, 188, 346; *Flacc.* 41-42).[61] He reports that Gaius regarded himself as a god before whom men had to prostrate themselves (*Legat.* 116).

Although Philo claims the title god for Moses, he is "god" in a relative sense. In relation to God, Moses as "god" is seen in a place "near" to God (*Sacr.* 9). This view is corroborated by the fact that Philo never describes Moses as object of sacrifice or *proskynēsis.* In this manner, Moses is Gaius's counterpart.

---

61. Josephus says of Caligula: "He wished to be considered a god and to be hailed as such" (*J.W.* 2.184).

Like the worship of Gaius, according to John the Seer Jesus Christ as the Lamb is worshiped by means of *proskynēsis* (Rev 5:12). Likewise, to Paul every tongue should confess that Jesus Christ is Lord of the world (Phil 2:10-11).

Cosmic authority over the world

In *Legat.* 8, Philo states that Emperor Gaius held sovereignty over the whole earth and sea. Philo's description of Moses' sovereignty coincides with and exceeds his characterization of the area under the Roman emperor's control. Thus, God not only granted Moses the whole earth and sea and rivers (*Mos.* 1.155), but also gave him the whole cosmos as his portion. In *Mos.* 1.155, Philo elaborates on Moses, who renounced his inheritance as the son of Pharaoh's daughter; having rejected material power, God made Moses a partner in the divine rule of the universe:

> And so, as he abjured the accumulation of lucre and the wealth whose influence is might among men, God rewarded him by giving instead the greatest and most perfect wealth. That is the wealth of the whole earth and sea and rivers, and of all the other elements and the combinations they form. For, since God judged him worthy to appear as a partner of his own possessions, he gave into his hands the whole world as a portion well fitted for his heir.

Correspondingly, Jesus, as the Lamb of God, was placed next to God and had cosmic authority, which he joined with God who is placed upon the throne (Rev 5:13). Similarly, Paul's description of Jesus' sovereignty coincides with and exceeds the area under the Roman emperor's control. Thus, God gave Jesus Christ the whole cosmos as his area of Lordship (Phil 2:10-11).

Inner-Jewish Conflicts and Punishments

Sabbath Controversy

Philo can throw further light on John beyond the area of exegetical methods and exegetical traditions. His writings illustrate how exegesis of the laws of Moses played a role in controversies within the Jewish community. Thus, he provides comparative material to the way in which exegesis of the laws of

Moses (for example, Gen 2:2-3 in John 5:1-18) was a factor in the controversy between the synagogue and the emerging Christian community.[62]

In *Migr.* 91, Philo gives the following advice and warning against those who draw wrong conclusions from the circumstance that God is active on the seventh day, as stated in Gen 2:2-3 according to Jewish exegesis:

> It is quite true that the Seventh Day is meant to teach the power of the Unorginate and the nonaction of created beings (cf. Gen 2:2-3). But let us not for this reason abrogate the enactments laid down for its observance, and light fires or till the ground or carry loads or demand the restoration of deposits or recover loans, or do all else that we are permitted to do as well on days that are not festival seasons. . . . If we keep and observe these, we shall gain a clearer conception of those things of which these are the symbols; and besides that we shall not incur the censure of the many and the charges they are sure to bring against us.

Migr. 91 has points of similarities with John 5:1-18. In both places the exegesis of Gen 2:2-3 is presupposed and employed, although this Old Testament passage is not quoted and therefore not interpreted in an explicit way. In both places the Scripture is applied to specific controversies related to Sabbath observance. The Sabbath gives witness to the understanding that God is always active. This understanding is what matters. Thus there is freedom as to the specific observances, such as the prohibition against carrying a load. In John 5:10, the load is the mat carried by the one healed. Moreover, the charge against Jesus because of the healing on the Sabbath might have been considered in general as overriding the prohibition of doing on the Sabbath what the Jews "are permitted to do as well on days that are not festival seasons" (*Migr.* 91). That such a basic rule was applied to the criticism of Jesus' healing on the Sabbath is evident from Luke 13:14: "There are six days on which work ought to be done; come on those days and be healed, and not on the Sabbath day."

There is a basic difference, however, between the spiritualizing Jews whom Philo criticizes and the views expressed in John. According to John, the activity of the "Father" is the basis for the activity of the "Son" on the

---

62. See Borgen, *Philo, John, and Paul,* 65-68; "The Sabbath Controversy in John 5.1-18 and Analogous Controversy Reflected in Philo's Writings," in *Heirs of the Septuagint: Philo, Hellenistic Judaism and Early Christianity. Festschrift for Earle Hilgert,* ed. David T. Runia, David M. Hay, and David Winston (SPhAn 3; BJS 230; Atlanta: Scholars, 1991) 209-21.

Sabbath, and the "Son" is the historical person Jesus of Nazareth. This view leads to the conclusion that the Sabbath proscriptions against healing and against the carrying of a load could be set aside. The spiritualists in Alexandria, on the other hand, referred to an idea and a doctrine of God's providential activity in defense of their freedom from Sabbath observances.

Various Attitudes on Circumcision

In *Migr.* 92 Philo states:

> It is true that receiving circumcision does indeed portray the excision of pleasure and all passions and the putting away of the impious conceit, under which the mind supposed that it was capable of begetting by its own power, but let us not on this account repeal the law laid down for circumcising.

At this point Philo draws on a scriptural tradition which relates bodily circumcision to ethical circumcision, often depicted as circumcision of the heart (cf. Deut 10:16; 30:6; Jer 4:4). Philo exhorts himself and the potential spiritualists probably known to him not to spiritualize circumcision and cease practicing its observance. Obviously, according to Philo the spiritualists had a right intellectual understanding of circumcision, but they were in danger of preferring a lifestyle stressing the ethical meaning at the expense of its literal observation. On this basis, Philo exhorts them to keep together the concrete and spiritual aspects of circumcision.

The issue of circumcision was a central issue to Paul. *Migr.* 92 can be compared with Gal 5 and Rom 2:25-9.[63] In Gal 5, Paul, like Philo, stresses doing away with pleasures: "do not gratify the desires of the flesh" (v. 16), "what the flesh desires" (v. 17), "crucified the flesh with its passions and desires" (v. 24). Philo's ethical interpretation of circumcision is similar: "excision of pleasure and all passions" (*Migr.* 92). In its literary context, Paul's ethical interpretation in Galatians is bound to the questions concerning Paul's own preaching of circumcision and whether Gentile converts to Christian faith should be circumcised or not. Paul makes clear that his views on circumcision have got him into trouble: "If I still preach circumcision, why am I still persecuted? In that case the offense of the cross has been

---

63. See John M. G. Barclay, "Paul and Philo on Circumcision: Romans 2.25-9 in Social and Cultural Context," *NTS* 44 (1998) 536-56.

removed" (Gal 5:11). The trouble seems to have derived from the Jewish community, and it is easy to understand why: If Paul insists that Gentile converts, whom he and the Jewish community would have treated like proselytes, were not to be circumcised, he undermines the role of the law of Moses as the constitution of the Jewish people of God. Such a relativizing of circumcision would certainly elicit such hostile reactions from the Jewish community as persecution, as informed by Philo as we shall see below. Thus, it is not surprising that Acts represents Paul as an apostate from the law of Moses who taught Diaspora Jews not to circumcise their children and follow the customs of the law (Acts 21:21). In Galatians, Paul delivers a twofold defense for his view: (1) The Christians are those who believe and so are reckoned as righteous, as following in the footsteps of Abraham. In this way the promise to Abraham was being fulfilled (Gal 3:2-9). As we saw above, Paul used a similar kind of reasoning, using the method of order of rank, in Rom 4:9-12. As in Gal 3:6, Paul here quoted Gen 15:6 about faith reckoned to him as righteousness, and asks: "How then was it reckoned to him? Was it before or after he had been circumcised?" The answer was: "It was not after, but before he was circumcised." Accordingly, in contrast to the view of the Galatian opponents, Paul meant that the "Christian" was reckoned as a "proselyte" by faith, with the consequence that the observance of circumcision was not to follow. (2) Moreover, the rationale for such a view was based on the message about the crucified Christ: if righteousness was based on doing according to the law of Moses, then circumcision of the flesh was logically to follow the step of faith (cf. Gal 3:3, which can be paraphrased: "Having started with the [circumcision of the heart as effected by the] Spirit, are you now ending with [the circumcision of] the flesh?"). However, according to Paul, such a thinking would have removed the offense of the cross (Gal 5:11) and made invalid the fact that Christ died as a crucified criminal, not for his own crimes, but for the crimes of humankind. Thus, actually, it is the heart of the gospel and the role of the crucified Christ which is at stake and endangered. If a life according to the law of Moses still mattered as a ground for righteousness, the consequence would inevitably become that Christ died for nothing, that is, as a regular criminal (Gal 2:21; 3:1). Against this background it is very understandable that Paul asked the Galatians: "Who has bewitched you, before whose eyes Jesus Christ was publicly portrayed as crucified?" (Gal 3:1).[64]

---

64. The function of Gal 3:1 and the emphasis on the crucified Christ in its immediate literary context (cf. 2:19-21) seems to have been neglected in the scholarly debate.

Migr. 89-92 sheds significant light on the presuppositions of Paul's reasoning in Rom 2:25-29. Here Paul moved in the direction of relativizing bodily circumcision as a necessary requirement of being a "Jew" by definition. In Rom 2:29 he has a statement that comes close to the attitude of the potential spiritualists in *Migr.* 89-93: "He is a Jew who is one inwardly, and real circumcision is a matter of the heart, spiritual and not literal." Thus, in Rom 2:28-29 Paul redefines what it means to be a "Jew" in a much more radical way than the Philonic spiritualists: the real contrast is not between the literal and spiritual meanings of circumcision, but between circumcision of the body as obedience to the written law and circumcision of the heart by the Spirit of God. Moreover, according to Paul, such a person receives praise or reputation from God and not from others, as, for example, by the Jewish community as is the result of combining an intellectual understanding and external observance of circumcision according to Philo. Thus, Paul was socially far more controversial than Philo and was willing to face hostile reactions from the Jewish community (cf. Gal 5:11), where Philo wished to avoid "censure of the many and the charges they are sure to bring against us" (*Migr.* 92).

The Danger of Blasphemy

Even though John 5:18 does not use any of the words for blasphemy with regard to Jesus' claiming of a divine prerogative, it is apparent from the accusation of the "Jews" and their violent response that they considered his words as blasphemous, "making himself equal to God."[65] In John 10:33, the charge is the same as in 5:18, but here we find the word "blasphemy" used for the first and only time in John: ". . . but for blasphemy, because you, being a man, make yourself God." In John 10:36, Jesus asks why the "Jews" accuse him of blasphemy on the ground that he claims to be Son of God: "Can you say that the one whom the Father has sanctified and sent into the world is blaspheming because I said, 'I am God's Son'?" Do the notions of blasphemy reflected in John have some verisimilitude in the Jewish cultural context of

---

65. It has often been noticed that Philo in many texts uses expressions close to John 5:18. The notion that no one is equal to God is particularly prominent and finds expression in several places. Philo says that "there is nothing equal to him" (*Sacr.* 92), or that "God is equal to himself and like himself" (*Aet.* 43), or "there is nothing equal or superior to God" (*Leg.* 2.3). Cf., e.g., James F. McGrath, *John's Apologetic Christology: Legitimation and Development in Johannine Christology* (SNTSMS 111; Cambridge: Cambridge University Press, 2001) 93.

the first century c.e.? The answer seems to be in the affirmative. It has been difficult to comprehend the references in the Gospel of John based on what is known of the Jewish law of blasphemy.[66] According to the regulation pre-scribed in *m. Sanh.* 7:5, the blasphemer is not culpable unless he pronounces the Name (the Tetragrammaton) itself. Such a teaching was most probably not in force in the first century c.e. However, some recent studies of the notion in Philo's writings have suggested that a broader understanding of blasphemy is documented in source material from the first century, which indicates that the charges made against Jesus by the "Jews" in John have some plausibility in its cultural Jewish context.[67] I will briefly point out their rel-evance for such a comparison.

In his writings *On the Embassy to Gaius* and *On Dreams,* Philo applies the words for blasphemy to mean a specific kind of insulting God, namely, the human arrogation and usurpation of a divine status to oneself. This par-ticular kind of blasphemy compromises the Jewish affirmation that only the God of the Jewish people is divine. Such evidence seems to provide a cultural context for the meaning of blasphemy in John, according to which Jesus as a human being is charged by the Jews of making himself God or equal to God by claiming for himself divine prerogatives.

In *Legat.* 353, Philo describes the meeting of the Jewish delegation with Emperor Gaius Caligula. Philo reports how Gaius first addressed the Jews: "Are you the god-haters who do not believe me to be a god, a god acknowl-edged among all the other nations but not to be named by you?" After the Jews had refuted accusations posed by the Alexandrian opponents present that they refuse to offer sacrifices of thanksgiving to the emperor, Gaius replied: "Alright, that is true, you have sacrificed, but to another, even if it was for me; what good is it then? For you have not sacrificed to me" (*Legat.* 357). Gaius finishes his complaints about the Jews with the remark that "they seem to me to be people unfortunate rather than wicked and to be foolish in re-fusing to believe that I have the nature of a god" (*Legat.* 367). In his response, Philo characterizes this experience as "torture, the racking of the whole soul through the blasphemies against God and the menaces launched upon us by this mighty despot" (*Legat.* 368). Apparently the most serious insult was

---

66. Thus, e.g., Raymond E. Brown makes the claim that "we are handicapped by lack of evidence as to what constituted blasphemy according to the Jewish law of this period"; *The Gospel According to John* (AB 29; Garden City: Doubleday, 1966) 1:408.

67. See Adela Yarbro Collins, "The Charge of Blasphemy in Mark 14.64," *JSNT* 26 (2004) 379-401, esp. 386-90; Darrell L. Bock, "Blasphemy and the Jewish Examination of Jesus," *BBR* 17 (2007) 53-114, esp. 79 n. 62.

Gaius's claim to be god himself and the expectation that the Jews should offer sacrifices to him as such.[68] This kind of blasphemy on his part obviously ignores the Jewish belief that only the God of the Jewish nation is divine, and that the Jews were expected to avoid worshiping any other gods than the only one and true God.

The second text, *Somn.* 2.130-32, involves an unnamed Roman governor of Egypt analogous to the passage about Gaius. Here Philo reports that this governor tried to persuade the Jews to do away with the Sabbath and asked as well that he himself be served on that day. Philo reacts, asking:

> What shall we say of one who says or even merely thinks these things? Shall we not call him an evil thing hitherto unknown: a creature of a strange land or rather one from beyond the ocean and the universe — he who dared to liken to the All-blessed his all-miserable self? (*Somn.* 2.130)

Philo further characterizes him as one who would not hesitate

> to utter blasphemies against the sun, moon, and the other stars, if what he hoped for at each season of the year did not happen at all or only grudgingly, if the summer visited him with scorching heat or the winter with a terrible frost, if the spring failed in its fruit-bearing or the autumn showed fertility in breeding diseases. (*Somn.* 2.131)

Philo concludes with the remark that "being a man he conceives himself to have been made superior to other living creatures" (*Somn.* 2.132). From this passage we can observe that the term for blasphemy is applied for a human being who claims authority and power that according to Philo is reserved for the God of Israel.

In sum, it is likely that in John the "Jews" defined blasphemy broad enough, like Philo in his portrayal of Gaius and the unknown Egyptian governor, to have considered Jesus' words as an encroachment upon divine prerogatives and a usurpation of a role not appropriate to his status as a human being. Thus, the notion of blasphemy attested by Philo illustrates most likely the Jewish environment and provides the cultural basis for un-

---

68. Cf. *Legat.* 75, where Philo says of Gaius, "sooner could God change into a human being than a human being into God." Cf. also *Virt.* 171-72, which the translator Leopold Cohn takes as alluding to Gaius: "the arrogant man is always filled with the spirit of unreason, holding himself, as Pindar says, to be neither man nor demigod, but wholly divine, and claiming to overstep the limits of human nature."

derstanding the reactions to Jesus and his claims in the Gospel of John to be of heavenly provenance.[69]

Trial and Execution on the Spot

Those whom Philo criticizes and warns in *Migr.* 91-93 for abrogating the observance of the Sabbath, circumcision, and other practices were in danger of crossing the boundaries of the Jewish community and thus of being subject to censure and accusations. Thus, according to the Letter to the Galatians, Paul was accused and persecuted for undermining the role of circumcision. Likewise, Jesus was charged by the Jewish leaders of a "double" crime: that he not only broke the Sabbath, but also made himself equal to God. For this reason the Jewish authorities sought to kill him (John 5:17-18). They probably understood Jesus' claim to mean ditheism, which qualified for the death penalty.

According to John 16:2b-3 also, the disciples might be put to death as a result of their separation from the Jewish community: "the hour is coming when whoever kills you will think he is offering service to God. And they will do this because they have not known the Father, nor me."

In this regard, scholars have noted Deut 13 as a probable judicial precedent, according to which enticement to serve other gods is a crime which carries the death penalty.[70] This understanding receives support from Philo, who in *Spec.* 1.315-18 has a paraphrased rendering of Deut 13. He applies the passage to the situation in which a person who claims to be an inspired prophet, among others, leads people to worship the gods recognized in the various cities.

There are several commonalities between this passage in Philo and John: (1) Those who commit the crime claim divine legitimation, as an inspired prophet (Philo) or Jesus as the Son of God (John). (2) The crime is that of partaking in polytheism (Philo) or ditheism (John). (3) The death penalty

69. *Pace* Raimo Hakola, who maintains that "it may be impossible to tell whether this response reflects the opinion of some actual Jews in John's surroundings or just John's expectations of what the response to the claims made for Jesus would be like"; *Identity Matters: John, the Jews and Jewishness* (NovTSup 118; Leiden: Brill, 2005) 127.

70. Cf., e.g., Torrey Seland, *Establishment Violence in Philo and Luke: A Study of Nonconformity to the Torah and Jewish Vigilante Reactions* (Biblical Interpretation 15; Leiden: Brill, 1995) 63-80, 98-107, 123-37.

may be executed without regular court procedure being followed. (4) The killing is seen as a service to God.

One difference is that Philo elaborates on the point in Deut 13 concerning polytheism in a pagan city, while the problem in John is the claim of a fellow Jew, Jesus, which is understood to represent ditheism. However, ditheism is one form of polytheism, and thus it is probable that John here presupposes juridical traditions which draw on Deut 13. Philo's paraphrasing exposition of this text shows that in contemporary Judaism there were those who defended the death penalty for Jews who accepted polytheistic views and practices, even sharpening Deut 13 to imply execution on the spot without a proper trial. Several scholars have claimed that Philo frequently attests a Jewish practice of lynch law that was called for without due process in cases where a fellow Jew had transgressed the law.[71] Thus, Philo seems to have endorsed actions to be taken on the spot against violaters of the law taken *in flagrante*. Scholars have proposed that New Testament texts such as Acts 6:1–8:3 and John 8:1-11 seem to be ample evidence that Jews, without reference to any Roman tribunal, freely followed their own instincts in dealing with apostates.

The narratives in John 5:10-18; 8:59; and 10:25-33 recording attempts on Jesus' life for such crimes as breaking the Sabbath and blasphemy have some verisimilitude in the cultural context provided by the Jewish evidence known to us from the first century c.e. On a judicial level, Philo's writings on lynch law (*Spec.* 1.54-57; 315-18; 2.252-53; 3.96) lend support to the view that the Jews might carry out execution without due court procedure. In light of Philo's expositions of the actions taken against violaters of the Torah,[72] John's records of the attempts on Jesus' life might offer illustrations of such cases. Thus, these texts seem to affirm that when some Jews did not conform to the established Jewish customs, they were in real danger as objects of hostility, censure, and violent reactions on the spot within their Jewish context.

---

71. See Erwin R. Goodenough, *The Jurisprudence of the Jewish Courts in Egypt: Legal Administration by the Jews under the Early Roman Empire as described by Philo Judaeus* (1929; repr., Amsterdam: Philo, 1968) 27-34.

72. See Gedalyahu Alon, *The Jews, Judaism and the Classical World: Studies in Jewish History in the Times of the Second Temple and Talmud*, trans. Israel Abrahams (Jerusalem: Magnes, 1977) 112-24; Seland, *Establishment Violence in Philo and Luke*, 59, 236, 253; Katell Berthelot, "Zeal for God and Divine Law in Philo and the Dead Sea Scrolls," *SPhAn* 19 (2007) 113-29.

Historical Information

Finally, we shall take a brief look at how historical data in Philo's writings might also provide help in locating New Testament passages within their Greco-Roman context. According to Pieter W. van der Horst, "a New Testament scholar can only neglect Philo's historical works to his or her detriment."[73] Such a statement is meant to emphasize the value of Philo's writings for shedding light on a broad spectrum of historical information in the New Testament. The following will highlight some historical aspects from the Gospels and the book of Acts in comparison with Philo's historical writings.

Philo's *Against Flaccus* and *On the Embassy to Gaius* provide information that can help us to locate the Gospel Passion Narratives within the broader context of the Greco-Roman world. So, for example, scenes from the Passion Narratives, namely, the mocking of Jesus as a royal figure, the use of scourging as part of his punishment, and the role of Pontius Pilate relative to the Jews, which have parallels in Philo's writings, may be illustrative.[74]

Flacc. 36-40 renders the Alexandrians' exploitation of an insane person named Carabas in order to mock king Agrippa I when he visited Alexandria in 38 C.E. The "theatrical farce" and mimetic scene is similar to the way Jesus is mocked by the Roman soldiers who dressed and equipped him as a royal figure:

> The rioters drove the poor fellow into the gymnasium and set him on high to be seen of all and put on his head a sheet of byblus spread out wide for a diadem, clothed the rest of his body with a rug for a royal robe, while someone who had noticed a piece of the native papyrus thrown away in the road gave it to him for his sceptre. And when as in some theatrical farce he had received the insignia of kingship and had been tricked out as a king, young men carrying rods on their shoulders as spearmen stood on either side of him in imitation of a bodyguard. . . . Then from the multitudes standing round him there rang out a tremendous shout hailing him as Marin, which I said to be the name for the "lord" in Syria. (*Flacc.* 37-39)

---

73. Pieter W. van der Horst, "Philo's *In Flaccum* and the Book of Acts," in *Philo und das Neue Testament: Wechselseitige Wahrnehmungen. I. Internationales Symposium zum Corpus Judaeo-Hellenisticum 1.-4. Mai 2003, Eisenach/Jena,* ed. Roland Deines und Karl-Wilhelm Niebuhr (WUNT 171; Tübingen: Mohr Siebeck, 2004) 95-105, esp. 105.

74. See Gregory E. Sterling, "Philo of Alexandria," in *The Historical Jesus in Context,* ed. Amy-Jill Levine, Dale C. Allison Jr., and John Dominic Crossan (Princeton: Princeton University Press, 2006) 296-308.

A second text describes the flogging of the Jewish magistrates in Alexandria by Flaccus, which according to Philo was a violent measure "commonly used for the degradation of the vilest malefactors" on the part of the Roman administration. The Gospels suggest that Jesus endured a similar kind of punishment as part of his examination by the Roman prefect before his crucifixion (cf. Matt 27:26; Mark 15:15; John 19:1):

> Then as they stood with their enemies seated in front to signalize their disgrace, he ordered them all to be stripped and lacerated with scourges, which are commonly used for the degradation of the vilest malefactors, so that in consequence of the flogging some had to be carried out on stretchers and died at once, while others lay sick for a long time despairing of recovery. (*Flacc.* 75)

The remarkable parallels between the Gospel accounts and Philo describing royal appurtances, clothing, stripping, and flogging correspond to the mimetic and mocking character of other Greco-Roman penal parodies,[75] in which the purpose often was to ridicule the endeavor to acquire royal power.[76]

A third text is one of the most important evidences in addition to the Gospels that describe Pilate, the Roman prefect who sentenced and executed Jesus. Philo's account is located in a letter of King Agrippa I to Emperor Gaius in *Legat.* 299-305. Agrippa tried to prevent Gaius from setting up a statue of him in the Jerusalem temple by contrasting the emperor with Pilate. Through his account of Pilate, Agrippa urged Gaius to respect Jerusalem in the same way as Tiberius had. The narrative reads, in brief, as follows: Pilate had set up in Jerusalem some golden shields bearing an inscription. According to Philo's account, the Jews, on the one hand, were afraid that Pilate could start a revolt and destroy the peace in Jerusalem. On the other hand, Pilate realized that the emperor would be furious and that the Jews would impeach him for the way he practiced his governorship. The outcome was that Pilate's action provoked the Jewish magistrates to write Emperor Tiberius letters of petition. As a result, Tiberius reproached and rebuked Pilate and ordered him to take down the shields and to transfer them to Caesarea by the sea.

Whether or not Philo's account on Pilate is historically reliable, it may

---

75. Cf. Dio Chrysostum's description of the Sacian feast of the Persians in *Orat.* 4.67-70 and Plutarch, *Mor.* 554b.

76. See Joel Marcus, "Crucifixion as Parodic Exaltation." *JBL* 125 (2006) 73-87.

be useful for bringing light to the trial of Jesus under Roman jurisdiction as recorded in the Gospel of John, namely, the circumstances which led Jesus to crucifixion. It has been assumed that partly due to pressure from the Jews that Pilate would be setting himself against the emperor if he refused to crucify an alleged king (John 19:12) and partly to prevent Jewish uprising and revolt, the Roman prefect crucified Jesus to ensure crowd control. Both aspects seem more comprehensible within the context of Philo's description of Pilate relative to the emperor and the Jews in *Legat.* 299-305.

A comparison of Acts and *Against Flaccus* and *On the Embassy to Gaius* makes clear that both Philo and Luke lived within the same geographical horizon.[77] Philo's geographical information is comparable with Acts because of its setting in a Jewish Diaspora context. The boundaries in Philo and Acts are similar. For the east, Acts mentions the nations of Medes and Elamites (2:9-11), while Philo even includes India (*Somn.* 2.56). In the north, Pontus and Bithynia at the Black Sea are listed by both Acts (2:9-11; 16:7) and Philo (*Legat.* 281-83). In the west Rome, Sicily, and Libya are names common to both Acts (2:9-11; 28:12-15) and Philo (*Somn.* 2.54; *Legat.* 283). For the south, both Acts (8.26-39) and Philo (*Flacc.* 43) mention Ethiopia. Both Luke and Philo refer to Jerusalem, Athens, and Rome as the main centers of the world. Both Luke and Philo describe how people come to worship in the temple of Jerusalem. Thus, Philo shows that Jews from all nations meet and enjoy fellowship and exchange information in Jerusalem, while Acts states that Jews from all nations are located in Jerusalem. The central role Jerusalem represents for both authors reflects the fact that they view the world from the perspective of Diaspora Judaism. In a similar way, Luke and Philo view Athens as a city of Greek culture and philosophy. As for Rome, both authors depict the city as the most westerly place where Jews reside. Most probably, Ephesus has the same function for Luke, corresponding to that of Alexandria for Philo, that is, as centers from which the geographical perspective of the world is viewed.

Much more historical information is common between *Against Flaccus* and Acts. It is sufficient for now to mention the names (Acts 6:9; *Flacc.* 53) and location near the sea of the synagogues in the Diaspora (Acts 16:13; *Flacc.* 122), the function of the city theater in the mob riots (Acts 19; *Flacc.* 41, 138), and the role of the personified goddess Dike (Acts 28:4; *Flacc.* 104). Likewise, it should be mentioned that Paul's sea voyage in Acts 27–28, of which the final stage was made by a ship from Alexandria to Rome, has been compared

77. See Peder Borgen, "Philo, Luke and Geography," in *Philo, John, and Paul,* 273-85.

to *Flacc.* 152-56. Both passages shed light on each other, not least regarding the difficulties of travel in the ancient Mediterranean.[78]

Conclusion

I could easily have extended the number of topics and texts, but these will suffice to get a sense of Philo's relevance for the study of the New Testament. The present essay has surveyed five categories reflected in the Philonic corpus and the New Testament writings: (1) Scripture and exegesis; (2) beliefs, motifs, and metaphors; (3) Jews' relation to non-Jews and pagan society; (4) inner-Jewish conflicts and punishments; (5) historical information. Some of the issues highlighted within these broad categories at the same time represent some of the challenges of identity to both Jews and Christians living in the cultural complexity and context of the first century C.E. Hopefully, the present study will stimulate and inspire further investigations of the potential of Philo's corpus to throw more light on the New Testament.

78. Cf. van der Horst, "Philo's *In Flaccum* and the Book of Acts," 105; Friedrich Avemarie, "Juden vor den Richterstühlen Roms: *In Flaccum* und die Apostelgeschichte im Vergleich," in Deines and Niebuhr, *Philo und das Neue Testament,* 107-26.

Philo in the Patristic Tradition: A List of Direct References

David T. Runia

There are two main reasons why the reception of Philo's writings and thought in early Christianity and the patristic tradition is important. First, there is no doubt that we owe almost all our knowledge of Philo to the church fathers. If they had not found his writings interesting and useful, they would not have preserved them for posterity. Second, because the church fathers read Philo, his thought exerted an influence on them in a number of areas. Philonic ideas are absorbed into the Christian tradition of biblical exposition and theology. The list of direct references to Philo in the patristic tradition, which forms the main body of this chapter, records the bare bones of Philo's reception in the church fathers. In order to understand its significance better, we first need to take a closer look at how Philo's writings survived and what influence they exerted in the centuries after his death.[1]

The Survival of Philo's Writings

From references in Philo's own writings and from small remains elsewhere, it is clear that an extensive body of writings was produced in the Greek-speaking Jewish community of Alexandria in the time of its flourishing from

---

1. The following account is based on my monograph, *Philo in Early Christian Literature: A Survey* (CRINT 3/3 (Assen: Van Gorcum; Mineapolis: Fortress, 1993). Further studies were presented in *Philo and the Church Fathers: A Collection of Papers* (VCSup 32; Leiden: Brill, 1995). See also "Philo and the Early Church Fathers," in *The Cambridge Companion to Philo*, ed. Adam Kamesar (Cambridge: Cambridge University Press, 2009) 210-30.

200 B.C.E. to 100 C.E. Sadly, these writings have almost wholly perished. It is likely that most of them were destroyed in the catastrophic events that took place in 115-17 C.E., when the Jewish community rose up against their Roman overlords and suffered huge losses, from which they did not recover for centuries. There are two great exceptions to this massive destruction. The Greek translation of the Hebrew Bible, generally known as the Septuagint, became part of the Scriptures of the Christian church and so survived in a large number of manuscripts. More surprisingly, the works of Philo also survived. Josephus in his *Antiquities* mentions Philo by name as the head of an Alexandrian Jewish delegation to the emperor in Rome (*Ant.* 18.257-60). Clearly, Philo was a highly respected member of the Jewish community. But it was hardly to be expected that his writings would survive as one of the larger bodies of writing to be preserved from the ancient world. Yet this did happen, and the story of how it happened makes fascinating reading.

As can be seen in the list below, the first church father to mention Philo explicitly by name is Clement of Alexandria. It is possible that some of the earlier Christian writers, such as the apologist Justin, were acquainted with Philo, but it cannot be proven. Clement was active in the Alexandrian church as a member of the so-called catechetical school from about 175 to 200 C.E., that is, more than a century after Philo's death.[2] We do not know how Philo's library escaped the holocaust of the Jewish revolt. But it is telling that his writings resurface in a Christian resource center. It is very likely that Clement's teacher Pantaenus, who founded the school, played a major role in their preservation. From the late second century onward, Philo's writings were disseminated throughout Egypt. This is demonstrated by the discovery of a number of papyri, notably a beautifully preserved small codex containing two complete treatises, which was found in Coptos hidden in a niche and was probably placed there by a Christian who feared persecution in the decades before Constantine's conversion.[3] We can be certain that the owner was a Christian, because the text contains so-called *nomina sacra,* abbreviations of sacred names only used by Christian scribes.

The next chapter in the history of the survival of Philo's writings is set in motion by Clement's successor in Alexandria, Origen. He too was active in the catechetical school and wrote a number of his major works there. But

2. On the catechetical school of Alexandria, see Annewies van den Hoek, "The 'Catechetical' School of Early Christian Alexandria and Its Philonic Heritage," *HTR* 90 (1997) 59-87.

3. On the Philonic papyri found in Egypt, see my "One of Us or One of Them? Christian Reception of Philo the Jew in Egypt," in *Shem in the Tents of Japheth: Essays on the Encounter of Judaism and Hellenism,* ed. James L. Kugel (JSJSup 74; Leiden: Brill, 2002) 203-22.

in 233 he accepted a call to move to Caesarea in Palestine and took with him his extensive library, which contained a complete set of Philo's treatises. This library formed the basis of the celebrated episcopal library of Caesarea, established by the presbyter Pamphilus and continued by his pupil Eusebius, who in time became the bishop of the city. Eusebius, in his history of the rise of the church in the first three centuries, devotes three chapters to Philo and gives a most valuable list of his writings, which is certainly based on the holdings of the library and allows us to see the extent of the corpus as it had survived at that time.[4] Two generations after Eusebius, one of his successors as bishop, Euzoius, noted that the copies of Philo's works were deteriorating and arranged for them to be transferred to parchment codices.[5] From Egypt and Caesarea, knowledge of Philo's writings spread to other major centers of the empire, including Constantinople, where in the sixth century a group of Armenian scholars translated about a quarter of the corpus into their native language, and to Rome, where in the fourth century some treatises were translated into Latin. Although in this long process of transmission from Philo's library to the Renaissance about a third of his vast output did not survive, what did remain was a very considerable corpus.[6] Its survival was entirely due to the efforts of generations of Christians who copied out and made use of his works. Between Josephus in the first century and the Renaissance there is not a single explicit reference to Philo in a Jewish or a non-Christian Greek or Latin source.[7]

Philo's Influence on Christian Thought

The second question we must ask is why the early Christians went to all this trouble to preserve such a large corpus. After all, writing and publishing

---

4. On the role of Caesarean library in the preservation of the Philonic corpus, see further my "Caesarea Maritima and the Survival of Hellenistic-Jewish Literature," in *Caesarea Maritima: A Retrospective after Two Millenia,* ed. Avner Raban and Kenneth G. Holum (DMOA 21; Leiden: Brill, 1996) 476-95.

5. As indicated in the famous "cross of Euzoius" preserved in the Codex Vindobonensis Theol. Gr. 29; see photo and discussion in Runia, *Philo in Early Christian Literature,* 20-22.

6. For a handy list of Philo's lost works as they can be reconstructed from references in his writings, see *SPhAn* 4 (1992) 78-80.

7. The first Jew to make a study of Philo's writings since antiquity was the Italian Azariah de' Rossi; see Joanna Weinberg, trans., *Azariah de' Rossi, The Light of the Eyes* (New Haven: Yale University Press, 2001).

materials were very expensive in antiquity, and it is also not so likely that the Christians would feel any loyalty toward Philo because of his Jewish background. We need to look more closely at the evidence of the list of references.

As noted above, the first church father to cite Philo by name is Clement. Although he refers to Philo explicitly only four times, actually this is only the tip of the iceberg of his usage of Philo, as demonstrated by Annewies van den Hoek and other scholars.[8] If Clement's usage is analyzed, it emerges that there are three main areas where he is indebted to Philo. First, Philo can help him explain the history of Israel, and particularly the role of the great Jewish lawgiver Moses. This history is important when understanding the relationship of the Old to the New Testament, and also for defending the new religion of Christianity in an apologetic context. Second, Philo provides a huge amount of material when explaining the books of Moses. Clement and his Alexandrian successors were impressed by Philo's use of the allegorical method and were keen to take over numerous allegorical themes, as well as other symbolic and more literal explanations. This might be why Clement rather puzzlingly calls Philo "the Pythagorean," because he is impressed by his supply of arithmological explanations of the many numbers in Scripture.[9] But there is also a third, more general debt that Clement has incurred to Philo. Having been educated in Greek philosophy — it is likely that he studied Platonic philosophy in Athens before he converted to Christianity — Clement is impressed by the way that Philo was able to use philosophical terminology and doctrine to explain the deeper truths of Scripture, particularly in theology and the doctrine of creation, but also for questions of epistemology and ethics. Philo thus helps Clement set out the first delineations of an orthodox theology. Its basis is primarily texts from the Gospel of John and the Pauline letters, but various themes relating to the Logos and to our understanding of God's presence in and remoteness from the world are also indebted to Philo.[10]

8. Annewies van den Hoek, *Clement of Alexandria and His Use of Philo in the* Stromateis: *An Early Christian Reshaping of a Jewish Model* (VCSup 3; Leiden: Brill, 1988). Van den Hoek's study covers only the Philonic material in the *Stromateis*. For recent discoveries of Philonic material in other works, see two articles by Andrew Dinan: "The Mystery of Play: Clement of Alexandria's Appropriation of Philo in the *Paedagogus* (1.5.21.3–22.1)," *SPhAn* 19 (2007) 59-80; "Another Citation of Philo in Clement of Alexandria's *Protrepticus* (10,93,1-2)," *VC* 64 (2010) 435-44.

9. See further David T. Runia, "Why Does Clement of Alexandria Call Philo 'the Pythagorean'?" *VC* 49 (1995) 1-22.

10. On Clement's theology and his debt to Philo, see the magisterial monograph of Eric F. Osborn, *Clement of Alexandria* (Cambridge: Cambridge University Press, 2005).

The main lines of usage are continued by Origen, who clearly knew the works of Philo in his library well and made extensive use of them. Like Clement, he does not often refer to Philo by name. There are, in fact, only three direct references, but more than twenty references couched in anonymous terms, for example, "as one of our predecessors has said."[11] In her analysis of all the passages where Origen makes use of Philo, van den Hoek concludes that about 80 percent focus on biblical interpretation and the theory of allegory, while the remaining 20 percent relate to philosophical questions and the doctrines of God and creation.[12] The preponderance of passages on exegesis might explain why most references to Philo are anonymous. He is regarded as a distinguished predecessor in the task of expounding Scripture (especially the Pentateuch), and there is no need to draw attention to his name or background. When, however, there is an apologetic context and Origen wishes to appeal to the authority of a Jewish author, he does cite Philo by name (*C. Cels.* 4.51). Origen's extensive use of Philo as an exegetical *Fundgrube* is continued by his Alexandrian successor Didymus the Blind, who more than one once describes Philo as a useful source for etymologies and arithmological material (*Comm. Gen.* 139.12, 147.17).[13]

When we turn to writings of Eusebius at the beginning of the fourth century, we observe that his use of Philo occurs almost exclusively in historical and apologetic contexts.[14] Wishing to describe the early history of the Christian church, Eusebius has very little material, so he uses what he can find. He believes that Philo can provide information on the very beginnings of the Alexandrian church. Erroneously, he identifies the community of the Therapeutae, whom Philo describes as living just outside the city, with the first Christians in Egypt (*Hist. eccl.* 2.17.2-24).[15] In his *Praeparatio evangelica*, that vast compilation of material from Greek and Hellenistic-Jewish authors intended to show how they prepared the way for Christian doctrine, about

11. See the thorough analysis of Annewies van den Hoek, "Philo and Origen: A Descriptive Catalogue of Their Relationship," *SPhAn* 12 (2000) 44-121.

12. See her further analysis of the data in "Assessing Philo's Influence in Christian Alexandria: The Case of Origen," in Kugel, *Shem in the Tents of Japheth*, 223-39.

13. On Philo and Didymus, see the research of Albert C. Geljon, "Didymus the Blind's Use of Philo in His Exegesis of Cain and Abel," *VC* 61 (2007) 282-312.

14. On Eusebius and Philo, see the thorough analysis of Sabrina Inowlocki, *Eusebius and the Jewish Authors: His Citation Technique in an Apologetic Context* (AGJU 64; Leiden: Brill, 2006).

15. On this passage, see Sabrina Inowlocki, "Eusebius of Caesarea's *Interpretatio Christiana* of Philo's *De vita contemplativa*," *HTR* 97 (2004) 305-28.

twenty passages are quoted verbatim from Philo's writings, to which Eusebius had access in the episcopal library in his see.

In the remainder of the fourth century, extensive use of Philo's writings continues, both in the East and now also in the West. Gregory of Nyssa adapts much material from Philo's *On the Life of Moses* for his own life of Moses.[16] But when he wants to explain how his opponent Eunomius obtained his heretical theological ideas on God and the Logos, he suggests that he might have been influenced by a statement of the Jew Philo (*C. Eun.* 3.5.24). Perhaps the most spectacular use that any church father made of the Philonic corpus is found in the exegetical commentaries of Ambrose, the bishop of Milan.[17] His borrowings have been estimated at more than six hundred in number,[18] and yet he refers to Philo explicitly only once, and in a critical vein at that (there are at least ten anonymous references similar to what we find in Origen). Writing in the theologically more contentious atmosphere of the fourth century, Gregory and Ambrose reveal an ambivalent attitude toward Philo and his legacy. They are happy to use the exegetical material he supplies, but in matters of theology one must exercise care. After all, Philo was a Jew, not a Christian, acquainted neither with Christ nor with the doctrine of the Trinity. Critical judgments could be negative or positive, depending on the context and one's point of view. In the Antiochene tradition of literalist biblical exegesis, Philo was heavily criticized for his allegorical method, which was seen as the source of Origen's wrongheaded ideas.[19] Augustine, in contrast, does accept some allegorical explanations of Scripture, but argues that Philo goes astray in his exegesis of Noah's ark because he does not take Christ into account (*Faust.* 12.39). But in a remarkable passage in one of his letters, the desert monk Isidore of Pelusium defends Philo and argues that his doctrine of the Logos, though lacking in precision, nevertheless anticipates true Christian dogma (*Epist.* 2.143).

From the fifth century onward, the number of explicit references to Philo declines. He is never named in the extensive bodies of works by John

16. See Albert C. Geljon, *Philonic Exegesis in Gregory of Nyssa's De vita Moysis* (SPhilMon 5; Providence: Brown Judaic Studies, 2002).

17. See the detailed study of Hervé Savon, *Saint Ambroise devant l'exégèse de Philon le Juif* (2 vols.; Paris: Études augustiniennes, 1977).

18. Enzo Lucchesi, *L'usage de Philon dans l'oeuvre exégétique de Saint Ambroise: une "Quellenforschung" relative aux commentaires d'Ambroise sur la Genèse* (ALGHJ 9; Leiden: Brill, 1977) 7.

19. Theodore of Mopsuestia, *Treatise against the Allegorists* pp. 14.27–16.5 Van Rompay (survived only in a Syriac translation).

Chrysostom and Cyril of Alexandria, and only briefly twice by Theodoret of Cyrrhus. To some degree, this may result from the fact that in the areas of biblical exposition and theology many of Philo's ideas had been absorbed into the tradition and were no longer referred to explicitly. A good example is the huge amount of Philonic exegetical material that Procopius of Gaza has included in his *Commentary on the Octateuch*.[20] It may also be the case, however, that scholars have not yet identified all the Philonic material that is hidden away in the vast corpus of patristic literature.

Although our knowledge of Philo's presence in the patristic tradition has greatly increased through the considerable amount of scholarship that has been carried out during the past two decades, there still remains much to explore and discover. Through the use of modern lexicographical instruments — particularly the database of the *Thesaurus Linguae Graecae* — it is likely that nearly all explicit references to Philo in Greek and Latin patristic sources have been identified. But there may still be quite a few anonymous references to him hidden away in the volumes of the *Patrologia graeca et latina*. These cannot be discovered by mechanical means, but only through detailed study of the sources. Moreover, the writings of Byzantine period and of other patristic traditions preserved in languages other than Greek or Latin have scarcely been researched. The list of references below is certainly incomplete. It is my hope that it will be supplemented in the future by enterprising scholars.

List of References[21]

From the very first edition of Philo's complete works it has been customary to include a list of ancient witnesses to Philo that can be gathered from the remains of patristic, Byzantine, and early medieval literature. These lists focused mainly on what the sources could tell us about Philo's life and the fate of his writings, but also included some references to exegetical and doctrinal use of Philonic material. The list below aims to include every explicit refer-

20. This material was extensively used by Françoise Petit in her edition of the fragments of Philo's *Questions and Answers*, *Quaestiones in Genesim et in Exodum: Fragmenta graeca* (Œuvres de Philon d'Alexandrie 33; Paris: Cerf, 1978).

21. This list is based on two previous publications: Runia, *Philo in Early Christian Literature*, 348-56; "References to Philo from Josephus Until 1000 AD," *SPhAn* 6 (1994) 111-21; repr. in *Philo and Church Fathers*, 228-39. I thank the Society of Biblical Literature for permission to reprint material from the original publication in *The Studia Philonica Annual*.

ence to Philo in Christian sources up to 1000 C.E. It therefore includes a number of references to the early Byzantine period and also to traditions in languages such as Syriac and Armenian, which fall outside the mainstream of the patristic tradition. It is to be admitted that the cutoff date is somewhat arbitrary. Extending the list, however, would make it very imcomplete because of the state of scholarship at present. The list also includes a number of anonymous references to Philo when it is certain that he is the author to whom allusion is made. These are indicated by an asterisk at the end of the reference. If possible, texts are cited as located in modern critical texts of the authors concerned (full details of these can be found in the peerless volumes of the *Clavis patrum graecorum* and *Clavis patrum latinarum*).[22] A very brief summary is given of the contents of the reference.[23]

If the reference to Philo has been included in earlier collections of testimonia, it is indicated in square brackets behind the reference. The abbreviations used are as follows:

T = Adrianus Turnebus, *Philonis Iudaei in libros Mosis, de mundi opificio, historicos, de legibus: Eiusdem libri singulares* (Paris, 1552): Περὶ τοῦ Φίλωνος (pages unnumbered)

V = Vulgate edition (Turnebus-Hoeschelius-Gelenius), *Philonis Ioudaei omnia quae extant opera,* published in various forms in 1613, 1640, 1691, 1729: *Illustrium et praecellentium scriptorum de Philone testimonia* (pages unnumbered).

M = Thomas Mangey, *Philonis Judaei opera quae reperiri potuerunt omnia.* 2 vols. (London, 1742): *Veterum testimonia de Philone Judaeo,* xxi-xxix.

C = Leopold Cohn and Paul Wendland, *Philonis Alexandrini opera quae supersunt.* 6 vols. (Berlin: Reimer, 1896-1915): *Testimonia de Philone eiusque scriptis* (1:lxxxv-cxiii, compiled by Cohn).

22. Mauritius Geerard, *Clavis patrum graecorum* (5 vols. and suppl.; Turnhout: Brepols, 1974-98); Eligius Dekkers, *Clavis patrum latinorum* (3rd ed.; Corpus christianorum; Steenbrugge: Brepols, 1995). See also the editions listed in *Thesaurus linguae graecae: Canon of Greek Authors and Works,* ed. Luci Berkowitz and Karl A. Squitier (3rd ed.; New York: Oxford University Press, 1990).

23. Full texts of the passages cited and an Italian translation can be found in David T. Runia, *Filone di Alessandria nella prima letteratura cristiana: Uno studio d'insieme, a cura di Roberto Radice* (Milan: Vita e Pensiero, 1999) 365-445.

List of references to Philo in the patristic tradition up to 1000 C.E.

Clement of Alexandria (ca. 150–ca. 215)

Stromateis 1.31.1, 20.5 Stählin: Etymologies of Hagar and Sarah [M,C]

Strom. 1.72.4, 46.17: Philo the Pythagorean gives many proofs that Jewish philosophy is more ancient than Greek philosophy [M,C]

Strom. 1.141.3, 87.25: On the kings of Judah (mistaken reference)[24] [C]

Strom. 1.152.2, 95.16: On the education of Moses as reported in On the Life of Moses [M,C]

Strom. 2.100.3, 168.2: On great natures hitting on the truth [C]

Canon Muratorianus (ca. 160-200)

Fol. 2a.7-9, = lines 69-71: Wisdom of Solomon written by Philo (if Tregelles's emendation is accepted)

Origen (ca. 185-254)[25]

Contra Celsum 4.51, 314.30 Borret SC:[26] Origen's opponent Celsus must be referring to the allegories of Philo and Aristobulus [M,C]

C. Cels. 5.55, 152.18: Allegorical exegesis of daughters of men (Gen 6:2) in terms of souls desirous of bodies*

C. Cels. 6.21, 232.17: Philo composed a book about Jacob's ladder (i.e., On Dreams) [M,C]

C. Cels. 7.20, 60.5: The Law as twofold, literal and figurative*

Homiliae in Genesim 14.3, 340.20 Doutreleau: Some have added that God created and rules everything through his Logos*

Selecta in Genesim 27, PG 12.97C: The six days in creation account for the sake of order (cf. Opif. 13, 26-28)*

Sel. Gen. 36, PG 12.116A: Origen questions Philo's interpretation of Sarai and Abram's confrontation in Gen 16:4-5*

Sel. Gen. 44, PG 12.129D: On Pharaoh the φαῦλος ("wicked man") who, enamored of genesis ("becoming"), celebrates his birthday (cf. Ebr. 208)* (perhaps paraphrase of Comm. Matt. 10.22)

Homiliae in Exodum 2.2, 74.3ff. Borret SC: On the Jewish midwives; exegesis of Exod 1:17 (cf. Her. 128)*

---

24. On this mistaken reference, see my Philo and the Church Fathers, 28.

25. Some additional anonymous references identified by van den Hoek in "Philo and Origen" (n. 11 above) have been added.

26. In what follows SC refers to the series Sources chrétiennes.

Hom. Exod. 9.4, 294.2 Borret SC: On the interpretation of the tabernacle and the high priest (cf. *Mos.* 2.135)*

Selecta in Exodum, PG 12.285A: Allegorical interpretation of God's command in Exod 12:22 to put blood on the lintel and doorposts*

Homiliae in Leviticum 8.6, 34.9ff. Borret SC: On the color of the leper; exegesis of Lev 13:14-15 (cf. *Deus* 125)*

Homiliae in Numeros 9.5, 61.8 Baehrens: Ethical interpretation of the alive and the dead; exegesis of Num 17:13 (cf. *Her.* 201)*

Hom. Num. 26.4, 244.25: Allegorical interpretation of the departure from Egypt*

Homiliae in Josua 16.1, 358.1 Jaubert SC: Presbyters in Scripture determined not by length of years (cf. *Sobr.* 17)*

Homiliae in Jeremiam 14.5, 74.26 Nautin SC: The wise man complains to Sophia; exegesis of Jer 15:10 (cf. *Conf.* 49)*

Commentarii in Matthaei. 10.22, 10.30.5 Klostermann-Benz: On Pharaoh the φαῦλος ("wicked man") who, enamored of *genesis* ("becoming"), celebrates his birthday (cf. *Ebr.* 208)*

Comm. Matt. 15.3, 10.354.30: According to Philo, it is better to be a eunuch than to rage after sexual intercourse (citation of *Det.* 176) [M,C]

Comm. Matt. 17.17, 10.635.16: On the principles of anthropomorphic language concerning God* [M,C]

Comm. Matt. frag. *ad* 25:31-34, 11.163.16: On the exegesis of Gen 1:2 (cf. *Opif.* 32ff.)*

Commentarii in Joannis 6.42.217, 151.16 Preuschen: On the descent of souls into bodies; exegesis of Gen 6:2*

Pseudo-Justin, *Cohortatio ad Graecos* (between 220 and 300)
    §9.2, 34.21 Marcovich: The "most wise historians" Philo and Josephus on Moses as ancient ruler of the Jews [M,C]
    §10.1, 36.8: Philo and Josephus on the life of Moses [M,C]
    §13.4, 41.29: Translation of the LXX is no myth; the author has seen the translators' cells himself and is corroborated by Philo and Josephus [M,C]

Anatolius of Alexandria, bishop of Laodicaea (died ca. 280)
    Cited at Eusebius *Hist. eccl.* 7.32.16: Evidence of Philo on the date of Easter [C]

Peter, bishop of Alexandria (*sed.* 300-311) and his opponent, the Montanist Tricentius
    Cited at *Chronicon paschale* PG 92.73B-C, 76B: Appeal to ancient Hebrew sages on the paschal question*

Eusebius of Caesarea (ca. 260-339)[27]

>Chronicon ad Olymp. 203, 213 Karst: Philo of Alexandria, a learned man, was prominent

>Chron. Olymp. 203, 213 Karst, 176.15-18 Helm: Sejanus attempts to destroy the Jewish people, as recorded in Philo's Legat.

>Chron. Olymp. 204, 214 Karst, 177.18–78.3 Helm: Flaccus descrates the Jewish synagagues at Alexandria, impelling Philo to undertake the embassy [MC]

>Chron. Olymp. 204, 214 Karst 178.17-20 Helm: Atatues of Gaius placed in synagagues, as Philo and Josephus report

>Historia ecclesiastica, preface to book 2, 100.20 Schwartz: This book put together from writings of Clement, Tertullian, Josephus, Philo

>Hist. eccl. 2.4.2–6.4 : Philo introduced and then used as a source for events during the reign of Caligula [T,V,M,C]

>Hist. eccl. 2.16.2–18.8: Philo as a source for the first Christians in Egypt, as witnessed in his On the Complative Life; inventory of Philo's writings [T,V,M,C]

>Hist. eccl. 6.13.7: Clement refers to Philo in his Stromateis

>Hist. eccl. 7.32.16: Extract from Canons of Anatolius on the date of Easter, referring to the evidence of Philo and other Jewish authors (see also above under Anatolius) [C]

>Praeparatio evangelica 1.9.20 Mras: Eusebius indicates that he means Philo of Byblus, not "the Hebrew"

>Praep. ev. 7.12.14–13.7: Three texts from Philo are quoted to prove biblical basis for the "theology of the second cause" [M]

>Praep. ev. 7.17.4–18.3: Again Philonic text used to interpret biblical doctrine, this time on the nature of man

>Praep. ev. 7.20.9–21.5: Philo quoted on the subject that matter is not uncreated (ἀγένητος)

>Praep. ev. 8.5.11–7.21: Quotes from Philo's Hypothetica on the flight from Egypt and the Mosaic constitution [M]

>Praep. ev. 8.10.19–12.20: Quote from same work and That Every Good Person Is Free on the Jewish ascetic way of life exemplified by the Essenes [M]

>Praep. ev. 8.12.21–14.72: Extracts from On The Creation of the World on creation and Prov. 2 on providence to illustrate Jewish theology [M]

---

27. I have not included the references to Philo in the summaries preceding the books of Historia ecclesiastica and Praeparatio evangelica, except the significant remark at the end of the summary of Hist. eccl. book 2.

Praep. ev. 11.14.10–15.7: Repetition of Philonic material on the second cause [M]

Praep. ev. 11.23.12–24.12: Three quotes from *On the Creation* on the Mosaic (and Platonic) theory of ideas

Praep. ev. 13.18.12-16: Quotes from *Spec.* 1 on the Mosaic injunction not to worship the heavenly bodies

Demonstratio evangelica 8.2.123, 390.5 Heikel: Philo's evidence on Pilate and the episode of the golden shields (*Legat.* 299) [M]

Eusebius of Emesa (ca. 300-359)

Fragment in *Catena in Genesim ad* Gen. 2:6, no. 194 Petit: Citation of fragment from *QG* 1.3 on how "spring" can be understood collectively

Didymus the Blind (313-98)

Commentarii in Genesim 118.24, 119.2, 19 Nautin SC: Exegesis of Gen 4:1-2; allegorization of Cain and Abel

Comm. Gen. 139.12: Exegesis of Gen 4:18; Philo is invoked as a useful source of information for etymologies (cf. *Post.* 66-75)

Comm. Gen. 147.17: Exegesis of Gen 5:3-5; Philo again a useful source if one wants a μυστικὸς λόγος for names and numbers

Comm. Gen. 235.28, 236.8: Exegesis of Gen 16; Philo gives a different allegorical interpretation than Paul for Sarah and Hagar

Commentarii in Ecclesiasten 276.19-22 Gronewald: Exegesis of Eccl 9:9a recalls Philo's interpretation of Hagar in Gen 16

Comm. Eccl. 300.15 Gronewald: Exegesis of Eccl 10:7-8, citing Philo's life of Moses on philosophers as kings (cf. *Mos.* 2.2)

Comm. Eccl. 356.10-14 Binder-Liesenborghs: Exegesis of Eccl 12:5 on the special nature of the almond tree (cf. *Mos.* 2.186)*

Commentarii in Zachariam 320.6-9 Doutreleau: Sword in Zech 11:17 recalls oracle to Abraham in Gen 12:1, which is given an allegorical interpretation*

Epiphanius (ca. 315-403)

Panarion (Adv. haer.) 1.29.5.1-3 Holl: One may learn more about the *Iessaioi* from the historical writings of Philo, who visited the early Christians at Lake Mareotis [MC]

Basil of Caesarea (ca. 330-79)

> *Epist.* 3.190, 74.23 Deferrari LCL: Philo interprets manna as if drawing on a Jewish tradition [M,C][28]

Gregory of Nyssa (ca. 338–ca. 395)

> *Contra Eunomium* 9.1, 1.16.20 Jaeger:[29] Eunomius's doctrine of God draws on Philo
>
> *C. Eun.* 3.5.24, 2.168.17: Eunomius glues together a ragbag of statements, for which Philo supplies some material
>
> *C. Eun.* 3.7.8-9, 2.217.19–18.3: Further explanation of Eunomius's theft from Philo
>
> *De vita Mosis* 2.113, 67.22 Musurillo: A literal justification of the *spoliatio Egyptiorum* is rejected*
>
> *Vita Mos.* 2.191, 98.15: Some predecessors have regarded the blue of the high priest's tunic as symbolizing the air*
>
> *De infantibus praemature abreptis* 77.23–78.23 Horner: Humanity was created so that the earth would not be bereft of intelligence*

Calcidius (*fl.* 350[?])

> *Commentarius Timaei* 278, 282.8 Waszink: Philo interprets the heaven and earth in Gen 1:1 in terms of ideas and compares them with the creation of archetypal man before corporeal man

Pseudo-Chrysostom (homily dated 387)

> *In sanctum Pascha sermo* 7.2, PG 59.748: The Hebrew sages Philo and Josephus assure us that Easter must take place after the spring equinox [M,C]

Ambrose (339-97)[30]

> *De paradiso* 2.11, 271.8–272.2 Schenkl: Exegesis of Adam and Eve in terms of νοῦς and αἴσθησις*
>
> *Parad.* 4.25, 281.19–282.5: Exegesis of Gen 2:15; man's double task in paradise; Philo as a Jew gives only a moral interpretation [M,C]

---

28. Basil probably refers here to Wis 16:20-21, of which Philo was thought to be the author; see the references below in Jerome and Julian of Eclanum and the article by Adam Kamesar, "San Basilio, Filone, e la tradizione ebraica," *Hen* 17 (1995) 129-40.

29. The summary was probably added by a later hand, as noted by Jaeger in his edition.

30. The list of anonymous references in Ambrose is necessarily incomplete.

De Cain et Abel 8.32, 367.2 Schenkl: The Word is not God's product (*opus*) (cf. *Sacr.* 65), but is himself producing *(operans)**

De Noe et arca 13.43-44, 441.8-21 Schenkl: Exegesis of Gen 7:4; rain for forty days and nights refers allegorically to man and woman*

Noe 14.47, 445.9-16: Exegesis of Gen 7:15; the double divine name*

Noe 15.52, 449.26: Our predecessors on the fifteen cubits of Gen 7:20*

Noe 17.63, 459.1-6: Exegesis of Gen 8:15; water as the force of the passions*

Noe 26.99, 482.17: On the exegesis of the repetition of "God" in Gen 9:6*

De Abraham 2.11.83, 634.14 Schenkl: A question raised by the seemingly excessive death sentence in Gen 17:14*

De fuga saeculi 4.20, 180.12 Schenkl: The etymology of Bethuel*

Rufinus (ca. 345–ca. 410)

Historia ecclesiastica 2.4-6, 2.16-18 Mommsen: Latin translation of Eusebius's work (see above)

Jerome (347-420)

Adversus Jovinianum 2.14, PL 23.317A: Philo has written a book on the Essenes

Chronicle, trans. of Eusebius (see above under Eusebius)

Commentariorum in Amos 2.9 CCL 76.238.314: Etymology of Esau as meaning "oak"

Comm. Am. 3.6, CCL 76.304.182: On the seven ages of life (cf. *Opif.* 103-5)

Commentariorums in Danielem 1.1.4a, CCL 75A.779.60: Philo thinks the language of Hebrews was Chaldean [M,C]

Commentariorum in Ezechielem 4.10b, CCL 75.171.1160: Philo on the hyacinth of the high-priestly robes (cf. also 8.7, 75.362.850)

De viris illustribus 11, 96.5 Ceresa-Gastaldo: Brief biographical notice, together with list of writings (Philo also briefly mentioned in §8.4 on the apostle Mark, §13.2 on Apion) [V,M,C]

Dialogus adversus Pelagianos 3.6.62, CCL 80.106.62: On the seven ages of life

Epistulae 22.35.8, CSEL 54.1.200.7: Philo reports on the sober meals of the Essenes at Pentecost [M]

Epist. 29.7.1, CSEL 54.1.241.17: Philo as interpreter of the high-priestly vestments [M]

Epist. 70.3.3, CSEL 54.1.704.12: Philo, whom critics call the Jewish Plato, cited in a discussion on sound usage of pagan learning [M]

Liber interpretationis Hebraicorum nominum, praefatio, CCL 72.1.59.1–60.3

Philo according to Origen author of a book of Hebrew etymologies [M,C]

Prefatio in librum Job, PL 28.1141A: Philo as one of the witnesses to the fact that Hebrews composed poetry (cf. *Contempl.* 80) [M,C]

Praefatio in libros Salomonis, PL 28.1308A: Some consider Philo to be the author of the Wisdom of Solomon [M]

Quaestionum hebraicarum liber in Genesim 17:15, CCL 72.21: Sarah's name-change by doubling the *r* is erroneous*[31]

Theodore of Mopsuestia (ca. 350-428)

Treatise against the Allegorists, CSCO.SS 190, p. 14.27–16.5 Van Rompay: Origen goes astray in learning the allegorical method from the Jew Philo

Augustine (354-430)

Contra Faustum 12.39, CSEL 25.366, PL 42.274: Philo goes astray in his allegorical exegesis of Noah's ark because he does not take Christ into account [M,C]

Isidore of Pelusium (ca. 370–ca. 435)

Epistulae 2.143, PG 78.585-589 (= *Epist.* 643 Évieux): Unlike other Jews, Philo was moved by the truth to gain some idea of the orthodox doctrine of God as one substance and three hypostases [MC]

Epist. 2.270, PG 78.700C (= *Epist.* 770 Évieux): Philo one of the sages who use μήποτε in the sense of ἴσως or ἔσθ' ὅτε [M,C]

Epist. 3.19, PG 78.746A-B (= *Epist.* 819 Évieux): The Jewish affirmation that the lawgiver spoke only literally is refuted by Philo, who converts nearly the entire Old Testament into allegory [C]

Epist. 3.81, PG 78.788C-D: Quotation from Philo proves that there are beneficent passions [M,C] (= *Epist.* 881 Évieux)

Orosius (ca. 378–after 418)

Historiae adversus paganos 7.5.6-7, 445.12 Zangemeister: Philo's embassy before Caligula fails

---

31. Other anonymous criticisms of Philonic etymologies are listed by Carl Siegfried, *Philo von Alexandria als Ausleger des alten Testaments* (Jena: Dufft, 1875) 396.

Maruta of Maipherkat (*fl.* ca. 410)

> *Canons* III, CSCO.SS 192 p. 9 Vööbus: The order of monks had different name in the old covenant, as testified in letters prepared by Philo for James, brother of the Lord

Pseudo-Prochorus (*fl.* 400-450)

> *Acta Johannis* 110.6-112.11 Zahn: Philo has an altercation with the apostle John, but is converted after John heals his wife from leprosy

Julian of Eclanum (386-ca. 454)

> At Augustine, *Contra secundam Juliani responsionem imperfectum opus* 4.123, PL 45.1420: Unless one should think that the Hebrews Sirach or Philo, who are thought to be authors of the Wisdom of Solomon, are Manichees

Theodoret of Cyrrhus (ca. 393-ca. 466)

> *Quaestiones in Exodum* 24, PG 80.251A: Philo interprets Pascha as "crossings" (διαβατήρια) [M,C]
>
> *Curatio affectionum Graecarum* 2.94 61.19 Raeder: Not Philo the Hebrew but Philo of Byblus is meant (taken over from Eusebius, *Praep. ev.* 1.9.20)

Salaminius Hermias Sozomen (ca. 400-ca. 460)

> *Historia ecclesiastica* 1.12.9-11, 26.4, 18 Bidez-Hansen: Philo describes the beginnings of the monastic movement [M,C]
>
> *Hist. eccl.* 7.18.7, 328.11 Bidez-Hansen: Anatolius on Philo on the Easter question (taken over from Eusebius, *Hist. eccl.* 7.32.16; see above)

Catena in Genesim, Catena in Exodum (end fifth century)

> Numerous exegetical extracts from Philo under the headings Φίλωνος ἐπισκόπου, Φίλωνος Ἑβραίου, Φίλωνος.[32]

Procopius of Gaza (ca. 465-ca. 529)

> Extensive, always anonymously presented exegetical extracts from QG and QE in *Commentary on the Octateuch*, PG 87*

---

32. In the apparatus to *Mos.* Cohn and Wendland also cite extracts from the *Catena in Numeros* and the *Catena in Psalmos*. On these titles and particularly the curious "Philo the Bishop," see David T. Runia, "Philonic Nomenclature," *SPhAn* 6 (1994) 1-27, esp. 20-21.

Cassiodorus (487–ca. 580)

Institutiones divinarum litterarum, PL 70.1117B: Jerome is right in attributing the Wisdom of Solomon to Philo [M]

Johannes Lydus (490–ca. 565)

De mensibus 4.47 103.14–104.1 Wuensch: Philo in *On the Life of Moses* writes of his Chaldean origin and the fact that his books were written in Hebrew

Anonymous Armenian translator of Philo's writings (ca. 550)

Praefatio in libris Philonis De providentia, p. vii-xi Aucher: Lengthy notice on Philo's life and description of translated works [C]

Isidore of Seville (ca. 570-636)

Etymologiae 6.2.30: Philo and the Wisdom of Solomon

Barhadbsabba 'Arbaya, bishop of Halwan (ca. 600)

Cause of the Foundation of the Schools, 375.6–376.4 Scher: Philo the Jew was director of the school of biblical exegesis in Alexandria[33]

Anastasius Sinaïta (ca. 610–ca. 700)

Duae Viae 13.10.1-96, CCG 8.251 Uthemann: Cites Ammonius of Alexandria, who in turn cites a dialogue between Philo and Mnason, in which Philo attacks the divinity of Christ [C]

Chronicon paschale (ca. 650)

PG 92.69A: Quotes *Mos.* 2.222-24 on the vernal equinox and the Passover feast [M]

Ananias Shirakatzi (ca. 650)

Armenian Easter treatise, containing extensive reference to Philo's interpretation of Exod 12:2, p. 126-27 Strobel[34]

Pseudo-Sophronius (seventh century)

Ἱερωνύμου ἐπιστολὴ πρὸς Δέξτρον (= Greek translation of Jerome, *De viris illustribus*) 12, 21, 23 von Gebhardt [C]

---

33. This rather inaccessible text is printed in Runia, *Philo in Early Christian Literature,* 269-70.

34. Further references to Philo in the Armenian tradition are not recorded in our list.

John of Damascus (c. 675–c. 750)
>   *Prol. in Sacra Parallela,* PG 95.1040B, 1044B: Philo (and Josephus) are cited, even though they are Jews, because they can make a valuable contribution [M,C]

Venerable Bede (ca. 673-735)
>   *In Marci evangelium praefatio,* CCL 120.431: Citation from Jerome on the beginnings of the church of Alexandria

George Syncellus (d. after 810)
>   *Ecloga chronographica* 399.5, 402.14, 19 Mosshammer: Philo on the reign of Gaius (taken from Eusebius) [M]

Anonymous Syrian commentator of the works of Gregory of Nazianzus (eighth-ninth century)
>   ms. London, Brit. Libr. Add. 17,147, fol. 98a and 144a: Some quotations are found from other writers, among them two quotations from "Philo the Hebrew"

Iso'dad of Merv (ca. 850)
>   *Commentary on Exodus* 23:19, 56.5 van den Eynde: Philo is cited on the injunction not to boil a lamb in its mother's milk (cf. *Virt.* 143-44)
>   *Commentary on Numbers* 7:11, 120.28 van den Eynde: On the phases of the moon and the ten sacrifices (cf. *Spec.* 1.177-78)

Freculphus, bishop of Lisieux (ca. 825–851)
>   *Chronicon* 2.1.11, PL 106.1126: On Philo and the fate of the Jews under Gaius [M]

Photius, bishop of Constantinople (ca. 820-91)
>   *Bibliotheca* 103-105, 2.71-72 Henry: Record of Philonic works read, with critical comments added, to which a biographical notice is appended [V,M,C]

George the Sinner (or the Monk) (ca. 830-ca. 890)
>   *Chronicon* 9.4 1.324.17 de Boor: In the reign of Gaius, Philo and Josephus, the Hebrew sages, were prominent

Anastasius Incertus (ninth century)
  In hexaemeron 7, PG 89.961D: Philo among those church fathers who allegorized paradise in terms of the church [C]

Arethas, archbishop of Caesarea (ca. 850–ca. 940)
  Commentary on the Apocalypse 1, PG 106.504D: On the Hebdomad [M,C]

Anonymous compiler of Nestorian exegesis (tenth century [?])
  Exegesis Psalmorum 29.1 Vandenhoff: Philo as "spiritual philosopher" in a long list of exegetes

Souda (ca. 1000)
  1.10.14 Adler: s.v. Ἀβραάμ; Philo's book on the life of the πολιτικός will testify to Joseph [M]
  1.18.32: On the term ἀγαλματοφορούμενος [M]
  1.472.3: On the term βίος (reference mistaken; actually Eusebius, *Suppl. min. ad quaest. ad Marinum* PG 22.1008)
  2.146.9: s.v. δύναμις; two powers enter into every soul [M]
  2.655.3: In the notice on Josephus it is mentioned that Apion accused Philo
  2.698.27: s.v. θεός; an extract from Isidore of Pelusium, *Epist.* 2.143 on Philo's doctrine of God (see above under Isidore) [M]
  2.705.29: s.v. θεραπευταί; Philo's account mentioned and name explained [M]
  4.737-38: s.v. Φίλων; biographical notice with list of writings [T,V,C,M][35]

---

35. Other Byzantine references printed by Mangey and Cohn and two intriguing Jewish texts in Mangey are later than 1000 C.E.

Bibliography

Abegg, Martin G. "The Covenant of the Qumran Sectarians." In Porter and de Roo, *The Concept of the Covenant in the Second Temple Period*, 81-97.

Adler, Maximililanus. *Studien zu Philon von Alexandreia*. Breslau: Marcus, 1929.

Alesse, Francesca, ed. *Philo of Alexandria and Post-Aristotelian Philosophy*. Studies in Philo of Alexandria 5. Leiden: Brill, 2008.

Alexander, Philip S. "Retelling the Old Testament." In *It is Written: Scripture Citing Scripture: Essays in Honour of Barnabas Lindars, SSF,* ed. Donald A. Carson and Hugh G. M. Williamson. New York: Cambridge University Press, 1988, 99-121.

Alexandre, Manuel, Jr. *Rhetorical Argumentation in Philo of Alexandria*. BJS 322. SPhilo Monographs 2. Atlanta: Scholars, 1999.

Alexandre, Monique. *De congressu eruditionis gratia*. Vol. 16 of Arnaldez, Mondésert, and Pouilloux, *Les oeuvres de Philon d'Alexandrie*. Paris: Cerf, 1967.

————. "La culture profane chez Philon." In *Philon d' Alexandrie. Actes du Colloque nationale de Lyon 11-15 Septembre 1996*, ed. Roger Arnaldez, Claude Mondésert, and Jean Poilloux. Paris: CNRS, 1967, 105-30.

Alon, Gedalyahu. *The Jews, Judaism and the Classical World: Studies in Jewish History in the Times of the Second Temple and Talmud*. Trans. Israel Abrahams. Jerusalem: Magnes, 1977.

Alston, Richard. "Philo's *In Flaccum*: Ethnicity and Social Space in Roman Alexandria." *Greece & Rome* 44 (1997) 165-75.

Ameling, Walter. "Zenon von Kition." In *DNP* 12/2 (2002) 744-48.

Amir, Yehoshua. "Philo and the Bible." *SPhilo* 2 (1973) 1-8.

————. "The Transference of Greek Allegories to Biblical Motifs in Philo." In Greenspahn, Hilgert, and Mack, *Nourished with Peace,* 15-25.

————. "Authority and Interpretation of Scripture in the Writings of Philo." In Mulder and Sysling, *Mikra,* 421-54.

Applebaum, Shimon. "The Legal Status of the Jewish Communities in the Diaspora." In Safrai and Stern, *The Jewish People in the First Century,* 1:420-63.

————. "The Social and Economic Status of the Jews in the Diaspora." In Safrai and Stern, *The Jewish People in the First Century,* 2:701-27.

Archer, Léonie. *Her Price Is Beyond Rubies: The Jewish Woman in Graeco-Roman Palestine.* JSOTSup 60. Sheffield: Sheffield Academic, 1990.

Argall, Randal A. "A Hellenistic-Jewish Source on the Essenes in Philo, *Every Good Man is Free* 75-91 and Josephus, *Antiquities* 18.18-22." In *For a Later Generation: The Transformation of Tradition in Israel, Early Judaism, and Early Christianity,* ed. Argall, Beverly A. Bow, and Rodney A. Werline. Harrisburg: Trinity Press International, 2000, 13-24.

Arnaldez, Roger, Jean Pouilloux, and Claude Mondésert, eds. *Les Oeuvres de Philon d'Alexandrie.* 36 vols. Paris: Cerf, 1961-92.

Arnim, Hans Friedrich August von. *Stoicorum veterum fragmenta.* 4 vols. Leipzig: Teubner, 1903-24.

Athanassiadi, Polymnia, and Michael Frede. *Pagan Monotheism in Late Antiquity.* Oxford: Clarendon, 1999

Attridge, Harold W. *The Interpretation of Biblical History in the* Antiquitates Judaicae *of Flavius Josephus.* HDR 7. Missoula: Scholars, 1976.

————. *The Epistle to the Hebrews.* Hermeneia. Philadelphia: Fortress, 1989.

Aucher, J. B. *Philonis Judaei paralipomena Armena: Libri videlicet quottuor* In Genesin, *libri duo* In Exodum, *sermo unus* De Sampsone, *alter* De Jona, *tertius* De tribus angelis Abraamo apparentibus. Venice: Lazarus, 1826.

Aune, David E., Torrey Seland, and Jarl Henning Ulrichsen, eds. *Neotestamentica et Philonica: Studies in Honor of Peder Borgen.* NovTSup 106. Leiden: Brill, 2003.

Avemarie, Friedrich. "Juden vor den Richterstühlen Roms: *In Flaccum* und die Apostelgeschichte im vergleich." In Deines and Niebuhr, *Philo und das Neue Testament,* 107-26.

Barclay, John M. G. *Jews in the Mediterranean Diaspora: From Alexander to Trajan (323 BCE–117 CE).* Edinburgh: T. & T. Clark, 1996.

————. "Paul and Philo on Circumcision: Romans 2.25-9 in Social and Cultural Context." *NTS* 44 (1998) 536-56.

————. "The Politics of Contempt: Judaeans and Egyptians in Josephus's *Against Apion.*" In *Negotiating Diaspora,* 109-27.

Barclay, John M. G., ed. *Negotiating Diaspora: Jewish Strategies in the Roman Empire*. LSTS 45. London: T. & T. Clark, 2004.

Barclay, John M. G., trans. *Flavius Josephus: Against Apion*. Translation and Commentary 10. Leiden: Brill, 2007.

Barraclough, Ray. "Philo's Politics: Roman Rule and Hellenistic Judaism." In *ANRW* 2.21.1 (1984) 417-553.

Bartlett, John R., ed. *Jews in the Hellenistic and Roman Cities*. London: Routledge, 2002.

Beavis, Mary Ann. "Philo's Therapeutai: Philosopher's Dream or Utopian Construction?" *JSP* 14 (2004) 30-42.

Beckwith, Roger T. *The Old Testament Canon of the New Testament Church and Its Background in Early Judaism*. London: SPCK, 1985; Grand Rapids: Eerdmans, 1986.

Bekken, Per Jarle. "Abraham og Ånden: Paulus' anvendelse av Genesis 15:6 i Galaterbrevet 3:6 belyst ut fra jødisk materiale." *TTKi* 71 (2000) 265-76.

———. "Misjon og eskatologi: Noen observasjoner til Paulus' misjonsteologi på bakgrunn av eskatologiske forventninger i tidlig jødedom." *Norsk Tidsskrift for Misjon* 54 (2000) 85-104.

———. *The Word Is Near You: A Study of Deuteronomy 30:12-14 in Paul's Letter to the Romans in a Jewish Context*. BZNW 144. Berlin: de Gruyter, 2007.

———. "The Controversy on Self-Testimony According to John 5:31-40; 8:12-20 and Philo, Legum Allegoriae III.205-208." In *Identity Formation in the New Testament*, ed. Bengt Holmberg and Mikael Winninge. WUNT 227. Tübingen: Mohr Siebeck, 2008, 19-42.

Belkin, Samuel. *Philo and the Oral Law: The Philonic Interpretation of Biblical Law in Relation to the Palestinian Halakah*. Cambridge, MA: Harvard University Press, 1940.

———. *The Midrash of Philo*. Vol. 1, ed. Elazar Hurvitz. New York: Yeshiva University Press, 1989. (Hebrew)

Bell, H. Idris. *Jews and Christians in Egypt: The Jewish Troubles in Alexandria and the Athanasian Controversy*. London: Oxford University Press, 1924.

Bennett, Robert Ernest. "The Prefects of Roman Egypt 30 B.C.-69 A.D." Ph.D. diss., Yale, 1971.

Berkowitz, Luci, and Karl A. Squitier, *Thesaurus linguae graecae: Canon of Greek Authors and Works*. 2nd ed. New York: Oxford University Press, 1986; 3rd ed., 1990.

Berthelot, Katell. "Zeal for God and Divine Law in Philo and the Dead Sea Scrolls." *SPhAn* 19 (2007) 113-29.

———. "Philo's Perception of the Roman Empire." *JSJ* 42 (2011) 166-87.

Beutler, Rudolf. "Okellos." In PW 17/2 (1937) 2361-80.

Biblia Patristica Supplément: Philon d'Alexandrie. Paris: Editions du Centre National de la recherche scientifique, 1982.

Bilde, Per. "The Essenes in Philo and Josephus." In Qumran between the Old and New Testaments, ed. Frederick H. Cryer and Thomas L. Thompson. JSOTSup 290. Sheffield: Sheffield Academic, 1998, 32-68.

———. "Filon som polemiker og politisk apologet: En undersøgelse af de to historiske skrifter Mod Flaccus (In Flaccum) og Om delegationen til Gaius (De legatione ad Gaium)." In Perspektiver på jødisk apologetik, ed. Anders Klostergaard Petersen and Kåre Sigvald Fuglseth. Antikken og Kristendommen 4. Copenhagen: ANIS, 2007, 155-80.

Bilde, Per, et al., eds. Ethnicity in Hellenistic Egypt. Studies in Hellenistic Civilization 3. Aarhus: Aarhus University Press, 1992.

Binder, Donald D. Into the Temple Courts: The Place of the Synagogues in the Second Temple Period. SBLDS 169. Atlanta: Society of Biblical Literature, 1999.

Bird, Michael F. Crossing Over Sea and Land: Jewish Missionary Activity in the Second Temple Period. Peabody: Hendrickson, 2010.

Birnbaum, Ellen. "What Does Philo Mean by 'Seeing God'? Some Methodological Considerations." In Society of Biblical Literature 1995 Seminar Papers, ed. Eugene H. Lovering Jr. Atlanta: Scholars, 1995, 535-52.

———. The Place of Judaism in Philo's Thought: Israel, Jews, and Proselytes. BJS 290. SPhilo Monographs 2. Atlanta: Scholars, 1996.

———. "Philo on the Greeks: A Jewish Perspective on Culture and Society in First-Century Alexandria." In Runia and Sterling, In the Spirit of Faith, 37-58.

———. "A Leader with Vision in the Ancient Jewish Diaspora: Philo of Alexandria." In Jewish Religious Leadership: Image and Reality, ed. Jack Wertheimer. New York: Jewish Theological Seminary of America, 2004, 1:57-90.

———. "Portrayals of the Wise and Virtuous in Alexandrian Jewish Works: Jews' Perceptions of Themselves and Others." In Harris and Ruffini, Ancient Alexandria between Egypt and Greece, 125-60.

———. "Two Millennia Later: General Resources and Particular Perspectives on Philo the Jew." Currents in Biblical Research 4 (2006) 241-76.

———. "Exegetical Building Blocks in Philo's Interpretation of the Patriarchs." In From Judaism to Christianity: Tradition and Transition: A Festschrift for Thomas H. Tobin, S.J., on the Occasion of His Sixty-fifth Birthday, ed. Patricia Walters. NovTSup 136. Leiden: Brill, 2010, 69-92.

————. "Who Celebrated on Pharos with the Jews? Conflicting Philonic Currents and Their Implications." In *Philon d'Alexandrie: un penseur à l'intersection des cultures gréco-romaine, orientale, juive et chrétienne*, ed. Sabrina Inowlocki-Meister and Baudouin Decharneux. Turnhout: Brepols, 2011, 63-82.

Boccaccini, Gabriele. *Middle Judaism: Jewish Thought, 300 B.C.E. to 200 C.E.* Minneapolis: Fortress, 1991.

Bock, Darrell L. "Blasphemy and the Jewish Examination of Jesus." *BBR* 17 (2007) 53-114.

Bokser, Baruch M. *The Origins of the Seder: The Passover Rite and Early Rabbinic Judaism.* Berkeley: University of California Press, 1984.

Bonazzi, Mauro. "Towards Transcendence: Philo and the Renewal of Platonism in the Early Imperial Age." In Alesse, *Philo of Alexandria and Post-Aristotelian Philosophy*, 233-51.

Booth, A. Peter. "The Voice of the Serpent: Philo's Epicureanism." In *Hellenization Revised: Shaping a Christian Response within the Graeco-Roman World*, ed. Wendy E. Helleman. Lanham: University Press of America, 1994, 159-72.

Borgen, Peder. *Bread from Heaven: An Exegetical Study of the Concept of Manna in the Gospel of John and the Writings of Philo.* NovTSup 10. Leiden: Brill, 1965.

————. *"Logos Was the True Light" and Other Essays on the Gospel of John.* Trondheim: Tapir, 1983.

————. *Paul Preaches Circumcision and Pleases Men and Other Essays on Christian Origins.* Relieff 8. Trondheim: Tapir, 1983.

————. "Aristobulus — A Jewish Exegete from Alexandria." In *Paul Preaches Circumcision and Pleases Men*, 179-90.

————. "Filo, Diasporajøde Fra Aleksandria." In *Blant skriftlærde og fariseere: Jødedommen i oldtiden*, ed. Hans Kvalbein. Oslo: Verbum, 1984, 143-56.

————. "Philo of Alexandria." In Stone, *The Literature of the Jewish People*, 233-82.

————. "Philo of Alexandria: A Critical and Synthetical Survey of Research since World War II." In *ANRW* 2.21.1 (1984) 98-154.

————. *Philo, John, and Paul: New Perspectives on Judaism and Early Christianity.* BJS 131. Atlanta: Scholars, 1987.

————. "The Sabbath Controversy in John 5.1-18 and Analogous Controversy Reflected in Philo's Writings." In Runia, Hays, and Winston, *Heirs of the Septuagint*, 209-21.

————. "Judaism: Judaism in Egypt." In *ABD* 3:1061-72.

————. "Philo and the Jews in Alexandria." In Bilde et al., *Ethnicity in Hellenistic Egypt*, -38.

———. "'There Shall Come Forth a Man': Reflections on Messianic Ideas in Philo." In *The Messiah: Developments in Earliest Judaism and Christianity,* ed. James H. Charlesworth et al. First Princeton Symposium on Judaism and Christian Origins. Minneapolis: Fortress, 1992, 341-61.

———. "Man's Sovereignty over Animals and Nature according to Philo of Alexandria." In Fornberg and Hellholm, *Texts and Contexts,* 369-89.

———. "'Yes,' 'No,' 'How Far?': The Participation of Jews and Christians in Pagan Cults." In *Paul in His Hellenistic Context,* ed. Troels Engberg-Pedersen. Edinburgh: T. & T. Clark; Minneapolis: Fortress, 1995, 30-59.

———. "Philo of Alexandria — A Systematic Philosopher or an Eclectic Editor?" *Symbolae Osloenses* 71 (1996) 115-34.

———. "The Gospel of John and Hellenism." In *Exploring the Gospel of John: In Honor of D. Moody Smith,* ed. R. Alan Culpepper and C. Clifton Black. Louisville: Westminster John Knox, 1996, 98-123.

———. *Philo of Alexandria: An Exegete for His Time.* NovTSup 86. Leiden: Brill, 1997.

———. *Early Christianity and Hellenistic Judaism.* Edinburgh: T. & T. Clark, 1998.

———. "Two Philonic Prayers and Their Contexts: An Analysis of *Who Is the Heir of Divine Things (Her.)* 24-29 and *Against Flaccum. (Flac.)* 170-175." *NTS* 45 (1999) 291-309.

———. "Application of and Commitment to the Laws of Moses: Observations on Philo's Treatise *On the Embassy to Gaius.* In Runia and Sterling, *In the Spirit of Faith,* 86-101.

———. "Greek Encyclical Education and the Synagogue: Observations from Philo of Alexandria's Writings." In *Libens Merito: Festskrift til Stig Strømholm på sjutioårsdagen 16 sept. 2001 Uppsala, 2001,* ed. O. Matsson, Aa. Frändberg, M. Hedlund, S. Lunell, and G. Sedin. Uppsala: Kungl. Vetenskapssamhället I Uppsala, 2001, 61-71.

———. "The Gospel of John and Philo of Alexandria." In *Light in a Spotless Mirror: Reflections on Wisdom Traditions in Judaism and Early Christianity,* ed. James H. Charlesworth and Michael A. Daise. Harrisburg: Trinity Press International, 2003, 45-76.

———. "Philo of Alexandria as Exegete." In Hauser and Watson, *A History of Biblical Interpretation,* 114-43.

Borgen, Peder, Kåre Fuglseth, and Roald Skarsten, *The Philo Index: A Complete Greek Word Index to The Writings of Philo of Alexandria.* Grand Rapids: Eerdmans; Leiden: Brill, 2000.

Borgen, Peder, and Roald Skarsten. "Quaestiones et Solutiones: Some Observations on the Forms of Philo's Exegesis." *SPhilo* 4 (1976-77) 1-15.

Bos, Abraham P. "Philo of Alexandria: A Platonist in the Image and Likeness of Aristotle." *SPhAn* 10 (1998) 66-86.

Boswell, John. *The Kindness of Strangers.* New York: Pantheon, 1988.

Bousset, Wilhelm. *Die Religion des Judentums im späthellenistischen Zeitalter.* Rev. Hugo Gressmann. 3rd ed. Tübingen: Mohr, 1926.

Box, Herbert. *Philonis Alexandrini* In Flaccum. London: Oxford University Press, 1939.

Boyancé, Pierre. "Le Dieu très haut chez Philon." In *Mélanges d'historie des religions offerts à Henri-Charles Puech.* Paris: Presse univeritairires de France, 1974, 139-49.

Brakke, David, Anders-Christian Jacobsen, and Jörg Ulrich, eds. *Beyond Reception: Mutual Influences Between Antique Religion, Judaism, and Early Christianity.* Early Christianity in the Context of Antiquity 1. Bern: Lang, 2006.

Braund, David C. "Agrippa." In *ABD* 1:98-100.

Breslauer, S. Daniel. "Philosophy in Judaism: Two Stances." In *The Blackwell Companion to Judaism,* ed. Jacob Neusner and Alan J. Avery-Peck. Oxford: Blackwell, 2000, 162-80.

Brewer, David Instone. *Techniques and Assumptions in Jewish Exegesis before 70 C.E.* TSAJ 30. Tübingen: Mohr Siebeck, 1992.

Brown, Raymond E. *The Gospel According to John.* 2 vols. AB 29-29A. Garden City: Doubleday, 1966-70.

Buber, Solomon, ed., *Midrash Tanḥuma.* Wilna: Romm, 1885.

Bubis, Gerald B. *Saving the Jewish Family: Myths and Realities in the Diaspora.* Lanham: University Press of America, 1987.

Burke, John Bruce. "Philo and Alexandrian Judaism." Ph.D. diss., Syracuse University, 1963.

Cantarella, Eva. *Pandora's Daughters.* Baltimore: Johns Hopkins University Press, 1987.

Carson, D. A., and H. G. M. Williamson, eds. *It is Written: Scripture Citing Scripture: Essays in Honour of Barnabas Lindars, SSF.* New York, Cambridge University Press, 1988.

Carson, D. A., Peter T. O'Brien, and Mark A. Seifrid, eds. *Justification and Variegated Nomism.* Vol. 1: *The Complexities of Second Temple Judaism.* Tübingen: Mohr Siebeck; Grand Rapids: Baker, 2001.

Catto, Stephen K. *Reconstructing the First-Century Synagogue: A Critical Analysis of Current Research.* LNTS 363. London: T. & T. Clark, 2007.

Cazeaux, Jacques. "Système implicite dans l'exégèse de Philon: un exemple: le *De Praemiis*." *SPhilo* 6 (1979-80) 3-36.

Clarysse, Willy, and Dorothy J. Thompson. *Counting the People in Hellenistic Egypt.* Vol. 2: *Historical Studies.* Cambridge: Cambridge University Press, 2006.

Christes, Johannes. "Erziehung." In *DNP* 4 (1996) 110-20.

Christiansen, Irmgard. *Die Technik der allegorischen Auslegungswissenschaft bei Philon von Alexandrien.* Beiträge zur Geschichte der biblischen Hermeneutik 7. Tübingen: Mohr, 1969.

Cohen, Jeremy. *Be Fertile and Increase, Fill the Earth and Master It: The Ancient and Medieval Career of a Biblical Text.* Ithaca: Cornell University Press, 1989.

Cohen, Naomi G. *Philo Judaeus: His Universe of Discourse.* BEATAJ 24. Frankfurt am Main: Lang, 1995.

———. *Philo's Scriptures: Citations from the Prophets and Writings: Evidence for a Haftarah Cycle in Second Temple Judaism.* JSJSup 123. Leiden: Brill, 2007.

Cohen, Shaye J. D. Foreword to Modrzejewski, *The Jews of Egypt,* xi-xv.

———. *The Beginnings of Jewishness: Boundaries, Varieties, Uncertainties.* Berkeley: University of California Press, 1999.

Cohen, Shaye J. D., ed. *The Jewish Family in Antiquity.* BJS 289. Atlanta: Scholars, 1993.

Cohn, Leopold, Isaak Heinemann, Maximilian Adler, and Willy Theiler, eds. *Philo von Alexandria, Die Werke in deutscher Übersetzung.* 7 vols. Breslau: Marcus, 1909-38; repr., Berlin: de Gruyter, 1962-64.

Cohn, Leopold, Paul Wendland, Siegfried Reiter, and Hans Leisegang, eds. *Philonis Alexandrini opera quae supersunt.* 7 vols. Berlin: Reimer, 1896-1930; repr., Berlin: de Gruyter, 1962-63.

Collins, Adela Yarbro. "The Charge of Blasphemy in Mark 14.64." *JSNT* 26 (2004) 379-401.

Collins, John J. "The Development of the Sibylline Tradition." In *ANRW* 2.20.1 (1987) 421-59.

———. *Jewish Wisdom in the Hellenistic Age.* OTL. Louisvillle: Westminster John Knox, 1997.

———. *Between Athens and Jerusalem: Jewish Identity in the Hellenistic Diaspora.* 2nd ed. BRS. Grand Rapids: Eerdmans; Livonia: Dove, 2000.

———. "Anti-Semitism in Antiquity? The Case of Alexandria." In *Ancient Judaism in Its Hellenistic Context,* ed. Carol Bakhos. JSJSup 95. Leiden: Brill, 2005, 9-29.

———. "Special Section: Philo and the Dead Sea Scrolls." *SPhAn* 19 (2007) 81-142.

Collins, John J., and Gregory E. Sterling, eds. *Hellenism in the Land of Israel.* Notre Dame: University of Notre Dame Press, 2001.

Colson, F. H., G. H. Whitaker, and Ralph Marcus, trans. *Philo.* 10 vols. LCL 275. London: Heinemann; Cambridge, MA: Harvard University Press, 1929-62.

Conroy, John T., Jr. "Philo's 'Death of the Soul': Is This Only a Metaphor?" *SPhAn* 23 (2011) 23-40.

Dahl, Nils A. "Messianic Ideas and the Crucifixion of Jesus." In *The Messiah: Developments in Earliest Judaism and Christianity,* ed. James H. Charlesworth. Minneapolis: Fortress, 1992, 382-403.

Dahl, Nils A., and Alan F. Segal. "Philo and the Rabbis on the Names of God." *JSJ* 9 (1978) 1-28.

Deines, Roland, and Karl-Wilhelm Niebuhr, eds. *Philo und das Neue Testament: Wechselseitige Wahrnehmungen. I. Internationales Symposium zum Corpus Judaeo-Hellenisticum 1.-4. Mai 2003, Eisenach/Jena.* WUNT 171. Tübingen: Mohr Siebeck, 2004.

Dekkers, Eligius. *Clavis patrum latinorum.* Corpus christianorum. 3rd ed. Steenbrugge: Brepols, 1995.

Delia, Diana. *Alexandrian Citizenship during the Roman Principate.* American Classical Studies 23. Atlanta: Scholars, 1991.

Delling, Gerhard. "Perspektiven der Erforschungen des hellenistischen Judentums." *HUCA* 45 (1974) 133-76.

Delorme, Jean. "Gymnasium." In *RAC* 13 (1983) 155-75.

Denis, Albert-Marie. *Introduction à la littérature religieuse Judéo-Hellénistique: Pseudépigraphes de l'Ancient Testament.* 2 vols. Turnhout: Brepols, 2000.

De Savignac, J. "Le Messianisme de Philon d'Alexandrie." *NovT* 4 (1960) 319-24.

Des Places, Édouard. *Numénius Fragments: Texte établi et traduit.* Paris: Les Belles Lettres, 1973.

Diels, Hermann, and Walter Kranz. *Die Fragmente der Vorsokratiker.* 3 vols. 12th ed. Dublin: Weidmann, 1966.

Dillon, John M. "Ganymede as the Logos: Traces of a Forgotten Allegorization in Philo." *SPhilo* 6 (1979-80) 37-40.

———. "Preface." In *Philo of Alexandria: The Contemplative Life, The Giants, and Selections.* Trans. David Winston. Classics of Western Spirituality. New York: Paulist, 1981, xi-xiv.

———. "A Response to Runia and Sterling." *SPhAn* 5 (1993) 151-55.

———. *The Middle Platonists, 80 B.C. to A.D. 220.* Rev. ed. Ithaca: Cornell University Press, 1996.

Dillon, John, and Anthony A. Long, eds. *The Question of "Eclecticism": Studies in Later Greek Philosophy.* Hellenistic Culture and Society 3. Berkeley: University of California Press, 1988.

DiMattei, Steven. "Moses' *Physiologia* and the Meaning and Use of *Physikos* in Philo of Alexandria's Exegetical Method." *SPhAn* 18 (2006) 3-32.

Dimant, Devorah. "Pesharim, Qumran." In *ABD* 5:244-51.

Dinan, Andrew. "The Mystery of Play: Clement of Alexandria's Appropriation of Philo in the *Paedagogus* (1.5.21.3–22.1)." *SPhAn* 19 (2007) 59-80.

————. "Another Citation of Philo in Clement of Alexandria's *Protrepticus* (10,93,1-2)." *VC* 64 (2010) 435-44.

Dines, Jennifer M. *The Septuagint*. London: T. & T. Clark, 2004.

Doering, Lutz. *Schabbat: Sabbathalacha und -praxis im antiken Judentum und Urchristentum*. TSAJ 78. Tübingen: Mohr Siebeck, 1999.

Donaldson, Terence L. *Judaism and the Gentiles: Jewish Patterns of Universalism (to 135 CE)*. Waco: Baylor University Press, 2007.

Döring, Klaus. "Aristippos." In *DNP* 1 (1996) 1103-4.

————. "Theodoros aus Kyrene." In *DNP* 12/1 (2002) 326-27.

Dörrie, Heinrich, and Hermann Dörries. "Erotapokriseis." In RAC 6 (1966) cols. 342-70.

Downing, F. Gerald. "Philo on Wealth and the Rights of the Poor." *JSNT* 24 (1985) 116-18.

Droysen, Johann Gustav. *Geschichte des Hellenismus*. 3 vols. Gotha: Perthes, 1836-43.

Dunn, James D. G. *Romans*. 2 vols. WBC 38a, 38b. Waco: Word, 1988.

Eccles, Robert S. *Erwin Ramsdell Goodenough: A Personal Pilgrimage*. Chico: Scholars, 1985.

El-Abbadi, Mostafa. *Life and Fate of the Ancient Library of Alexandria*. 2nd ed. Paris: UNESCO/UNDP, 1992.

Engberg-Pedersen, Troels. "Philo's *De vita Contemplativa* as a Philosopher's Dream." *JSJ* 30 (1999) 40-64.

Engels, Donald. "The Problem of Female Infanticide in the Greco-Roman World." *CP* 75 (1980) 112-20.

Erskine, Andrew, ed. *A Companion to the Hellenistic World*. Oxford: Blackwell, 2003.

Etienne, Stéphane. "Réflexion sur l'Apostasie de Tibérius Julius Alexander." *SPhAn* 12 (2000) 122-42.

Evans, Craig A. "Covenant in the Qumran Literature." In Porter and de Roo, *The Concept of the Covenant in the Second Temple Period*, 55-80.

Evans, Katherine G. "Alexander the Alabarch: Roman and Jew." In *Society of Biblical Literature 1995 Seminar Papers*, ed. Eugene H. Lovering Jr. Atlanta: Scholars, 1995, 576-94.

Feldman, Louis H. *Philo's Portrayal of Moses in the Context of Ancient Judaism*. Notre Dame: University of Notre Dame Press, 2007.

Fernández Marcos, Natalio. "Rewritten Bible or *Imitatio?* The Vestments of the High-Priest." In *Studies in the Hebrew Bible, Qumran, and the Septuagint Presented to Eugene Ulrich,* ed. Peter W. Flint, Emanuel Tov, and James C. VanderKam. VTSup 101. Leiden: Brill, 2006, 321-36.

Festugière, A. J. "Sur une nouvelle édition du 'De Vita Pythagorica' de Jamblique." *REG* 50 (1937) 470-94.

Fischer, Ulrich. *Eschatologie und Jenseitserwartung im hellenistischen Diasporajudentum.* BZNW 44. Berlin: de Gruyter, 1978.

Fitzmyer, Joseph A. *Romans.* AB 33. New York: Doubleday, 1993.

Flandrin, Jean Louis. *Families in Former Times: Kinship, Household, and Sexuality.* Cambridge: Cambridge University Press, 1972.

Fletcher-Louis, Crispin H. T. *All the Glory of Adam: Liturgical Anthropology in the Dead Sea Scrolls.* STDJ 42. Leiden: Brill, 2002.

Fornberg, Tord, and David Hellholm, eds. *Texts and Contexts: Biblical Texts in Their Textual and Situational Contexts: Essays in Honor of Lars Hartman.* Oslo: Scandinavian University Press, 1995.

Fortenbaugh, William W., and Johannes van Opphuijsen. "Theophrastus." In *DNP* 12/1 (2002) 385-93.

Fraser, P. M. *Ptolemaic Alexandria.* 3 vols. Oxford: Clarendon, 1972.

Frede, Michael. "Chaeremon der Stoiker." In *ANRW* 2.36.3 (1989) 2067-2103.

Frey, Jean-Baptiste. *Corpus inscriptionem Judaicarum.* 2 vols. Rome: Pontifico instituto, 1936-52.

Fritsch, Charles T. *The Anti-Anthropomorphisms of the Greek Pentateuch.* Princeton: Princeton University Press, 1943.

Fuchs, Harald. "Enkyklios Paideia." In *RAC* 5 (1962) 365-98.

Fuglseth, Kåre Sigvald. *Johannine Sectarianism in Perspective.* NovTSup 119. Leiden: Brill, 2005.

―――. "The Reception of Aristotelian Features in Philo and the Authorship Problem of Philo's De Aeternitate Mundi." In Brakke, Jacobsen, and Ulrich, *Beyond Reception,* 57-67.

Gambetti, Sandra. "The Jewish Community of Alexandria: The Origins." *Hen* 29 (2007) 213-39.

―――. *The Alexandrian Riots of 38 c.e. and the Persecution of the Jews: A Historical Reconstruction.* JSJSup 135. Leiden: Brill, 2009.

García Martínez, Florentino. "Divine Sonship at Qumran and in Philo." *SPhAn* 19 (2007) 85-99.

Geerard, Mauritius, *Clavis patrum graecorum.* 5 vols. and suppl. Turnhout: Brepols, 1974-98.

Gehrke, Hans-Joachim. "Ephebeia." In *DNP* 3 (1997) 1072-75.

Geljon, Albert C. *Philonic Exegesis in Gregory of Nyssa's* De vita Moysis. SPhilMon 5. Providence: Brown Judaic Studies, 2002.

————. "Didymus the Blind's Use of Philo in His Exegesis of Cain and Abel." *VC* 61 (2007) 282-312.

Geljon, Albert C., and David T. Runia. *Philo of Alexandria: On Cultivation.* PACS 4. Leiden: Brill, 2013.

Glock, Andreas. "Museion." In *DNP* (2000) 507-11.

Glucker, John. *Antiochus and the Late Academy.* Hypomnemata 56. Göttingen: Vandenhoeck & Ruprecht, 1978.

Goldberg, Shari. "The Two Choruses Become One: The Absence/Presence of Women in Philo's *On the Contemplative Life.*" *JSJ* 39 (2008) 459-70.

Golden, Mark. "Demography and the Exposure of Girls at Athens." *Phoenix* 85 (1951) 316-31.

————. *Children and Childhood in Classical Athens.* Baltimore: Johns Hopkins University Press, 1990.

Goodenough, Erwin R. "Philo and Public Life." *JEA* 12 (1926) 77-79.

————. *The Jurisprudence of the Jewish Courts in Egypt: Legal Administration by the Jews under the Early Roman Empire as Described by Philo Judaeus.* 1929; repr., Amsterdam: Philo, 1968.

————. "Philo's Exposition of the Law and His De Vita Mosis." *HTR* 26 (1933) 109-25.

————. *By Light, Light: The Mystic Gospel of Hellenistic Judaism.* 1935; repr., Amsterdam: Philo, 1969.

————. *The Politics of Philo Judaeus: Practice and Theory.* New Haven: Yale University Press, 1938.

————. *Jewish Symbols in the Greco-Roman Period.* 13 vols. New York: Pantheon, 1953-68.

————. *An Introduction to Philo Judaeus.* 2nd ed. Oxford: Blackwell, 1962; repr., Brown Classics in Judaica. Lanham: University Press of America, 1986.

Goodman, Martin. "Early Judaism." In *Judaism in the Roman World: Collected Essays.* AGJU 66. Leiden: Brill, 2007, 1-19.

Goudriaan, Koen. "Ethnical Strategies in Graeco-Roman Egypt." In Bilde et al., *Ethnicity in Hellenistic Egypt,* 74-89.

Goulet, Richard. *La philosophie de Moïse: Essai de reconstition d'un commentaire philosophique préphilonien du Pentateuque.* Histoire des doctrines de l'Antiquité classique 11. Paris: Vrin, 1987.

Goulet-Cazé, Marie Odile. "Diogenes von Sinope." In *DNP* 3 (1997) 598-600.

Grabbe, Lester L. *Etymology in Early Jewish Interpretation: The Hebrew Names in Philo.* BJS 115. Atlanta: Scholars, 1988.

————. *Judaism from Cyrus to Hadrian*. 2 vols. Minneapolis: Fortress, 1994.

————. "Eschatology in Philo and Josephus." In *Judaism in Late Antiquity*. Pt. 4: *Death, Life-after-Death, Resurrection and the World-to-Come in the Judaisms of Antiquity*. HO 1: *Der Nahe und Mittlere Osten* 49. Leiden: Brill, 2000, 163-85.

————. "The Hellenistic City of Jerusalem." In Bartlett, *Jews in the Hellenistic and Roman Cities*, 6-21.

————. "Did All Jews Think Alike? 'Covenant' in Philo and Josephus in the Context of Second Temple Judaic Religion." In Porter and de Roo, *The Concept of the Covenant in the Second Temple Period*, 251-66.

Gradl, Hans-Georg. "Kaisertum und Kaiserkult: Ein Vergleich zwischen Philos *Legatio ad Gaium* und der *Offenbarung des Johannes*." *NTS* 56 (2009) 116-38.

Graver, Margaret. "Philo of Alexandria and the Origins of the Stoic ΠΡΟΠΑΘΕΙΑΙ." In Alesse, *Philo of Alexandria and Post-Aristotelian Philosophy*, 197-221.

Green, William Scott. "What Do We Really Know about the Pharisees, and How Do We Know it?" In Neusner and Chilton, *In Quest of the Historical Pharisees*, 409-23.

Greenspahn, Frederick E., Earle Hilgert, and Burton L. Mack, eds. *Nourished With Peace: Studies in Hellenistic Judaism in Memory of Samuel Sandmel*. Homage Series 9. Chico: Scholars, 1984.

Gruen, Erich S. *Diaspora: Jews amidst Greeks and Romans*. Cambridge, MA: Harvard University Press, 2002.

————. "Jews and Greeks." In Erskine, *A Companion to the Hellenistic World*, 264-79.

————. "Caligula, the Imperial Cult, and Philo's Legatio." *SPhAn* 24 (2012) 135-47.

Haacker, Klaus. *The Theology of Paul's Letter to the Romans*. Cambridge: Cambridge University Press, 2003.

Hadas, Moses, ed. and trans. *Aristeas to Philocrates*. New York: Ktav, 1973.

Hadas-Lebel, Mireille. *Philo of Alexandria: A Thinker in the Jewish Diaspora*. Trans. Robyn Frechet. Studies in Philo of Alexandria 7. Leiden: Brill, 2012.

Hadot, Ilsetraut. "Gymnasion." In *DNP* 5 (1998) 19-27.

Hakola, Raimo. *Identity Matters: John, the Jews and Jewishness*. NovTSup 118. Leiden: Brill, 2005.

Hamerton-Kelly, Robert G. "Sources and Traditions in Philo Judaeus: Prolegomena to an Analysis of His Writings." *SPhilo* 1 (1972) 3-26.

Harich-Schwarzbauer, Henriette. "Erziehung." In *RGG*[4] 2 (1999) 1505-9.

Harker, Andrew. *Loyalty and Dissidence in Roman Egypt: The Case of the* Acta Alexandrinorum. Cambridge: Cambridge University Press, 2008.

Harris, William V. "The Theoretical Possibility of Extensive Infanticide in the Graeco-Roman World." *CQ* 32 (1982) 114-16.

Harris, William V., and Giovanni Ruffini, eds. *Ancient Alexandria between Egypt and Greece.* Columbia Studies in the Classical Tradition 26. Leiden: Brill, 2004.

Hauser, Alan J., and Duane F. Watson, eds. *A History of Biblical Interpretation.* Vol. 1: *The Ancient Period.* Grand Rapids: Eerdmans, 2003.

Hay, David M. "Philo's References to Other Allegorists." *SPhilo* 6 (1979-80) 41-75.

―――. "Politics and Exegesis in Philo's Treatise on Dreams." In *Society of Biblical Literature 1987 Seminar Papers,* ed. Kent Harold Richards. Atlanta: Scholars, 1987, 429-38.

―――. "References to Other Exegetes." In Hay, *Both Literal and Allegorical,* 81-97.

―――. "Putting Extremism in Context: The Case of Philo, *De Migratione* 89-93." *SPhAn* 9 (1997) 126-42.

―――. "The Veiled Thoughts of the Therapeutae." In *Mediators of the Divine: Horizons of Prophecy, Divination, Dreams, and Theurgy in Mediterranean Antiquity,* ed. Robert M. Berchman. South Florida Studies in the History of Judaism 163. Atlanta: Scholars, 1998, 167-84.

―――. "Foils for the Therapeutae: References to Other Texts and Persons in Philo's 'De Vita Contemplativa.'" In Aune, Seland, and Ulrichsen, *Neotestamentica et Philonica,* 330-48.

Hay, David M., ed. *Both Literal and Allegorical: Studies in Philo of Alexandria's Questions and Answers on Genesis and Exodus.* BJS 232. Atlanta: Scholars, 1991.

Hayward, C. T. R., ed. *The Jewish Temple: A Non-biblical Sourcebook.* London: Routledge, 1996.

Hecht, Richard D. "Preliminary Issues in the Analysis of Philo's De Specialibus Legibus." *SPhilo* 5 (1978) 1-55.

―――. "The Exegetical Contexts of Philo's Interpretation of Circumcision." In Greenspahn, Hilgert, and Mack, *Nourished With Peace,* 43-79.

―――. "Philo and Messiah." In *Judaisms and Their Messiahs at the Turn of the Christian Era,* ed. Jacob Neusner, William Scott Green, and Ernest Frerichs. Cambridge: Cambridge University Press, 1987, 139-68.

Heinemann, Isaak. *Philons griechische und jüdische Bildung: Kulturvergleichende Untersuchungen zu Philons Darstellung der jüdischen Gesetze.* Breslau: Marcus, 1932; repr., Hildesheim: Olms, 1962.

————. *Altjüdische Allegoristik*. Breslau: Marcus, 1936.

Heinemann, Isaak, ed. *Die Werke Philos von Alexandria*. Vol. 2. Breslau: Marcus, 1910.

Heinisch, Paul. *Der Einfluss Philos auf die älteste christliche Exegese*. Alttestamentliche Abhandlungen 1/2. Münster: Aschendorff, 1908.

Helleman, Wendy E. "'Philo of Alexandria on Deification and Assimilation to God.'" *SPhAn* 2. BJS 226 (1990) 51-71.

Hengel, Martin. *Judaism and Hellenism: Studies in Their Encounter in Palestine during the Early Hellenistic Period*. Trans. John Bowden. 2 vols. London: SCM; Philadelphia: Fortress, 1974; repr. in 1 vol. 1981.

————. "Messianische Hoffnung und politischer 'Radikalismus' in der 'jüdischen Diaspora.'" In *Apocalypticism in the Mediterranean World and the Near East: Proceedings of the International Colloquium on Apocalypticism, Uppsala, August 12-17, 1979*, ed. David Hellholm. 2nd ed. Tübingen: Mohr Siebeck, 1989, 655-86.

Herzer, Jens. "'Von Gottes Geist durchweht': Die Inspiration der Schrift nach 2Tim 3,16 u. bei Philo von Alexandrien." In Deines and Niebuhr, *Philo und das Neue Testament*, 223-40.

Hilgert, Earle. "Bibliographia Philoniana 1935-1981." In *ANRW* 2.21.1 (1984) 47-97.

————. "A Survey of Previous Scholarship on Philo's *De Josepho*." In *Society of Biblical Literature 1986 Seminar Papers*, ed. Kent Harold Richards. Atlanta: Scholars, 1986, 262-70.

————. "The Quaestiones: Texts and Translations." In Hay, *Both Literal and Allegorical*, 1-15.

————. "Philo Judaeus et Alexandrinus: The State of the Problem." In Kenney, *The School of Moses*, 1-15.

Hoek, Annewies van den. *Clement of Alexandria and His Use of Philo in the Stromateis: An Early Christian Reshaping of a Jewish Model*. VCSup 3. Leiden: Brill, 1988.

————. "The 'Catechetical' School of Early Christian Alexandria and Its Philonic Heritage." *HTR* 90 (1997) 59-87.

————. "Philo and Origen: A Descriptive Catalogue of Their Relationship." *SPhAn* 12 (2000) 44-121.

————. "Assessing Philo's Influence in Christian Alexandria: The Case of Origen." In Kugel, *Shem in the Tents of Japheth*, 223-39.

Holladay, Carl R. *Fragments from Hellenistic Jewish Authors*. Vol. 1: *Historians*. SBLTT 20. SBLPS 10. Chico: Scholars, 1983.

————. *Fragments from Hellenistic Jewish Authors*. Vol. 2: *Poets*. SBLTT 30. SBLPS 12. Atlanta: Scholars, 1989.

————. *Fragments from Hellenistic Jewish Authors.* Vol. 3: *Aristobulus.* SBLTT 39. SBLPS 13. Atlanta: Scholars, 1995.

Horbury, William, and David Noy, eds. *Jewish Inscriptions of Graeco-Roman Egypt.* Cambridge: Cambridge University Press, 1992.

Horsley, Richard A. "The Law of Nature in Philo and Cicero." *HTR* 71 (1978) 35-59.

Horst, Pieter Willem van der. *The Sentences of Pseudo-Phocylides.* SVTP 4. Leiden: Brill, 1978.

————. *Chaeremon: Egyptian Priest and Stoic Philosopher.* EPRO 101. Leiden: Brill, 1984.

————. "Pseudo-Phocylides Revisited." *JSP* 3 (1988) 3-30.

————. *Philo's Flaccus: The First Pogrom: Introduction, Translation, and Commentary.* PACS 2. Leiden: Brill, 2003.

————. "Philo's *In Flaccum* and the Book of Acts." In Deines and Niebuhr, *Philo und das Neue Testament,* 95-105.

Hübner, Hans, ed. *Die Weisheit Salomos im Horizont biblischer Theologie.* Biblisch-theologische Studien 22. Neukirchen-Vluyn: Neukirchener, 1993.

Hülser, Karlheinz. "Pythagoreer/Pythagoreismus." In *RGG⁴* 6 (2003) 1846-48.

Hutt, Curtis. "Qumran and the Ancient Sources." In *The Provo International Conference on the Dead See Scrolls — Technological Innovations, New Texts, and Reformulated Issues,* ed. Donald W. Parry and Eugene Ulrich. STDJ 30. Leiden: Brill, 1999, 274-93.

Inwood, Brad. "Chrysippus." In *DNP* 2 (1997) 1177-83.

————. "Kleanthes." In *DNP* 6 (1999) 499-500.

Inowlocki, Sabrina. "Eusebius of Caesarea's *Interpretatio Christiana* of Philo's *De vita contemplativa.*" *HTR* 97 (2004) 305-28.

————. *Eusebius and the Jewish Authors: His Citation Technique in an Apologetic Context.* AGJU 64. Leiden: Brill, 2006.

Jaffee, Martin S. *Early Judaism.* Upper Saddle River: Prentice Hall, 1997.

Janácek, Karel. "Philon von Alexandreia und skeptische Tropen." *Eirene* 19 (1982) 83-97.

Jaubert, Annie. *La notion d'alliance dans le judaïsme aux abords de l'ère chrétienne.* Paris: Éditions du Seuil, 1963.

Josephus, Flavius. 10 vols. LCL 203-456. London: Heinemann; Cambridge, MA: Harvard University Press, 1926-81.

Kamesar, Adam. "San Basilio, Filone, e la tradizione ebraica." *Hen* 17 (1995) 129-40.

————. "The Literary Genres of the Pentateuch as Seen from the Greek Perspective: The Testimony of Philo of Alexandria." In *Wisdom and Logos: Studies in Jewish Thought in Honor of David Winston,* ed. David T. Runia and Greg-ory E. Sterling. SPhAn 9. BJS 312. Atlanta: Scholars, 1997, 143-89.

―――. "Biblical Interpretation in Philo." In Kamesar, *The Cambridge Compan-ion to Philo,* 65-91.

Kamesar, Adam, ed. *The Cambridge Companion to Philo.* Cambridge: Cambridge University Press, 2009.

Kasher, Aryeh. "The Jewish Attitude to the Alexandrian Gymnasium in the First Century A.D." *American Journal of Ancient History* 1 (1976) 148-61.

―――. *The Jews in Hellenistic and Roman Egypt: The Struggle for Equal Rights.* TSAJ 7. Tübingen: Mohr Siebeck, 1985.

Katz, Peter. *Philo's Bible: The Aberrant Text of Bible Quotations in Some Philonic Writings and Its Place in the Textual History of the Greek Bible.* Cambridge: Cambridge University Press, 1950.

Kaufman, Michael. *Love, Marriage, and Family in Jewish Law and Tradition.* Northvale: Aronson, 1992.

Keck, Leander E. *Romans.* ANTC. Nashville: Abingdon, 2005.

Kenney, John Peter, ed. *The School of Moses: Studies in Philo and Hellenistic Re-ligion in Memory of Horst R. Moehring.* BJS 304. SPhilo Monographs 1. At-lanta: Scholars, 1995.

Kerkeslager, Allen. "The Absence of Dionysios, Lampo, and Isidoros from the Violence in Alexandria in 38 CE." *SPhAn* 17 (2005) 49-94.

―――. "Agrippa and the Mourning Rites for Drusilla in Alexandria." *JSJ* 37 (2006) 367-400.

―――. "Agrippa I and the Judeans of Alexandria in the Wake of the Violence in 38 CE." *REJ* 168 (2009) 1-49.

Koester, Helmut. "Die Auslegung der Abraham-Verheissung in Hebräer 6." In *Studien zur Theologie der alttestamentlichen Überlieferungen,* ed. Rolf Rend-torff und Klaus Koch. Neukirchen: Neukirchener, 1961, 95-109.

―――. "ΝΟΜΟΣ ΦΥΣΕΩΣ: The Concept of Natural Law in Greek Thought." In *Religions in Antiquity: Essays in Memory of Erwin Ramsdell Goodenough,* ed. Jacob Neusner. SHR 14. Leiden: Brill, 1968, 521-41.

Koskenniemi, Erkki. *Der Philostrateische Apollonios.* CHL 94. Helsinki: Societas Scientiarum Fennica, 1991.

―――. "Greeks, Egyptians and Jews in the Fragments of Artapanus." JSP 13 (2002) 17-31.

―――. *The Old Testament Miracle-workers in Early Judaism.* WUNT ser. 2 206. Tübingen: Mohr Siebeck, 2005.

―――. "Josephus and Greek Poets." In *The Intertextuality of the Epistles,* ed. Thomas L. Brodie. Sheffield: Sheffield Phoenix, 2006, 46-60.

————. "Philo and Classical Drama." In *Ancient Israel, Judaism, and Christianity in Contemporary Perspective: Essays in Memory of Karl-Johan Illman,* ed. Jacob Neusner et al. Lanham: University Press of America, 2006, 137-51.

————. "Moses — A Well-Educated Man: A Look at the Educational Idea in Early Judaism." *JSP* 17 (2008) 281-96.

————. "Philo and Greek Poets." *JSP* 41 (2010) 301-22.

————. "Philo and the Sophists" (forthcoming).

Kraemer, David, ed. *The Jewish Family: Metaphor and Memory.* New York: Oxford University Press, 1989.

Kraft, Robert A. "Tiberius Julius Alexander and the Crisis in Alexandria According to Josephus." In *Of Scribes and Scrolls: Studies of the Hebrew Bible, Intertestamental Judaism and Christian Origins Presented to John Strugnell on the Occasion of His Sixtieth Birthday,* ed. Harold W. Attridge, John J. Collins, and Thomas H. Tobin S.J. Lanham: University Press of America, 1990, 175-84.

————. "Philo and the Sabbath Crisis: Alexandrian Jewish Politics and the Dating of Philo's Works." In *The Future of Early Christianity: Essays in Honor of Helmut Koester,* ed. Birger A. Pearson. Minneapolis: Fortress, 1991, 131-41.

————. "Philo's Bible Revisited: The 'Aberrant Texts' and Their Quotations of Moses." In *Interpreting Translation: Studies on the LXX and Ezekiel in Honour of Johan Lust,* ed. Florentino García Martínez and Marc Vervenne. BETL 192. Leuven: Peeters 2005, 237-53.

Kugel, James L. *Traditions of the Bible: A Guide to the Bible As It Was at the Start of the Common Era.* Cambridge, MA: Harvard University Press, 1998.

Kugel, James L., ed. *Shem in the Tents of Japheth: Essays on the Encounter of Judaism and Hellenism.* JSJSup 74. Leiden: Brill, 2002.

Kuiper, G. J. 1986 "Jewish Literature Composed in Greek." In Schürer, *The History of the Jewish People in the Age of Jesus Christ,* 3/1:470-704.

Lange, Nicholas de. "The Celebration of the Passover in Graeco-Roman Alexandria." In *Manières de penser dans l'Antiquité méditerranéenne et orientale: Mélanges offerts à Francis Schmidt par ses élèves, ses collègues et ses amis,* ed. Christophe Batsch and Mădălina Vârtejanu-Joubert. JSJSup 134. Leiden: Brill, 2009, 157-66.

Lange, Tineke de. *Abraham in John 8,31-59: His Significance in the Conflict between Johannine Christianity and Its Jewish Environment.* Amsterdam: Amphora, 2008.

Laporte, Jean. *La doctrine eucharistique chez Philon d'Alexandrie.* ThH 16. Paris: Beauchesne, 1972.

Larcher, Chrysostome. *Études sur le Livre de la Sagasse*. RBib. Paris: Gabalda, 1969.

Lauterbach, J. Z. "Ancient Jewish Allegorists." *JQR* n.s. 1 (1991) 291-333, 503-31.

Lefkowitz, Mary R., and Maureen B. Fant, eds. *Women in Greece and Rome*. Toronto: Stevens, 1977.

Levine, Lee I. *The Ancient Synagogue: The First Thousand Years*. 2nd ed. New Haven: Yale University Press, 2005.

Levinson, Bernard M. *Deuteronomy and the Hermeneutics of Legal Innovation*. Oxford: Oxford University Press, 1997.

Leonhardt, Jutta. *Jewish Worship in Philo of Alexandria*. TSAJ 84. Tübingen: Mohr Siebeck, 2001.

Lévy, Benny. *Le logos et la lettre: Philon d'Alexandrie en regard des pharisiens*. Lagrasse: Verdier, 1988.

Lévy, Carlos. "Deux problèmes doxographicques chez Philon d'Alexandrie: Posidonius et Enésidème." In *Philosophy and Doxography in the Imperial Age*, ed. Aldo Brancacci. Accademia Toscana di scienze e lettere. La Colombaria Studi 228. Florence: Olschki, 2005, 79-102.

———. "Philo's Ethics." In Kamesar, *The Cambridge Companion to Philo*, 146-71.

———. "L'aristotélisme, parent pauvre de la pensée philonienne?" In *Plato, Aristotle, or Both? Dialogues between Platonism and Aristoteliansim in Antiquity*, ed. Thomas Bénatouïl, Emanuele Maffi, and Franco Trabattoni. Hildesheim: Olms, 2011, 17-33.

Lewis, Naphtali. *Life in Egypt Under Roman Rule*. Oxford: Clarendon, 1983.

Lieberman, Saul. *Greek in Jewish Palestine; Hellenism in Jewish Palestine*. New York: Jewish Theological Seminary of America, 1994.

Lombardi, Sara Mancini, and Paola Pontani, eds. *Studies on the Ancient Armenian Version of Philo's Works*. Studies in Philo of Alexandria 6. Leiden: Brill, 2011.

Long, Anthony A. "Philo on Stoic Physics." In Alesse, *Philo of Alexandria and Post-Aristotelian Philosophy*, 121-40.

Long, Anthony A., and David N. Sedley, eds. *The Hellenistic Philosophers*. 2 vols. Cambridge: Cambridge University Press, 1987.

Lucchesi, Enzo. "La division en six livres des *Quaestiones in Genesim* de Philon d'Alexandrie." *Mus* 89 (1976) 383-95.

———. *L'usage de Philon dans l'oeuvre exégétique de Saint Ambroise: une "Quellenforschung" relative aux commentaires d'Ambroise sur la Genèse*. ALGHJ 9. Leiden: Brill, 1977.

Lüderitz, Gert. "What is the Politeuma?" In *Studies in Early Jewish Epigraphy*, ed. Jan Willem Van Henten and Pieter Willem van der Horst. AGJU 21. Leiden: Brill, 1994, 183-225.

Mach, Michael F. "Choices for Changing Frontiers: The Apologetics of Philo of Alexandria." In *Religious Apologetics — Philosophical Argumentation,* ed. Yossef Schwartz and Volkhard Krech. Religion in Philosophy and Theology 10. Tübingen: Mohr Siebeck, 2004, 319-33.

Mack, Burton L. "Exegetical Traditions in Alexandrian Judaism: A Program for the Analysis of the Philonic Corpus." *SPhilo* 3 (1974-75) 71-115.

―――. *Logos und Sophia: Untersuchungen zur Weisheitstheologie im hellenistischen Judentum.* SUNT 10. Göttingen: Vandenhoeck & Ruprecht, 1973.

―――. "Philo Judaeus and Exegetical Traditions in Alexandria." In *ANRW* 2.21.1 (1984) 227-71.

―――. "Wisdom and Apocalyptic in Philo." In Runia, Hays, and Winston, *Heirs of the Septuagint,* 21-39.

Mansfeld, Jaap, and David T. Runia. *Aëtiana: The Method and Intellectual Context of a Doxographer.* 3 vols. Philosophia antiqua 73, 114, 118. Leiden: Brill, 1997-2010.

Marcovich, Miroslav. *Heraclitus: Greek Text with a Short Commentary.* Mérida: Los Andes University Press, 1967.

Marcus, Joel. "Crucifixion as Parodic Exaltation." *JBL* 125 (2006) 73-87.

Marmorstein, Arthur. *The Old Rabbinic Doctrine of God.* Vol. 1: *The Names and Attributes of God.* 1927; repr., New York: Ktav, 1968.

―――. "Philo and the Names of God." *JQR* 22 (1932) 295-306.

Marrou, Henri Irénée. *Histoire de l'éducation dans le antiquité.* Paris: du Seuil, 1948. Eng. trans.: *A History of Education in Antiquity.* Trans. George Lamb. 1956; repr., Madison: University of Wisconsin Press, 1982.

Martín, José Pablo, ed. *Filón de Alejandría obras completas.* 5 vols. Madrid: Editorial Trotta, 2009-12.

Martola, Nils. "Eating the Passover Lamb in House-Temples in Alexandria: Some Notes on Passover in Philo." In *Jewish Studies in a New Europe: Proceedings of the Fifth Congress of Jewish Studies in Copenhagen 1994 under the Auspices of the European Association for Jewish Studies,* ed. Ulf Haxen, Hanne Trautner-Kromann, and Karen Lisa Goldschmidt-Salamon. Copenhagen: Reitzel, 1998, 521-53.

Mason, Steve. "Should Any Wish to Enquire Further (*Ant.* 1.25): The Aim and Audience of Josephus's *Judean Antiquities/Life.*" In *Understanding Josephus: Seven Perspectives.* JSPSup 32. Sheffield: Sheffield Academic, 1998, 64-103.

―――. "Josephus's Pharisees: The Philosophy." In Neusner and Chilton, *In Quest of the Historical Pharisees,* 41-66.

Maybaum, Siegmund. *Die Anthropomorphien und Anthropathien bei Onkelos und den spätern Targumim.* Breslau: Schletter, 1870.

Mayer, Günter. *Index Philoneus.* Berlin: de Gruyter, 1974.

McCready, Wayne O., and Adele Reinhartz, eds. *Common Judaism: Explorations in Second-Temple Judaism.* Minneapolis: Fortress, 2008.

McGing, Brian. "Population and Proselytism: How Many Jews Were There in the Ancient World?" In Bartlett, *Jews in the Hellenistic and Roman Cities,* 88-106.

McGrath, James F. *John's Apologetic Christology: Legitimation and Development in Johannine Christology.* SNTSMS 111. Cambridge: Cambridge University Press, 2001.

McKnight, Scot. "*De Vita Mosis* 1.147: Lion Proselytes in Philo?" *SPhAn* 1 (1989) 58-62.

Mealand, David L. "Philo of Alexandria's Attitude to Riches." *ZNW* 69 (1978) 258-64.

———. "The Paradox of Philo's Views on Wealth." *JSNT* 24 (1985) 111-15.

Méasson, Anita. *Du char ailé de Zeus à l'Arche d'Alliance: Images et mythes platoniciens chez Philon d'Alexandrie.* Paris: Études Augustiniennes, 1986.

Meecham, Henry G. *The Oldest Version of the Bible: "Aristeas" on Its Traditional Origin.* London: Holborn, 1932.

Meeks, Wayne A. *The Prophet-King.* NovTSup 14. Leiden: Brill, 1967.

———. "The Divine Agent and His Counterfeit in Philo and the Fourth Gospel." In *Aspects of Religious Propaganda in Judaism and Early Christianity,* ed. Elisabeth Schüssler Fiorenza. Notre Dame: University of Notre Dame Press, 1976, 43-67.

Mendelson, Alan. *Secular Education in Philo of Alexandria.* Monographs of the Hebrew Union College 7. Cincinnati: Hebrew Union College Press, 1982.

———. *Philo's Jewish Identity.* BJS 161. Atlanta: Scholars, 1988.

———. "'Did Philo Say the Shema?' and Other Reflections on E. P. Sanders' *Judaism: Practice and Belief.*" *SPhAn* 6 (1994) 160-70.

Menken, Maarten J. J. *Old Testament Quotations in the Fourth Gospel: Studies in Textual Form.* Contributions to Biblical Exegesis and Theology 15. Kampen: Kok Pharos, 1996.

———. "The Image of Cain in 1 John 3,12." In *Miracles and Imagery in Luke and John: Festschrift Ulrich Busse,* ed. Jozef Verheyden, Gilbert Van der Belle, and Jan G. Van der Watt. BETL 218. Leuven: Peeters, 2008, 195-211.

Mercier, Charles Petit, trans. *Quaestiones et Solutiones en Genesim I et II e Versione Armeniaca.* Les œuvres de Philon d'Alexandrie 34a. Paris: Cerf, 1979.

————. *Quaestiones et Solutiones en Genesim III-IV-V-VI e Versione Armeniaca.* Les œuvres de Philon d'Alexandrie 34b. Paris: Cerf, 1984.

Meyer, Rudolf. *Hellenistisches in der rabbinischen Antropologie.* BWANT 74. Stuttgart: Kohlhammer, 1937.

Mitchell, Margaret M. "New Testament Envoys in the Context of Greco-Roman Diplomatic and Epistolary Conventions: The Example of Timothy and Titus." *JBL* 111 (1992) 641-62.

Mitchell, Stephen, and Peter Van Nuffelen, eds. *Monotheism between Pagans and Christians in Late Antiquity.* Leuven: Peeters, 2010.

Modrzejewski, Joseph Mélèze. "How To Be a Greek and Yet a Jew in Hellenistic Alexandria?" In *Diasporas in Antiquity,* ed. Shaye J. D. Cohen and Ernest S. Frerichs. BJS 288. Atlanta: Scholars, 1993, 65-92.

————. *The Jews of Egypt: From Rameses II to Emperor Hadrian.* Trans. Robert Cornman. Edinburgh: T. & T. Clark; Philadelphia: Jewish Publication Society, 1995.

Moehring, Horst. "Moses and Pythagoras: Arithmology as an Exegetical Tool in Philo." In *Studia Biblica 1978: Sixth International Congress on Biblical Studies, Oxford 3-7 April 1978,* ed. Elizabeth A. Livingstone. JSOTSup 11. Sheffield: Sheffield University Press, 1979, 205-8.

————. "Arithmology as an Exegetical Tool in the Writings of Philo of Alexandria." In Kenney, *The School of Moses,* 141-76.

Mondésert, Claude. "Philo of Alexandria." In *Cambridge History of Judaism.* Vol. 3: *The Early Roman Period,* ed. William Horbury, W. D. Davies, and John Sturdy. Cambridge: Cambridge University Press, 1999, 877-900.

Moore, George Foot. *Judaism in the First Centuries of the Christian Era.* 2 vols. New York: Schocken, 1971.

Morgan, Teresa. *Literate Education in the Hellenistic and Roman Worlds.* Cambridge: Cambridge University Press, 1998.

Morris, Jenny. "The Jewish Philosopher Philo." In Schürer, *The History of the Jewish People,* 3/2:809-89.

Moxnes, Halvor. *Theology in Conflict: Studies in Paul's Understanding of God in Romans.* NovTSup 53. Leiden: Brill, 1980.

Mulder, Martin Jan, and Harry Sysling, eds. *Mikra: Text, Translation, Reading and Interpretation of the Hebrew Bible in Ancient Judaism and Early Christianity.* CRINT 2/1. Assen: Van Gorcum; Philadelphia: Fortress, 1990.

Musurillo, Herbert A., ed. *The Acts of the Pagan Martyrs: Acta Alexandrinorum.* Oxford: Clarendon, 1954.

Najman, Hindy. "The Law of Nature and the Authority of the Mosaic Law." *SPhilo* 11 (1999) 55-73.

———. "Cain and Abel as Character Traits: A Study in the Allegorical Typology of Philo of Alexandria." In *Eve's Children: The Biblical Stories Retold and Interpreted in Jewish and Christian Traditions,* ed. Gerald P. Luttikhuizen. Leiden: Brill, 2003, 107-18.

———. *Seconding Sinai: The Development of Mosaic Discourse in Second Temple Judaism.* JSJSup 77. Leiden: Brill, 2003.

———. "Philosophical Contemplation and Revelatory Inspiration in Ancient Judean Traditions." *SPhAn* 19 (2007) 101-11.

Nelson, Carroll A. *Status Declarations in Roman Egypt.* ASP 19. Amsterdam: Hakkert, 1979.

Neusner, Jacob. *Method and Meaning in Ancient Judaism.* Ser. 1. BJS 10. Missoula: Scholars, 1979.

———. *Major Trends in Formative Judaism.* Vol. 3: *The Three Stages in the Formation of Judaism.* BJS 99. Chico: Scholars, 1985.

———. *Judaism and Its Social Metaphors: Israel in the History of Jewish Thought.* Cambridge: Cambridge University Press, 1989.

———. *Judaic Law from Jesus to the Mishnah: A Systematic Reply to Professor E. P. Sanders.* South Florida Studies in the History of Judaism 84. Atlanta: Scholars, 1993.

———. *The Way of Torah: An Introduction to Judaism.* 6th ed. Belmont: Wadsworth, 1997.

———. *The Rabbinic Traditions about the Pharisees before 70.* Vol. 3: *Conclusions.* South Florida Studies in the History of Judaism 204. Atlanta: Scholars, 1999, 244-46.

———. "Rabbinic Traditions about the Pharisees before 70 CE: An Overview." In Neusner and Chilton, *In Quest of the Historical Pharisees,* 297-31.

Neusner, Jacob, trans. *The Tosefta.* Fourth Division: *Neziqin.* New York: Ktav, 1981.

Neusner, Jacob, and Bruce D. Chilton, eds. *In Quest of the Historical Pharisees.* Waco: Baylor University Press, 2007.

Nickelsburg, George W. E. "The Bible Rewritten and Expanded." In Stone, *The Literature of the Jewish People,* 89-156.

Niehoff, Maren Ruth. *The Figure of Joseph in Post-Biblical Jewish Literature.* AGJU 16. Leiden: Brill, 1992.

———. "Jewish Identity and Jewish Mothers: Who Was a Jew According to Philo?" *SPhAn* 11 (1999) 31-54.

———. *Philo on Jewish Identity and Culture.* TSAJ 86. Tübingen: Mohr Siebeck, 2001.

———. "Response to Daniel R. Schwartz." *SPhAn* 17 (2005) 99-101.

―――――. "Philo's Contribution to Contemporary Alexandrian Metaphysics." In Brakke, Jacobsen, and Ulrich, *Beyond Reception,* 35-55.

―――――. *Jewish Exegesis and Homeric Scholarship in Alexandria.* Cambridge: Cambridge University Press, 2011.

Nikiprowetzky, Valentin. *Le Commentaire de l'écriture chez Philon d'Alexandria.* ALGHJ 11. Leiden: Brill, 1977.

―――――. "L'exegese de Philon d'Alexandrie dans le *De Gigantibus et le Quod Deus.*" In Winston and Dillon, *Two Treatises of Philo of Alexandria,* 5-75.

Nilsson, Martin P. *Die hellenistische Schule.* München: Beck, 1955.

Oehler, J. "Gymnasium." In PW 7:2004-26.

―――――. "Gymnasiarchos." In PW 7:1969-2004.

Osborn, Eric F. *Clement of Alexandria.* Cambridge: Cambridge University Press, 2005.

Paget, J. N. B. Carleton. "The Christian Exegesis of the Old Testament in the Alexandrian Tradition." In Sæbø, *Hebrew Bible/Old Testament,* 1/1:478-542.

Palfrey, John, and Urs Gasser. *Born Digital: Understanding the First Generation of Digital Natives.* New York: Basic Books, 2008.

Pearce, Sarah J. K. "Jerusalem as 'Mother-City' in the Writings of Philo of Alexandria." In Barclay, *Negotiating Diaspora,* 19-36.

―――――. *The Land of the Body: Studies in Philo's Representation of Egypt.* WUNT 208. Tübingen: Mohr Siebeck, 2007.

Pearson, Birger A. "Philo and Gnosticism." In *ANRW* 2.21.1 (1984) 295-342.

Pelletier, André. *Flavius Josèphe, adaptateur de la Lettre d'Aristée: Une reaction atticisante contre la Koiné.* Paris: Kincksieck, 1962.

―――――. *Lettre d'Aristée à Philocrate.* SC 89. Paris: Cerf, 1962.

Petit, Françoise. *L'ancienne version latine des Questions sur la Genèse de Philon d'Alexandrie.* 2 vols. TUGAL 113-14. Berlin: Akademie, 1973.

―――――. *Quaestiones in Genesim et in Exodum: Fragmenta graeca.* Œuvres de Philon d'Alexandrie 33. Paris: Cerf, 1978.

Pomeroy, Sarah B. *Goddesses, Whores, Wives, and Slaves.* New York: Schocken, 1975.

―――――. "Infanticide in Hellenistic Greece." In *Images of Women in Antiquity,* ed. Averil Cameron and Amélie Kuhrt. Detroit: Wayne State University Press, 1983, 207-22.

Porter, Stanley E., and Jacqueline C. R. de Roo, eds. *The Concept of the Covenant in the Second Temple Period.* JSJSup 71. Leiden: Brill, 2003.

Porton, Gary G. "Midrash." In *ABD* 4:818-22.

Pucci Ben Zeev, Miriam. "New Perspectives on the Jewish-Greek Hostilities in Alexandria During the Reign of Emperor Caligula." *JSJ* 21 (1990) 227-35.

————. *Jewish Rights in the Roman World: The Greek and Roman Documents Quoted by Josephus Flavius.* TSAJ 74. Tübingen: Mohr Siebeck, 1998.

Rad, Gerhard von. *Weisheit in Israel.* Neukirchen-Vluyn: Neukirchener Verlag, 1970. Eng. trans. James D. Martin. *Wisdom in Israel.* London: SCM; Nashville: Abingdon, 1972.

Radice, Roberto. *Filone di Alessandria: bibliografia generale 1937-1982.* Elenchos 8. Naples: Bibliopolis, 1983.

————. "Observations on the Theory of the Ideas as the Thoughts of God in Philo of Alexandria." *SPhAn* 3 (1991) 126-34.

————. *La filosofia di Aristobulo e I suoi nessi con il* De Mundo *attribuito ad Aristotele.* Pubblicazioni del Centro di Ricerche di Metfisica: Collana Temi metafisici e problem del pensiuero antico. Studi e Testi 33. Milan: Via e pensiere, 1994.

————. "Philo and Stoic Ethics: Reflections on the Idea of Freedom." In Alesse, *Philo of Alexandria and Post-Aristotelian Philosophy,* 141-68.

————. "Philo's Theology and Theory of Creation." In Kamesar, *The Cambridge Companion to Philo,* 124-45.

Radice, Roberto, and David T. Runia. *Philo of Alexandria: An Annotated Bibliography, 1937-1986.* VCSup 8. Leiden: Brill, 1988.

Rajak, Tessa. "Ethnic Identities in Josephus." In *The Jewish Dialogue with Greece and Rome: Studies in Cultural and Social Interaction.* Leiden: Brill, 2002, 137-46.

Reed, Stephen A. "The Role of Food as Related to Covenant in Qumran Literature." In Porter and de Roo, *The Concept of the Covenant in the Second Temple Period,* 129-64.

Reese, James M. *Hellenistic Influence on the Book of Wisdom and Its Consequences.* AnBib 41. Rome: Biblical Institute Press, 1970.

Räisänen, Heikki. "Paul, God and Israel: Romans 9–11 in Recent Research." In *The Social World of Formative Christianity and Judaism: Essays in Tribute to Howard Clark Kee,* ed. Jacob Neusner et al. Philadelphia: Fortress, 1988, 178-206.

Reinhartz, Adele. "The Meaning of Nomos in Philo's Exposition of the Law." *SR* 15 (1986) 337-45.

————. "Philo on Infanticide." *SPhAn* 4 (1992) 42-58.

————. "Parents and Children: A Philonic Perspective." In *The Jewish Family in Antiquity,* ed. Shaye D. Cohen. BJS 298. Atlanta: Scholars, 1993, 61-87.

————. "Philo's *Exposition of the Law* and Social History: Methodological Considerations." In *Society of Biblical Literature 1993 Seminar Papers,* ed. Eugene H. Lovering Jr. Atlanta: Scholars, 1993, 6-21.

Renehan, Robert. "The Greek Philosophic Background of Fourth Maccabees." *Rheisches Museum für Philologie* 115 (1972) 223-38.

Reydams-Schils, Gretchen. "Philo of Alexandria on Stoic and Platonist Psycho-Physiology: The Socratic Higher Ground." In Alesse, *Philo of Alexandria and Post-Aristotelian Philosophy,* 169-95.

Royse, James R. "The Original Structure of Philo's Quaestiones." *SPhilo* 4 (1976-77) 41-78.

———. "Further Greek Fragments of Philo's *Quaestiones.*" In Greenspahn, Hilgert, and Mack, *Nourished with Peace,* 143-53,

———. "Philo's *Quaestiones in Exodum* 1.6." In Hay, *Both Literal and Allegorical,* 17-27.

———. "Philo's Division of His Works into Books." *The Studia Philonica Annual* 13 (2001) 76-85.

———. "The Works of Philo." In Kamesar, *The Cambridge Companion to Philo,* 32-64.

———. "Some Observations on the Biblical Text in Philo's *De Agricultura.*" *SPhAn* 22 (2010) 111-29.

———. "Philo of Alexandria *Quaestiones in Exodum* 2.62-68: Critical Edition." *SPhAn* 24 (2012) 1-68.

Runesson, Anders, Donald D. Binder, and Birger Olsson. *The Ancient Synagogue from Its Origins to 200 C.E.: A Source Book.* Leiden: Brill, 2008.

Runia, David T. "Philo's *De aeternitate mundi:* The Problem of Its Interpretation." *VC* 35 (1981) 105-51.

———. *Philo of Alexandria and the Timaeus of Plato.* Philosophia antiqua 44. Leiden: Brill, 1986.

———. Review of *La philosophie de Moïse. JTS* 40 (1989) 590-602.

———. *Exegesis and Philosophy: Studies on Philo of Alexandria.* Aldershot: Variorum, 1990.

———. "How To Read Philo." In *Exegesis and Philosophy,* 185-98.

———. "Philo, Alexandrian and Jew." In *Exegesis and Philosophy,* 1-18.

———. "Polis and Megalopolis: Philo and the Founding of Alexandria." In *Exegesis and Philosophy,* 398-412.

———. *Philo in Early Christian Literature: A Survey.* CRINT 3/3. Assen: Van Gorcum; Mineapolis: Fortress, 1993.

———. "Was Philo a Middle Platonist? A Difficult Question Rrevisited." *SPhAn* 5 (1993) 112-40.

———. "Philonic Nomenclature." *SPhAn* 6 (1994) 1-27.

———. "References to Philo from Josephus Until 1000 AD." *SPhAn* 6 (1994) 111-21.

—————. *Philo and the Church Fathers: A Collection of Papers.* VCSup 32. Leiden: Brill, 1995.

—————. "Why Does Clement of Alexandria Call Philo 'the Pythagorean'?" *VC* 49 (1995) 1-22.

—————. "Caesarea Maritima and the Survival of Hellenistic-Jewish Literature." In *Caesarea Maritima: A Retrospective after Two Millenia,* ed. Avner Raban and Kenneth G. Holum. DMOA 21. Leiden: Brill, 1996, 476-95.

—————. "The Text of the Platonic Citations in Philo of Alexandria." In *Studies in Plato and the Platonic Tradition: Essays Presented to John Whittaker,* ed. Mark Joyal. Aldershot: Hampshire; Brookfield: Ashgate, 1997, 261-91.

—————. *Filone di Alessandria nella prima letteratura cristiana: Uno studio d'insieme, a cura di Roberto Radice.* Milan: Vita e Pensiero 1999, 365-445.

—————. "Philo of Alexandria and the Greek *Hairesis*-model." *VC* 53 (1999) 117-47.

—————. "Philo's Longest Arithmological Passage: *De opificio mundi* 89-128." In *De Jérusalem à Rome: Mélanges offerts à Jean Riaud,* ed. Lucian-Jean Bord and David Hamidovic. Paris: Guethner, 2000, 155-74.

—————. *Philo of Alexandria: On the Creation of the Cosmos according to Moses: Introduction, Translation and Commentary.* PACS 1. Leiden: Brill, 2001.

—————. "One of Us or One of Them? Christian Reception of Philo the Jew in Egypt." In Kugel, *Shem in the Tents of Japheth,* 203-22.

—————. "Philo of Alexandria, 'Legatio Ad Gaium' 1-7." In Aune, Seland, and Ulrichsen, *Neotestamentica et Philonica,* 349-70.

—————. "Philo and Hellenistic Doxography." In Alesse, *Philo of Alexandria and Post-Aristotelian Philosophy,* 13-52.

—————. "Philo and the Early Christian Fathers." In Kamesar, *The Cambridge Companion to Philo,* 210-30.

—————. "The Theme of Flight and Exile in the Allegorical Thought-World of Philo of Alexandria." *SPhAn* 21 (2009) 1-24.

—————. "Philon d'Alexandrie." In *Dictionnaire des philosophes antiques,* ed. Richard Goulet. Paris: Editions du Centre national de la recherche scientifique, 2011, 5:362-90.

Runia, David T., ed. *Philo of Alexandria: An Annotated Bibliography, 1987-1996.* VCSup 57. Leiden: Brill, 2000.

—————. *Philo of Alexandria: An Annotated Bibliography, 1997-2006.* VCSup 109. Leiden: Brill, 2012.

Runia, David T., David M. Hay, and David Winston, eds. *Heirs of the Septuagint: Philo, Hellenistic Judaism and Early Christianity. Festschrift for Earle Hilgert.* SPhAn 3; BJS 230. Atlanta: Scholars, 1991.

Runia, David T., and Gregory E. Sterling, eds. *In the Spirit of Faith: Studies in Philo and Early Christianity in Honor of David Hay.* SPhAn 18; BJS 332 (2001).

Runia, David T., Gregory E. Sterling, and Hindy Najman, eds. *Laws Stamped with the Seals of Nature: Law and Nature in Hellenistic Philosophy and Philo of Alexandria.* SPhAn 15; BJS 337. Providence: Brown University Press, 2003.

Ryle, Herbert E. *Philo and Holy Scripture, or the Quotations of Philo from the Books of the Old Testament.* London: Macmillan, 1895.

Sæbø, Magne, ed. *Hebrew Bible/Old Testament: The History of Its Interpretation.* Vol. 1/1: *Antiquity.* Göttingen: Vandenhoeck & Ruprecht, 1996.

Safrai, Shemuel, and Menahem Stern, eds. *The Jewish People in the First Century: Historical Geography, Political History, Social, Cultural, and Religious Life and Institutions.* 2 vols. CRINT 1/1-2. Assen: Van Gorcum; Philadelphia: Fortress, 1974-76.

Sandelin, Karl-Gustav. *Die Auseinandersetzung mit der Weisheit in 1. Korinther 15.* Meddelanden från Stiftelsens för Åbo Akademi forskningsinstitut 12. Åbo: Åbo Akademi, 1976.

―――. "Zwei kurze Studien zum Alexandrinischen Judentum." *ST* 31 (1977) 147-52.

―――. *Wisdom as Nourisher: A Study of an Old Testament Theme, Its Development within Early Judaism, and Its Impact on Early Christianity.* Acta Academiae Aboensis ser A. Humaniora 64/3. Åbo: Åbo Akademi, 1986.

―――. "The Danger of Idolatry According to Philo of Alexandria." *Temenos* 27 (1991) 109-50.

―――. "Philo's Ambivalence towards Statues." In Runia and Sterling, *In the Spirit of Faith,* 122-38.

―――. "Drawing the Line: Paul on Idol Food and Idolatry in 1 Cor 8,1–11,1." In Aune, Seland, and Ulrichsen, *Neotestamentica et Philonica,* 108-25.

―――. "Philo and Paul on Alien Religion: A Comparison," In *Lux Humana, Lux Aeterna: Essays on Biblical and Related Themes in Honour of Lars Aejmelaeus,* ed. Antti Mustakallio et al. Helsinki: Finnish Exegetical Society; Göttingen: Vandenhoeck & Ruprecht, 2005, 211-46.

―――. "Jews and Alien Religious Practices during the Hellenistic Age." In *Ancient Israel, Judaism, and Christianity in Contemporary Perspective: Essays in Memory of Karl-Johan Illman,* ed. Jacob Neusner et al. Lanham: University Press of America, 2006, 365-92.

―――. *Sophia och hennes värld: Exegetiska uppsatser från fyra årtionden.* Studier i exegetik och judaistik, Teologiska fakulteten vid Åbo Akademi 6. Åbo: Åbo Akademi, 2008.

Sanders, E. P. *Judaism: Practice and Belief, 63 BCE–66 CE.* London: SCM; Philadelphia: Trinity Press International, 1994.

Sandmel, Samuel. "Parallelomania." *JBL* 81 (1962) 1-13.

———. *Philo's Place in Judaism: A Study of Conceptions of Abraham in Jewish Literature.* Augmented ed. New York: Ktav, 1971.

———. *Philo of Alexandria: An Introduction.* Oxford: Oxford University Press, 1979.

———. "Philo Judaeus: An Introduction to the Man, His Writings, and His Significance." In *ANRW* 2.21.1 (1984) 3-46.

Satlow, Michael L. *Creating Judaism: History, Tradition, Practice.* New York: Columbia University Press, 2006.

———. "Defining Judaism: Accounting for 'Religions' in the Study of Religion." *JAAR* 74 (2006) 837-60.

Savon, Hervé. *Saint Ambroise devant l'exégèse de Philon le Juif.* 2 vols. Paris: Études augustiniennes, 1977.

Schäfer, Peter. *Judeophobia: Attitudes Toward the Jews in the Ancient World.* Cambridge, MA: Harvard University Press, 1997.

Schaublin, Christoph. *Untersuchungen zu Methode und Herkunft der antiochenischen Exegese.* Theophaneia 23. Cologne: Hanstein, 1974, 49-51.

Scheidel, Walter. "Creating a Metropolis: A Comparative Demographic Perspective." In Harris and Ruffini, *Ancient Alexandria between Egypt and Greece,* 1-31.

Schenck, Kenneth. *A Brief Guide to Philo.* Louisville: Westminster John Knox, 2005.

Schiffman, Lawrence H. *Understanding Second Temple and Rabbinic Judaism.* Jersey City: Ktav, 2003.

Schimanowski, Gottfried. *Juden und Nichtjuden in Alexandrien: Koexistenz und Konflikte bis zum Pogrom unter Trajan (117 n. Chr.).* Münsteraner judaistische Studien 18. Berlin: LIT, 2006.

Schmitt, Armin. "Struktur, Herkunft, und Bedeutung der Beispielreihe in Weish 10." *BZ* n.s. 21 (1977) 1-22.

Schulz-Flogel, Eva. "The Latin Old Testament Tradition." In Sæbø, *Hebrew Bible/ Old Testament,* 1/1:642-62.

Schürer, Emil. *The History of the Jewish People in the Age of Jesus Christ (175 B.C.–A.D. 135).* Rev. and ed. Geza Vermes and Fergus Millar. 3 vols. Edinburgh: T. & T. Clark, 1973-87.

Schwartz, Daniel R. "Philonic Anonyms of the Roman and Nazi Periods: Two Suggestions." *SPhilo* 1 (1989) 63-73.

———. *Agrippa I: The Last King of Judaea.* TSAJ 23. Tübingen: Mohr Siebeck, 1990.

―――. "Did the Jews Practice Infant Exposure and Infanticide in Antiquity?" *SPhAn* 16 (2004) 61-95.

―――. "Philo, His Family, and His Times." In Kamesar, *The Cambridge Companion to Philo,* 9-31.

―――. "Philo and Josephus on the Violence in Alexandria in 38 CE." *SPhAn* 24 (2012) 149-66.

Schwartz, Seth. "How Many Judaisms Were There? A Critique of Neusner and Smith on Definition and Mason and Boyarin on Categorization." *Journal of Ancient Judaism* 2 (2011) 208-38.

Schwemer, Anna Maria. "Zum Verhältnis von Diatheke und Nomos in den Schriften der jüdischen Diaspora Ägyptens in hellenistich-römischer Zeit." In *Bund und Tora: Zur theologischen Begriffsgeschichte in alttestamentischer, frühjüdischer und urchistlicher Tradition,* ed. Friedrich Avemarie und Hermann Lichtenberger. WUNT 92. Tübingen: Mohr, 1996, 67-109.

Seckel, Emil, und Wilhelm Schubart, eds. *Der Gnomon des Idios Logos.* BGU 5/1. Berlin: Weidmannsche, 1919; repr., Milan: Cisalpino Goliardica, 1973.

Sedley, David. ed., *The Philosophy of Antiochus.* Cambridge: Cambridge University Press, 2012.

Seland, Torrey. *Establishment Violence in Philo and Luke: A Study of Nonconformity to the Torah and Jewish Vigilante Reactions.* Biblical Interpretation 15. Leiden: Brill, 1995.

―――. "Philo and the Clubs and Associations of Alexandria." In *Voluntary Associations in the Graeco-Roman World,* ed. John S. Kloppenborg and Stephen G. Wilson. London: Routledge, 1996, 110-27.

―――. *Strangers in the Light: Philonic Perspectives on Christian Identity in 1 Peter.* Biblical Interpretation 76. Leiden: Brill, 2005.

―――. "The 'Common Priesthood' of Philo and 1 Peter: A Philonic Reading of 1 Peter 2:5 & 9." In *Strangers in the Light,* 79-115.

―――. "'Conduct Yourselves Honorably among the Gentiles' (1 Peter 2:12): Assimilation and Acculturation in 1 Peter." In *Strangers in the Light,* 147-89.

―――. "'Colony' and 'Metropolis' in Philo: Examples of Mimicry and Hybridity in Philo's Writing Back from the Empire?" In *Études Platoniciennes 7: Philon d'Alexandrie,* ed. J.-F. Pradeau. Paris: Les Belles lettres, 2010, 13-36.

Shaked, Gershon. "Alexandria: On Jews and Judaism in America." *Jerusalem Quarterly* 49 (1989) 47-84.

Sharples, Robert. "Kritolaos." In *DNP* 6 (1999) 855.

Shroyer, Montgomery J. "Alexandrian Jewish Literalists." *JBL* 55 (1936) 261-84.

Siegert, Folker. *Philon von Alexandrien, Über die Gottesbezeichnung "wohltätig verzehrendes Feuer" (De Deo): Rückübersetzung des Fragments aus dem Ar-*

menischen, deutsche Übersetzung und Kommentar. WUNT 46. Tübingen: Mohr Siebeck, 1988.

————. "Early Jewish Interpretation in a Hellenistic Style." In Sæbø, *Hebrew Bible/Old Testament,* 1/1:130-98.

————. "The Philonian Fragment *De Deo:* First English Translation." *SPhAn* 10 (1998) 1-13.

————. "Die Inspiration der Heiligen Schriften: Ein philonisches Votum zu 2 Tim 3,16." In Deines and Niebuhr, *Philo und das Neue Testament,* 205-22.

————. "Philo and the New Testament." In Kamesar, *The Cambridge Companion to Philo,* 175-209.

Siegfried, Carl. *Philo von Alexandria als Ausleger des Alten Testaments.* Jena: Dufft, 1875.

Sijpesteijn, Pieter J. *Nouvelle liste des gymnasiarques des métropoles de l'Égypte Romaine.* Studia Amsteolodamensia ad epigraphicam, ius antiqum et papyrologicam perintentia 28. Zutphen: Terra, 1986.

Sjöberg, Erik. "Wiedergeburt und Neuschöpfung im palästinischen Judentum." *ST* 4 (1950) 44-85.

Skarsaune, Oskar. "The Development of Scriptural Interpretation in the Second and Third Centuries — Except Clement and Origen." In Sæbø, *Hebrew Bible/Old Testament,* 1/1:373-442.

Skarsten, Roald. *Forfatterproblemet ved De aeternitate mundi i corpus philonicum.* Bergen: Universitetet i Bergen, 1987.

Skarsten, Roald, Peder Borgen, and Kåre Fuglseth. *The Complete Works of Philo of Alexandria: A Key-Word-In-Context Concordance.* 8 vols. Piscataway: Gorgias, 2005.

Sly, Dorothy. *Philo's Perception of Women.* BJS 209. Atlanta: Scholars, 1990.

Smallwood, E. Mary. *The Jews under Roman Rule: From Pompey to Diocletian.* 2nd ed. Leiden: Brill, 1981.

Smallwood, E. Mary, ed. *Philonis Alexandrini Legatio ad Gaium.* 2nd ed. Leiden: Brill, 1970.

Smith, Jonathan Z. "Fences and Neighbors: Some Contours of Early Judaism." In *Imagining Religion: From Babylon to Jonestown.* Chicago: University of Chicago Press, 1982, 1-18.

Sowers, Sidney G. *The Hermeneutics of Philo and Hebrews: A Comparison of the Interpretation of the Old Testament in Philo Judaeus and the Epistle to the Hebrews.* Basel Studies of Theology 1. Zurich: EVZ; Richmond: John Knox, 1965.

Stager, Lawrence E. "Eroticism and Infanticide at Ashkelon." *BAR* 17/4 (1991) 35-53.

Stein, Edmund. "Der Begriff der Palingenesie im Talmudischen Schrifttum." *MGWJ* n.s. 47 (1939) 194-205.

Stein, Siegfried. "The Dietary Laws in Rabbinic and Patristic Literature." In *Studia Patristica,* ed. Kurt Aland and Frank L. Cross. Berlin: Akademie (1957) 2:141-54.

Sterling, Gregory E. "Platonizing Moses: Philo and Middle Platonism." *SPhAn* 5 (1993) 96-111.

―――. "'Athletes of Virtue': An Analysis of the Summaries in Acts (2:41-47; 4:32-35; 5:12-16)." *JBL* 113 (1994) 679-96.

―――. "Recluse or Representative? Philo and Greek-Speaking Judaism Beyond Alexandria." In *Society of Biblical Literature 1995 Seminar Papers,* ed. Eugene H. Lovering Jr. Atlanta: Scholars, 1995, 595-616.

―――. "'Thus Are Israel': Jewish Self-Definition in Alexandria." *SPhAn* 7 (1995) 1-18.

―――. "'The School of Sacred Laws': The Social Setting of Philo's Treatises." *VC* 53 (1999) 148-64.

―――. "Judaism between Jerusalem and Alexandria." In Collins and Sterling, *Hellenism in the Land of Israel,* 263-301.

―――. "Ontology versus Eschatology: Tensions between Author and Community in Hebrews." *SPhAn* 13 (2001) 190-211.

―――. "'Philo Has Not Been Used Half Enough': The Significance of Philo of Alexandria for the Study of the New Testament." *PRSt* 30 (2003) 251-69.

―――. "The Place of Philo of Alexandria in the Study of Christian Origins." In Deines and Niebuhr, *Philo und das Neue Testament,* 21-52.

―――. "'Day One': Platonizing Exegetical Traditions of Genesis 1:1-5 in John and Jewish Authors." *SPhAn* 17 (2005) 118-40.

―――. "The First Theologian: The Originality of Philo of Alexandria." In *Renewing Tradition: Studies in Texts and Contexts in Honor of James W. Thompson,* ed. Mark Hamilton, Thomas H. Olbricht, and Jeffrey Patterson. Eugene: Wipf & Stock, 2006, 145-62.

―――. "Philo of Alexandria." In *The Historical Jesus in Context,* ed. Amy-Jill Levine, Dale C. Allison Jr., and John Dominic Crossan. Princeton: Princeton University Press, 2006, 296-308.

―――. "'The Queen of the Virtues': Piety in Philo of Alexandria." *SPhAn* 18 (2006) 103-23.

―――. "Philosophy as the Handmaid of Wisdom: Philosophy in the Exegetical Traditions of Alexandrian Jews." In *Religiöse Philosophie und philosophische Religion der frühen Kaiserzeit,* ed. Rainer Hirsch-Luipold, Herwig Görgemanns, and Michael von Albrecht. STAC 51. Tübingen: Mohr Siebeck, 2009, 67-98.

————. "The Interpreter of Moses: Philo of Alexandria and the Biblical Text." In *A Companion on Biblical Interpretation in Early Judaism,* ed. Matthias Henze. Grand Rapids: Eerdmans, 2012, 415-35.

————. "'Prolific in Expression and Broad in Thought': Internal References to Philo's Allegorical Commentary and Exposition of the Law." *Euphrosyne* 40 (2012) 55-76.

Stern, Menahem, ed. *Greek and Latin Authors on Jews and Judaism.* 3 vols. Jerusalem: Israel Academy of Sciences and Humanities, 1974-84.

Stone, Michael E., ed. *The Literature of the Jewish People, in the Period of the Second Temple and the Talmud.* Vol. 2: *Jewish Writings of the Second Temple Period: Apocrypha, Pseudepigrapha, Qumran Sectarian Writings, Philo, Josephus.* CRINT 2/2. Assen: Van Gorcum; Philadelphia: Fortress, 1984.

Strecker, Georg. "Der vorchristliche Paulus: Überlegungen zum biographischen Kontext biblischer Überlieferung — zugleich eine Antwort an Martin Hengel." In Fornberg and Hellholm, *Texts and Contexts,* 713-41.

Stuckenbruck, Loren T. "To What Extent did Philo's Treatment of Enoch and the Giants Presuppose a Knowledge of the Enochic and Other Sources Preserved in the Dead Sea Scrolls?" *SPhAn* 19 (2007) 131-42.

Swete, Henry Barclay. *An Introduction to Old Testament in Greek.* Cambridge: Cambridge University Press, 1902.

Taylor, Joan E. *Jewish Women Philosophers of First-Century Alexandria: Philo's "Therapeutae" Reconsidered.* Oxford: Oxford University Press, 2003.

————. "Philo of Alexandria on the Essenes: A Case Study on the Use of Classical Sources in Discussions of the Qumran-Essene Hypothesis." *SPhAn* 19 (2007) 1-28.

Taylor, Joan E., and Philip R. Davies. "The So-Called Therapeutae of *De Vita Contemplativa*: Identity and Character." *HTR* 91 (1998) 3-24.

Tcherikover, Victor A. *Hellenistic Civilization and the Jews.* Trans. S. Applebaum. New York: Atheneum, 1985.

————. "Jewish Apologetic Literature Reconsidered." *Eos* 48 (1956) 169-93.

————. "The Decline of the Jewish Diaspora in Egypt in the Roman Period." *JJS* 14 (1963) 1-32.

Tcherikover, Victor A., Alexander Fuks, and Menahem Stern, eds. *Corpus papyrorum Judaicarum.* 3 vols. Cambridge, MA: Harvard University Press, 1957-64.

Terian, Abraham. "A Critical Introduction to Philo's Dialogues." In *ANRW* 2.21.1 (1984) 272-94.

————. "Had the Works of Philo Been Newly Discovered." *BA* 57 (1994) 86-97.

Terian, Abraham, trans. *Philonis Alexandrini De animalibus: The Armenian Text with an Introduction, Translation, and Commentary.* Chico: Scholars, 1981.

————. *Quaestiones et Solutiones in Exodum, e versione armeniaca et fragmenta graeca.* Les œuvres de Philon d'Alexandrie 36. Paris: Cerf, 1988.

————. *Alexander, e versione armeniaca.* Les œuvres de Philon d'Alexandrie 34c. Paris: Cerf, 1992.

Termini, Cristina. *Le potenze di Dio: Sudio su dunamis in Filone di Alessandria.* Rome: Institutum Patristicum Augustinianum, 2000.

————. "Taxonomy of Biblical Laws and φιλοτεχνία in Philo of Alexandria: A Comparison with Josephus and Cicero." *SPhAn* 16 (2004) 1-29.

————. "Philo's Thought within the Context of Middle Judaism." In Kamesar, *The Cambridge Companion to Philo,* 95-123.

Thesleff, Holger. *An Introduction to the Pythagorean Writings of the Hellenistic Period.* Åbo: Åbo Akademi, 1961.

————. *The Pythagorean Texts of the Hellenistic Period.* Åbo: Åbo Akademi, 1965.

Thompson, Dorothy J. "The Ptolemies and Egypt." In Erskine, *A Companion to the Hellenistic World,* 103-20.

Tobin, Thomas H. *The Creation of Man: Philo and the History of Interpretation.* CBQMS 14. Washington: Catholic Biblical Association of America, 1983.

————. "Tradition and Interpretation in Philo's Portrait of the Patriarch Joseph.'" In *Society of Biblical Literature 1986 Seminar Papers,* ed. Kent Harold Richards. Atlanta: Scholars, 1986, 271-77.

————. "Was Philo a Middle Platonist?: Some Suggestions." *SPhAn.* 5 (1993) 147-50.

————. "Philo and the Sibyl: Interpreting Philo's Eschatology." *SPhAn* 9 (1997) 84-103.

————. "The Beginning of Philo's *Legum Allegoriae.*" *SPhAn* 12 (2000) 29-43.

Townsend, John T. "Education (Greco-Roman Period)." In *ABD* 2:312-17.

Tracy, Sterling. *Philo Judaeus and the Roman Principate.* Williamsport: Bayard, 1933.

Triviño, José Maria, trans. *Obras completas de Filón de Alejandría.* 4 vols. Colección Valores en el tiempo. Buenos Aires: Acervo Cultural, 1975-76.

Turner, E. G. "Tiberius Iulius Alexander." *JRS* 44 (1954) 54-64.

Ulmer, Rivka. *Egyptian Cultural Icons in Midrash.* SJ 52. Berlin: de Gruyter, 2009.

Urbach, Ephraim E. *The Sages; Their Concepts and Beliefs.* Trans. Israel Abrahams. 2 vols. Jerusalem: Magnes, Hebrew University, 1975.

Uxkull-Gyllenband, Woldemar Graf. *Aegyptische Urkunden aus den Königli-*

chen Staatlichen Museen zu Berlin: Griechische Urkunden. 15 vols. 1895-1983; Berlin: Weidmanssche Buchhandlung, 1934; repr., Milano: Cicalpino Goliardica, 1973.

Victor, Royce M. *Colonial Education and Class Formation in Early Judaism: A Postcolonial Reading.* LSTS 72. London: T. & T. Clark, 2010.

Villari, Elisabetta. *Il morso e il cavaliere: Una metafora della termperanza e del dominio di sé.* Genova: Il melangolo, 2001.

Völker, Walther. *Fortschritt und Vollendung bei Philo von Alexandrien.* Tugal ser. 4, 4/1. Leipzig: Hinrich, 1938.

Vollenweider, Samuel. "Der 'Raub' der Gottgleichheit: Ein Religionsgeschichtlicher Vorschlag zu Phil 2,6(-11)." *NTS* 45 (1999) 413-33.

Walter, Nikolaus. *Der Thoraausleger Aristobulus: Untersuchungen zu seinen Fragmenten und zu pseudepigraphischen Resten der jüdisch hellenistischen Literatur.* TUGAL 86. Berlin: Akademie, 1964.

————. "Hellenistische Diaspora-Juden an der Wiege Des Urchristentums." In *The New Testament and Hellenistic Judaism,* ed. Peder Borgen and Søren Giversen. Aarhus: Aarhus University Press, 1995; Peabody: Hendrickson, 1997, 37-58.

Wan, Sze-kar. "Philo's *Quaestiones et solutiones in Genesim:* A Synoptic Approach." In *Society of Biblical Literature 1993 Seminar Papers,* ed. Eugene H. Lovering Jr. Atlanta: Scholars, 1993, 22-53.

Wasserman, Emma. *The Death of the Soul in Romans 7.* WUNT ser. 2, 256. Tübingen: Mohr Siebeck, 2008.

Wasserstein, Abraham, and David J. Wasserstein. *The Legend of the Septuagint: From Classical Antiquity to Today.* Cambridge: Cambridge University Press, 2006.

Watts, Sheldon J. *A Social History of Western Europe, 1450-1720.* London: Hutchinson University Library, 1984.

Wegner, Judith Romney. "Leviticus." In *The Women's Bible Commentary,* ed. Carol A. Newssom and Sharon H. Ringe. Louisville: Westminster John Knox, 1992, 36-44.

Weinberg, Joanna, trans. *Azariah de' Rossi, The Light of the Eyes.* New Haven: Yale University Press, 2001.

Weinfeld, Moshe. "Deuteronomy, Book of." In *ABD* 2:168-83.

Weiss, Herold. "Philo on the Sabbath." *SPhAn* 3 (1991) 83-105.

————. *A Day of Gladness: The Sabbath among Jews and Christians in Antiquity.* Columbia: University of South Carolina Press, 2003.

Whitehorne, J. E. G. "The Ephebate and the Gymnasial Class in Roman Egypt." *BASP* 19 (1982) 171-84.

Wiedemann, Thomas E. J. *Adults and Children in the Roman Empire*. London: Routledge; New Haven: Yale University Press, 1989.

Wilcken, Ulrich, and Ludwig Mitteis. *Grundzüge und Chrestomathie des Papyruskunde*. 2 vols. Leipzig: Teubner, 1912.

Wilson, Walter T. *Philo of Alexandria, On Virtues: Introduction, Translation, and Commentary*. PACS 3. Leiden: Brill, 2011

Winston, David. *The Wisdom of Solomon*. AB 43. Garden City: Doubleday, 1979.

———. "Philo's Ethical Theory." In *ANRW* 2.21.1 (1984) 372-416.

———. "Response to Runia and Sterling." *SPhAn* 5 (1993) 141-46.

———. "Philo's *Nachleben* in Judaism." *SPhAn* 6 (1994) 103-10.

———. "Philo and Rabbinic Literature." In Kamesar, *The Cambridge Companion to Philo*, 231-53.

Winston, David, and John Dillon, eds. *Two Treatises of Philo of Alexandria: A Commentary on* De Gigantibus *and* Quod Deus sit immutabilis. BJS 25. Chico: Scholars, 1983.

Winter, Bruce W. *Philo and Paul among the Sophists: Alexandrian and Corinthian Responses to a Julio-Claudian Movement*. 2nd ed. Grand Rapids: Eerdmans, 2002.

Wise, Michael O. "The Concept of a New Covenant in the Teacher Hymns from Qumran (1QHᵃ x-xvii)." In Porter and de Roo, *The Concept of the Covenant in the Second Temple Period*, 99-128.

Wolfson, Elliot R. "Traces of Philonic Doctrine in Medieval Jewish Mysticism: A Preliminary Note." *SPhAn* 8 (1996) 99-106.

Wolfson, Harry Austryn. *Philo: Foundations of Religious Philosophy in Judaism, Christianity, and Islam*. 2 vols. Cambridge, MA: Harvard University Press, 1948.

Yonge, C. D., trans. *The Works of Philo: Complete and Unabridged*. Peabody: Hendrickson, 1993.

Zeller, Dieter. "The Life and Death of the Soul in Philo of Alexandria." *SPhAn* 7 (1995) 19-55.

Zuckerman, Constantine. "Hellenistic *Politeumata* and the Jews: A Reconsideration." *Scripta Classica Israelica* 8/9 (1985-88) 171-85.

Zuckermandel, Moses Samuel, ed. *Tosefta, Mischna und Boraitha in ihrem Verhältnis zu einander, oder palästinensische und babylonische Halacha*. 2 vols. Frankfurt: Band, 1908-9.

Index of Modern Authors

323

Index of Biblical References and Other Ancient Literature